THE SEARCH FOR QUALITY INTEGRATED EDUCATION

Recent Titles in
Contributions to the Study of Education

Black Students in Higher Education:
Conditions and Experiences in the 1970s
Edited by Gail E. Thomas

The Scope of Faculty Collective Bargaining:
An Analysis of Faculty Union Agreements
at Four-Year Institutions of Higher Education
Ronald L. Johnstone

Brainpower for the Cold War: The Sputnik
Crisis and National Defense Education Act
of 1958
Barbara Barksdale Clowse

In Opposition to Core Curriculum: Alternative
Models for Undergraduate Education
Edited by James W. Hall with Barbara L. Kevles

Peer Teaching: Historical Perspectives
Lilya Wagner

School Law for the Practitioner
Robert C. O'Reilly and Edward T. Green

THE SEARCH FOR QUALITY INTEGRATED EDUCATION

Policy and Research on Minority Students in School and College

MEYER WEINBERG

CONTRIBUTIONS TO THE STUDY OF EDUCATION, NUMBER 7

GREENWOOD PRESS
WESTPORT, CONNECTICUT • LONDON, ENGLAND

Library of Congress Cataloging in Publication Data

Weinberg, Meyer, 1920–
   The search for quality integrated education.

   (Contributions to the study of education, ISSN 0196-
707X; no. 7)
   Bibliography: p.
   Includes index.
   1. School integration—United States.   2. Educational
equalization—United States.   3. Education, Urban—
United States.   4. Minorities—Education—United States.
I. Title.   II. Series.
LC214.2.W44   1983   370.19'342   82-12016
ISBN 0-313-23714-X (lib. bdg.)

Library of Congress Catalog Card Number: 82-12016
ISBN: 0-313-23714-X
ISSN: 0196-707X

First published in 1983

Greenwood Press
A division of Congressional Information Service, Inc.
88 Post Road West
Westport, Connecticut 06881

Printed in the United States of America

10   9   8   7   6   5   4   3   2   1

Contents

Tables

Acknowledgments

I wish to thank Gertrude Martin for editing the first draft of the present volume with taste and effectiveness, and for her aid in compiling the comprehensive index. Mary von Euler was my program officer at the National Institute of Education and she helped in many concrete ways. Toward the end, she was succeeded by Oscar Uribe. Lynn Sedlak edited the work with an expert eye for accuracy and clarity. She deserves the readers' gratitude. The manuscript was typed expeditiously and carefully by Sharon Charow, Betty Craker, Lorraine DiAnne, Susan Reid, Ella Kolasienski, Nancy Scott, and Nancy Arnold. Elaine Grennan aided in keeping track of the extensive research materials as the work proceeded.

The research report herein was developed under a contract from the National Institute of Education, Department of Education. However, the content does not necessarily reflect the position or policy of that agency, and no official endorsement of these materials should be inferred.

Introduction

This book examines critically a large amount of research on the schooling of poor and minority children, carried out during the 1970s and the earliest 1980s. Higher education is also discussed. The principal viewpoint of the analysis emerges from a conviction that effectiveness of schooling is closely bound up with equality and equity of education. Class and race barriers ensure that poor and minority children will receive ineffective education. Those who seek to abstract educational effectiveness from its social and racial context are mistaken. Decade upon decade of experience and research, both here and abroad, suggest as much. The search for equal and equitable education, on the other hand, seems short-sighted in the absence of a concern for educational effectiveness.

As one sifts through the mass of research reported here a realization dawns that we are beginning to overcome the heritage of the 1960s. That decade, deservedly renowned for its rebirth of social conscience, also bequeathed to us a surfeit of sentimental paternalism which only now has begun to ebb. Educational researchers and policy-makers, especially, embodied a social philosophy and a methodology profoundly unfitted to solve the challenges of that decade or of the following two. The earmarks of this orientation were a view of the uneducated as having brought their ignorance upon themselves, and a stance of neutral innocence of schools in this process of uneducating. Omitted, however, were an acknowledgment of the structural racism that largely guided the schools, and the significance of growing parental organization as part of the burgeoning civil rights movement.

The sweeping ineffectiveness of America's urban schools was first made into a national issue by that movement, as was a concern for equality and equity of education. Educational research, however, resisted these issues as "political" and continued, more or less, in the usual pursuit of knowledge with images of raceless, benevolent classrooms. Instructional failures were attributed to individual failings of students whose race or economic status was other than "standard." An intricate tangle of theorizing produced will-of-the-wisps resembling the ancient Aether, to whose existence most of the learned gave assent but whom they could never lay on the table, for the life of them. Such, for example, was the presumed inability of some children to learn "because" of their social class; the exact mechanisms involved were never specified. Another was the supposed inevitability of lower achievement among minority children; once more, the alleged mechanisms remained undescribed.

Recent research, however, reveals a far more realistic direction. In part, this can be explained by the growing presence of minority researchers in the field. This is clearest in the case of Hispanic researchers. During the 1940s, 1950s, and 1960s, Anglo researchers were preeminent in research on Hispanic children. Since the late 1960s, however, Hispanics with a strong tie to their communities have largely taken over the field. Numerous works and studies on the history of specific Hispanic communities, analyses of the generally wretched level of schooling for Hispanic children, and explorations of legal and pedagogical aspects of bilingualism have emerged. Politics in these newer works takes on a two-fold meaning: it is used as an explanatory framework for community analysis, and it frequently becomes part of the researcher's prescription for future community organization.

Since the 1960s, educational research has begun to live a more public life. The advent of special legislation and advocacy groups has meant that the researchers are much more frequently called upon to testify in trials and congressional hearings. Out of this novel experience have come some misgivings, widely circulated, about the value of social science research. The issue of desegregation has elicited much of this discussion.[1]

Often, social science evidence is said to be "soft" while that of physical science is described as "hard." This distinction is a myth. Purveyors of the myth usually point to contradictions between social scientists in testimony as evidence of a certain lack of substance. If social science evidence were solid, it is declared, social scientists would agree more wholeheartedly on it.

The fact is that most of the "softness" of social science evidence arises from the happenstance that it is usually used in a clash over policies. Social science witnesses are asked whether proposed policies are securely anchored in fact. And they disagree.

In congressional hearings, it is quite customary to hear opposing viewpoints from qualified physical scientists. In patent litigation, both sides frequently come well fortified with physicists, chemists, geologists, among others. When confronted with conflicts among these specialists, we do not denounce their evidence as soft. Instead, we acknowledge the complexity of the situations under dispute. The same should be done with situations in which social scientists testify.

---

1. The following eight paragraphs are taken from the author's invited testimony of October 19, 1981, before the Subcommittee on Civil and Constitutional Rights of the U.S. House of Representatives' Committee on the Judiciary.

We need to ask: Is social science evidence hard or soft with respect *to what*? The effect of desegregation on academic achievement is among the most extensively researched questions in American social science. If one wishes to pick and choose selected evidence to build a case, this is possible to do. Since research on academic achievement has conflicting findings—*as does nearly every other significant research problem known to me*—it is not difficult to manipulate one's evidence to produce whatever conclusion one wishes. This is not science—nor is it honest. It should be exposed whenever encountered.

Differences between social scientists that arise out of ignorance of previous research are inexcusable. We can say the same of shoddy work by some social scientists who read a three-paragraph abstract of a research work that runs upwards of three hundred pages and then claim to have "reviewed" the study. Nor need we respect the righteously pronounced claim of one or another researcher to having discovered the "only true way" to study a topic. Desegregation is complex enough to call upon the research perspectives of many fields, including law, history, and economics, as well as the more customary social sciences.

Some disagreements among social scientists can be highly productive, especially if they lead to the uncovering of hitherto ignored factors or to the rejection of conventional beliefs which are shown to be without foundation. Disagreements about facts are constructive if they are followed by heightened efforts to establish the facts.

It is astonishing to note how little attention is paid by researchers and writers to actual cases of desegregation. The question is debated as though desegregation were a purely theoretical construct. In fact, however, it is being applied in thousands of American schools. Today, no adequate overview of the workability of desegregation can be made without extensive reference to practices in specific cities. A judgment of the success or failure of parent participation cannot be made without examination of Charlotte and Boston, for example. The role of academic innovation under desegregation should include the experience of Minneapolis and Milwaukee. How to construct a well-organized student busing plan is illustrated by the success of Tampa; a horrible example is San Francisco. The limits of voluntary desegregation can be studied by reference to San Bernardino and Dallas. A good rule would seem to be: If concrete practices in specific cities are not mentioned in an analysis of desegregation, chances are it does not merit much attention. Such a study may be more significant for debate classes than for serious policy making.

A final point on conflicting opinions: People who have extensive practical experience as well as researchers who have conducted studies are entitled to express opinions on disputed or unresolved practical problems. I would argue that it is their obligation to do so.

Twenty years ago, the research literature of desegregation and integration was exceedingly slight and no researcher was known as a specialist in this field alone. The learned journals of education and the social sciences were bare of articles dealing with the subject. Federal and foundation research funds for studies in the field simply did not exist. Doctoral students here and there happened on the subject and so a few dissertations were written. A single journal, *Integrated Education*, begun in 1963, dealt wholly with the subject.

Today, no single person can possibly read everything written on desegregation and integration. A corps of research specialists exists and findings are published in a wide variety of journals and reports. Dissertation research has expanded significantly. Research funds have grown, but only meagerly. A single federal agency, the National Institute of Education, had a research budget for this field. President Reagan's budget-slashing all but eliminated it. Private foundations always tip-toed gingerly around the subject although a handful spent a tiny portion of their funds on the subject. (Late in 1981, a large, well-known foundation informed one applicant for desegregation-related funds that the organization felt it necessary to trim its sails in accordance with changing public opinion.)

Yet, little attention is paid by academe or the media to the findings of the growing research community. During the Fall and Winter of 1981, two congressional committees held prolonged hearings on legislation to regulate desegregation and busing. Afterwards, various members quoted only those witnesses who conformed with their own opinions. The press did not point this out; indeed, some parts of it followed the same practice. As is demonstrated in a later chapter, many researchers are unaware of studies by others. Thus, antiquated findings parade as the most recent. Also, other research is often cited selectively, thus creating a lop-sided and partial view of what is known. In some cases, ancient canards are revived and placed in new scholarly contexts, as in the case of "racial differences" in intelligence.

The following chapters are written for three types of readers: practitioners, parents, and policymakers. Practical applications are the dominant concern. Studies which have a bearing for practice are highlighted. Studies without such an orientation are criticized for it. By no means does the writer believe theory is irrelevant to equity and equality of education. Rather, the viewpoint is that the dignity of theory and the richness of application are mutually enhancing. Since, however, educational theorizing has been notably barren in the subject under examination there is little to report.

In Chapter 1 we review recent research on historical aspects of the Mexican-American and black communities, especially in regard to the development of education. Wherever possible attention is paid to organized efforts of both groups to achieve a greater measure of equality and equity. Locales include California, Texas, and Harlem. In Chapter 2, the legal framework for the education of minority children is analyzed not so much in terms of formal legal enactments as in terms of community and institutional aspects of implementation of legal commands. Subject matter ranges from bilingual education to classification problems in special education to desegregation in the Deep South.

Chapter 3 investigates whether historical and genetic evidence sustains a view that intelligence differs among the races. Among the subjects examined are the history of the issue, genetic research, IQ tests, and the relation of malnutrition to intelligence. The next chapter is devoted to an analysis of how desegregation, even after ordered by a court, is frequently resisted and contraverted by school authorities. Equal attention is paid to studies of the behavior of black, white, and Hispanic teachers in non-segregated classrooms.

In Chapter 5, historical and contemporary evidence is reviewed for its bearing on the question of whether high-quality education has been or is being offered in all-black or heavily black schools. Specific schools are studied, primarily located in the South or Border states. Chapter 6 presents an overall view of the subject of intradistrict inequalities, that is, variations in per-pupil expenditure among schools in a single district. This problem, virtually ignored by researchers on school finance, is shown to be highly significant.

The relationship between desegregation and academic achievement is examined in Chapter 7. This most researched aspect of desegregation surveys the major works in the field, as well as some very recent and lesser-known works. In Chapter 8, the process of transforming desegregation into integration is studied. Among the specific problems reviewed are racial self-concept of both white and black students and the capacity of schools to generate a process of integration.

Chapter 9 is a detailed examination of a body of research dating from the 1970s that studies a broad range of life among Mexican Americans and American Indians. In some cases, parallel lines of inquiry can be found in both subjects, especially with respect to ethnic character and assimilation. Minority public opinion on desegregation and busing, usually treated as nonexistent, is examined in Chapter 10 through the medium of national, state, and local polls. In addition, a considerable number of exhaustive studies of parent participation are analyzed, ranging from places such as Detroit, Rochester, and New York City to Orange County, California.

Chapters 11 and 12 review comprehensively research on minority students in higher education. In the first of these chapters studies of the higher schooling of Alaskan Natives, Mexican Americans, and blacks are presented. The historically black colleges are given special attention. In Chapter 12 topics such as desegregation are dealt with, as well as the reception of black students on predominantly white campuses. A number of specific universities are reviewed. Chapter 13 is a conclusion to the book as a whole.

THE SEARCH FOR QUALITY INTEGRATED EDUCATION

The Historical Background

During the past decade there has been a significant increase in scholarly historical research on minorities. A large part of it has come not from university departments of education, but from history departments. Courses on the history of minority education, however, are still exceptional, whatever the department. The historical consciousness of American educators remains meager and conventional, and not a little stereotypical. The general run of educational research reflects more or less the same pattern.

Historical research on Mexican Americans has begun to emerge from a comparative void.

Two younger historians, writing a year apart, have dealt with the life of the *Tejanos*—native Mexicans of Texas—during a thirty-year period covering Mexican independence from Spain (1821), Texan independence from Mexico (1836), and absorption of Texas into the United States (1846). In 1900, more than a half-century later, nine of ten Mexican Americans in the United States still lived in Texas. What basic patterns of life were established during these decades?

Andrew Tijerina points out that the *Tejanos* were a racially diverse group: "Tlascan, Indian-Spanish, and European, the *Tejanos* were culturally receptive to persons of various racial origins."[1] From earliest time a distinctive set of cultural features began to emerge. Tijerina writes:

The single most characteristic trait of the *Tejano* culture was the strong sense of community. The early Spaniards had brought there a strong neighborhood concept of the barrio. After this was superimposed over the Mexican Indian's traditional unit, the *calpulli*, the result was a reinforced sense of social unity.[2]

The barrio became the organizational framework for discharging communal tasks.

Social welfare and administrative matters were implemented by an official, the *comisario*, whose jurisdiction was a single barrio. Under Mexican rule, state-owned lands were given to municipalities, which were expected to use some as sites for schools. (It was customary for the schools to be free to the poor.)

Tijerina stresses that this Mexican pattern of encouragement of local schooling from a governmental center was unknown to American settlers in Texas: "Actually the Anglos scarcely understood or considered the Tejano concept of local full responsibility for financing and managing schools. Anglos were accustomed to private, home education, or "old field" schools."[3] It should be recalled that Anglo-Texans came overwhelmingly from the American South where state-financed systems of public education did not become the norm until after the Civil War (1861–1865). During the latter half of the nineteenth century, privately organized communal schools in the barrios continued to operate without state funds. Teachers were hired by a board of directors. Around the end of the century, occasional public schools for "Mexicans" were opened but on a strictly segregated basis.

Anglo-Texans depended heavily upon the *Tejano* community for knowledge about more than school organization. The livestock industry, soon to be an economic mainstay of the state, was a product of Mexico. *Tejanos* provided intimate knowledge of herding skills as well as resource management.[4] "As the 1840s progressed," Tijerina notes, "Anglos flooded in and took the ranches, the livestock, and indeed the livelihood of the old *Tejanos* around Bexar, Goliad, and Nacodoches."[5]

In other dimensions of community life, including local government and law, the *Tejano* heritage persisted during the nineteenth century. Yet, it is ironic that the first full-scale work to study that heritage was not written until 1977! Tijerina's careful research should be represented in the textbooks of Texas schools as well as in larger historical syntheses.

Crisp, a year earlier than Tijerina, dealt with the same general subject matter but was concerned with Anglo attitudes toward *Tejanos* rather than with reconstructing *Tejano* life and culture. The bulk of the work thus examines evidence of these attitudes as expressed in letters, diaries, newspapers, and contemporary books.

In the 1836 constitution of the Texas republic all residents were declared citizens except blacks and Indians. *Tejanos* were thus citizens, but by no means did this indicate a universal Anglo predisposition in favor of *Tejanos*. Indeed, in the same year, Texas leader Stephen F. Austin had characterized the Texas war for independence as "a war of barbarism and despotic principles, waged by the mongrel Spanish-Indian and Negro race, against civilization and the Anglo-American race."[6] During debates at the constitutional convention of 1845, the word "white" as a prerequisite for voting was rejected since it might also lead to exclusion of *Tejanos* from the franchise. Three years later, Senator John C. Calhoun, arguing against incorporation of all Mexico into the United States, declared: "Ours, sir, is the government of a white race. . . . [The] Mexican States . . . [have] a population of . . . [predominantly] mixed blood[,] equally ignorant and unfit for liberty."[7] Anglo definitions of race combined biology with politics.

While Anglo consideration for *Tejanos* could be discerned here and there in Texas, the dominant element in their attitude was contempt. Unlike the cases of blacks and Indians, however, explicit statutory racism against *Tejanos* did not appear. Crisp puts the matter well: "Mexican Americans came to endure a quasi-citizenship in which their constitutional equality with Anglos was usually overwhelmed by the practical consequences of everyday informal discrimination."[8] By the turn of the century, when *Tejanos* were far outnumbered by recent immigrants from Mexico, Anglo authorities were readier to revert to explicit discrimination. As noted earlier, one school board after another adopted resolutions that segregated the descendants and successors of the *Tejanos*.

In 1853, the United States bought a relatively small area known as the Gadsden Purchase from Mexico and annexed it as part of southern Arizona. Goldstein has studied the social processes at work in the area during the period 1853–1880. Her special interest is the Mexican elite in the area. She found that that group was, for the most part, "wealthy, educated in the United States and had close personal as well as family and economic ties to the Anglo-Americans."[9]

The leaders of the elite, the *ricos* (the rich), eagerly entered into advantageous business arrangements with the Anglos, but their wealth predated the Gadsden Purchase. As Goldstein explains: "The elite of the Anglo-American period were the sons of earlier generations of *ricos*, not a recently formed group taking advantage of traditional Anglo-American freedoms and social mobility."[10] Assimilation into Anglo society was their social ideal; they were unconcerned with maintaining traditional Mexican culture.

Not only were sons of the elite sent to American schools; in the Purchase area the elite advocated attendance at public schools as another measure of Americanization. Lower-class, more traditional, elements refused to turn away from the parochial schools.

The *ricos* undoubtedly were powerful but they acted under an overarching restraint: Politically and economically they measured their actions by the lights of Anglo leadership. Where the two interests coincided, there was cooperation. Otherwise, the Mexican elite served, in Goldstein's word, as an "adjunct."[11] Americanization after 1853, she observes, produced a "sharply divided" Mexican community in southern Arizona.[12] Increasing assimilation among the *ricos* widened the cultural gap between themselves and the greater number of poor Mexicans. During the generation following the Purchase, it was the latter who constituted the majority of miners who worked in southern Arizona. The *ricos* did not share a common economic interest with the Mexican lower classes who, declares Goldstein, "did not find acceptance let alone support in the new society."[13]

Fernando Chacon Gomez, searching for a legal-historical basis for biculturalism in the United States, has analyzed the significance of Article VIII of the Treaty of Guadalupe Hidalgo, which ended the Mexican-American war of 1846–1848. That measure provided that (1) inhabitants of the former Mexican territory could choose to move to other Mexican land or to remain where they were; (2) if they remained, they had a year to choose American or Mexican citizenship; and (3) the security of Mexican-owned property in the new American territories was guaranteed. Article IX provided that until the territories became states, Mexicans living there were to be "maintained and protected in the full enjoyment of their liberty and property, and secured in the free exercise of their religion without restriction."

Chacon's primary point is that the Mexican government was most concerned to protect the rights of those nationals and ex-nationals who chose to remain in the new American territories, and he stated that a study of the negotiations leading to the treaty shows as much.[14] Specifically, Chacon writes: "The intent of the negotiators was to provide specific and wide-reaching rights and guarantees to the Mexican inhabitants of the ceded territories. . . . Yet subsequent to cession, no institutional protections were established to safeguard Mexican civil rights."[15] The treaty contemplated an integration of ex-Mexicans. Instead, they were segregated and isolated.

American treaties with Indian tribes usually acknowledged the identity of the various tribes. In the Treaty of Guadalupe Hidalgo, except for Articles VIII and IX, this was not done. Thereafter, whatever territorial courts or western state supreme courts adjudicated the rights of Mexicans, the outcomes could almost be foretold. They would be decided against the Mexicans.[16] Chacon regards this strain of American law as fundamental to the ethnic philosophy of the United States. The failure of the United States to ratify the International Declaration of Human Rights and International Covenants of Human Rights further illustrates the same philosophy. He regards these failures as motivated by a refusal to acknowledge the right of Mexicans "to be culturally different."[17]

A study by Baldarrama complements Chacon's interpretation. The former studied the role of Mexican consulates in aiding Mexican Americans to oppose official school segregation in various California communities. Baldarrama reports:

As early as the summer of 1919, San Francisco Consul General Rafael de Negris had protested to California Governor William D. Stephens about the segregation of Mexican students in the state's elementary schools. De Negris's protest was directed primarily at the El Centro, Santa Paula, and Gloreyetta school authorities who had compelled Mexican children to attend schools designated exclusively for them.[18]

On another occasion the Mexican government commissioned two Mexican-American scholars at the University of Texas—Ezequel A. Chavez and Herschel T. Manuel—to report on anti-Mexican discrimination.

In Lemon Grove, a suburb of San Diego, the school board in 1930 built a two-room center for all Mexican Americans regardless of their English language competence. Parents, most of whom were poor workers, protested. The San Diego Mexican consul unobtrusively pushed for a lawsuit, which was filed. (It was known as *Roberto Alvarez* v. *Lemon Grove School District*.) Early the next year, the consulate also encouraged a parental boycott of the two-room school. Eventually, a court ordered the board of education to admit Mexican Americans to the regular school but unofficial school segregation continued throughout the state.[19]

Baldarrama's research is of a very high order. Given the virtual absence of printed discussions of his topic, he depended almost wholly on manuscripts and other primary sources—diplomatic correspondence and confidential reports—to be found in the archives of Mexico and elsewhere.

Dr. Hector Garcia is a physician in Corpus Christi, Texas. In one room of his house are kept seventy steel filing cabinet drawers. These constitute the files of the American G.I. Forum, an association initially of Mexican-American veterans of World War II organized by Dr. Garcia in 1948. In Mercedes, where he had grown up, he had attended a segregated school (*"solamente Mexicano"*). Signs in Garcia's Texas frequently used the word *solamente*, as, *"Se sirve solamente a raza blanca"* (Only whites are served), and *"Este bano solamente para Americanos"* (This restroom for Americans only). State school funds designed for Mexican-American children were frequently misappropriated for Anglo students. Over the period 1937–1947, only 79 of 6,511 high school graduates in Austin were Mexican Americans.[20] Housing, health, and employment were shot through with discrimination. In such a setting the G.I. Forum took shape. In 1976, Allsup studied the record of that process.

The organization concerned itself essentially with education. It found, for example, that in heavily Mexican-American San Antonio through 1948 no Mexican American had ever served on the school board. In one town after another segregated schools were the rule. Sometimes a state official would condemn the practice in a single town but usually little changed afterward. In 1940, for example, the League of United Latin American Citizens (LULAC) complained to state authorities about segregation in Ozona. The state superintendent ruled that "under the laws of this state children of Latin-American extraction are classified as white and therefore have a right to attend the Anglo American schools in your community in which they live."[21]

Seven years later three student groups investigated segregation in Bastrop, Beeville, Cotulla, Elgin, and Sinton. The most frequent response of the districts was that language difficulties required a separate education. Parents in Bastrop and two other towns sued the districts. In *Delgado* v. *Bastrop County* a federal district court approved separation only for the first grade and for no more than one year; after that it could continue on the basis of the results of standardized tests administered to all pupils.

The G.I. Forum organized statewide teams to determine whether *Delgado* was being implemented. Violations were found in Robstown, George West, Mathis, Orange Grove, Bishop, Driscoll, Sinton, Taft, Three Rivers, Edcouch, Encinal, Beeville, Rio Hondo, and Del Rio. At its 1949 annual convention, the Forum called upon the federal government to cut the flow of federal aid to school districts guilty of segregation. (This prescient demand predated *Brown* v. *Board of Education of Topeka* by five years and the Civil Rights Act by ten more.) It included a compilation of segregated districts among which were some of those listed above as well as Lubbock, San Angelo, Samora, Ozona, Sanderson, Alpine, Pecos, Marattan, Rock Springs, Santa Cruiz, Kyle, Oden, Harlingen, Lockheart, and Cuero. The state turned aside all offers by the Forum to cooperate in enforcing *Delgado*. Instead, the Forum filed a series of legal actions during 1952–1957 and finally won its point.

Unlike its peer organization, LULAC, the Forum organized poor people. One reason was that better-off persons tended to underestimate the racism of Anglos. During 1953–1954, the Forum supported a job action by the predominantly Mexican-American garbage workers of Albuquerque. It is no wonder that the Forum set its first annual membership dues at only twenty-five cents. (Another historical parallel presses upon our attention. At the very close of Dr. Martin Luther King's life, he began focusing more attention on economic issues. In 1968 he was killed in Memphis where he had come to support a strike for higher wages and union recognition by black garbage workers.)

The six works just reviewed add up to a significant body of research. They relate to a number of important issues in Mexican-American education. For one thing, they document the continuing struggle of a people to maintain its ethnic identity. The destructive effects of Anglo racism are described plainly. Formal law is presented as a thin reed to lean on, especially in the absence of political power. Continued resort to collective action by parents and others is a constant theme in the education of Mexican-American children.

All six works are unpublished although each is of monograph or book length. Commercial publishers do not wish to issue materials in this field. University presses are somewhat more open, although to date none has distinguished itself by its receptivity to research works on Mexican-American education. One consequence is that sections of this or that dissertation may appear as articles in learned journals, read by few scholars and even fewer practitioners. The oldest standard university-affiliated education journals almost never carry articles or reviews of research on Mexican-American history or education. Worse yet, this silence is not itself a subject of discussion in educational circles. As a result there is a widely shared illusion that "nothing solid is known in this area."

The history of black Americans continues to attract first-rate work.

Lang studied the ideology that actuated the activity of abolitionist educators of blacks in the pre-Civil War generation. By entitling his study *Black*

Bootstraps, he suggests that the educators preached a philosophy of self-help to free blacks during the years 1828–1860. This, however, was only one of three elements in the ideology. Others were that blacks had to work on their moral character development and, simultaneously, that Afro-American life styles had to be reformed. Basically, the educators believed that improvements in black life depended upon changes in individual blacks.

Since the educators opposed slavery and personally worked with free blacks, it would appear difficult to challenge their devotion. Lang, however, finds that "the abolitionists might have been equalitarian but they were not sure equality was possible nor that it was desirable."[22] Education, they were convinced, would prove the key to individual mobility and social acceptance of blacks. "What the educators failed to recognize," Lang observes, "was that racism had become a social norm, and therefore to most [white] Americans racial prejudice seems natural and even rational."[23] Few abolitionist educators pointed to white racism as an obstacle to improvement, except in order to spur blacks to surmount the obstacle. Little if any stress was placed upon the need for the white community to overcome its own racism. By implication, at least, the white man was treated by the abolitionist educators as though he were the standard by which blacks were properly gauged. Abolitionist educator and racist accepted the same standard.

Abolitionist educators were enemies of "the demon rum," as, indeed, were most educators during this period of American history, although Lang does not deal with this larger fact. Black middle-class abolitionists, as well as white, assailed drunkenness among poorer blacks. They attributed a vague "shiftlessness" to the same poorer blacks. Abolitionist educators considered both drinking and lack of interest in work as character defects. They therefore spoke much of moral development.

Lang criticizes the contention of the abolitionist educators that in order to succeed in American society blacks had to be "better" than whites. He characterizes this argument as a "desire to see Afro-Americans acculturated by a racist society."[24] He attributes this belief to Booker T. Washington also and—surprisingly!—to W.E.B. Du Bois. Does Lang hold then that education in a racist society is a blind alley for blacks? No. Instead, he writes:

The abolitionist educators' experience does not warrant the conclusion that education is a useless means to provide Afro-Americans the opportunity to participate fully in American society, but their experience does suggest that an education which does not face the problem of racism and provide Afro-Americans with some means of combatting it is doomed to failure.[25]

Lang does not go on to specify the elements of such an education although black educators, including Du Bois, have done so.[26]

It is important to note that Lang does not equate the abolitionist educators with the leaders of racist movements. After all, the latter burnt down black schools and cultural institutions while the former helped build them up. But the racism of the abolitionist educators was expressed in paternalism, a mode of interaction marked by a sense of superiority, of "knowing what's good for" people who are thought to be unable to know for themselves. This attitude has lived a long life to the present.

During the years 1866–1870, immediately following the Civil War, a federal agency, the Freedmen's Bureau, became a prime factor in black education. It supplied buildings and some equipment while private associations provided teachers and maintenance expenses. At times, this division of functions was indistinct. Morris has made the second major study of the educational functions of the Bureau.[27] His primary interest is the ideology of the Bureau educators. Independently of Lang's work, Morris reached parallel conclusions about abolitionist educators:

From the beginning of the nineteenth century, abolitionists and other reformers promoted Negro education as a moderate or even conservative solution to the race problem, a solution which stressed "moral suasion" rather than civil rights activism as the chief mode of eliminating prejudice and discrimination.[28]

Interestingly Morris, like Lang, calls this a "bootstrap" philosophy.

Bureau educators, according to Morris, extended this philosophy into the post-Civil War years. He conducted an exhaustive study of the official and personal correspondence of officials of the Bureau, as well as of the official reports concerning each district of the agency. This work constitutes the most comprehensive documentation yet of the subject. A private agency, the American Missionary Association (AMA), which had been prominent in abolitionist movements and in pre-Civil War education, entered into close relations with the Bureau and operated many Bureau-built schools. A number of the officials in the Bureau's educational structure were AMA members or were affiliated with other evangelical groups.

Morris lists the major nonacademic goals of Bureau schools as follows: "Obedience to law, respect for personal and property rights, honesty, economy, sectional and racial harmony. . . ."[29] Bureau officials counselled moderation and patience to the freedmen. "They sought to convince white leaders," according to Morris, "that education would transform the recently freed slaves into efficient, dependable, and contented laborers."[30]

A powerful sense of paternalism took hold of Bureau educators. Thus, "most AMA policy-makers were reluctant to accept increased Negro 'self-sufficiency' in school affairs if this meant a substantial decrease in their own authority."[31] At the same time, "Bureau state school superintendents were rarely true radicals when it came to racial and sectional matters."[32]

Morris is the first historian to describe the large number of black teachers who worked in Bureau schools. Most of them had been free before the war. A small number came from the North. Following is a listing of the number of black and white teachers in Bureau schools:[33]

Date	Black	White	Black as Percentage of Total
January 1867	458	972	32.0
July 1867	699	1388	33.5
January 1868	1031	1171	46.8
July 1868	1296	1495	46.4
January 1869	1186	1081	52.3
July 1869	1742	1551	52.9
July 1870	1764	1536	53.5

The increase of black teachers was in part the direct result of a deliberate Bureau policy of spurring teacher-training institutions to prepare blacks for teaching. In large part, however, the increase was a response "to a growing desire on the part of freedmen to attend schools taught by members of their own race."[34] It is known from earlier research that the number of black teachers was greater in private black colleges operated by black churches than in institutions run by white churches.[35] Many black teachers were ministers.

A strong sense of class and status pervaded the ranks of black teachers: "Individual free black teachers frequently expressed a sense of superiority over the former slaves."[36] In Louisiana some black schools excluded children of ex-slaves.[37] All in all, black teachers, as a middle-class group, shared the general philosophy of their white peers. Nevertheless, former slaves managed to play "a major part" in Bureau schools though formerly free blacks were dominant.

The issue of textbooks for freedmen's schools was a contentious one. Devotees of the old order expressed shock at the books and called them biased and inflammatory. Morris, who examined a number of the books, came to quite the opposite conclusion.

Teachers in Bureau schools often made political statements but Morris characterized these as extremely moderate and conciliatory. Morris reports that "in every southern state high-ranking Bureau officials frequently used their considerable influence to prevent freedmen's teachers from becoming too political or too vindictive in their approach to sectional issues."[38] Citing a book by Maria Child, a well-known former abolitionist, Morris writes that she "advised the ex-slaves to turn the other cheek when abused by southern whites . . . ."[39] In an organ of a missionary society, "always the emphasis was on self-improvement as a means of eliminating racial prejudice."[40] Black children, all of whom had lived under slavery, welcomed stories about slavery and emancipation.

In 1877, federal troops were removed from the South, an act that signalled the impending end of Reconstruction policy. By that time, the Bureau had been extinct for seven years. Educators in freedmen's schools were all too ready to close the door. "Convinced that compromise was essential to the success of the Bureau program," comments Morris, "school officials and teachers were often willing to follow southern racial etiquette and to tolerate racial segregation and discrimination in their own ranks."[41] Accommodating to southern racism led, according to Morris, to an educational policy of accommodation later in the century: "Emphasizing self-help, hard work, and strict morality, this philosophy encouraged the growth of the individual education movement and prepared the way for the leadership of Booker T. Washington."[42]

Morris's conclusions should be subjected to critical examination. For one thing, he identifies black education with Bureau education. He never discusses black public education. Yet, by 1880, one-third of all school-age black children attended public schools; in 1870, it had been only one-tenth.[43] The growth of enrollment in public schools was almost wholly a black achievement, based on careful use of political power, however precarious it was. Northern missionaries played no role in it. We have no way of knowing what educational philosophy reigned in the public schools. Also, Morris identifies Washington's accommodationist educational philosophy with the general run of black education. While this assumption is frequently made, recent research suggests that it is defective. Sherer has shown that most black educators in Washington's own state of Alabama rejected his philosophy.[44] These black contemporaries refused to convert their schools into mere appendages of an industrial shop. What were the sources of such opposition? How were they related to the education of the freedmen? Were the resisters exempt from the Bureau's purported influence or was that influence both less pervasive and more intermittent than Morris suggests? However one responds to these queries, Morris's work is still excellent and thorough as well as provocative.

Histories of education are often written in an historical vacuum. That is, detailed accounts of schools and districts are given, and changes over time are explained by these same factors. The typical history is seamless and self-contained. Little or no account is taken of the society "out there" except as an inert backdrop. The same defect can be found in works dealing with contemporary education.

Nieman studied the role of the Freedmen's Bureau from 1865 to 1868 in its attempt to insure freedmen their legal rights. The most difficult problem was to bring them under the protection of local and state laws in the South. The Bureau failed in this effort, largely because of self-imposed limitations.

Within two weeks after becoming head of the Bureau, General O. O. Howard decided to convince freedmen to remain on their old plantations and work for wages. The Bureau would police the contracts for fairness and protect the freedmen from exploitation. Throughout the South, however, local courts and law enforcement officials were frank and flagrant partisans of planters, who were frequently immune from legal penalty even in cases of assault on their black employees.

Although the Bureau did help protect freedmen's contractual rights, very often its agents failed to do so. They discouraged blacks from engaging in strikes against planters. In at least one case, involving interpretation of a wage contract, leaders of a protest were arrested by soldiers on the complaint of a Bureau agent.[45] Before they were ordered to stop by the secretary of war, many Bureau agents instituted a pass system for urban blacks: "When these agents arrested blacks who did not have a paper, they put them to work on the public works and subsequently hired them to planters who came to town looking for additional laborers."[46]

On the other hand, when agents tried to help freedmen who had been assaulted by their employers to gain redress it was always in vain: "Justices often placed every impediment they could in the way of freedmen who brought suits against planters."[47] Further, writes Nieman: "Across the South, judges and magistrates refused to admit black testimony in cases in which one of the parties was a white man."[48] Frequently, military commanders meddled in Bureau efforts to settle cases involving blacks.

The Bureau was of two minds when it came to freedmen's rights. It protected their right to select or change jobs with only a moderate degree of consistency. In the face of obdurate local courts and law officers the Bureau tried fitfully to translate the freedmen's legal rights into reality. By 1868, a scant three years after war's end, few Bureau representatives remained in the South. Congress ended the agency's existence and no successor appeared. The "white massive resistance" to racial change foreclosed the rule of law for blacks. During the next decade or so, blacks struggled along with minimum federal assistance, at least on the local and state level. All the more wonder, therefore, that blacks succeeded during that time in establishing and securing their hold on southern public education.

Federal enforcement of the freedmen's right to vote, during the period 1877–1893, was the subject of Robert Goldman's research. In what is apparently the first study of its kind, he found that the Department of Justice filed over 1,200 prosecutions involving election violations. Yet, this was a period of falling black participation in voting, a period which closed when southern states began disfranchising blacks through poll taxes, literacy tests, and other devices. Why did federal activity from 1877 to 1893 accomplish so little?

Goldman points out that although before 1870, the attorney general was a member of the presidential cabinet, it was only after that date that the Department of Justice operated as an executive department. Prior to that, the attorney general was merely an adviser to the president and others who had to depend upon enforcement by local federal court officers. The latter were autonomous before 1870; after that date they remained so in all but name. The local federal district attorney, the federal marshal, and federal deputies were the hope of the freedmen. As Goldman observes of the mid-1880s: "Black politicians, educators, writers, and conventions of black organizations, all spoke out against the emergence of segregation and the growing violence and intimidation against black voters."[49] At the same time, district attorneys found it difficult to get white grand juries to vote indictments in voting rights cases.[50] Judges in Arkansas levied absurdly light sentences, such as ten dollars and court costs.[51]

In 1893, Congress repealed the two statutes under which the Department of Justice had filed cases. The Democratic party, secure in its white southern base, took the lead in this action. But Republicans did not protest greatly. In fact, they won the congressional elections of 1894 without black votes. Since the Republicans no longer needed black votes to win and the Democrats' power in the South required an end to black voting, cynicism and despotism made a mockery of the Fifteenth Amendment.

Let us return to the work of Morris, discussed earlier. He viewed the former abolitionists' philosophy of accommodation to southern racism as a prime cause of the rise of industrial education and the political and educational leadership of Booker T. Washington. Yet, it is clear from the research of Nieman and Goldman that a racist system had been reestablished in the postwar southern economy and polity. The failure of the federal government to consolidate the rights of freedmen left the latter at the mercy of local oppressors. The freedmen fought back but after a certain point acquiescence became their dominant strategy. In education, acquiescence became accommodation to the view that blacks needed a special kind of education that would "fit" them for a subordinate life position. But contrary to Morris's view, this educational philosophy was of little importance in creating the system of southern racism. Rather, the reverse is more accurate. Preconditions for the racism lay in economics, politics, and law rather than in educational philosophy.[52]

Smith has studied the rise of racially discriminatory systems of school finance in the South from 1870 to 1910. A central question concerned whether blacks "paid for" their schools through their taxes or whether they were subsidized. He summarized his findings as follows: "By 1900, blacks were subsidizing white education. In fact, there are only two [census] years in which black education was being subsidized [by whites], 1880 and 1890. . . ."[53] Thus, blacks paid for their own and for part of whites' schooling at least between 1900 and 1910.

On a per child basis, Smith found that blacks carried a far heavier burden of subsidization than did whites: "Expenditures for black education could have been more than double their actual 1910 level if no transfers [to whites] had taken place while white expenditures would have been only 9.81 percent lower without the subsidy from blacks."[54] Another way of putting it is that the educational deprivation of black children resulting from black subsidies to whites was greater by far than the advantages white students gained thereby. This inequality in impact was due to the general disparity of financial support between black and white schools. The greater the disparity, the more unequal the impact of subsidies.

Smith attributes the disparity not to impersonal economic factors but to "racial attitudes and relationships and [to] the decision-making process in education. . . ."[55] As we saw above, these attitudes, relationships, and processes operated in one overall direction—to the disadvantage of blacks. State school authorities as well as local school boards and superintendents failed to challenge either the method employed or the outcome. Disfranchisement sealed the doom of black equality in the public schools as they came to operate as an adjunct to the plantation system.

The past decade has seen a welcome increase in historical research on black education in northern cities. Helping to dispel the myth of de facto segregation is a valuable by-product of this work. De facto segregation is the widespread belief that school segregation in the North is merely a reflex to housing segregation and that no intentional discrimination is involved.

Rosenbaum's study of Chicago, Philadelphia, and Indianapolis suggests otherwise. Chicago's historical record is well-documented.[56] Early in the present century, the issue of blacks in the schools became a matter of public discussion in Philadelphia. Superintendent Martin G. Brumbaugh, who advocated outright segregation, also devised what may be the earliest formulation of the so-called tipping point. In his annual report for 1907, he wrote, "When the percentage of colored children reaches thirty or more the other children begin gradually to withdraw from the school."[57] Thus began a folk-belief that was described by its author as a "fact." As a halfway measure to outright segregation, Brumbaugh proposed that, in non-segregated schools, separate black classes could be established and taught by black teachers.

This proposal was interpreted by some as an invitation to black teachers to apply for jobs, even if only in segregated schools. Presumably in response to such willingness, Brumbaugh set up lists for teacher applicants on a racial basis. This lasted until 1937. Rosenbaum comments:

Thus a practice of never hiring Negro teachers for mixed classes hardened into official policy. . . . In no school in which even one percent of the pupils was white was a black teacher placed. Thus little benefit accrued to the black community as far as increased jobs for Negro educators.[58]

In the few schools enrolling both black and white children, investigators found in 1912 "that in some rooms Negro children were instructed to sit on one side of the room away from the white pupils."[59]

Indiana, which did not abolish legally required school segregation until 1949 (the last northern state to do so), is a good example of how the system worked. During the 1920s the bulk of the black community in Indianapolis opposed the school board's intention to build the city's first all-black high school, to be named after Crispus Attucks. By 1929, writes Rosenbaum, Indianapolis was "the largest segregated system in any northern metropolitan area."[60] Although the city housed the headquarters for the politically influential Ku Klux Klan, which warmly endorsed school segregation, the Klan was not the prime mover. In Indianapolis as well as in Chicago and

Philadelphia, Rosenbaum notes, "discriminatory policies emanated from the mainstream educators and civic leaders . . ."[61] and could not be attributed to extremist minorities or street mobs. As early as 1897, for example, the Committee of Fifteen of the National Education Association has recommended the creation of "distinctive schools for Negro youth," with black teachers.[62]

Maskin is the first historian to examine the effects of Franklin D. Roosevelt's New Deal on black education. The primary mechanism for that influence was the Emergency Education Program (EEP) which operated as part of the federal relief program. Maskin used two principal kinds of evidence: correspondence and unpublished reports in federal agencies, and unpublished fact-finding memoranda of the Gunnar Myrdal investigation which resulted in the 1944 publication, *The American Dilemma*. Maskin was concerned with federal policy decisions and concrete conditions of black schooling in New York City, Chicago, and Philadelphia, especially during the years 1935-1943.

Federal officials did not challenge the racially segregated structure of northern education. Frequently, local blacks were warned by federal representatives—some of them black—to moderate their demands for equality. Nevertheless, encouraged by the demands of local black communities, EEP organized the first adult education classes in such areas. It offered courses in black history, modest vocational training, tutorial services, and other activities. In most cases, the local school systems were none too eager to welcome what many regarded as federal meddling.

Most revealing, however, were conditions that EEP found in the local schools.

In Harlem, for example, "any attempt to move beyond the confines of the established curriculum, such as the teaching of Negro history, was severely frowned upon by the authorities."[63] A white principal of P.S. 89, in Harlem, wrote a correspondent that the problem in the area's schools

is not to bring up the pupil standard to the curricular level, but to minimize the course of study to fit the pupil. An extension of manual training work is the only answer if we are to fit the children of this neighborhood for a good, profitable life after their education is completed.[64]

Low expectations and other techniques of academic discouragement were also the rule in secondary education.

Maskin explains:

The bulk of the problem grew out of the [School] Board's policy of allowing the Dean of Boys in each junior high school in Harlem to decide whether or not a student's choice of a high school was a wise one. The Dean also reserved the right not to send a written statement to this effect along with the student's high school application. As a result of this policy black graduates from junior high schools in Manhattan were invariably sent to Wadleigh, Textile, and Haaren High Schools—all inferior with regard to facilities and equipment. In addition to their inadequate lunchrooms, gymnasiums and laboratories, these schools were staffed by socially insensitive administrators. At Wadleigh, for example, Negro girls were told by the principal not to register for commercial courses on the grounds that "they would not have opportunity after graduation to use such knowledge."[65]

During the 1920s, a principal in a Harlem junior high school ordered the removal of typewriters because "the course was not practicable in a colored neighborhood."[66]

Parents and civic groups formed an organization, the Permanent Committee for Better Schools in Harlem, whose straightforward slogan was: "Don't give our children a half-assed education."[67] The Committee, which consisted of some eighty-five groups, included organizations with a broad range of interests, from the American Legion to the Communist party. They called for, among other things, a lessening of segregation in Harlem schools. In 1937, part of Harlem was rezoned into the all-white George Washington High School.

The same activist protest against the school system also led, after an initial period of suspicion, to their welcoming EEP activities. Harlem's EEP program was a highly active one.

In Chicago's black schools the story was not essentially different. The principal of Doolittle Elementary School set up what he called "lower vocational training," especially for children newly arrived from the South. At Doolittle, according to Maskin, "Boys made letter openers and bookends, and girls learned to cook, sew, and make beds. Both girls and boys judged "mentally unfit" were assigned to wash walls in the hallways and in the school's kitchen."[68] This approach, Maskin adds, resembled that of the school board mentioned above.

He also found that the school board took pains to enforce segregation along with deprivation. In 1935, for example, fourteen schools were on double shift, that is, so crowded that children attended for less than a whole day. Thirteen of the schools were black. Maskin comments: "This situation was particularly ironic since many of the schools adjacent to the Black Belt were experiencing an average decline in enrollment of about five percent and had many seats vacant and no black students to fill their empty classrooms."[69] The school system's only black principal told an investigator that whites who staffed black schools "often expected their students not to succeed scholastically, or to behave in a respectable manner."[70]

Philadelphia's school board, as we saw earlier, had formally segregated its teachers by race since before World War I. During the 1920s, Maskin reports, "the trend toward separate facilities was enhanced by a ruling from the [School] Board . . . which allowed the principal of any school to reject or accept pupils at will and to provide ready transfers to those students wishing to attend school elsewhere."[71] As in New York City and Chicago, vocational educators in Philadelphia selected black students for menial tasks: "Black girls were found disproportionately enrolled in beauty culture and home economics courses in high school, while black boys were guided into auto mechanics courses which prepared them for jobs as car washers or greasers."[72]

Two black citizen groups emerged during the thirties in Philadelphia. One was the Educational Equity League, founded by Floyd Logan. It fought successfully to eliminate racially segregated faculties and was able to gain the reinstatement of fifty-eight black teachers who had been discharged. A second group was the North Philadelphia United Committee for Better Schools whose slogan called for "a full day in school for every child."[73]

EEP, as indicated above, did not attempt to deal with basic inequities in the three school systems. When the contrast between black and white schooling was especially glaring—as in New York City at a time when the school system was regarded as a national leader—federal officials worked at the outer edge of things, providing marginal services that would not disturb the fundamentals of the system. Maskin evaluates the effort more positively: "The New Deal sought to pull together the threads of community life in these three black neighborhoods, and to activate an untapped mine of human creativity which lay below a shroud of poverty and neglect."[74] Nearly 100,000 blacks had shared in one or another EEP program, but it was only a momentary gleam in an otherwise dull future.

Only rarely do research studies concern more than a single minority and almost never do they expand their terms of reference to an entire state. In 1975, two studies—by Beck and Wollenberg—did both at one time. With some overlap between them, both authors examined the history of the education of minority children in California largely since 1850. Beck stressed the earlier period, Wollenberg the latter half. Both dealt with blacks, Mexican Americans, Indian Americans, and Asians.

Beck found discrimination against all the groups. Foreshadowing the present, the Los Angeles superintendent, T. H. Rose, is quoted in 1868: "Many, indeed, most of the children, are Spanish, and a teacher, to succeed, should know something of that language."[75] While state law required instruction in English only, theory frequently yielded to practice and both languages were used. When English-only was stressed, parents of Mexican-American children sometimes sent them to parochial schools where Spanish usually was used. Indian children were segregated, provided, of course, they went to any school at all prior to 1890. Ten years earlier, Beck reports, only about 8 percent of school-age Indian children attended school.[76]

In 1859 Chinese children were given a one-room public "school" located in the basement of the Chinese Chapel in San Francisco. It was completely segregated. After it was closed in 1870 sixteen more years passed before the state provided another one. Meanwhile, Protestant missionaries provided the children a combination of schooling and salvation.

Blacks in California were few in number and better off than their peers elsewhere:

Blacks in San Francisco were significantly more skilled, educated, informed and organized . . . than in almost any other American city. . . . The statewide illiteracy rate for California's 11,322 blacks in 1890 was 26.5 percent, compared to 57.1 percent for the nation.[77]

In the state as a whole, they were outnumbered by the Chinese in a ratio of 6.5 to 1.

Nevertheless, black children were segregated by law and practice. In 1854, the first publicly financed segregated school for blacks was established in San Francisco; it was funded by the city. The next year, the state legislature provided that school tax funds were to be apportioned on the basis of a census of white children only. Four years later, the state superintendent of schools, Andrew Jackson Moulder, declared: "Our Schools must be maintained exclusively for whites, or they will soon become tenanted by blacks alone."[78] After unremitting pressure by black parents the law was changed, but their children were required to attend black schools.

Wollenberg fashioned his work around six court decisions, each significant for a minority group's search for educational equality in California. He brought, however, far more than legal knowledge to his task. Each episode is set in a historical framework that greatly enhances the comprehension of legal detail. The writing is notably clear, unlike so much work in this field.

Ward v. *Flood* was a response to a highly organized black community campaign to abolish black segregated schools. Instead, the court adopted a separate-but-equal doctrine that had first been applied in Boston twenty-two years earlier. On the face of it the decision was a total defeat, yet it accomplished one goal of the blacks: the court declared that the state had a legal obligation to educate blacks. In fact, the next year black children in San Francisco, Sacramento, Oakland, and Vallejo entered previously all-white schools.

Chinese parents challenged the virtual exclusion of their children from public schools in *Tape* v. *Hurley* (1885). One ground for their case was a claim that the 1868 treaty between China and this country "assured Chinese children living in America the right to attend public schools."[79] Mamie Tape, a Chinese student, had applied to enter a white school in San Francisco but had been turned away. The state supreme court ruled in her favor, thus settling the question of a Chinese child's right to attend a public school. (A lower court had declared it "unjust" for the state to levy a "forced tax on Chinese parents to help maintain our schools, and yet prohibit their children born here from education in those schools.")[80] The high court did not strike down segregation but only the total exclusion of Chinese children from public schools. Within hours after the decision, however, the state legislature authorized the establishment of a separate school for "Mongolians."

Aoki v. *Deane* (1906) concerned the right of Japanese-American children to attend non-segregated schools in San Francisco. Wollenberg points out some distinctive cultural traits of this group:

The Japanese may well have been the best educated immigrant group ever to come to America, with over 90 percent . . . literate in their own language. . . . The new Japanese residents had long experience with public education [in Japan] and a belief that it could promote their economic and social well-being. These values were passed on to their children.[81]

Unlike the Chinese children in the same city, Japanese-American students attended neighborhood schools.

In 1906, the school board ordered Japanese students to attend the Redding Elementary School and no other, arousing a storm of protest among Japanese-Americans. The Japanese government declared the action was in violation of the 1894 treaty between the United States and Japan and demanded its recision. The treaty provided that Japanese would not be subjected to any disability from which the nationals of any other country were exempt. Since no Europeans were segregated, neither should any Japanese be.

The conflict was settled finally more as an aspect of world politics than as an educational matter. Around this time, the United States regarded Japan as a valuable potential ally in world political competition in the Far East. Late in 1906, President Theodore Roosevelt, in his annual message to Congress, referred to the Japanese-American students and called the segregation order "a wicked absurdity."[82] Racism ran deep on this issue in California and the president was attacked for siding with the "Yellow Peril." Especially criticized was the court suit Roosevelt said would be filed. The matter was finally settled out of court. The school board rescinded its order and the Japanese government undertook to suspend the emigration of unskilled Japanese laborers, thus calming white Californian complaints, largely fanciful, of unfair low-wage competition from the Japanese in America.

During the 1920s and 1930s, Japanese Americans attended "after-school" classes in Japanese language schools. These did not resemble their Chinese counterparts as the Japanese-American emphasis was upon assimilation into the larger American society. Most of the schools "also taught English to very small children in order to prepare them for public schools, and some language schools purposely hired whites to teach these English classes."[83] Tragically, however, both first- and second-generation Japanese Americans (Issei and Nisei) were deprived of their rights during World War II and placed in camps as potential spies and saboteurs.

The right of Indian Americans to attend public schools was established by *Piper* v. *Big Pine School District* (1924). Until then, the practice in California was to require Indians to attend a federal Indian school even if a public school were located in the same area. The court held that since Alice Piper, an Indian, was a citizen, she could attend the school of her choice.

The ruling, however, did not challenge the historic separate-but-equal rule: to establish a "separate school for Indians . . . does not offend either the federal or state constitutions."[84]

Piper did not touch on other problems. The content of Indian education was one of these. Two years after *Piper*, a Commonwealth Club study reported, according to Wollenberg:

Sherman Institute in Riverside was judged to be "by far the best" of the boarding schools "in equipment and grade of teacher," but even it was described as based on "the conception that the Indian is inferior to the whiteman. . . . Every Indian girl is viewed as a potential house servant and every boy as a farm hand."[85]

These conditions resisted change.

In *Mendez* v. *Westminster* (1946) Mexican-American parents challenged the practice of segregating their children. They asked a federal court to permit transfers out of the "Mexican" to the "white" school. Four school districts were involved. Judge Paul J. McCormick rejected the separate-but-equal contention of school district lawyers. Instead, he held: "A paramount requisite in the American system of public education is social equality. It must be open to all children by unified school association regardless of lineage." The court agreed that separation of children on the basis of language might be acceptable in early grades but not for eighth grade. The ruling was upheld by a United States Appeals Court.

Segregation of blacks was involved in *Jackson* v. *Pasadena* (1963). The state supreme court approved a finding of deliberate conscious segregation by the Pasadena school board. Gerrymandering of junior high school boundaries and permitting whites to transfer from an increasingly black junior high school were the major violations. The court, however, proceeded to lay down a novel principle: a court could order desegregation even in the absence of a showing of deliberate discrimination. "The right to equal opportunity for education and the harmful consequences of segregation," stated the court, "require that school boards take steps, insofar as reasonably feasible, to alleviate racial imbalance in schools regardless of its cause."[86] Thus was established by a court, for the first time, the potentially powerful principle that segregation as such—whether de jure or de facto—was unacceptable in California.

Wollenberg's study remedied in part the situation that "California's long history of school segregation and exclusion has been virtually ignored by educators and historians, let alone politicians and the general public."[87]

Overall, the picture that emerges from the recent historical research is one of pervasive and enduring racial discrimination. Another of the findings is the ordinariness of the discriminatory structures. That is, the history of racial discrimination in education is one of normal institutions of education introducing practices that severely penalize large groups of children. School boards, central administrations, state departments of education, and state superintendents, courts and administrative agencies have all participated in restricting equality in the schools. Another feature of the research is the congruence of discrimination in education and in society. Perhaps the most striking feature of all is the resort to collective protest by parents whose children feel the greatest impact of discrimination.

Notes

1. Andrew Anthony Tijerina, *Tejanos and Texas: The Native Mexicans of Texas, 1820-1850* (doctoral diss., University of Texas, 1977), p. 44. (University Microfilms Order No. 78-7397.)

2. Ibid., p. 97.

3. Ibid., p. 136.

4. Ibid., p. 158.

5. Ibid., p. 320.

6. Quoted in James Ernest Crisp, *Anglo-Texan Attitudes Toward the Mexicans, 1825-1845* (doctoral diss., Yale University, 1976), p. 97. (University Microfilms Order No. 76-29, 828.)

7. Ibid., p. 273.

8. Ibid., p. 455.

9. Marcy Gail Goldstein, *Americanization and Mexicanization: The Mexican Elite and Anglo-Americans in the Gadsden Purchase Lands, 1853-1880* (doctoral diss., Case Western Reserve University, 1977), p. 43. (University Microfilms Order No. 77-18855.)

10. Ibid., p. 311.

11. Ibid., p. 136.

12. Ibid., p. 310.

13. Ibid., p. 312.

14. Fernando Chacon Gomez, *The Intended and Actual Effect of Article VIII of the Treaty of Guadalupe Hidalgo: Mexican Treaty Rights Under International and Domestic Law* (doctoral diss., University of Michigan, 1977), p. 36. (University Microfilms Order No. 78-4709.)

15. Ibid., p. 38.

16. Ibid., p. 187.

17. Ibid., footnote 139, p. 77.

18. Francisco Enrique Baldarrama, *En Defensa de la Raza: The Los Angeles Mexican Consulate and Colonia Mexicana during the Great Depression* (doctoral diss., University of California, Los Angeles, 1978), pp. 104-5. (University Microfilms Order No. 7901331.)

19. Meyer Weinberg, *A Chance to Learn* (New York: Cambridge University Press, 1977), pp. 156-59.

20. Vernon Carl Allsup, *The American G. I. Forum: A History of a Mexican-American Organization* (doctoral diss., University of Texas, 1976), pp. 11-12. (University Microfilms Order No. 77-3855.) See also Carl Allsup, "Education is our Freedom: The American G.I. Forum and the Mexican American School Segregation in Texas, 1948-1957," *Aztlan*, 8 (Spring-Fall 1977), pp. 27-50.

21. Quoted in Allsup, *The American G.I. Forum*, p. 114.

22. William L. Lang, *Black Bootstraps: The Abolitionist Educators' Ideology and the Education of the Northern Free Negro, 1828–1860* (doctoral diss., University of Delaware, 1974), p. 10. (University Microfilms Order No. 74-27,858.)

23. Ibid., p. 16.

24. Ibid., p. 228.

25. Ibid., p. 229.

26. See W.E.B. Du Bois, "The Negro College," *Crisis* (August 1933); and Charles S. Johnson, *The Negro College Graduate* (Chapel Hill: University of North Carolina Press, 1938).

27. The first was written twenty-five years earlier by Marjorie H. Parker: "The Educational Activities of the Freedmen's Bureau" (doctoral diss., University of Chicago, 1951).

28. Robert C. Morris, "Reading, 'ritin and Reconstruction: Freedmen's Education in the South" (doctoral diss., University of Chicago, 1976), p. 211.

29. Ibid., p. 217.

30. Ibid., p. 61.

31. Ibid., p. 41.

32. Ibid., p. 153.

33. Ibid., p. 154.

34. Ibid.

35. James W. McPherson, "White Liberals and Black Power in Negro Education, 1865–1915," *American Historical Review*, 75 (June 1970).

36. Morris, "Reading, 'ritin and Reconstruction," p. 178.

37. Ibid., pp. 177–78.

38. Ibid., p. 265.

39. Ibid., p. 296.

40. Ibid., p. 297.

41. Ibid., p. 360.

42. Ibid.

43. See Weinberg, *A Chance to Learn*, p. 44.

44. Robert G. Sherer, Jr., *Subordination or Liberation: The Development and Conflicting Theories of Black Education in Nineteenth Century Alabama* (University: University of Alabama Press, 1976).

45. Donald G. Nieman, *To Set the Law in Motion: The Freedmen's Bureau and the Legal Rights of Blacks, 1865–1868* (doctoral diss., Rice University, 1975), p. 270. (University Microfilms Order No. 75-22,051.)

46. Ibid., p. 117.

47. Ibid., p. 281.

48. Ibid., p. 22.

49. Robert Michael Goldman, *"A Free Ballot and a Fair Count": The Department of Justice and the Enforcement of Voting Rights in the South, 1877–1893* (doctoral diss., Michigan State University, 1976), p. 219. (University Microfilms Order No. 76-27,098.)

50. Ibid., p. 228.

51. Ibid., p. 243.

52. The same criticism can be made of James Douglas Anderson, *Education for Servitude: The Social Purposes of Schooling in the Black South, 1870–1930* (doctoral diss., University of Illinois, 1973). (University Microfilms Order No. 73-17,493.)

53. Richard Kent Smith, *The Economics of Education and Discrimination in the*

U.S. South: 1870–1910 (doctoral diss., University of Wisconsin, 1973), p. 100. (University Microfilms Order No. 74-10,269.)

54. Ibid.

55. Ibid., pp. 139–40.

56. See Michael W. Homel, "Negroes in the Chicago Public Schools, 1910–1941" (doctoral diss., University of Chicago, 1972).

57. Quoted in Judy J. Rosenbaum, *Black Education in Three Northern Cities in the Early Twentieth Century* (doctoral diss., University of Illinois, 1974), p. 149. (University Microfilms Order No. 75-11,741.)

58. Ibid., pp. 150, 152.

59. Ibid., p. 153.

60. Ibid., p. 216.

61. Ibid., pp. 239–40.

62. Ibid., p. 147.

63. Melvin Reuben Maskin, *Black Education and the New Deal: The Urban Experience* (doctoral diss., New York University, 1973), p. 143. (University Microfilms Order No. 73-19,948.)

64. Ibid., p. 138.

65. Ibid., pp. 143–44.

66. Ibid., p. 144.

67. Ibid., p. 149.

68. Ibid., p. 216.

69. Ibid., p. 221 (emphasis in original).

70. Ibid., p. 222.

71. Ibid., p. 270.

72. Ibid., p. 275.

73. Ibid., p. 283.

74. Ibid., p. 337.

75. Nicholas P. Beck, *The Other Children: Minority Education in California Public Schools from Statehood to 1890* (doctoral diss., University of California, 1975), p. 21. (University Microfilms Order No. 75-22,604.)

76. Ibid., p. 45.

77. Ibid., pp. 95, 96.

78. Ibid., p. 103.

79. Charles M. Wollenberg, *All Deliberate Speed: Segregation and Exclusion in California Schools: 1855–1975* (doctoral diss., University of California, Berkeley, 1975), p. 36. (University Microfilms Order No. 76-15,425.) This dissertation was published by the University of California Press in 1978 but references here are to the unpublished dissertation.

80. Ibid., p. 43.

81. Ibid., p. 59.

82. Ibid., p. 68.

83. Ibid., p. 79.

84. Ibid., p. 113.

85. Ibid., p. 115.

86. Ibid., p. 167.

87. Ibid., p. 211.

2

The Legal Framework

The legal framework for the education of minority children consists of far more than laws and court decisions. Equally important are the community conditions that give rise to movements for legal change. No less significant are the consequences of legal change as exemplified by the implementation or—just as frequently—nonimplementation of legal declarations. Yet, all but a few studies concern themselves with the formal change and pay little if any attention to preconditions and consequences. In this chapter we will examine a series of recent researches that exemplify a great improvement over the traditional approach. Their central concern is not the legal enactments as such but their consequences, both anticipated and unanticipated.

Sarah Nieves studied the operation of legislation in New York State affecting bilingual education, which stipulates that "subject matter such as reading and mathematics will be learned in the dominant language with the goal of achieving fluency in both languages." The law also requires "programs which impart the history, traditions, culture, life styles, and values associated with the languages." Nieves found that implementation of the law usually involved "pulling out" students from their regular classroom for forty-five minutes, three to five days a week. During these periods, instruction in Spanish was given. Nieves holds that such periods are too short for language instruction, let alone for cultural instruction as well.

It is somewhat difficult to understand from Nieves's account how the formal bilingual program actually worked. The researcher seemed more interested in characterizing the schools' putative abuse of the programs in terms of broad social theory. For example, one of her conclusions is as follows:

Within the confines of a compensatory education conception, bilingual education for Puerto Ricans in the United States is little more than an anesthetic to distract the recipients from the causes of their problems and, therefore, from achieving the concrete solutions to those problems.[1]

Since Nieves analyzes neither the causes nor the solutions of the problems the reader is unable to assess the soundness of the conclusion.

She does, however, point to an assimilatory mind-set among educational decision-makers that leads to "the imposition of the Anglo-Saxon world view upon children of differing backgrounds and assumptions."[2] This point is made repeatedly. She also emphasizes the failure of schools in New York City to take the home and parents into account in curriculum matters as well as in educational planning. Earlier writers have repeatedly made both these points. The work as a whole sheds little fresh light on the dynamics of implementation of the state bilingual statute.

Three years after Nieves completed her study, Lois Steinberg analyzed the implementation of federal bilingual statutes. (In 1968, Congress passed the Bilingual Act of 1968, Title VII, as an amendment to the Elementary and Secondary Education Act (ESEA) of 1965. In 1974, Congress amended Title VII to restrict the participation of English-dominant children in federal bilingual programs.) Steinberg's basic interest was in the political consequences of the legislation. Specifically, she traced "the mobilization of an informal network of Puerto Rican educators whose careers have been promoted through federal initiatives and their participation in efforts to use federal resources to change New York City's educational policy."[3]

As of 1969, the Puerto Rican presence among the staff of the city's schools was minimal. Of 3,700 Puerto Ricans employed, 68 percent or nearly 2,500 were paraprofessionals. Of non-Puerto Ricans employed, only 14 percent were paraprofessionals.[4] Overall, Puerto Ricans made up only 3.8 percent of all school board personnel. By 1972, the situation had improved. During 1969–1972, for example, the number of Hispanic principals rose by 288 percent; this figure reflected a net increase of merely twenty-three principals. The number of Hispanic teachers rose by 470 but this was a minuscule increase in a teaching force of some 60,000.

Until 1970, state law prohibited the use of a language of instruction other than English. That year the law was amended, but bilingualism did not sweep all before it. Between 1970 and 1972–1973, the number of New York City students enrolled in bilingual classes rose from 6,000 to 13,815.[5] By 1973, some 72,000 students were in bilingual or English as a Second Language classes, mostly the latter.

During the years 1968–1973, Steinberg observes, an informal network of Puerto Rican educators took shape in New York City. She lists among the leaders in the network Evelyn Colon, Hernan La Fontaine, Awilda Orta, Carmen S. Perez, Sonia Rivera, and Jose Vasquez. They socialized together, had founded the Puerto Rican Educators Association (PRED) in 1965, and were early practitioners of bilingual education in the city. Principalships and supervisory positions in the school system went to members of the network. While a number of such positions became available, Steinberg emphasizes that "the Puerto Rican's upward mobility was confined to federally-funded bilingual positions."[6] In other words, the growing Puerto

Rican impact was severely restricted within the school system as a whole. "By isolating Puerto Rican educators and confining their advancement to the limited roles provided by compensatory bilingual programs or administrative positions in schools with high Puerto Rican enrollments," comments Steinberg, "the policies erode their opportunities to exert significant influence within the bureaucracy as well as limit their professional advancement."[7]

What was the relationship of the informal network to the broader Puerto Rican community in the city? According to Steinberg, the community remained largely unorganized during 1968–1973. To be sure, Aspira, which had been organized in 1961, had thirty-six clubs in the city during 1971 and thirty-two four years later. Its main use was to encourage Puerto Rican youth to complete high school and college. Membership was modest in any case, standing at 2,800 and 1,199 respectively during the two years.[8] Aspira's affiliates were located in five states. Steinberg refers to "Aspira's limited and unstable funds which [make] the group dependent on middle class Puerto Ricans many of whom, particularly educators, have a professional rather than a community oriented perspective."[9]

What of the issue of bilingualism within the Puerto Rican community? According to Steinberg, "there is no evidence to indicate Puerto Rican interest in language maintenance" before 1967 or thereabouts.[10] Undoubtedly, after that date the issue rose in saliency within the community. At the same time, however, a certain tension existed between "grass roots" representatives and the network of educators. Thus, at the Fourth International Conference on Bilingual/Bicultural Education, held in New York City in May, 1974, the militant United Bronx Parents (UBP) distributed a leaflet containing the following message:

Without our *children*, you would not be making the nice fat salaries you make. Parents have opened up a whole new field of opportunity of "professionals" who have been unsure of their ethnicity. We're sick and tired of being used as stepping stones for opportunists to walk on. . . . Without the struggle of parents, their sacrifices, arrests, and battles, there would be no bilingual education today.[11]

Whatever lay behind this embittered outburst, UBP's conclusion was undoubtedly correct. Alone, the network would have been ineffectual. As part of a larger movement, it had a limited effect.

While Steinberg does not deal with the United Federation of Teachers (UFT) in great detail, she does sketch the general importance of the organization in the struggle over bilingualism. In 1968, a UFT-led teachers' strike "galvanized the network of Puerto Rican educators to pursue more aggressive tactics."[12] UFT feared that demands for community control of schools would endanger union controls of employment, wages, and working conditions. It also feared that bilingualism would call for special teaching licenses that would dilute UFT's control over entry into the work force. During the early 1970s, when Puerto Rican groups were lobbying in the state legislature for stronger bilingual legislation, UFT constituted a strong counterforce. In 1973, UFT opposed continued employment of Luis Fuentes as community superintendent of heavily Puerto Rican School District 1 on the grounds that he was anti-Semitic, a charge Fuentes denied. Dr. Kenneth B. Clark accused UFT of "racial incitement." Both in District 1 and in Ocean Hill-Brownsville, a community-controlled experimental district during the late 1960s, writes Steinberg, "the union has helped to generate and then publicize throughout the city inter-ethnic hostilities surrounding controversial minority administrators in one district."[13]

Steinberg's study is a solid work that is well informed and straightforward. Because she has made similar studies in earlier years, she is familiar with the local scene and knowledgeable about shadings and distinctions that might escape other observers. We will return to her work in connection with the next study to be reviewed.

In September, 1972, Aspira filed a complaint in federal court charging that the New York City school board had "failed to take into account the plaintiffs' inability to speak and understand English, and learn in classes conducted in the English language." It asked the court to mandate an educational plan. "The elements that the proposed plan should incorporate," the complaint stipulated, were "bilingual services, bilingual courses of study, procedures for evaluation and classification of language ability and achievement, and special programs to compensate, to the extent possible, for the Board's past failure to provide plaintiffs and their classes with an equal opportunity."[14] Almost two years later, United States District Judge Marvin E. Frankel ruled in favor of the plaintiffs.

Asaura Santiago has studied the events leading up to filing of the lawsuit, the courtroom presentations, Aspira's strategy, and the final court order. In addition, and perhaps most valuable of all, she has analyzed the implementation process as it unfolded, lurch by lurch. Especially instructive is the process by which the federal judge found the school board in contempt of court for failing to carry out the order. Santiago's treatment also succeeds in conveying vividly an "inside" sense of how a school system bureaucracy alternately lumbers or skips, depending on the issue and the state of affairs at a particular time.

Within two months of the filing of the complaint, plaintiffs confronted the school board with more than 392 interrogatories, that is, requests for specific information to which they were entitled by virtue of standard litigative procedures. These were not answered until July, 1973, nearly nine months later. During this same period, Judge Frankel denied the board's request to dismiss the case. It began to seem clear that a finding of guilt on the part of the board of education was in the works. In January, 1974, the United States Supreme Court unanimously decided *Lau* v. *Nichols*, a case involving the rights of Chinese children in San Francisco who, their parents claimed, were being denied equal education by their school's refusal to use a language other than English as an instructional language. While *Lau* was encouraging, Aspira feared their own case would be resolved by some arrangement short of bilingualism.

The organization began collecting statements by teachers and others in the schools as further evidence to be presented in court. School board employees were warned not to cooperate with Aspira and were threatened with prosecution for a misdemeanor if they persisted. Judge Frankel ordered the board to cease this activity.

By Spring, 1974, resolution of the case was imminent. School board representatives bargained with Aspira representatives on specific terms. When the board pled poverty, Judge Frankel turned aside the argument. As Santiago writes:

He stated that the city was obligated to fulfill its responsibilities and that a federal court had within its authority the right to order the city to float bonds, if necessary, to meet this commitment. Furthermore, he clarified that a federal court decision would supersede any agreements or contractual obligations.[15]

By April, 1974, negotiations dealt with concrete plans. The judge closely supervised resolution of disputed issues. In June, the case was decided.

Santiago summarized the contents of the plan as follows:

Eligible students were those "whose English-language deficiency prevents their effective participation in the learning process and who participate more effectively in Spanish." The board was directed to develop devices to "identify children eligible for the program on the basis of their ability to read, write, and speak both Spanish and English." The principal elements of the program included "(1) intensive instruction in English, (2) instruction in subject areas in Spanish, and (3) instruction to reinforce the child's Spanish language skills." Culture sensitive materials were to be used whenever possible.

An affirmative action program was to be implemented to employ professionals "fluent in the Spanish and English languages" and possessing "the necessary professional skills." September 1975 was set as the deadline for the complete implementation of the program. Preceding that date, a set of pilot schools was to be used as of October 30, 1974 to demonstrate program elements and to train personnel. Aspira was to receive the board's monthly progress reports that were to be submitted to the court.[16]

Santiago does not underestimate the significance of the decree: "The policy of requiring native language instruction in substantive subject areas constituted a major reform based on its compulsory nature."[17] The school board, however, chose to minimize progress, as Santiago's analysis clearly shows.

When Fall, 1975, arrived, the time established for full implementation, the board had accomplished little. In nine community districts, the percentage of eligible Spanish-surname students who were not participating in any bilingual program ranged from 70 to 100. Six months later, in February,

1976, nearly 25 percent of all eligible Spanish-surname students were still without any services. So sweeping a default could only have occurred by a combination of intent and incompetence. Aspira asked the court to find the board guilty of contempt of court. Judge Frankel so ruled in October, 1976.

He found that the board "failed steadily and repeatedly to exercise their power and authority so that those they controlled would proceed promptly and in good faith to accomplish the tasks commanded by the consent decree. This failure reflected their own lack of concentrated will to achieve substantial compliance."[18] Further, he ruled:

Defendants have fallen far short of the requisite diligence. They have neglected to marshal their own resources, assert their high authority, and demand the results needed from subordinate persons and agencies in order to effectuate the court of action required by the consent decree. . . . The failure of supervision and control extended to extravagantly long and benign tolerance of outright defiance as well as footdragging and evasion in the district.[19]

Judge Frankel faced squarely the issue of whether sufficient numbers of qualified bilingual personnel were available:

Adequate [numbers of] people were available by the fall of 1975 to staff the program. . . . Responsible officials . . . had knowledge . . . that many districts were neglecting to hire these available and necessary persons, and were subverting the program by employing unqualified people. Despite this awareness of critical default, the Board's officials took none of the possible and effective actions that would have remedied it.[20]

Conventional textbooks on school administration undoubtedly omitted this particular reality of urban schooling. Their authors had no way of acknowledging that under some political circumstances administrators would prefer the least qualified personnel.

Initiation of contempt motions immediately resulted in a flare of board activity. As Judge Frankel observed in his contempt ruling, "the institution of the contempt proceedings triggered a notable access of attention and energy."[21] The received wisdom of explaining school board inaction by pointing to inevitable delays due to large-scale bureaucracy was confounded by the judge's analysis. The giant nodded when it was prodded. Who could guess at its potential if it ever fully awakened?

The *Aspira* v. *Board of Education of the City of New York* decree effected a basic change in financing methods. Hitherto, funding for bilingual programs—such as they were—had come from federal sources on the theory that these services were "special" and thus not the responsibility of local authorities. Now, however, local tax funds were to be used to supply bilingual services, over and above the cost of basic instruction to all students. In other words, funds to implement *Aspira* came from the city even though they were compensatory in nature. Administrative efforts were made to guard against the *Aspira* bilingual funds being used for instructional services due to all students.

By June, 1976, writes Santiago, "a broad-based bilingual educational program was in operation in New York City public schools serving over 58,000 pupils and involving approximately 1,500 bilingual personnel."[22] Clearly, the program was a direct product of the *Aspira* decree. Yet, as Santiago sagely observes: "Policy change is often a cyclical process. Change causes further change."[23] Four specific questions remained unanswered.

First, is the *Aspira* legal route viable over the long run? Can a minority community count on the courts when serious educational problems arise? The ability of such a community to finance court fights is also problematical. Second, Santiago asks: Is the school board now "pedagogically committed" to bilingual education or has it merely given in where it had to? She notes there are very few bilingual programs for non-Spanish minorities, even though Special Circular No. 114, issued by the board in June, 1975, announced such programs would be created. A third, related question deals with whether the board views bilingual education as an alternative for children who "can effectively participate in the educational process in English."[24] Santiago finally asks whether the *Aspira* program fits the needs of limited-English-speaking children who are in special education.

Certain general problems still remain, despite the achievements of the *Aspira* decree. Santiago observes that "there would seem to be a resistance to define bilingualism in any but a compensatory context."[25] Yet, bilingualism could be viewed as one mark of giftedness and thereby an educational advantage. One test of this proposition, Santiago suggests, would be to study those Spanish-speaking students who scored barely high enough on a test to become ineligible for the bilingual program. Did they fare as well as the *Aspira* children?

Santiago raises the issue of language maintenance, that is, the right of non-English language speakers to cultivate further their ability to use their native language. The dominant approach is one of native language-as-transitional, that is, retaining it until English is mastered. Santiago places the question in a novel framework that applies more to Puerto Rican than to other language minorities:

The issue is not the desirability of one language as opposed to the other but rather whether the Puerto Rican should be required to give up one for the other. . . . The constitution of Puerto Rico stipulates that two cultures, American and Puerto Rican, shall co-exist on the island. . . . It would seem that the mainland Puerto Rican has an additional burden should he return to Puerto Rico after years in an educational system which has deprived him of the opportunity to maintain his first language.[26]

While Santiago does not do so, one could extend her arguments by analogy to embrace the constitutional right of citizens of one state to move to other states without impairing their rights. (Formally, this is known as the principle of interstate comity.)[27] In addition, it is well known that residence in monolingual mainland communities frequently unfits island—or mainland—born children to return to live in Puerto Rico.[28]

Santiago discusses still another general problem related to the effectiveness of bilingual instruction. In 1976, Jose Cardenas had acknowledged that "there is no widely recognized body of knowledge that says there are pedagogical advantages to a bilingual program."[29] But this was more a critique of the state of knowledge than of bilingualism. Santiago comments on experience under Title VII of ESEA, the bilingual legislation: "Ineffective monitoring and evaluation procedures by the federal government have resulted in what has been criticized as the lack of 'substantial evidence' that bilingual education makes a difference in student achievement."[30] Further, she writes:

Institutions must be held accountable for providing the administrative checks, the leadership, and the funds necessary to ensure that bilingual educational programs are carried out appropriately and that their impact and findings are responsibly reported to the public and analyzed by public educational authorities in terms of their relevance to existing educational policies.[31]

In short, Santiago contemplates the New York City experience and implies two possibilities. (1) If the city's earliest implementation of *Aspira* had been evaluated, the certain negative findings would have reflected their responsible manner in which the school board operated the program. Yet, the findings could be misinterpreted to the unwary as a judgment of bilingualism. (2) Similarly, if evaluations of bilingual education programs elsewhere are evaluated without reference to the manner and efficiency of implementation, how meaningful are the findings? This is especially true, one might add, in the absence of a federal district court to superintend the entire process.

Santiago touches on another issue which Steinberg also discussed. The former recognized that "there is not unanimity about the efficacy of bilingual education in the Hispanic community."[32] When terms of the decree were under consideration by the court, *Aspira* lawyers contended that the program should be compulsory for all eligible children. Judge Frankel disagreed, and held that the decree "imposed no *duties* upon the members of the class to 'enjoy' those rights."[33] Santiago calls for further study of factors that lead to parents opting out of the program.

Santiago agrees with Steinberg about the role of the United Federation of Teachers in opposing bilingualism:

The UFT had demonstrated its lack of support for bilingual education as defined by *Aspira* in a variety of instances: legislative memoranda against proposed bilingual legislation in New York State, opposition to special and separate licenses for bilingual teachers instead of teachers with greater seniority, opposition to the designation of bilingual teachers as a form of ethnic selection and discrimination, and opposition to quota systems to insure minorities equal employment opportunity.[34]

Santiago's work is an outstanding contribution to the study both of what might be called the ecology of bilingualism and of the realities of urban education. Her own involvement in some of the events she describes adds a sense of authenticity to the narrative as well as an unprecedented amount of documentation. And, although she wrote it as a doctoral dissertation, it has now been published.

By the time the *Aspira* decree was fully implemented, the fiscal crisis of New York City was in an advanced state. Regular teachers were being discharged in order to save funds. At the same time, bilingual teachers were being employed in accordance with the decree. Some regular teachers advised Puerto Rican parents to opt out of the *Aspira* program in order to save their own jobs. Actually, there was no relationship between *Aspira* and the loss of jobs, but many had the opposite impression. Anemoyanis studied the reasons why this was so.

She examined the attitudes of 135 teachers, bilingual and monolingual, as well as those of some supervisors in thirty schools, half with a high enrollment of Spanish-speaking pupils and half with a low enrollment of such pupils. All the schools had some kind of bilingual program. Essentially, Anemoyanis sought to discover which teachers (1) regarded the *Aspira* decree positively and (2) thought the decree was responsible for the firing of certain teachers. Her findings can be summarized briefly:

1. Bilingual teachers in schools with both high and low percentages of Spanish-speaking pupils had more positive attitudes toward the *Aspira* Consent Decree.

2. In schools with both high and low percentages of Spanish-speaking pupils the number of monolingual teachers who felt that the *Aspira* Consent Decree was a factor in the layoff of monolingual teachers was greater than the number who did not. In the bilingual group, however, the number who did not perceive the *Aspira* Consent Decree as a factor in the layoff of monolingual teachers was greater than the number who did.[35]

But self-interest alone could explain such a pattern.

Anemoyanis's work contains an interesting sidelight. As mentioned above, Special Circular No. 114, released in 1975, had required bilingual programs for non-Spanish language minority students. In the course of her research on *Aspira*, Anemoyanis found that the 1975 circular had not been heeded.

This circular . . . was ignored throughout the New York City schools, since the Central Board of Education neither monitored the non-Hispanic bilingual programs, nor required that school compliance data be submitted for the non-Hispanic, non-English speaking student population, as was the case with the *Aspira* Consent Decree program.[36]

This observation tends to support Santiago's judgment about the lack of school board commitment to bilingualism, let alone to the goal of enforcing its own rules.

In addition to bilingualism, a series of studies has examined a newer subject of inquiry—racial and ethnic factors in the classification of children as mentally retarded. This subject is deeply embedded in a legal framework.

In 1968, Mexican-American parents, with the aid of the NAACP Legal Defense Fund, filed suit in Santa Ana, California, charging that the school board was violating the rights of their children by placing them in classes for the mentally retarded without observing due process of law. This case, *Arreola*, became the first of a series filed in that state.

Henry J. Casso, in 1973, studied *Arreola* v. *Board of Education* and two other cases, *Diana* v. *State Board of Education* and *Cavarrubias* v. *San Diego Unified School District*. Besides lack of due process, another issue present in the *Arreola* case involved disproportionately high minority enrollment in classes for the mentally retarded. Julian Nava, historian and member of the Los Angeles school board, commented to Casso: "Many thousand[s] have been kept longer in these EMR [educable mentally retarded] programs. Many should not have been there in the first place. This is a good example of man's inhumanity to man, man's inhumanity to children."[37] This interpretation touched a profound chord of community sentiment that fueled one legal action after another.

In one lawsuit, plaintiffs called on the expert testimony of psychologist Alfredo Castaneda, who dealt with some pedagogical aspects of the case:

It is our contention that the learning environments in the majority (if not all) the schools in the Southwest along with the testing procedures are not geared to allow Mexican American youngsters to succeed. The curricula and teaching strategies do not take into account the unique cognitive, incentive-motivational and learning styles which these youngsters bring with them as a result of their prior interaction with the family and their ethnic community. As long as this is the case, Mexican American youngsters will continue to fail in disproportionate numbers in the school system, and it is irrelevant what instruments are used to predict success, whether or not these instruments are standardized for Mexican American youngsters.[38]

Clearly, Castaneda's diagnosis deals with the overall educational scene rather than with the EMR classroom as such. In the process, he also played down an issue which came increasingly to the fore—that is, the cultural bias of tests. In terms of the legal matter at hand, testing was not crucial. The general neglect of schools attended by Mexican-American children was more important, he believed.

The cases revealed a plethora of curious school practices. Josiah L. Neeper, a leading lawyer for the plaintiffs in the San Diego case *Cavarrubias*, reported: "Parents were told the child was going into a Special Education Program but were not told it was EMR. Often the parents were told the child was put in a class in order to catch up.''[39] During early negotiations, San Diego school authorities asked plaintiffs to sue other districts instead and even supplied names of some districts. Apparently, many educators were aware of violations.

In the three suits Casso discusses settlements favorable to parents were reached. He points out how proud parents were at having won their cases. He notes, too, that these victories influenced federal policies on the same issue.

Enriquetta Lopez Ramos, who taught in the schools of Santa Ana while that town's case was being litigated, adds much detail to the story in that case as well as in a number of others. Just prior to filing of *Arreola*, she reports, minorities in Santa Ana made up one-fifth of the city, one-third of the schools, and nearly three-quarters of EMR classes. One day Ray Villa, an insurance salesman, was making his rounds and struck up a conversation with a group of children. Some said they attended "special" classes. When they recounted the limited nature of these classes, Villa spoke with their parents and with school authorities. The parents did not know about the limited educational objectives of such "special" classes. Out of this accidental encounter a lawsuit was filed; among the lawyers for the plaintiffs were representatives of the League of United Latin American Citizens, the Mexican American Political Association, and the Mexican American Legal Defense Fund, as well as the NAACP's LDF.

Lopez also examined *Diana* v. *State Board of Education*, which originated in Soledad, California, a community of some 7,000 people. As a result of the litigation, testing for placement in special education classes was to be done in English as well as in the child's primary language. The court also ordered state psychologists to construct an IQ test appropriate to non-English speaking children. Another case Lopez discusses is *Guadalupe* v. *Tempe*, filed in 1971. She notes, however, that "the local district has never agreed to the stipulated agreement, and program changes have resulted primarily from new rules and regulations that have come from the Arizona Department of Education.''[40] In the San Diego case, *Cavarrubias*, while the court ruled in favor of the plaintiffs, it awarded damages of only one dollar rather than $20,000 to the parents of each student.

The classification cases, according to Lopez, had certain features in common. For one thing, each one "evolved from community concerns which generated outside the schools.''[41] Once more we see how little genuine change arises from efforts generated inside the schools. Viewing the past decade or so, Lopez asserts that "the major educational changes have come about because of legal mandates, rather than through the creative voluntary efforts of professional educators.''[42]

She cites a study made by Julius Cohen, one-time deputy director of the President's Committee on Mental Retardation. The Cohen study covered long-term effects of various litigative changes. Cohen observed a certain parochialism, as did Lopez, who summarized: "The schools have not incor-

porated the decisions of one suit pertaining to one ethnic group very extensively in their dealing with other ethnic groups."[43] Cohen also was "struck
by the amount of pervasive negative feelings [he] saw on the part of the
school personnel and many Anglos in the communities against Chicanos."[44]
After visiting a number of teacher-training institutions to learn how these
have responded to recent legal changes in classification, Cohen wrote: "The
impact of litigation is considered, but little emphasis is placed on the basic
ethical and moral issues that are raised when the legal questions are
raised."[45]

Lopez views the rise of legal action from a context of the educational
default of educators. Indeed, she hails the emergence of "forensic educational psychology" as a necessary development. She credits the civil rights
movement with having made a major contribution to this new field.

Both Casso and Lopez concentrated on specific cases and extracted their
general implications. John G. Richardson, on the other hand, placed the
subject in a historical and sociological framework. He analyzed California
state education laws during the long period 1860–1976 and found a total of
twenty-four exceptionalities. He uses this term to mean legal stipulations ex-
cluding a category of students from the benefits of attendance in the public
schools. Three stigmas accounted for all the exceptionalities: stigmas of
health (physical and mental), of race, and of character (as expressed by certain behavior). In 1947, the clause of the Education Code that permitted
racial segregation was repealed, as a direct consequence of a federal court's
Mendez v. *Westminister* ruling. (See Chapter 1.) The same year, as it happened, the legislature provided for special education classes of mentally
retarded children. Richardson declares that this double action by public
school authorities led "to the evolution of special education classes as a
form of extralegal exemption from normal school status for particular types
of mentally able minority children."[46] It should be recalled that use of the
stigma of health or race did not assume that the affected children were intellectually unable to learn. They were excluded on other grounds. Now public
school authorities found they could use special education as a means of getting around the court's decision that the use of race and character exceptionalities was illegal.

The 1947 special education laws were the product of agitation and organization by white middle-class parents and their allies. Nevertheless, Richardson observes, "special education served the needs of local districts facing
the immigration of 'divergent youth,' children of migrant origins and minority status."[47]

Also, the districts' strong tradition of autonomy precluded the development of firm state guidelines governing implementation of new laws. Local
districts tended to view special education as a means of controlling bother-
some students who did not fit into customary categories of acceptability.
When students proved incapable of relating effectively to these young
people, the special education laws could, in Richardson's words, "relieve
conflict by 'exempting' these students from regular education."[48]

Richardson tries to recreate the state of research understanding on retardation during the 1950s and 1960s, a time of very great expansion of special classes for the retarded. After reviewing the principal studies, he concludes:

The weight of the studies does not lend support to the "efficacy" of special class placement. In the main, they indicate that (1) retarded children remaining in the regular classes are equal or superior in academic performance and development to those assigned to special classes, and (2) although the seriously handicapped may benefit from special class placement, the "mild" or "borderline" mentally handicapped, those who comprise the bulk of the EMR classes in public schools, are hurt.[49]

In 1967, Lloyd Dunn, past president of the Council for Exceptional Children, declared: "We have been living at the mercy of general educators who have referred their problem children to us."[50] By "problem children" Dunn did not mean profoundly retarded or even moderately retarded. As Richardson comments, Dunn's complaint "was coupled with an observation that special classes for mildly retarded children were being used as educational dumping grounds for minority children."[51]

Whether children are referred for testing that can lead to placement in classes for the mentally retarded may have little to do with the actual number of retarded children in a school. Summarizing a number of studies, Richardson finds that "considerations of school size, and class size, ethnic composition, attitudes of principals and the number of special class vacancies, will influence special class placement procedures more than they will academic tracking ostensibly based on ability."[52] Misplacement can serve also to deflect criticism from the school, as social psychologist Carl Jorgensen writes: "As long as the children are labeled 'retarded,' then poor learning, disruption, disinterest, rebellion and other disapproved behaviors can be blamed on the child's deficiencies, and no consideration need be given to the influence of the institution."[53]

To test some of his insights from the literature, Richardson conducted a small-scale study in Oakland, concentrating on grades two through four, which he called "prime referral grades."[54] He found a moderate, significant correlation between socioeconomic status and referral and placement. Children in the referral group as well as in the EMR class tended to be those born in southern and southwestern states; the same could be said of students from Oakland whose families had moved comparatively often. Greater mobility apparently affects a child's school adjustment. "It suggests," according to Richardson, "that 'adjustment' problems coupled with low academic achievement are the central factors in a teacher's decision to refer and only afterward is place of birth or geographic mobility brought to bear upon the student's evaluation."[55]

Richardson's interpretation is a long distance from a literal view of testing and classification. According to him, the presence of mental retardation as such is not the crucial consideration in explaining the classification of mentally retarded children. The social process whereby some children are labeled as "retarded" serves ends other than education.

In the process of studying historical materials, Richardson found that exclusionary structures were removed only by what he calls "the process of challenges." Parents of the excluded children were almost invariably the ones who challenged the schools. Precisely the same could be said of the latest version of bars to regular attendance in the shape of retardation-classification procedures.

In October, 1979, United States District Judge Robert F. Peckham of San Francisco ruled in *Larry P.* v. *Riles.*[56] He found the state education department guilty of violating the rights of black children who were over-represented in classes for the mentally retarded. Ample evidence established the failure of the state to exercise its statutory and constitutional obligations to guard against the misclassification. The *Larry P.* decision is notable for its close analysis of the consistent violation of state laws and regulations by the state department of education. It is also important for its treatment of various technical aspects of testing theory. Finally, it broke certain ground in legal doctrine. While a court decision is not a work of original research, it may constitute an instructive exercise in forensic psychology and politics.

Judge Peckham recalled the declaration of IQ founder Alfred Binet, cited in testimony: "It was necessary to protest the brutal pessimism of those who regarded the test as measuring some fixed and unchanging quality."[57] The early years of the IQ test, especially, the court observed, were "a history of racial prejudice, of Social Darwinism, and of the use of the scientific 'mystique' to legitimate such prejudices." Even the most renowned psychologists shared those prejudices; one example was Stanford psychologist Lewis Terman, who was quoted in a work dated 1916. Feeblemindedness, he wrote, represents "the level of intelligence which is very, very common among Spanish-Indian and Mexican families of the Southwest and also among negroes. Their dullness seems to be racial or at least inherent in the family stocks from which they come."[58]

It was in such an intellectual climate that California first authorized classes for the mentally retarded during 1921. The state superintendent of public instruction explained: "Children who are hopeless, so far as ordinary education is concerned, could then be sent to a proper institution, thus relieving society from any menace from them."[59] This declaration stressed the educational hopelessness of retarded children and the danger they constituted to nonretarded children, themes that became watchwords in the special education of the time.

Beginning in 1947, the law was altered frequently. That year, an amendment stipulated that children could be assigned to classes for the retarded only after a "careful individual examination by a competent psychologist."[60] During 1968–1969, it was discovered that while blacks made up only 9 percent of the state's school enrollment, they constituted three times as many of the children enrolled in classes for the retarded. Public knowledge of these data led to demands for reform. A 1969 law required that assignment to EMR classes be made "only on the basis of an individual recommendation of a local admissions committee which shall include a teacher, a school nurse or social worker, a school psychologist or other pupil personnel worker authorized to serve as a school psychologist who has individually examined the minor, a principal or supervisor, and a licensed physician."[61] Consultation with parents before enrollment as well as annual reviews of placement were also required.

The very next year, 1970, the legislature resumed a program of action. Judge Peckham summarized a number of the measures. In classifying children as mentally retarded an IQ test was to be used from a list approved by the state board of education. In addition:

The law provided for the testing of children in their primary home language, and it prohibited placement into an EMR class if a child scores better than two standard deviations below the norm on the test. Written parental consent, obtained after an explanation of the EMR program, was required before placement . . . and the Department of Education was required to prepare an annual report for the state legislature on placements into the EMR classes.[62]

All children already in EMR classes were to be retested according to the new cut-off scores. School districts enrolling minorities in EMR programs to a disproportionately high degree were required to submit annual reports. Remedial work was mandated for children in EMR classes who were found to be qualified for regular classes.

Nor was this all. The torrent continued the following year, 1971. First, in Judge Peckham's words, there was "a clarion declaration": "The legislature hereby finds and declares that there should not be disproportionate enrollment of any socioeconomic, minority, or other ethnic group pupils in classes for the mentally retarded."[63] If IQ test scores indicated retarded intellectual development, this finding would need to be substantiated by "a complete psychological examination by a credentialed school psychologist investigating such factors as developmental history, cultural background, and school achievement."[64] The court noted that "studies of adaptive behavior—the ability to engage in social activities and perform everyday tasks—were also called for, as well as home visits, with the consent of the parent or guardian."[65]

These, then, were the principal legal safeguards created by the state legislature. Together, they were to protect children from being improperly classified as retarded. The educational significance of such misclassification was enormous, according to Judge Peckham. "The educational goals for the educable mentally retarded are not reading, writing, and arithmetic per se. . . . The [EMR] classes are conceived of as 'dead-end' classes." Further, as an assistant superintendent of the San Francisco schools put it:

"The object is for the children to remain in the [EMR] program from the time of placement until graduation from senior high school."[66] The longer they stayed in the program, the greater the gap between them and their peers in classes for the nonretarded. Thus, misclassification condemned able children to an educational situation in which it was all but impossible to demonstrate and nurture their abilities.

Evidence brought before the court showed that "in the 20 [school] districts accounting for 80 percent of the enrollment of black children [in the state], black students comprised about 27.5 percent of the EMR population."[67] The odds against such an outcome occurring by chance were more than one million to one. Judge Peckham found that the state department of education—State Superintendent Wilson Riles was the first-named defendant in the case—had contributed significantly to such sweeping misclassification.

In 1969, for example, the department had drawn up a list of approved IQ tests to be used in EMR classification work. The state official in charge was not an expert in testing. Nor was any outside expert consulted other than employees of testing companies. No heed was paid to a protest against such a procedure lodged by the co-chair of the Testing Committee of the California Association of School Psychologists and Psychometrists.[68] Apparently, frequency of use in the field was the principal criterion for choice of a test by the state department of education. The state board of education, however, was apparently under the impression that experts had selected the test and had taken into account the matter of cultural bias.

In August, 1977, the state department's Uslan Report was completed. It examined EMR placement during July, 1975–June, 1976. It found twenty-six school districts with an overenrollment of blacks in EMR classes exceeding by 15 percent or more enrollment in the district as a whole. This violated the legislative policy of six years before. Judge Peckham summarized other findings:

The report stated that, even using a "liberal interpretation of what constituted an estimate of adaptive behavior" almost one third of the pupil records contained no estimates of pupil adaptive behavior. Furthermore, 16 of 25 districts admitted they made little or no use of adaptive behavior information in the placement process. The report also revealed that more than one-quarter of the files surveyed revealed no "developmental history." In San Francisco, for example, the study team found that a request for adaptive behavior information was found in 23 of the 47 files sampled, developmental histories were located in 35 of the 47, and records indicated the I.Q. scores in 46 of the 47.[69]

Other studies had shown black persons usually scored higher on adaptive measures than on formal IQ tests.[70] By underutilizing the former in favor of the latter, school districts were in effect stacking the cards against minority persons.

The state failed to enforce those of its laws that were supposed to preclude any such practice. As Judge Peckham noted of the Uslan Report, the

state department of education—which had itself commissioned the study—
"did nothing but file this report, even where it revealed severe deficiencies
in compliance with statutory norms, and the particular results were not even
conveyed to the [State] Board of Education."[71]

The validity of IQ tests was a central consideration in *Larry P.* v. *Riles*.
Judge Peckham grew increasingly skeptical about the use of the tests in
EMR placement. Testimony was especially revealing on the issue of whether
or not "innate" mental capacity could be tapped by IQ tests. Dr. Leo Mun-
day, vice-president and general manager of the test department of Hough-
ton Mifflin, publishers of the Stanford-Binet IQ test, stated outright: "It is
safe to say that . . . no one in aptitude testing today believes that intelligence tests measure innate capacity."[72]

The court remarked more than ever on the failure of testing companies to
investigate the persistent fifteen-point gap on IQ scores between blacks and
whites. Judge Peckham suggested that either an explanation of the gap
could be sought or companies could mount an effort to eliminate the disparity by means of "testing redesign." Here he was referring to the well-
known early finding on IQ tests of a systematic male-female score gap. This
disparity was eliminated deliberately by testers through a system of
weighting and special care with the writing of test items. As a result, IQ tests
are now sex-neutral.

Judge Peckham emphasized that testers have taken a very different approach to racial disparities in IQ scores:

No such modification on racial grounds . . . has ever been tried by the testing companies according to the testimony at this trial. Rather, the experts have from the
beginning been willing to tolerate or even encourage tests that portray minorities,
especially blacks, as intellectually inferior.[73]

This observation is particularly striking in view of the vast collection of data
in the hands of testing firms, which could easily have tried to devise an IQ
test that was racially neutral.

Does this continuing reluctance imply that testers subscribe to racial inferiority doctrines? No study has examined this question. Judge Peckham,
however, reports that "a number of key state officials . . . testified that
they were familiar with Professor [Arthur R.] Jensen's writings, and they
would not rule out the genetic explanation for disparities between [black
children] and white children in I.Q. scores and EMR enrollment."[74] (The
work of Jensen and others is discussed in the following chapter.) Such an attitude, one may add, might have helped predispose these state officials
toward a complacency on the matter of large-scale minority overrepresentation in EMR classes, even though this condition violated state law.

A further issue deserves attention. Several times Judge Peckham dis-
claimed interest in whether IQ tests as such were valid or scientific. Instead,
he wanted to know whether the tests were valid as a means of classifying

black children for EMR classes. Studies of this question were rare or nonexistent. In examining correlations of IQ scores with later school performance, the judge observed a differential validity: predictability was greater for whites than for blacks. Accordingly, declared the court, "differential validity means that more errors [based on IQ scores] will be made for black children than whites, and that is unacceptable."[75]

In his rulings on the more technical legal issues of the case, Judge Peckham began with *Lau* v. *Nichols*, discussed earlier in this chapter. In that case, a unanimous Supreme Court ruled that a number of Chinese-speaking students were denied the benefits of the Civil Rights Act of 1964 by being offered instruction in English only. The high court stressed that although no "purposeful design" to discriminate was present in the school board's practice, the effect of the practice was still discriminatory.

Judge Peckham regarded use of an IQ test to place black children in EMR classes as equivalent to the *Lau* situation:

The failure [in *Lau*] to provide [an alternative to] English language teaching foreclosed substantial numbers of students from any meaningful educational opportunity. This same result occurs from the use of I.Q. tests and a biased placement process [to place students in EMR classes].[76]

Since these classes have a minimal educational objective, misplacement in them is a denial of equal educational opportunity.

Once more Judge Peckham returned to the matter of IQ test validity in EMR placement:

If tests can predict that a person is going to be a poor employee, the employer can legitimately deny that person a job, but if tests suggest . . . a young child is probably going to be a poor student, the school cannot on that basis alone deny the child the opportunity to improve and develop the academic skills necessary to success in our society. . . . Placing children with lower I.Q. scores in these [retarded] classes . . . necessarily is a self-fulfilling prophecy. The results of such placements cannot be the basis for test validation in an educational setting.[77]

Indeed, Judge Peckham continued, it is not the disparity of enrollment but the failure to validate the classifying instrument that offends the law.

In the end, the state department of education (SDE) failed to uphold the law and thereby violated the rights of *Larry P.* and his class. "Throughout the period covered by this lawsuit," concluded Judge Peckham, "the SDE set policy as if the legislative findings about testing and disproportionate enrollments meant nothing, and the [State] Board [of Education] in turn has compelled no investigation nor indeed taken any position about these problems."[78]

Larry P. v. *Riles* is still in the process of being appealed. Further proceedings may confirm or upset Judge Peckham's findings. It is well, however, to examine the case as it presently stands. Since the trial transcript runs to around 10,000 pages, and Judge Peckham's ruling some 100 typed pages, obviously there was much we could not discuss here. The record, however, may be regarded as a testament to the educational costs of political power-lessness as well as a treasure trove of applied research.

One of the gravest errors in writings on minorities is a tendency to portray them as passive victims. For whatever reason, this view is illustrated by one defeat after another until the reader is moved toward pity rather than respect. Both white and black writers share this error.

This mood of chronic defeatism can also be found in discussions of recent legal developments bearing on desegregation and related topics. Consider-able evidence contradicts this orientation. Let us examine some of it.

Jimmy Lee Peterson studied educational changes in three Alabama coun-ties—Greene, Lowndes, and Macon—during the years 1960-1974. He wanted to discover whether these changes might be, in part, the result of heightened black political participation and increased federal involvement. Both in 1960 and 1970, the counties were at least three-quarters black. His-torically blacks had been severely subordinated and had not dared to vote. In Greene, the fifth poorest county in the country, "most of the blacks live in tar paper shacks or whitewashed cottages set on cinder blocks along un-paved country roads."[79] At the same time, "the white overlords have kept industry out because they do not want to change the status quo."[80] In Macon County, blacks controlled both Tuskegee Institute and the Veterans Hospital and thus to that extent exercised economic power.

The civil rights movement swept the three counties in the early 1960s. In Greene and Lowndes, where no blacks had registered to vote in 1960, more than half those of voting age did so in 1966. By 1972, the proportion had risen. In Macon, where a small number voted in 1960, no blacks held a cen-tral school administrative position in any of the counties. The situation changed quickly after black voting spread. Greene County elected an all-black school board (it had been all-white) and appointed a black superinten-dent. By 1974, organized blacks in Lowndes achieved a parallel victory: "Blacks presently have a definite control of the Lowndes County school system."[81]

A review of Tables 2.1-4 demonstrates that the political power was used to buttress the position of blacks in the three school systems. As white children were withdrawn by their parents, enrollment fell. But the proportion of blacks among teachers and other certificated personnel rose between 1960 and 1974. This was contrary to customary patterns of employment in Ala-bama's black belt. Without concerted political action by blacks it could not have happened.

In October, 1969, the United States Supreme Court decided *Alexander* v. *Holmes County Board of Education* and ordered sweeping desegregation in Mississippi. In January, 1970, the plan was implemented. Throughout the South, desegregation sometimes involved large-scale discharge of black

Table 2.1
Changes in Educational Leadership in Macon County

	1960	1961	1962	1963	1964	1965	1966	1967	1968	1969	1970	1971	1972	1973	1974
Board Member	5	5	5	5	5	5	5	5	5	5	5	5	5	5	5
Black	0	0	0	0	1	1	1	1	2	2	2	4	4	4	4
White	5	5	5	5	4	4	4	4	3	3	3	1	1	1	1
Supt. of Education	1	1	1	1	1	1	1	1	1	1	1	1	1	1	1
Black	0	0	0	0	0	0	0	0	0	0	1	1	1	1	1
White	1	1	1	1	1	1	1	1	1	1	0	0	0	0	0
Central Office Administrator	1	1	1	1	2	2	2	2	3	3	3	5	5	5	5
Black	0	0	0	0	0	0	0	0	0	2	2	4	4	4	4
White	1	1	1	1	2	2	2	2	3	1	1	1	1	1	1
Principals	19	19	18	18	14	13	11	11	11	11	11	11	11	11	11
Black	17	17	16	16	12	11	9	9	9	9	10	10	10	10	10
White	2	2	2	2	2	2	2	2	2	2	1	1	1	1	1
Vice Principals	0	0	0	0	0	0	0	0	0	0	2	2	2	2	2
Black	0	0	0	0	0	0	0	0	0	0	2	2	2	2	2
White	0	0	0	0	0	0	0	0	0	0	0	0	0	0	0

Table 2.2
Changes in Educational Leadership in Greene County

	1960	1961	1962	1963	1964	1965	1966	1967	1968	1969	1970	1971	1972	1973	1974
Board Member	5	5	5	5	5	5	5	5	5	5	5	5	5	5	5
Black	0	0	0	0	0	0	1	1	1	5	5	5	5	5	5
White	5	5	5	5	5	5	4	4	4	0	0	0	0	0	0
Supt. of Education	1	1	1	1	1	1	1	1	1	1	1	1	1	1	1
Black	0	0	0	0	0	0	0	0	0	0	1	1	1	1	1
White	1	1	1	1	1	1	1	1	1	1	0	0	0	0	0
Central Office Administrator	3	3	3	3	3	3	3	4	4	4	6	6	6	6	6
Black	0	0	0	0	0	0	0	0	0	0	6	6	6	6	6
White	3	3	3	3	3	3	3	4	4	4	0	0	0	0	0
Principals	6	6	6	6	6	6	6	6	6	6	5	5	5	5	5
Black	5	5	5	5	5	5	5	5	5	5	4	4	4	4	4
White	1	1	1	1	1	1	1	1	1	1	1	1	1	1	1

Table 2.3
Changes in Educational Leadership in Lowndes County

	1960	1961	1962	1963	1964	1965	1966	1967	1968	1969	1970	1971	1972	1973	1974
Board Member	5	5	5	5	5	5	5	5	5	5	5	5	5	5	5
Black	0	0	0	0	0	0	0	0	0	0	0	0	0	0	3
White	5	5	5	5	5	5	5	5	5	5	5	5	5	5	2
Supt. of Education	1	1	1	1	1	1	1	1	1	1	1	1	1	1	1
Black	0	0	0	0	0	0	0	0	0	0	0	0	0	0	0
White	1	1	1	1	1	1	1	1	1	1	1	1	1	1	1
Central Office Administrator	3	3	3	3	3	5	5	5	5	5	6	6	6	6	9
Black	0	0	0	0	0	0	0	0	0	0	0	0	0	0	6
White	3	3	3	3	3	5	5	5	5	5	6	6	6	6	3
Principals	11	11	11	11	10	10	10	8	8	8	8	8	8	8	8
Black	9	9	9	9	8	8	8	7	7	7	7	7	7	7	7
White	2	2	2	2	2	2	2	1	1	1	1	1	1	1	1
Vice Principals	0	1	1	2	2	2	2	2	2	2	2	2	2	2	4
Black	0	1	1	2	2	2	2	2	2	2	2	2	2	2	4
White	0	0	0	0	0	0	0	0	0	0	0	0	0	0	0

44

Table 2.4
Teachers and Other Certified Personnel—Racial Composition in the Three Counties Between 1960 and 1974

County	1960	1961	1962	1963	1964	1965	1966	1967	1968	1969	1970	1971	1972	1973	1974
Greene															
Black	116	113	111	107	103	104	100	109	106	108	138	139	127	126	149
White	31	31	31	31	31	30	31	31	30	30	31	16	17	20	25
Lowndes															
Black	147	142	142	130	134	134	130	136	133	133	140	141	139	138	144
White	30	30	30	30	33	33	26	26	26	26	26	27	26	24	28
Macon															
Black	212	214	203	187	193	199	233	217	212	212	209	222	222	229	228
White	58	59	63	43	33	36	43	28	40	39	23	31	19	27	27

teachers as white school administrators sought to avoid assigning black teachers to teach white children in desegregated schools. What happened to black teachers in Mississippi?

Bobby G. Cooper studied the effect of desegregation in Mississippi during 1970–1973.[82] He used the 1969–1970 school year as a benchmark since the schools were still largely segregated at the beginning of that year but less so at its close. In the state as a whole, of school districts consisting of 20 percent to 90 percent blacks, the total number of teachers increased by 1.3 percent; the number of white teachers increased by 8.7 percent; while the number of black teachers declined by 11.4 percent. Clearly net displacement of black teachers had occurred as a result of desegregation. Where did the displaced teachers go? What new jobs did they get?

In the absence of any centralized comprehensive records, Cooper had to depend on a more restricted pool of names. These were drawn from names of displaced black teachers who had registered with the Tougaloo Training Coordination Center during the years 1970–1973. A random sample of 120 names was drawn from this pool. Questionnaires were sent to the sample. Ninety-four or 78.3 percent responded.

Nearly two-thirds of the respondents were women, most under forty years of age. Over three-quarters taught in districts whose population was less than 10,000. Following is a listing of various actions undergone by the ninety-four respondents reported:[83]

Respondents	Number	Percentage
Promoted	4	4.3
Demoted	18	18.0
Terminated	42	44.6
Resigned	7	7.4
Displaced	7	7.4
Transferred to federal program	2	2.1
No answer	14	14.8

Nearly half of the ninety-four had succeeded in obtaining a professional position since displacement; just over half were teaching at the time of Cooper's study.

Teachers were somewhat reluctant to discuss the effects of displacement on income. Forty-one of the ninety-four reported that their income was higher on the new job; seventeen reported lower salaries; thirty-four did not reply to this question.[84] In general, displaced teachers experienced something of a downward movement. "The majority of displaced teachers," Cooper writes, "were reassigned as classroom teachers. Many became teacher aides and hardly any remained department heads."[85]

Teachers who bore the brunt of displacement were women, those who worked in rural areas, and teachers with fewer than ten years experience. Desegregation in Mississippi did not affect the employment of some 88 percent of the state's black teachers. Judging from Cooper's analysis, the remainder underwent a broad range of experiences. While overall the movement was downward, a considerable number of displaced teachers were able to maintain or even to improve their positions, at least in a material sense.

Yet, the basic racial discrimination involved in displacement remained clear. The United States Court of Appeals for the Fifth Circuit ruled against Mississippi school boards in five separate cases. Displaced teachers were ordered reinstated, with or without back pay, or were given priority in the filling of future vacancies.[86] Favorable court decisions were helpful in slowing displacement. In urban areas, the power of organized black teachers was apparently sufficient to prevent any significant displacement.

Peterson's study embraces only three counties in a single state while Cooper deals with ninety-four teachers in another state. Does the problem appear any differently if we examine the country as a whole, or, at least, a number of states?

Richard B. Freeman has, in fact, made a study that attempts to do just that. He set out to investigate possible interrelations among the employment of black teachers, the occurrence of desegregation, and the level of black voting, especially in the South. The time covered was 1950–1970. He states his major findings as follows:

Increased black voting power appears to have substantially raised demand for black school teachers, offsetting most of the reduction in demand due to desegregation. . . . Relative employment of blacks in teaching was maintained, and relative incomes rose in the 1950s and 1960s.[87]

Thus the "economic position of black teachers did not deteriorate" during decades of desegregation.

Two tables pretty well summarize the principal evidence brought forward by Freeman. First, here is a listing of the percentages of black teachers in nine states during 1950–1970:[88]

States	1950	1960	1970
Alabama	31.3	33.2	28.1
Louisiana	26.9	31.7	30.7
South Carolina	37.2	35.0	31.3
Virginia	21.7	20.7	16.4
Connecticut	0.4	1.5	2.9
Illinois	3.4	5.6	8.2
New York	1.6	2.8	4.5
Ohio	2.0	3.7	5.9

Percentages of black teachers fell in four southern states but this was more than compensated for by rises in Louisiana and the four northern states.

In the next listing, covering 1960–1970, one may see how salaries of black teachers rose relative to those of white teachers (Parity is 1.0):[89]

States	1960 Male	1970 Male	1960 Female	1970 Female
Alabama	0.81	0.97	1.01	1.08
Louisiana	0.85	0.99	0.99	1.16
South Carolina	0.84	0.92	0.91	0.98
Virginia	0.92	0.95	1.05	1.114
Kentucky	1.03	1.15	1.03	1.15
Connecticut	—	1.05	0.84	1.06
Illinois	0.91	1.10	1.16	1.22
New York	0.84	0.98	0.97	1.07
Ohio	0.94	1.09	1.12	1.18

Thus, while in 1960 black male teachers received higher salaries than whites in only one state, ten years later this was the case in four states. The figures for female teachers were five states in 1960 and eight in 1970. Improvement was uniform.

Economic improvement was in turn dependent on electoral activity. "Between 1960 and 1970 the black share of the electorate jumped from 9 percent to 23 percent in South Carolina and from 4 percent to 17 percent in Alabama," according to Freeman, "despite declines in the relative number of blacks of voting age."[90] So regular was the rise that Freeman found "a 10 percent increase in the black share of voters increases black teacher employment by about 2 percent."[91]

Freeman asks about the precise mechanisms that link political activity and increased employment of teachers but does not answer his own question. Clearly, he observes, one such link is the election of black public officials. Admittedly, however, this is not sufficient to account for the entire difference. One may perhaps "borrow" from Peterson's study to suggest several other links. In the Alabama counties, increased electoral activity led to the election of black school boards which employed black superintendents and black central administrative staff. It is these latter persons who most directly control the process of teacher employment, especially in the absence of teacher unions in rural areas.

Neither Peterson, Cooper, nor Freeman deals adequately with one group of school employees—the black principals. To be sure, each one notes the overwhelming numbers of such principals who were discharged or demoted in the process of desegregation in the South. Freeman observes: "By the time court and federal actions were initiated in the late 1960s/early 1970s to prevent further displacement of black school officials and endangered teachers as well, desegregation and consolidation of school districts had eliminated most black principals in the South."[92]

Why did the burgeoning civil rights movement of the sixties fail to make defense of black principals a central issue? For one thing, the firings took place very rapidly, confronting black communities with *faits accomplis*. But there may have been a political reason as well. Economic penalties were frequently the response to civil rights activity in the South of the sixties. Fannie Lou Hamer, a legendary figure from Mississippi, recalled to a friend:

Until 1962 I did not even know that I could vote. When SNCC [Student Non-Violent Coordinating Committee] students and others convinced me that I could vote and must make the effort, someone reported my intention to my boss on the plantation where I had worked for eighteen years. I was fired. In a few weeks he also fired my husband, and we had to move from our house on the plantation to Ruleville. The day he fired me was a good day for me because from that moment on I have supported every effort to free the Negro in Mississippi.[93]

While Hamer was too poor to welcome loss of her job, there was nothing unexceptionable about the action itself. She treats it as a fact of life.

But to a black principal, loss of job was the ultimate penalty. Historically, his status in the black community was high. At the same time his role was charged with ambiguity. He was part of the black community and could "get things" for it. But he was utterly subordinated to the dominant white leadership and felt constrained to satisfy it. When blacks in the South began their political organizing, some black principals secretly helped out, thus reenacting the classic role of Booker T. Washington. But many black principals adopted an openly antagonistic stance toward the civil rights movement. Thus, their high status in the community strained against the community's increasingly militant stand. The ambiguity of the principal's role was tested as never before.

But ambiguity was out of step with the requirements of the sixties in the South. At one time, Hamer had noted that things must really be bad because *even* black principals started showing up at civil rights meetings. And so, while the communities opposed firing of black principals they put comparatively little energy behind such protests. In a sense, the black principal was victimized by a system that had used him for its advantage as long as segregation could be maintained. Racism was the clear cause of these firings as it was of the displacement of black teachers. The black principal, however, could not turn for protection to powerful national organizations.

This chapter has tried to put some flesh—muscle, fat, and all—onto that gaunt creature known as "the legal framework." We have reviewed a number of scholarly research works including the text of a lengthy court decision. In each we were interested in an issue of substance, in the more formal legal aspects, and in the community and school settings that help determine what the legal measures will mean as they are implemented. We were also interested in the deliberate failure of public institutions to carry out their legal obligations.

Bilingual education has thus far been inextricably involved with legislation and court decisions. The studies by Nieves, Steinberg, and Santiago clarify why this has been the case. Lacking the sustained pressure of community power, advocates of bilingual education sought through formal means what earlier generations had enacted through informal, local efforts. The self-interest of knowledgeable professionals proved a vital prod to promotion of bilingualism. Court orders on behalf of bilingualism were not self-enforcing. Indeed, in the *Aspira* case, school authorities flouted the order.

Classification of minority children as retarded has been a legal issue for more than a decade. Lopez Ramos, Richardson, and Casso traced the process whereby a seemingly technical question came to be viewed as a political question. (Not that it ever was a *non*political question.) As with bilingual education, the issue of classification bore most heavily on minority communities. This further guaranteed that governmental remedies would be sought. *Larry P.* is a textbook on the politics of selective enforcement by California state educational authorities. In light of this fact, to counsel minorities to foreswear courtroom approaches to equal education is to counsel despair.

The ability of organized black teachers and communities to protect their educational interests through concerted civic action such as voting is made clear in studies by Peterson, Cooper, and Freeman. Despite the potential in desegregation to reduce job opportunities for black teachers, Freeman's study especially shows how this possibility was largely avoided during 1950–1970.

Notes

1. Sarah Nieves, *A Sociolinguistic Critique of Bilingual Education Curricula and the Bilingual Education Act in Terms of Adequacy for the Puerto Rican Collectivity* (doctoral diss., Columbia University, 1975), p. 105. (University Microfilms Order No. 75-18,690.)

2. Ibid., p. 90.

3. Lois S. Steinberg, *The Bilingual Education Act and the Puerto Rican Community: The Role of a Network in the Implementation of Federal Legislation at the Local Level* (doctoral diss., Fordham University, 1978), pp. 2–3.

4. Basic data in ibid., p. 91.

5. Ibid., p. 87.

6. Ibid., p. 149.

7. Ibid., p. 194.

8. Ibid., p. 69.

9. Ibid., p. 221.

10. Ibid., p. 137.

11. Ibid., p. 215.

12. Ibid., p. 143.

13. Ibid., p. 213.

14. Asaura Santiago Santiago, "Aspira v. Board of Education of the City of New York: A History and Policy Analysis" (doctoral diss., Fordham University, 1978), p. 149. (University Microfilms Order No. 78-9014.) This work has been published as *A Community's Struggle for Equal Educational Opportunity: Aspira v. Board of Education* (Princeton, N.J.: Office for Minority Education, Educational Testing Service, 1978). Page references are to the unpublished work.

15. Ibid., p. 184.

16. Ibid., pp. 212–13.

17. Ibid., p. 225.

18. Ibid., p. 239.

19. Ibid., p. 253.

20. Ibid., p. 293.

21. Ibid., p. 335.

22. Ibid., p. 320.

23. Ibid.

24. Ibid., p. 324.

25. Ibid., p. 330.

26. Ibid., pp. 330–31.

27. See Laurence H. Tribe, *American Constitutional Law* (Mineola, N.Y.: Foundation Press, 1978).

28. See, for example, Izzy Sanabria, "The Newyorican in Puerto Rico," *Latin New York*, 26 (September 1974), pp. 22–25.

29. Quoted in Steinberg, p. 243.

30. Santiago, p. 343.

31. Ibid., p. 344.

32. Ibid., p. 341.

33. Ibid., p. 248.

34. Ibid., p. 182.

35. Vivian K. Anemoyanis, "Teachers' Attitudes Toward the Aspira Consent Decree and Perceptions of Teachers and Supervisors of Teachers' Classroom Behavior in Bilingual and Non-Bilingual Programs" (doctoral diss., Fordham University, 1979), pp. 74, 76.

36. Ibid., p. 2.

37. Henry J. Casso, "A Descriptive Study of Three Legal Challenges for Placing Mexican American and Other Linguistically and Culturally Different Children Into Educably Mentally Retarded Classes" (doctoral diss., University of Massachusetts, 1973), p. 55.

38. Ibid., pp. 63–64.

39. Ibid., p. 85.

40. Enriguetta Lopez Ramos, *A Study of the Classification of Mexican American Students as Educable Mentally Retarded Through the Use of Inappropriate Culturally Biased Intellectual Assessment and Procedures*, 2 vols. (doctoral diss., University of California, Irvine, 1978), p. 63. (University Microfilms Order No. 78-19,056.)

41. Ibid., p. 64.

42. Ibid., p. 82.

43. Ibid., pp. 76–77.

44. Ibid., p. 77.

45. Ibid.

46. John G. Richardson, *Special Education and Minority Misclassification: An Historical and Sociological Explanation* (doctoral diss., University of California, Davis, 1976), p. 2. (University Microfilms Order No. 76-21,001.)

47. Ibid., p. 55.

48. Ibid.

49. Ibid., p. 92.

50. Ibid., p. 93.

51. Ibid.

52. Ibid., p. 111.

53. Ibid., p. 113.

54. Ibid., p. 132.

55. Ibid., p. 129.

56. *Larry P.* v. *Riles*, October 11, 1979, p. 8.

57. Ibid., p. 8.

58. Ibid., p. 9.

59. Ibid., p. 10.

60. Ibid., p. 11.

61. Ibid., p. 13.

62. Ibid., pp. 13–14.

63. Ibid., p. 15.

64. Ibid.

65. Ibid.

66. Ibid., p. 18.

67. Ibid., p. 23.

68. Ibid., p. 28.

69. Ibid., p. 33.

70. See, for example, M. Weinberg, *Minority Students: A Research Appraisal* (Washington, D.C.: U.S. Government Printing Office, 1977), p. 59.

71. *Larry P.* v. *Riles*, p. 91.

72. Ibid., p. 38.

73. Ibid., p. 41.

74. Ibid., p. 42.

75. Ibid., p. 72.

76. Ibid., p. 59.

77. Ibid., p. 66.

78. Ibid., p. 89.

79. Jimmy Lee Peterson, *The Changes in the Educational System Resulting from the Growth of Black Political Participation and the Involvement of the Federal Government—A Select Study of Three Blackbelt Counties in Central Alabama Between 1960–1974* (doctoral diss., University of Michigan, 1976), p. 43. (University Microfilms Order No. 76-27,567.)

80. Ibid., p. 44.

81. Ibid., p. 109.

82. Basic data in Bobby G. Cooper, *The Effects of Desegregation on Black Elementary and Secondary Teachers in Mississippi 1970–1973* (doctoral diss., University of Colorado, 1977), p. 20. (University Microfilms Order No. 77-24,199.)

83. Ibid., p. 57.

84. Ibid., p. 67.

85. Ibid., p. 74.

86. See *Armstead* v. *Starkville*, 461 F. 2d 276 (1972), *Baker* v. *Columbus*, 462 F. 2d 1112 (1972), *Ward* v. *Kelly*, 476 F. 2d 963 (1973), *Adams* v. *Rankin*, 485 F. 2d 324 (1973), and *MacLaurin* v. *Columbia*, 486 F. 2d 1049 (1973).

87. Richard B. Freeman, "Political Power, Desegregation, and Employment of Black Schoolteachers," *Journal of Political Economy*, 85 (1977), p. 301.

88. Ibid., p. 303.

89. Ibid.

90. Ibid., p. 314.

91. Ibid.

92. Ibid., p. 302.

93. Anna Arnold Hedgman, *The Gift of Chaos. Decades of American Discontent* (New York: Oxford University Press, 1977), p. 130.

3

Race and Intelligence in America

Over the broad sweep of evolution, man developed a cultural mode of existence. At the core of culture lay not only "a capacity for highly complex forms of learning," but also "a capacity for transcending what is learned; a potentiality for innovation, creativity, reorganization, and change."[1] Both capacities were crucial from the outset since the earliest human civilizations were established in the face of awesome natural obstacles. On each continent adaptations to the most varied challenges had to be made. During some 150,000 generations of history and prehistory, men and women of every race demonstrated their capacity to learn, unlearn, and learn anew. While mankind came to differ in color, in social and economic forms, and in other respects, only very recently did doctrines develop alleging that some persons were less capable of being fully human.

Race prejudice was not peculiar to slavery. Slavery in the ancient world and in medieval Europe and Asia did not, apparently, eventuate in labeling slaves as inferior human beings. Most of these slaves were white.[2] Nor did antiblack prejudice require slavery for its succor. In the early Islamic world, such prejudice was widespread despite religious strictures against it.[3] Full-scale denial of the humanity of black slaves developed first in colonial America. By the mid-eighteenth century, white colonists began to conceive of the slaves "as primarily and merely physical creatures."[4] And in case nature failed to attend to the new preachment, the legislature of South Carolina in 1740 forbade the instruction of black slaves. As black theologian Alexander Crummell later wrote of the enactment: "It was done . . . with the knowledge that the Negro had brain power. There was *then*, no denial that the Negro had intellect. That denial was an afterthought."[5] In the 1780s, Thomas Jefferson declared blacks to be intellectually inferior. He never withdrew this judgment. Blacks were thus excluded from his general prescription of universal education.[6]

Both in Europe and America, doctrines of racial inferiority became formalized by the 1850s. Such declarations, as a later black writer noted, "were always blessed with a singular freedom from effective protest."[7] Objections from blacks, however, persisted—even before the Civil War.

It was not a scholarly writer but the Judiciary Committee of the Ohio legislature that defended exclusion of black children from the common schools in 1834: "The security of our government rests and remains in the morality, virtue, and wisdom of our free white citizens. . . . The common school fund is not the offspring of the offices of charity."[8] To this practical racism black parents posited an equally practical opposition, not rhetorical but political. They conducted a statewide campaign to open the public schools to their children; within fifteen years they succeeded.

In opposition to direct contentions that blacks were inferior, black spokesmen presented a variety of refutations. Rather than consisting of learned subtleties, these usually referred the detractor to a study of then contemporary reality. Black abolitionist Robert B. Forten declared: "And there are innumerable living instances . . . that the color of the skin affects not the elements of human nature, nor the principles upon which men move on from ignorance to knowledge and refinement."[9] James McCune Smith, a physician and the leading black intellectual in New York City, declared in 1844:

During the last 30 years, the Northern States have been the scene of a silent struggle. . . . the free blacks [are] taught to believe themselves naturally inferior, barely admitted to common school instruction, shut out from the temple of higher literature, and taunted with ignorance. . . . Freedom has . . . strengthened our minds by throwing us upon our own resources, and has bound us to American institutions with a tenacity which nothing but death can overcome.[10]

Blacks opened their own schools but would not give up equal claim to the common schools.

School boards sometimes made a weapon of the issue of intellectual inferiority in order to justify segregation. Black parents in Boston during the 1840s sought to abolish an all-Negro school. School authorities refused. In 1846, the school board majority dragged out a new argument—one that was to reappear a century later under more scholarly auspices:

Their [Negro children's] peculiar physical, mental, and moral structure, requires an educational treatment, different, in some respects, from that of white children. Teachers of schools in which they are intermingled remark, that, in those parts of study and instruction in which progress depends on memory or on the imitative faculties, chiefly, the colored children will often keep pace with the white children; but when progress comes to depend chiefly on the faculties of invention, comparison, and reasoning, they quickly fall behind.[11]

Complaints like this were not heard in New Bedford, Salem, Nantucket, and Lowell, where black and white children attended common schools. Nor should it be forgotten that in Boston's black school, the principal—probably the source of the above-described theory—was under heavy attack by Negro parents for racist and neglectful educational practices.

Allegations of inferiority were often put forward in the name of public opinion. Educator Horace Mann wrote approvingly to a Negro group in 1851: "I suppose the almost universal opinion to be, that, in intellect, the blacks are inferior to the whites; while in sentiment and affection, the whites are inferior to the blacks."[12] He was answered by a public meeting of black citizens who denounced "that partial judgment which measures men by their complexion and stamps them with inferiority when their color or nationality appears unlike their own."[13] Black academician William G. Allen criticized Mann's racial theory, contending that blacks were not a distinct African race so much as "essentially a mixed race." Accordingly, strictly racial characteristics could not properly be delineated.[14] Black Boston lawyer John Rock summarized the Negro response to the allegations with his customary force: "Abject as our condition has been, our whole lives prove us superior to the influences that have been brought upon to crush us."[15]

After the 1860s, two new elements became a part of racist thought: imperialist expansion and the doctrine of evolution. In Europe as well as the United States, doctrines of racial superiority served to "justify" expansion into Africa. "Imperialism," writes Stocking, "not only nourished, but indeed required, theories of western European racial superiority."[16] Africa was viewed by Western historians as a land without history where a deadening sameness characterized the centuries. As two African historians noted later: "This attempt to cut the African adrift from his historical experience and in effect to undermine his basic humanity was the most upsetting feature of European colonialism."[17]

Darwin's evolutionary thought was soon translated into the same idiom. He had theorized that evolution depended on a process of natural selection, characterized by a struggle for existence among the various species of plants and animals. Social Darwinists transported this doctrine into the realm of human life and argued for a racist interpretation. First, they held, natural selection was tending toward pure races. Second, racial prejudice was adaptive toward this goal because it sped up the eventual emergence of pure races.[18] Races and nationalities were placed on an evolutionary scale, which was led invariably by white Anglo-Saxon populations. In time, the theory arose that all races were capable of development but that the lower ones required the guidance of the higher ones. Lamarckianism, the belief in the inheritance of acquired characteristics, complemented the argument for race development. Thus, changes in the environment of "lower" races could become their permanent acquisitions.

Around the turn of the century, some American social scientists began to develop the concept of culture. This view universalized the capacity to be human. During the early years of the new century, most social scientists rejected the idea that "racial differences were significant factors in determining cultural development."[19] By 1912, sociologist W. I. Thomas, who had believed otherwise a decade earlier, reported: "Present-day anthropology does not pretend that any of the characteristic mental powers, such as memory, inhibition, abstraction [or] logical ability, are feeble or lacking in any race."[20] Preeminent in the new stream of thought was anthropologist Franz Boas, who held that all races were equally potential carriers of culture.[21] He wrote of the black person: "We do not know of any demand made on the human body or mind in modern life that anatomical or ethnological evidence would prove to be beyond his powers."[22]

A number of social scientists retained beliefs in racial and ethnic inferiority. In 1904, sociologist Edward R. Ross wrote in the leading journal of his field that "the [N]egro is not simply a black Anglo-Saxon deficient in schooling, but a being who in strength of appetites and in power to control them differs considerably from the white man."[23] By the eve of World War I the doctrine of racial inferiority was less often stated than implied.

Racism took its toll in the various institutions of American society, including education, government, and economic life. Yet, the rise of formal justifications for racism strengthened the resolve of those who discriminated. As black intellectual W.E.B. Du Bois wrote in 1901: "If the Negro will blindly go to the devil and make haste about it, then the American conscience can justify three centuries of shameful history; and hence the subdued enthusiasm which greets a sensational article or book that proves all Negroes worthless."[24] Some social scientists condemned racism. Few, however, attempted to establish institutional challenges to racism.

Boas was one of these. Around 1907, he began a long, fruitless attempt to gain foundation support to establish an African Museum which would "combine public exhibits with facilities for extensive scholarly research on the Negro."[25] The proposal was rejected by all major foundations. In 1910 he turned to the Smithsonian Institution's Bureau of Ethnology but officials rejected the idea as likely to arouse the "race feelings" of Congress as well as endanger the bureau's budget. Three decades later, Boas reported continuing failure of researchers to take up the subject of the Negro in America:

We have reason to be ashamed to confess that the scientific study of these questions has never received the support either of our government or of any of our great scientific institutions; and it is hard to understand why we are so indifferent toward a question which is of paramount importance to the welfare of our nation.[26]

Boas's experience paralleled that of Du Bois, who also sought in vain to obtain foundation funds for a program of systematic research on the Negro.

The Uses of Genetics

Prior to 1900, knowledge of the mechanism of genetic inheritance was more fanciful than scientific. Extremely little was known about precise paths of transmission of traits, or even about what was inheritable. Ignorance, however, was no bar to the growth of a body of intellectual speculation known as eugenics, namely, the improvement of the quality of the human race. Much of the eugenic literature was little more than an intellectualization of dominant social prejudices. The existing social order was accepted as the standard of evaluation; position on the social scale was equated with relative quality. In the United States, eugenicists found the lower classes lacking in biological endowments possessed by successful Anglo-Saxon elements in the population. Eugenicists as a whole considered blacks to be biologically inferior to whites.[27]

After 1900, genetics became a modern science. That year, the pioneering experimental work of Gregor Mendel was rediscovered. In addition, August Weismann's disproof of the inheritance of acquired characteristics became known. With the knowledge that a single gene might control the inheritance of a single trait, the possibility of controlled breeding became apparent. Eugenics fastened upon the new knowledge and interpreted it within a framework of superiority versus inferiority. The lower class, for example, was said by Charles B. Davenport, a leading eugenicist, to have inferior genes.[28] In 1910, a federal legislative commission concluded that "immigrants from Mediterranean regions were biologically inferior to other immigrants."[29] Objections to such interpretations were heard occasionally. Jacques Loeb, experimental biologist from the Rockefeller Institute, protested in 1914 that "there is absolutely no basis for saying that the color of the skin or the shape of the eyes, or any other bodily characteristic has anything to do with the intellectual or moral inferiority of an individual or a race."[30] A number of geneticists apparently disagreed; perhaps as many as half of all geneticists in the country became identified with the eugenics movement."[31]

Eugenicists were emboldened to make excessive scientific claims for their beliefs. Science, it was declared, supported the advocacy of sterilization of the "unfit" and limitations on the further immigration of "inferiors" from southern and eastern Europe and elsewhere. By 1917, sixteen states had passed sterilization laws. Restriction of immigration became a reality during the early 1920s. By then, most geneticists had become disenchanted with eugenics. Raymond Pearl, a prominent biologist and one-time eugenicist, charged in 1927: "The literature of eugenics has largely become a mingled mess of ill-grounded and uncritical sociology, economics, anthropology, and politics, full of emotional appeals to class and race prejudices, solemnly put forth as science, and unfortunately acknowledged as such by the general public."[32]

Emergence of Intelligence Testing

The modern intelligence test originated in France. There, in 1904, a government commission resolved to establish special schools for the feebleminded. The commission decided that "no child suspected of retardation should be eliminated from the ordinary school and admitted into a special class, without first being subjected to a pedagogical and medical examination from which it could be certified that because of the state of his intelligence, he was unable to profit, in an average measure, from the instruction given in the ordinary schools."[33] The goal, then, was to discover how to retain rather than reject a child. Alfred Binet's intelligence test, created in 1905, was designed to facilitate this goal.

Binet sought to ascertain not what the child had learned but his intelligence. The latter he regarded as "judgment, otherwise called good sense, practical sense, initiative, the faculty of adapting oneself to circumstances. To judge well, to comprehend well, to reason well, these are the essential activities of intelligence."[34] Binet feared that the quantitative aspects of the test results might mislead psychologists to treat the child routinely or mechanically:

Notwithstanding appearances it is not an automatic method comparable to a weighing machine in a railroad station on which one need but stand in order that the machine throw out the weight printed on a ticket. . . . The results of our examination have no value if deprived of all comment; they need to be interpreted.[35]

The process of intelligence testing, in other words, "must be used with intelligence."[36] Binet stressed, too, the personal consideration and kindness that testers owed the tested.

Binet considered the role of cultural and social factors in intelligence. At first, he declared confidently that "it is the intelligence alone that we seek to measure, by disregarding in so far as possible, the degree of instruction which the subject possesses."[37] It proved less possible to do this than Binet imagined. He made it clear that the children with whom he worked were not from selected social groups but from Parisian working-class families.

In a study of Belgian children, Binet found that "the intellectual level of the children is modified according to the wealth of the population."[38] This, he emphasized, was not an absolute rule. Indeed, in the Parisian schools he studied it did not hold true. There he found little difference in achievement among children of varying social conditions. He attributed this outcome principally to the fact that "in the primary school . . . they all receive the same kind of instruction in class."[39] Also, the social contrasts were wider in Belgium than in Paris.

Binet stressed intelligence as a practical activity: "The faculty of adapting oneself is the property of intelligence and . . . the power of adaptation is the measure of it."[40] He regarded as "brutal pessimism" the view of intelligence as an unchangeable quantity. Instead, he proposed a system of "mental orthopedics" to raise the intelligence level.[41] In any event, intelligence tests were only one potentially useful means of reaching a judgment about a single child.

Transferred to an American setting, intelligence tests underwent fundamental changes. Within a decade after Binet's death in 1911, his invention was barely recognizable. H. H. Goddard, psychological director of a school for the feebleminded in Vineland, New Jersey, adapted the test in accordance with his firm belief in the hereditary determination of intelligence level. Binet had rejected such a view, pointing out that teachers often fell into this error in explaining comparative performance of their students.[42] Goddard also held that intelligence was not the complex phenomenon that Binet postulated but rather an unambiguous single faculty.

In 1916, Lewis Terman of Stanford University revised the Binet test, giving it the name Stanford-Binet. It was modified in accordance with American conditions and standardized on 1,000 white children of average social status born in California. Terman believed that IQ tests would ultimately reveal "enormously significant racial differences in general intelligence, differences which cannot be wiped out by any scheme of mental culture."[43] Through his long tenure at Stanford, Terman retained his belief in racial differentials and taught the doctrine to a generation of educators. He was joined by Columbia University's E. L. Thorndike in teaching the hereditary basis of intelligence. Given the great influence of Stanford and Teachers College, Columbia University, large numbers of future teachers, school administrators, and researchers imbibed both doctrines.

During World War I, intelligence tests lost their character as individual testing instruments and became group tests. Binet had declared it necessary "to abandon the idea that a method of investigation can be made precise enough to be entrusted to the first comer."[44] A group of psychologists drew up two tests—Alpha and Beta—to help the Army select potential officers. Alpha tests were verbal while Beta tests were designed for non-English speakers. Rapidly trained testers administered the tests en masse. The tests were of practical value as officer candidates were selected on the basis of test scores.[45]

The scientific significance of the Army tests was less clear. Organizers of the testing effort were devotees of the American trend: they stressed the hereditary significance of intelligence, insisted they were discovering "native" intelligence, and interpreted test results in a racist framework.

In 1923, Princeton psychologist Carl C. Brigham wrote the authoritative analysis of the Army tests from this viewpoint. He reported that changes in the places of origin of new immigrants were driving down American intelligence levels. As fewer persons of "Nordic blood" came, the number of persons from non-Nordic countries increased. "There can be no doubt," wrote Brigham, "that recent history has shown a movement of inferior peoples or inferior representatives of peoples to this country."[46] He asserted that one could only deny "in the teeth of the facts, the superiority of the Nordic race. . . ."[47] Brigham equated the negative influence of non-Nordics with that of blacks. He wrote of "the most sinister development in the history of this continent, the importation of the [N]egro."[48] Critics had already observed that northern black recruits had scored consistently higher than southern blacks, thus casting doubt on any racial theory of intelligence.

Brigham agreed, in part. He wrote:

The superior intelligence measurements of the northern [N]egro are due to three factors: first, the greater amount of educational opportunity, which does affect, to some extent, scores on our present intelligence tests; second, the greater amount of admixture of white blood; and third, the operation of economic and social forces, such as higher wages, better living conditions, identical school privileges, and a less complete social ostracism tending to draw the more intelligent [N]egro to the North.[49]

He concluded that it was "impossible to dissect out of this complex of forces the relative weight of each factor."

While Brigham made this admission, he nevertheless also held that the incorporation of blacks into the American "racial stock" produced a "taint" that Europe had been spared. Racial mixture—both via blacks and "inferior" Europeans—would, he predicted, accelerate the decline in American intelligence. He stated that further immigration must be strictly controlled and that in addition: "The really important steps are those looking toward the prevention of the continued propagation of defective strains in the present population."[50]

In 1924, Congress passed a general immigration statute that established quotas for each country of origin. Immigrants from favored countries—the "Nordics"—were given higher quotas while those from "inferior" countries in eastern and southern Europe entered under lower quotas. Of the twenty-seven states with sterilization laws by 1930, twenty had been passed since 1918, the end of World War I. Works by eugenicists such as Brigham were an important factor in the passage of this legislation.

The analysis of black intelligence contained in Brigham's book was an amalgam of old and new elements. Along with earlier commentators, he acknowledged that intelligence was in part, at least, an indication of or the result of one's education. (Why Brigham failed to apply the same reasoning to "inferior" immigrants is not clear.) He repeated the ancient tale that high black achievement reflected the presence of "white blood" in black achievers.[51] While about a quarter of the genes of American Negroes are derived from whites, neither in Brigham's day nor after was it possible to correlate skin hue with IQ scores. Explaining higher IQ scores by northern Negroes as being due to the migration of persons of superior intelligence was a fairly novel contention. A decade later, a standard work on psychological testing by Henry E. Garrett and M.R.S. Schenck stated that the selective migration argument was unproven.[52] Brigham simply assumed the general adequacy of the Alpha and Beta tests as a measure of "innate" intelligence. In fact, so culture-bound were the testmakers that they sought to determine innate intelligence on one question by asking which one of four different automobiles used the Knight engine.[53] Social prejudices were transformed into signs of innate intelligence in a series of questions purportedly testing "practical judgment."[54]

The public learned of the Alpha and Beta tests in 1919, the year following the end of the war, when colleges and other educational institutions started using them on a wide scale. Researchers also used them to probe into racial and ethnic elements of intelligence. Thus, Kimball Young, working at Stanford under L. M. Terman, wrote a dissertation based on use of the tests in six places in northern California: "We must accept the facts that intellectual traits are to considerable if not complete degree transmissible and subsumable to the laws of heredity."[55] When he ranked the students by socioeconomic status, he found Anglo and Mexican-American children differed greatly. Four out of ten Anglo children but fewer than one out of ten Mexican-American children came from the two highest status groups; about two out of ten Anglo children but nearly seven out of ten Mexican-American children came from the two lowest groups. Despite these sizable disparities, Young declared: "The writer stands firmly on the ground that the cause of school difficulties must be found in the more innate intellectual differences."[56]

Brigham and Young expressed the almost universal faith among American psychologists and educators that intelligence was innate and genetically inherited. Evidence to support the interpretations was exceedingly slim, consisting mainly of IQ scores derived from the Alpha and Beta tests. Geneticists tended to stay away from the question inasmuch as they regarded their science as incapable of resolving it, at least at the then current stage of knowledge. This reticence only encouraged less qualified persons to speak out.

One geneticist, H. J. Muller, a future Nobel laureate, did undertake an analysis in 1925. Referring to IQ tests, he wrote: "the genetic significance of these tests . . . [is] most dubious."[57] In a study of a pair of thirty-year-old identical twins who had been raised separately, he found they scored almost the same on both the Alpha and Otis IQ tests. "For most individual sections of these tests . . . when applied to persons of a given social class and territory," specified Muller, "they provide a fairly reliable index of genetic or inherent capability for work of this nature."[58] He avoided commitments to any concept of general intelligence or to intelligence that transcended class and habitat. Such, in fact, was the prevailing conception in the educational and psychological literature. Muller also warned that his twin study could not support "the more sweeping conclusion . . . that environmental influences in general would have little effect upon scores attained, because the twins were, after all, raised in the same kind of community, and in families of similar status. . . ." It was invalid to attribute the similarity of IQ scores to hereditary forces in the absence of any real environmental variation. A valid experiment would require the identical twins to be placed in very different environments. All in all, Muller remarked, scientific studies should prepare one to appreciate "the great latitude of genetic indetermination to which many psychic characters of man must be subject."[59]

Muller's emphasis on the indeterminacy of human development was directly opposed to the dominant psychological-educational view. Little attention was paid to his study. Workers in other fields, however, also probed IQ tests and found reason to doubt the prevailing interpretations.

In 1922, Alexander reexamined the Army Alpha scores for white draftees and was struck by the apparent importance of schooling. To test this hunch, he correlated state median Alpha scores with state index numbers of school adequacy on a scale invented by Ayres. (The scale measured tangible factors such as teachers' pay, length of school year, and the like.) The states with the most adequate school systems were also those with the highest test medians. "Army Alpha," concluded Alexander, "appears as a test of what has been learned rather than what *can* be learned."[60]

In 1924, a twenty-year-old black student at the University of Chicago, Horace Mann Bond, replicated Alexander's study and found the correlation between Alpha and Ayres scores to be .74, an extremely high figure. Bond went further and studied the relation of black to white scores. He found that blacks from Illinois scored 47.35 while whites from four different southern states averaged 41.0.[61] The so-called racial differences in intelligence were social differences. It will be recalled that Brigham explained higher scores by northern Negroes as partly a consequence of selective migration. Bond speculated: "One wonders how Mr. Brigham squares the facts of southern white deficiency with his theory?" Would Brigham, in other words, claim that the higher scoring northern whites had migrated selectively? Or, would he concede the overwhelming influence of differential opportunities? Leading testers such as Terman contended that racial status played only a minor role in the scores.

Bond also viewed the issue from the viewpoint of the black community. "To the list of inferiorities to which the Negro is assigned," he wrote, "is [now] to be added one of helpless and unsurmountable natural mental deficiency; a barrier indeed difficult to hurdle."[62] Bond charged that distribution of racist interpretations of the Alpha test results was socially destructive. He maintained that "they have given to the professional race-hatred agitator a semblance of scientific justification for his mouthings, and, in the writings of popular and ill-informed publicists, they are rapidly molding a public opinion in support of the most reactionary and inequable measure of general policy and welfare."[63] He called upon every black university student to "comprise himself into an agent whose sole purpose is the contravention of such half-truths."[64] The 1920s were marked by increased lynchings and comparatively low educational opportunity for blacks in the South, but those oppressions were ignored by the theorists of genetic inferiority.

Reorientation During the 1930s

During the 1930s genetics and eugenics in the United States came to a complete parting of the ways. When Hitler took power in 1933, he installed a far-reaching program of negative eugenics. In 1933, hereditary health courts were established to single out persons who were hereditarily defective and order their sterilization. Some quarter-million persons were sterilized. In 1939, euthanasia was legalized and during 1939–1941 about 50,000 persons were killed. American eugenicists praised the Nazi program of sterilization as exemplary. Geneticists in this country, however, were horrified at the distortion of their science, and began public attacks on the eugenicists. During the decade, reports Ludmerer, "among most geneticists there grew such a suspicion that human genetics would be used only for political purposes that many who might have contributed to the field now refused to do so."[65]

The spectre of Nazi racism also muted psychological and educational doctrines of racial intellectual inferiority. It failed, however, to encourage research in the area. At the 1940 annual meeting of the National Society for the Study of Education, a comprehensive yearbook on intelligence was presented. Paul Witty summarized research on the American Negro and observed acerbically that "one leaves the literature with the impression that the Negro child constitutes hopeless school material."[66] Leta Hollingworth spoke on the problem of comparative racial intelligence but did little more than bemoan the state of the field. She recommended "that in the proper course of events a whole yearbook in this series be devoted to the subject of racial characteristics, especially in regard to comparative mentality, as the matter bears upon the interests of school and society."[67] Apparently, no action was taken on this recommendation.

Curiously, such a study had been done six years before but, because it was conducted under the auspices of a black publication, it remained a non-event as far as the literature in the field was concerned. This was standard practice in American social science research.

For the July, 1934, yearbook issue of the *Journal of Negro Education*, published by Howard University, the editor assembled an interracial group of specialists in intelligence and race who represented a number of viewpoints. Editor Charles H. Thompson polled these outstanding psychologists, sociologists, anthropologists, and educators. He reported that "only 4 percent indicate[d] *unequivocally* that experimentation to date reveals any *inherent* mental differences."[68] Contributors to the journal kept their conclusions very much in line with those of geneticists in general. On racial differentials in intelligence, Dearborn and Long reported, "everywhere findings are inconclusive" and "inherent, mental inequalities among races have not been proved."[69]

University of Chicago psychologist Frank N. Freeman concluded: "It seems hardly possible . . . to secure data which will be unaffected by differences in environmental influence without a more widespread and radical control of social and economic conditions than a mere scientific experiment can provide."[70] (A decade earlier, Freeman had encouraged his student, Horace Mann Bond, to undertake a study of the Alpha tests.) District of

Columbia school researcher Long compared the IQs of local black and white children. They were separated by 4.7 points. Long examined the conditions of segregation in the city to reveal how formal equality of condition was contravened by everyday realities. "The wonder," Long concluded, "is not that the colored children of Washington fail to equal the whites in IQ score, but that their IQs are as high as they are."[71] A veteran researcher in the field, Joseph Peterson, speculated about ultimate findings: "We should not be surprised to find that racial differences in psychological traits (if any are finally proved to exist) may turn out to be differences in *emphasis only* of various capacities common to both races compared."[72]

Substantively, the special issue of the *Journal of Negro Education* constituted the most extensive discussion of intelligence and race then available. Its tone was balanced, its canvassing of prior research thorough, and its conclusions judicious. The educational world paid it little heed.

The 1930s witnessed a change of view by one of the principal architects of the scientistic racism of the 1920s. Brigham, a few years after publication of his tract in 1923, wrote a private memorandum in which he labeled belief in native intelligence as "one of the most serious fallacies in the history of science."[73] IQ scores, he now held, were "a composite including schooling, family background, familiarity with English, and everything else, relevant and irrelevant." In 1930, he published an article in which he reversed his earlier judgment and now held that "comparative studies of various national and racial groups may not be made with existing [intelligence] tests. . . ."[74] He labeled as "without foundation" his own book, which he judged "one of the most pretentious of these comparative racial studies." Unfortunately, as Weinland notes, "Brigham's recantation was not widely published and some continued to cite his book as evidence for racial differences. . . ."[75] In 1932, he repudiated the concept of biologically inherited aptitudes and viewed them simply as ways of thinking derived from a specific culture. "From this point of view," Brigham wrote, "test findings would not be construed as necessarily revealing unalterable psychological characteristics of the individual, but merely as exposing what is happening to the individual in his culture."[76]

We have been told that heaven rejoices more over the arrival of one repentant sinner than over ten holy men. It is different on earth. The harm done by racist ideologies could not be undone. Whereas Brigham's book had received an enormous amount of publicity upon publication, the retraction of its principal doctrines seven years later was whisper-like.

While Brigham apparently did not explain his change of view in detail, one may guess at possibly significant reasons. Soon after 1923, he worked increasingly with the College Entrance Examination Board (CEEB) and eventually left Princeton to work at CEEB full time. The empirical realities of testing must have impressed him deeply. Any mystique that once attached to tests was soon dissolved. In 1932 he was ridiculing the "phantom formulae" of the testing movement's "pseudo-scientific contacts with laboratory psychology."[77] (That a bright black applicant had not the least chance of being admitted to Princeton—whatever his score on College Board exams—however, was a problem that Brigham did not address.)

Before World War I, anthropologists took the most consistent social science stand against racial inferiority. Their major spokesman was Franz Boas and this resistance continued during the 1920s and 1930s. Boas dealt on several occasions with the import of IQ scores and race. In his presidential address to the American Association for the Advancement of Science in 1931, he declared:

> We do not need to assume that our modern intelligence tests give us a clue to absolutely biologically determined intelligence—whatever that may mean. . . . A careful examination of the tests shows clearly that in none of them has our cultural experience been eliminated. . . . There is no reason to believe that one race is by nature so much more intelligent, endowed with great will power, or emotionally more stable than another, that the difference would materially influence its culture.[78]

Boas continued to hold, as he had for years, that science knew no way to judge whether, in some ultimate sense, all races were equal intellectually. "It is hardly possible," he wrote in 1938, "to predict what would be the achievements of the Negro if he were able to live with the whites on absolutely equal terms."[79] Racists, Boas pointed out, were still unable to specify human behavior which was "characteristic of all genetic lines composing the race" and in which "considerable variations in the behavior of different genetic lines composing the race do not occur."[80]

Boas also stimulated research in the area of race differences. Otto Klineberg examined the hypothesis of selective migration as an explanation of higher black IQ scores in the North, but found it wanting.[81] Melville Herskovits studied the purported role of "white blood" in Negro behavior,[82] and denied that black behavior was affected by the presence of such "blood." He concluded that from a genetic point of view, the characteristics of a population depended on the capabilities of the ancestors. The racial character of the ancestors was unrelated to cultural behavior. Numerous other graduate students of Boas contributed to the research on race differences.

As World War II was getting under way in 1939, the issue of race and intelligence had become relatively quiescent. The traditional eugenic position was largely discredited; at least it could no longer claim scientific support for its prescriptions. Scientific researchers defended their integrity more by criticizing those who misapplied research than by enlarging the pool of research findings. In the balance, neither the hereditarian nor the racial interpretation of intelligence had been strengthened. Geneticists made no discoveries that invalidated Muller's open-ended position of 1925. In any event, some of the worst features of racial oppression had abated. Yet, this welcome development was due only in the smallest degree to the aid of social or biological scientists.

Since World War II

During the first postwar decade, psychologists seemed to have stabilized their views on possible racial and social implications of intelligence testing. In 1947, Garrett, testing expert and chairman of the psychology department at Columbia University, wrote: "The differences between American Negroes and American whites are not true racial differences. . . . Comparison of Negroes and whites within the United States can hardly reveal true race differences. . . ."[83] Seven years later, testing specialist Ernest Haggard criticized the makers of IQ tests for their overconcentration upon a narrow span of school abilities, and for ignoring cultural and socialization processes in intelligence formation.[84]

A rebirth of scientistic racism followed issuance of the *Brown* decision in 1954. Shortly after the *Brown* ruling, Mississippi Senator James O. Eastland told the U.S. Senate: "Southerners know that legislation and court decrees are powerless to . . . abolish distinctions based upon physical differences. . . ."[85] Two years later, W. C. George, an embryologist at the University of North Carolina, contended in a lecture at Dartmouth College that the Army Alpha tests of World War I had established the innate intellectual inferiority of blacks.[86] He warned, as had Senator Eastland, that desegregation would result in the debility of the white race.

During the decade after *Brown*, Garrett was the leader of the scientistic racists. As recently as 1947, he had denied the likelihood of racial differences in intelligence. Some time after his retirement from Columbia in 1956 and the beginning of his employment that year at the University of Virginia, he changed his mind. In none of his subsequent writings did he mention his previous views. Nor did he account for his directly opposite interpretations of the same evidence.

In 1960 Garrett first published his new view of race and intelligence.[87] He criticized Otto Klineberg's analysis of selective migration although in 1933 he had adopted a contrary evaluation of the hypothesis. Now, he also stressed the innate element in mental ability between races. Race mixture, he forecast, would have dire social consequences. He made no references to desegregation.

In 1961, Garrett published a paper in a scholarly journal in which he attacked what he called "the equalitarian dogma."[88] By this he meant the view that denied the existence of racial differentials in mental ability. Garrett contended, to the contrary, that "Negro-white differences in mental tests are so regular and persistent as strongly to suggest a genetic basis."[89] Almost immediately, the Society for the Psychological Study of Social Issues (SPSSI) adopted a resolution stating that "there is no direct evidence that supports the view that there is an innate difference between members of different racial groups."[90]

Garrett replied by citing thirteen studies; nine of these were published before 1957. One additional one came out in 1958. The remaining three references were to studies or sources that opposed Garrett's interpretation. Once again Garrett did not include an explanation of his reversal in judgment.

From 1962 on, Garrett elaborated his viewpoint within the context of opposition to desegregation. He published articles in the principal organ of the (White) Citizens Councils of America, the main organizer in the South of opposition to desegregation. Large numbers of Garrett's pamphlets were distributed throughout the country. He testified in court suits, defending segregation in terms of the mental inferiority of blacks. In 1961, racial test differences "suggested" innate differences; by 1962, the evidence "strongly favored" the view that the differences were "probably genetic."[91]

A greater leap in Garrett's reasoning occurred in 1963 when he testified in the *Stell* v. *Board of Education of Savannah* case, a desegregation action against Chatham County, Savannah, Georgia. U.S. District Judge Frank M. Scarlett described the testimony:

Dr. Garrett then gave his opinion that the differences in educability between Negro and white children were inherent, and that only minor changes could be achieved by educational readjustment or other environmental change. There was no scientific possibility that learning rate differences of the degree shown by Dr. Osborne's tests and the confirming national studies were either caused by or could be substantially altered by the student's environment.[92]

Garrett also told the court that most of the higher scorers among blacks were those whose ancestors included white persons. The next year he more or less repeated his testimony in a desegregation case involving Jackson, Mississippi.[93]

In 1965, Garrett reported that "Negro-white mental differences are chiefly innate and are inherited."[94] On the basis of studies of twins, he continued, "differences between Negro and white children . . . can be predicted to arise in the ratio of three-to-one from heredity over environment." A year later, Garrett again held that heredity was far more important than environment: "nurture can work only with the tools supplied by nature."[95]

In 1967, Garrett testified on a civil rights matter before a U.S. Senate subcommittee chaired by Senator Sam J. Ervin. He stated:

Black people are immature relative to the white. They are more primitive, they are more childlike, their abstract intelligence is on the average considerably lower. All of the evidence . . . shows that . . . [with respect to] intelligence on the abstract level [the Negro] falls down. . . . He doesn't have it. . . .[96]

In 1968, he testified in a federal desegregation proceeding in Mississippi. When a government attorney asked for evidence in support of his statement that Africans were intellectually inferior to Europeans, Garrett pointed to the contrast between the Caucasian Gothic cathedrals of Europe and the black-built "mud huts of the Congo."[97] During his last year of life, 1973,

Garrett revised a pamphlet in which he once more repeated every major argument he had put forward over the preceding thirteen years.[98]

As one-time president of the American Psychological Association—in 1943—and as a Southerner who had "made good" up North, Garrett was a figure of some prestige. He became a celebrity of sorts as he shaped his doctrine into a weapon against desegregation. But neither courts nor legislatures based any lasting action on his arguments. Southern school boards fighting desegregation found the doctrine a useful if secondary ideological weapon. The scientific content of Garrett's writings was exceedingly slender and rarely did he discuss opposing viewpoints. The most straightforward aspect of his material is the frank racism contained in it. Utterly convinced of the superiority of whites and openly contemptuous of blacks, Garrett was eager to put his theories into practice. His favored remedy was a perfected segregation—for the allegedly inferior blacks he prescribed separate black schools, controlled by Negroes and equal to those of whites. Garrett was overtaken by the practical progress of desegregation. By the opening of the 1970s he had sunk into scholarly obscurity.

Human Behavioral Genetics

After World War II, scientists created a new coherent field—human behavioral genetics. Perspectives and methods that had proved productive in general genetics were being applied to man, wherever appropriate.

Curiously, at least to non-geneticists, the advance of genetic knowledge did not strengthen the viewpoint that organic life was "determined" by genetic processes. Rather, the greater the appreciation of genetics, the more open-ended the organism's "future" seemed to be, as demonstrated by vastly expanded possibilities of plant and animal breeding. Geneticists, by altering both the hereditary and the environmental conditions of a plant, could produce a new plant. What of those qualities that distinguish man from other beings? Could these, too, be specified, measured, and controlled? What of human intelligence?

A standard approach to such inquiries is to seek the heritability ratio for the pertinent trait. Heritability describes the degree to which, at a given time and place, variations in a trait within a single population are related to genetic conditions. Scientists obtain varying values for a heritability ratio over an array of randomly selected environments. Where, however, environments have been deliberately manipulated for selected populations, heritability ratios are meaningless. The array of environments then consists of both privileged and disfavored types which cannot be equated. This effect is inherent in any racist or class society. If man were an experimental animal, to be shifted from one test environment to another, even such an obstacle could be overcome.[99] As Caspari notes, if one desires to understand behavior, it is not very helpful to arrive at a heritability ratio. The

more important question "is how genetic individuality, which is a demonstrated fact, will express itself under the influence of diverse social and environmental conditions."[100] Similarly, Dobzhansky writes:

Genes determine the pattern of the development in the sense that, given a certain
sequence of environmental influences, the development follows a certain path . . .
but the development of the carrier of a given genotype might also follow different
paths in different environments.[101]

One might say, along with Gottesman, "heritability today and gone tomorrow."[102]

What fleeting light was cast on the heritability of intelligence? Since experimental manipulation of man is impossible in this area, the nearest to a
"natural" experiment is to study the intelligence of identical twins. The pair
may be said to share an identical heredity, so any IQ differences between
them may be attributed to environment. Clearly, if they grow up in the same
home, under more or less identical life circumstances, there is no "room"
for variation of IQ. A test of relative genetic weight in determining IQ
would require separating the twins and rearing them in greatly differing circumstances. So long as the twins share both an identical heredity and a
common environment, there is no way to separate the relative contribution
of the two factors.

Until 1973-1974, the genetic and psychological literature cited a series of
twin studies by Burt as the most extensive evidence that the heritability of
IQ ran around .80.[103] This meant that 80 percent of the variance of IQ
scores within a population could be attributed to genetic inheritance rather
than to environment. In 1973, Kamin examined the evidence for Burt's
findings and concluded: "The numbers left behind by Professor Burt are
simply not worthy of serious scientific attention. . . . I see no unambiguous
evidence whatever in these studies for any heritability of IQ test scores."[104]
Shortly afterwards, Arthur R. Jensen—a psychologist who had earlier cited
Burt's work very favorably—also restudied the Burt data.[105] He, too, concluded that the data were unreliable, though he did not withdraw his own
earlier conclusion that twin studies established the heritability of IQ.

Rejection of Burt's data raised two questions: (1) did any scientific basis
remain for belief in the inheritance of intelligence—or, more properly, IQ
scores, and (2) had Burt deliberately faked his data?

McAskie and Clarke dealt with the first question. After examining a mass
of studies they concluded that "the correlation results indicate that the
degree to which offspring IQ is attributable to the IQs of their parents is
much less than that predicted on the basis of the genetic and environmental
models, individually or combined."[106] Did, however, that degree still constitute an adequate basis for belief and further work? The researchers were
doubtful: "Neither our understanding of the mechanisms involved in transmission, nor our knowledge about the origin and nature of sample differ-

ences is adequate to make generalizations concerning parent-offspring resemblances with any degree of confidence."[107] Such were their conclusions in 1976.

That same year, the medical correspondent for the London *Times*, Oliver Gillie, wrote several articles, published soon after in a book that charged Burt with fraud.[108] In 1977, Oxford sociologist A. H. Halsey lent support to a supposition of dishonesty on Burt's part who, he wrote, "to some greater or lesser degree . . . distorted opinion and policy on matters affecting the lives of people and . . . betrayed the trust which enables scientists to bring rationality to bear on the conduct of human affairs."[109]

In 1978, McAskie, co-author of the McAskie-Clarke study reviewed above, contended that Burt had "effectively misled" Jensen. He acknowledged that "clear evidence for fraud" had not yet been presented but seemed confident that it would.[110] Jensen, in his reply, angrily rejected any charge of fraud as baseless. He looked forward confidently to a biography of Burt being written by a well-known British psychologist, Leslie Hearnshaw. Jensen declared:

Burt's biographer . . . is fully aware of these questions and, I trust, will leave no avenue unexplored for getting at the relevant facts. His excellent credentials as an objective and impartial biographer and historian of psychology lead me to recommend that we wait for his forthcoming judgment on Burt's career.[111]

About a year afterwards, late in 1979, Hearnshaw's book was published.

He had uncovered numerous outright fabrications of data and distortions by Burt. Using such words as "cheat," "irresponsible," and "unscrupulous," Hearnshaw came to the central issue of fraud: "The charge of fraud no doubt brought Burt far greater public attention after his death than his achievements ever brought him during his lifetime. The evidence reviewed earlier in this book has shown beyond any reasonable doubt that these charges were true. . . ."[112] Hearnshaw's severe verdict related to Burt's twin studies that purported to establish scientific proof for the genetic inheritance of intelligence. Jensen's work on test bias, which must have been at the printer's when Hearnshaw's book was published, still speaks of Burt as one of the "great names" of modern psychology.[113]

Actually, Burt had never offered test data—fraudulent or not—bearing on the issue of genetic differences in IQ between races. His work related only to genetic processes within a single race. It was Jensen who, in his 1969 article, had alleged a genetic component in interracial IQ differences. He had leapt from intraracial to interracial differences, and, in so doing, attracted undoubtedly valid criticisms that such a leap was unwarranted. Intraracial genetic differences bore no necessary relationship to interracial differences. Thus, the exposure of Burt's fakery did not weaken the genetic case for interracial IQ differences. That case was weak enough without Burt's assistance. Jensen, however, had attempted in 1969 to use the erstwhile authority of Burt's research to support his own thesis of interracial inferiority.

The genetic case for race differences in intelligence was almost nonexistent at mid-twentieth century. R. Ruggles Gates, a British geneticist who had argued for such differences, was widely regarded by many of his peers as a "racist or at best racist-influenced."[114] The subject became an issue of international debate in 1969 upon the publication of an article by Jensen.[115] In it he wrote that "there seems to be little question that racial differences in genetically conditioned behavioral characteristics, such as mental abilities, should exist, just as physical differences."[116] In the light of a persistent fifteen-point IQ lag of blacks in relation to whites, Jensen held, "it seems not unreasonable, in view of the fact that intelligence variation has a large genetic component, to hypothesize that genetic factors may play a part in this picture."[117] Further, he speculated that since lower-class blacks had more children than middle- and upper-class blacks, that this "possible dysgenic effect," linked with current national welfare policies to help the poor, could lead to "the genetic enslavement of a substantial segment of our population."[118]

Blacks—and poor whites, as well as other ethnic minorities—were not deficient in every aspect of intelligence, according to Jensen. He contended that there were varieties of intelligence: type I, which was expressed in memory and rote learning or what he called simple associative learning; and type II, expressed in conceptual learning, as in problem solving and an ability to handle abstract ideas. All children, according to Jensen, were more or less equal in type I intelligence. Poor and ethnic minority children, however, were seriously deficient in type II intelligence. Jensen's hypothesis was that these two types of intelligence are "two genotypically distinct basic processes."[119] In other words, they were genetically determined. Compensatory education, Jensen held, had failed and inevitably so, since educators were trying to develop type II intelligence in children who were genetically incapable of such reasoning. Schools, he insisted, must "find ways of utilizing strengths in children whose major strength is not of the cognitive variety [that is, type II]."[120]

While Jensen stated the hypothesis of racial differences in tentative terms, his article treated it in every other respect as more or less established. For example, in discussing consequences of such a hypothesis, his terminology was more definite. His own viewpoint was apparently in a state of flux. Early in 1967—in a paper published the next year—he had written:

As far as I can tell from my search of the relevant literature, research on racial differences does not even begin to permit one to sort out the hereditary and environmental components of the demonstrated phenotypic differences in mental abilities. Therefore, statements concerning the relative importance of genetic and environmental factors in racial differences can at present be nothing but conjecture and surmise.[121]

He referred to "intellectually irrelevant racial characteristics such as skin color. . . ."[122] In another article, published in 1967, he wrote, "Since we know that the Negro population has for the most part suffered socioeconomic and cultural disadvantages for generations past, it seems a reasonable hypothesis that their low-average IQ is due to environmental rather than to genetic factors."[123] Once more, in 1968, he wrote that "data that would permit firm conclusions about the genetic basis of differences among ethnic groups in measured intelligence do not yet exist."[124]

But in 1969, less than a year later, Jensen reversed himself and abruptly found the hypothesis of a racial difference in intelligence reasonable. He neither took public note of the change nor did he cite any new, decisive evidence which had brought it about. He failed to explain why he had reconsidered the implications of existing evidence. Somewhat like Garrett's transformation in viewpoint a decade earlier, Jensen's shift was inexplicable. He denied he was a racist but his doctrine satisfied the central precondition of a racist thesis: it alleged an inborn inferiority based on race. Unlike Garrett, Jensen affirmed his belief in racial integration.[125]

During the five years following the appearance of his 1969 article, Jensen wobbled on the question of evidence for racial differences. In addressing the American Education Research Association in 1972, he counseled that "it is probably wise for educators to assume an openly agnostic position with regard to the genetic issue as it involves racial differences. . . ."[126] In 1973, he wrote in a popular magazine: "I do not claim any direct or definite evidence, in terms of genetic research, for the existence of genotype intelligence differences between races or other human population groups."[127] Yet, just two years later, Jensen called it "highly probable that genetic factors are involved to a substantial degree in the lower average IQ of American Negroes."[128] In 1980, he adopted an agnostic stance on the question, writing that he omitted any discussion of the issue of genetics. Indeed, he proceeded to note—as many of his critics had earlier—that "test scores—all test scores—are measures of *phenotypes*, not *genotypes*. . . ."[129] Therefore, they could not establish anything at all about a genetic component in IQ across races.

In the light of the above, it is hardly surprising that Jensen's basic view should be subject to broad misinterpretation. Langdon E. Longstreth, for example, wrote in 1978 that "just for the record I have read Jensen extensively and nowhere, to my knowledge, does he speak of any group as being innately inferior to any other group."[130] Jensen did just this in his 1969 article and suggested it once more in 1975, as indicated in the preceding paragraph. An English colleague of Jensen's wrote in 1972: "Both Jensen and I agree that the purely genetic evidence [about race differences in IQ] is indirect and inconclusive. . . ."[131]

Some writers who agreed with one or another aspect of Jensen's writings parted company with him on the matter of racial differences. Geneticist James F. Crow wrote: "It is clear . . . that a high heritability of intelligence in the white population would not, even if there were similar evidence in the black population, tell us that the differences between the groups are genetic."[132] Psychologist Herrnstein stated: "Concerning racial and ethnic differences in IQ, I am not ready to move from the agnostic position."[133] In examining Jensen's evidence psychologist P. E. Vernon expressed the view that "I . . . doubt whether genetic differences in ability between such groups as American whites and Negroes are as important as this evidence seems to suggest."[134]

Thus, neither Jensen nor his supporters succeeded in bringing forth evidence on behalf of his genetic hypothesis of racial inequality. Jensen's failure was not one of insufficient rhetoric nor of unfamiliarity with the findings of psychometry. It was simply an inability to produce relevant and binding genetic evidence in the precise area under contention.

Criticism of Jensen came from many quarters. Numerous geneticists expressed negative views about his racial hypothesis. Theodosius Dobzhansky observed that "class and race differences in IQ averages . . . may be genetic, which is pleasing to racists and reactionaries, but not espoused by any reputable scientist."[135] Walter F. Bodmer reported:

Many geneticists, including myself believe that there is no case on present evidence either for assuming, or for not assuming, the existence of a significant genetic component [in IQ differences between races]. The data are inadequate and the methodology for answering the question properly is not yet available.[136]

Cavalli-Sforza held that "present knowledge gives no basis on which to draw any conclusion whatsoever on the genetic component of attributed behavioral differences among races."[137] Richard C. Lewontin and Jerry Hirsch came to the same conclusion.[138] They were joined by M. F. Elias.[139] It should be noted that the book by Audrey M. Shuey, so frequently cited by both Garrett and Jensen as an authoritative and comprehensive review of IQ studies, does not contain, in the opinion of geneticist Gottesman, a "single study . . . [that] qualifies as a genetic analysis."[140] Yet, the book concludes that the fifteen-point IQ gap is genetically caused.

Over the past five years or so, the issue of a possible genetic element in IQ differences between races has continued to attract comment. In 1977, a majority of the members of the Genetics Society of America declared: "In our views, there is no convincing evidence as to whether there is or is not an appreciable genetic difference in intelligence between races."[141] The statement went on: "Whether or not there are significant genetic inequalities in no way alters our ideal of political equality, nor justifies racism or discrimination in any form."[142]

If a black child were adopted into an advantaged white or integrated family, would the IQ test scores of the child rise? Sandra Scarr and Richard A. Weinberg studied this problem. In the Twin Cities, Minnesota, area, 101 such families with 176 adopted children were selected. Of the children, 130 were black, 25 white, and 21 other, including part-white. Also included were 145 biological children of the adopting families. IQ tests were administered to all children and parents. The adoptive parents were "highly educated and above average in occupational status and income," considerably higher than the natural parents of the adoptees.[143]

While IQ scores of adopted children were average, they registered lower than those of adoptive parents and their own children. Among adoptees, average IQ scores were higher for children adopted earlier than for those adopted later (111.0 and 97.5). In school, adopted black children performed somewhat above national norms for all children on standardized achievement tests.

There were four findings:[144]

(1) Children who were adopted earlier, who had spent more years in the adoptive homes, who had fewer preadoptive placements, and who had better quality placements had higher IQ scores. In addition, adopted black and interracial children who had better educated and higher-IQ adoptive parents had higher IQs. Thus, the adopted child profited from a more stable background and, presumably, more complete incorporation within the adoptive family.

(2) "The interracial children scored about twelve points higher than those with two black parents. . . ."[145] Did this indicate that they scored this much higher because they were "less black"? Not at all. Scarr and Weinberg found that the difference was largely accounted for by "large differences in maternal education and preplacement history."

(3) The researchers also investigated the ethnic distribution of adoptee IQ scores and found that blacks ranked below whites and Asians but above American Indians. Again, duration of adoption seemed important for "the black/interracial early adoptees . . . performed at IQ 110, on the average."[146] Scarr and Weinberg stress that this above-normal score must have depended greatly upon beneficial adoptive family environments.

(4) "Black/interracial adoptees . . . [scored] slightly above average on school-administered achievement and aptitude tests, as predicted by their IQ scores."[147] This outcome is consistent with an earlier comment by the researchers that the black children were "fully exposed to the culture of the tests and the schools. . . ."[148]

All in all, then, the transracial adoption process was intellectually stimulating to the black children. Scarr and Weinberg declare, in fact, that "if all black children had environments such as those provided by the adoptive families in this study, we would predict that their IQ scores would be 10-20 points higher than the scores are under current rearing conditions."[149] Implicitly, therefore, the researchers are saying that the traditional fifteen-point gap in IQ scores between black and white can be eliminated by environmental action.

In describing beneficial environmental action, Scarr and Weinberg are somewhat indefinite. Clearly they mean, at the very least, that income and educational levels of black families must be raised sharply. But what more is required?

It was the indefiniteness of the study at this point that gave rise to a criticism by Chester W. Oden and W. Scott MacDonald. They charged that the Scarr-Weinberg study reflected "white values."[150] This view assumed that Scarr and Weinberg regarded the whiteness—separate from the middle-class status—of the adoptive parents as an intellectual benefit. Clearly, black parents are not white. Thus, they charge, the two researchers maintain that "the family atmosphere is the cause of black children with low IQs and seem . . . to imply removal of children from that environment—or a changing of the environment."[151]

Oden and MacDonald also ask why the researchers did not study white adoptees of black families or black adoptees of middle-class black families. Either of these cases might show the irrelevance of the skin color of adoptive families, and thus the families studied by Scarr and Weinberg. The latter reply that white child/black family adoptions are rare while studies of black-black adoptions are unreported.[152] Further, however, Scarr and Weinberg note that blacks who are biological children of middle-class black families score lower on IQ and achievement tests than do lower-status white children. They do not, however, attribute the lag to racial-genetic factors but to black-white cultural differences and the whiteness of tests.

Oden and MacDonald refuse to accept the IQ tests as an adequate measure of children's intellectual development. Thus, they see little point in elevating it into a standard for black as well as white children. Accordingly, they reject Scarr and Weinberg's utilization of the IQ test. The latter respond to the criticism by writing that black children were shown by their study not to be "genetically inferior in 'intelligence' by the same standard of IQ that is used for whites, once access to the culture sampled by the tests is assured."[153]

Scarr and Weinberg attribute relatively high IQ scores of black children to the interracial adoption process, which includes a major social class factor as well. While Oden and MacDonald do not mention it, a question might be raised about such an interpretation: How do we know whether the children would have scored high even in the absence of adoption? They were not tested before adoption. Nor were they a randomly selected population. It is thus questionable whether their achievement of a relatively high IQ score can be compared with the black population as a whole, as Scarr and Weinberg do.

Both pairs of authors agree that some kind of program of environmental change can benefit black children. Both deny that genetic obstacles to such a program can be overcome, if indeed they exist at all. They disagree on the efficacy of transracial adoption as one means of effecting change.[154]

IQ test scores of middle-class whites and blacks often differ greatly. Is this because a racial factor is at work, depressing black performance regardless of social position? Jensen said as much in his 1969 article. Frances K.

Trotman recently conducted a study into the matter. She asked: "Do middle-class black and white ninth-grade girls experience similar home environments in those areas related to intelligence test performance?"[155] Even, that is, if parental education and employment are similar, can one take it for granted that the intellectual content of the homes is also the same?

Trotman found that "among middle-class families with similar SES ratings, there was a significant difference in the intellectual home environments of blacks and whites."[156] The socioeconomic status (SES) ratings included data on occupation, source of income, housing type, and dwelling area. In these respects the homes were quite comparable. But this was not the case on home environment which included, among other things, intellectual expectations, rewards for accomplishments, parents' language usage, provisions for enlarging vocabulary, and others.

Trotman regards her study as providing evidence to counter the hereditarian contention that sizable IQ test differentials remain even when black and white groups are comparable in socioeconomic composition.

Trotman was countered by two critics. Longstreth[157] agrees with Trotman that equal social rankings do not necessarily mean that the intellectual environments of the homes are the same. But he rejects any contention that the Trotman study undermines the argument that genetic factors play a part in IQ differences. Joseph L. Wolff rejects Trotman's conclusions on several grounds.[158] First, he doubts the accuracy and objectivity of her ratings of home intellectual environments. Second, he cites a reliable study by Tulkin and Newbrough which found black and white middle-class homes comparable in family and cultural participation, contrary to Trotman's findings. Wolff cites several other studies, the implications of which are also contrary to Trotman's study. In response, Trotman emphasizes that suspicions are not enough to contradict a study.[159] She deals with a number of the specific criticisms.

One of the most frequently repeated assertions in racist writings concerns the supposed deficiency of grey matter in the cerebral cortex of the brain of blacks. This is said to account for their lower intellectual performance on IQ tests and the like. Recently, anatomist Philip V. Tobias examined almost every study which had come to such a conclusion. He sought to discover whether the evidence in each sufficed to support the conclusion. His central finding was that "there is no scientifically acceptable proof that the cerebral cortex of Negroes is thinner in whole, or in any layer, than that of Europeans."[160] Thus, he concluded, "there is no acceptable evidence . . . which provides a satisfactory anatomical basis for explaining any difference in IQ or in other mental and performance tests, in temperament or in behavior."[161]

The earlier investigations Tobias reviewed had measured the brain size of blacks and whites. In some cases the actual brain was measured but in many other cases where only skeletal remains were available, the volume of the brain case was measured. But Tobias notes: "The brain case accommodates a great deal more than simply brain."[162] In most cases, the age of the person whose brain was measured (or imputed) was unknown, thus confounding the measurement since the brain shrinks with age. Or, as Tobias puts it, with passage of the years "one's head may become progressively filled more and more with emptiness."[163]

It is true, Tobias found, that the average brain of blacks weighed somewhat less than that of whites. But none of the investigators apparently was aware of a crucial fact about brain weight which has more recently been established: the weight of the brain varies significantly with body height. A person with a larger body frame (but not a fatter one!) usually tends to have a larger brain than a smaller-framed person. Thus, the weight of a brain has to be related to body height before we can go on to further interpretation. After making an adjustment for this factor, Tobias concluded that "on this basis alone, all comparisons between Negro and white brain-sizes to date are invalid."[164]

Nutrition is also related to brain size. While Tobias reports that loss of brain weight due to malnutrition has not yet been established, it seems reasonable to expect smaller brains to result from undernutrition than would result from favorable nutrition. Previous studies had not taken this possibility into account.

Sickness is another factor in brain weight. Most brains available for study come from hospitals in which the person involved was ill and then died. How a sickness affects brain weight is well known in general but such information does not generally accompany specific brains from dead persons. Further, a certain number of brains are available from presumably well, normal persons killed in sudden accidents. Forensic medical institutes in Europe have, according to Tobias, the best collections of such brains. But they are all from white persons. Tobias observes: "No series of brain-weights is available for healthy, normal Negroes who have died a sudden death; no Negro series can therefore be compared validly with the best available European series. . . ."[165] It is thus undetermined how much of the black-white differential in unadjusted brain weight is due to differential illness history.

Certain technical considerations also tend to invalidate previous measurements of black-white brain differences. Thus, brain weight depends in part on the time elapsed between death and actual removal of the brain. Before removal, brain weight depends somewhat on the temperature at which the cadaver is kept. This controls the process of chemical change in the body and thus the brain. Another problem arises from the lack of standardization in determining the precise location at which the brain proper should be severed from connecting parts. Also, was the brain weighed before or after it was drained of all liquids?

Tobias, it should be recalled, was not seeking to *settle* an argument so much as to establish the physical facts underlying the argument. "It is totally invalid at this stage of our knowledge," he concluded, "to cite the alleged smaller brain-weight of Negroes as the physical basis for differences in intelligence and behavior tests."[166] Differences in behavior between individuals with large or small brains were not evident. From the viewpoint of evolution, a larger brain was significant for heightened adaptability. Tobias asserts, however, that "beyond a certain stage in the increase of brain-size, we have no evidence that further increase in any way improved man's adaptive abilities."[167] It is true that the brain-body ratio of the gorilla is 1:600 while that of man is 1:45. But Tobias reminds us that the ratio for spider monkeys is 1:12.

The controversy about race and intelligence is a matter of both science and politics. And inevitably so. Politics enter science at two points: by influencing the investigator through his world outlook, and by helping determine what kind of problems will be studied and what methods will be used to do so. Until recently, however, few social scientists have examined the race-intelligence controversy from this point of view.

Jonathan Harwood is the first to have done so in a systematic way. He selected fifteen participants in the controversy, all well known. Five he classified as "hereditarian" and ten as "environmentalists." In the first part of the study he tried to determine whether the particular position they adopted reflected the special training they had received. This proved not to be the case. Psychologists, for example, could be found on either side. Geneticists, who might be thought to tend toward a hereditarian view, were found among the environmentalists. (In an aside, Harwood writes that "strictly speaking . . . more appropriate labels for the two sides would be 'pro-Jensen' and 'anti-Jensen.' ")[168]

What, then, of the political elements, or, as Harwood phrases it, "external" elements, in the controversy? He recalls an earlier study by Nicholas Pastore of the nature-nurture problem. The latter had concluded that environmentalists were generally liberals or radicals while hereditarians tended to be conservatives. Harwood comments that "my observations of the modern race-IQ debate support this correlation. . . ."[169]

Contemporary hereditarianism, he declares, expresses its proponents' view of an ideal society. Such a society would maximize the freedom of the individual and cultivate both individual and group differences. Environmentalists, on the other hand, stress the similarities of individuals and groups. These distinctions emerge in current debates over educational policy, with hereditarians taking a traditionalist stance. They tend to emphasize the superiority of traditional arrangements embodying stratified schooling based presumably on objectively existent ability differences which are relatively fixed.

At this point, Harwood becomes more concrete:

The traditionalists' concern with the decay of boundaries, structure and order in the educational sphere . . . neatly reflects their increasingly threatened social situation. Since World War II, the formerly secure middle-class distinctions and privileges in Britain have been eroded through quasi-socialist political reform. In striking back at the collectivist ideal of their political opponents, the traditionalists have invoked hereditarianism in order to legitimate their case for individualism and hierarchical policy.[170]

The hereditarian-traditionalist position centers on "disorders" produced by recent changes in education that have increased access to education for previously excluded groups. This complaint often takes the shape of charges that "standards have been lowered."

Environmentalists or reformers, as Harwood dubs them, have a very different concern: "The reformers appear to be worried that racial minorities will become so alienated from 'mainstream' society that they will opt out altogether. For reformers the danger of hereditarianism is that it will foster societal fragmentation."[171] While Harwood does not go on to tie this view to a specific social base—as he did for the opposing view—one might easily do so. The reformers seem to be recruited from the same sectors of society as the traditionalists, principally middle-class families. Their prescription for curing the apparent break-up of traditional society is to enlarge the arena of individual rewards—through compensatory education avenues—rather than rejecting a stratified social order altogether.

Harwood hopes to make clear the shortcoming of any account of a scientific controversy which does not go beyond a simple listing of the formal research findings and methodology. How researchers "line up" on an issue is more than a matter of intellectualism alone. Yet, Harwood is not saying that politics is all. "In understanding the construction of scientific knowledge," he writes, "a major sociological problem remains: under what conditions is a scientist's specialist (or 'professional') role more (or less) important than his various lay roles in channelling his cognition?"[172] Harwood is not denying that scientists sometimes come to a conclusion that contradicts their general world view. He is merely calling our attention to the fact that in the race-IQ controversy this has happened infrequently.

Jane Mercer's study represents another way of understanding science and politics, as related to race and intelligence. She approached the issue by examining a controversy in psychological measurement regarding test validity, test bias, and test fairness. Spokespersons for the American Psychological Association (APA) took one position and representatives of minority psychologists, especially blacks and Mexican Americans, took an opposing one.

Mercer's starting point was to characterize the opposing belief systems that have evolved around each group. "The world," she notes, "appears different to rising minority groups than it does to the intelligentsia who are providing an interpretation of the world from the perspective of the politically dominant group."[173] The testing controversy is thus far more than a clash between two bodies of specialized knowledge, according to Mercer. She views it as "a confrontation between the ideology of politically dominant groups and the counter-ideology of rising minorities."[174] How does she arrive at such conclusions?

She begins with Karl Mannheim's sociology of knowledge in which systems of thought are seen as arising out of the collective activities of groups. Each system of ideas reflects the distinctive position of subgroups within the larger collectivity. Accordingly, persons within each subgroup develop a distinctive conception of the larger world. When society changes rapidly, different conceptions of the world come into conflict over which view will prevail in society at large. Socially dominant groups tend to regard their outlook as self-evident, as beyond doubt. Thus, only technical questions are admissible. The system as a whole is accepted as a fact of life.

Within each society, the dominant group develops an intelligentsia which acts as a priesthood of intellectual orthodoxy. The intelligentsia defines terms and delimits controversies but, if unchallenged, it shows a tendency over time to separate the development of knowledge from the real world. Science becomes increasingly "scholastic." When, however, new rising groups appear on the social horizon, a conflict of views bares the partial nature of the prevailing thought system.

Today, Mercer states, opposing groups articulate two conflicting views. "One group," she writes, "consists of the psychologists who control the American Psychological Association and are the intelligentsia for those established elites in American society which control American governmental, industrial, educational, financial, and military institutions." She continues: "All of these institutions use tests designed by psychologists to screen *in* those persons whose behavior fits their expectations and to screen *out* those whose behavior does not fit their expectations."[175] The other group consists of psychologists identified with "groups in Western society who are rising from lower status levels." (It is appropriate to recall from Chapter 2 that one of the groups helping plaintiffs in the *Larry P.* case was an association of black psychologists.)

Since the appearance of the IQ test in America, the Anglo-conformity model of appraisal has been in force. As Mercer writes: "In making inferences about children's 'intelligence' or 'aptitudes,' present procedures presume that America is a culturally homogeneous society in which all children are being socialized into essentially the same Anglo tradition."[176] Dominant practice is not to discuss the construction of tests that would accept cultural models other than the Anglo-only one. As a result, the existing tests "are to be used for diagnosis, prognosis, and prescription in education so that all children can be socialized to the existing social structure, i.e., the Anglo core culture."[177] Consequently, school success is assumed to involve success in one culture only. Spokespersons for minority groups have attacked this view as rejecting the legitimacy of their own groups' cultures.

How can one-culture tests be fair to children who do not fully share in that culture? Mercer points out that the validity of IQ tests is said to be verified because children scoring high also usually do well in the Anglo-centered school. Adherents to the APA view tend to see only the "school" and to dismiss the "Anglo-centered" feature as irrelevant. To rising groups, however, the truth may seen quite the contrary. Yet their view falls outside pre-vailing definitions of scientific truths. They advocate assessing intelligence by children's success in adapting to given circumstances in everyday life, but APA adherents reject this approach. Evaluating minority children by their ability to succeed in "Anglo-oriented and Anglo-dominated institutions" is, to minority spokesmen, unfair, notwithstanding statistical demonstra-tions to the contrary.

Mercer points out a peculiarity in technical discussions of test validity and fairness. To minority spokesmen, an IQ test is biased if minority children on the average score significantly less than white children. As Mercer puts it, in the Anglo-oriented view, "the greater the sociocultural distance be-tween the individual and the dominant core culture, the lower his or her score will be. Thus, persons more culturally distant from the Anglo core culture will score lower and will be considered 'subnormal,' ineligible for job placement, and inadmissible to college and graduate school."[178]

In conclusion, Mercer returns to the general problem. Since the inception of mental testing, the psychometric intelligentsia has succeeded in detaching the issue of test fairness from real-world considerations such as persistent penalizing of minority children because of failure to master Anglo-only tests. Instead, test fairness has become a matter of satisfying certain ab-stract mathematical conditions. This way, attention is distracted from the justice of existing arrangements and the discussion remains purely techni-cal.[179] The status quo remains unchallenged.

The careful reader will observe that Mercer is not casting the APA school of thought as a villain for expressing the interests of the powerful in the so-ciety. The "other side" also expresses a group interest, but it happens to be one without great power. "Issues concerning the use and interpretation of tests," Mercer predicts, "will be settled in the political arena, not in the halls of academe."[180] This is the way problems of power are customarily re-solved, however they may be disguised in statistical garb.

Azinna Nwafor, Barbara Tizard, and Hilary and Steven Rose have, in separate statements, presented a coherent view of science and politics which stresses the social usefulness of what they regard as unscientific work on race and intelligence. Nwafor writes: "For at crucial historical moments when the hegemony of the ruling ideas of a social order [is] threatened by the insurgent activity of the oppressed and exploited of that society, at such periods it is seen as imperative for the preservation of the existing pattern of domination to reinforce the ideological instruments of class control."[181] All in all, this is not very different from Mercer's approach. Nwafor goes on, however, to contend that bourgeois ruling groups value highly any ideology that portrays a given class and racial structure as "an eternal category," determined by genetic forces. Tizard declares that "in a world where power and environmental advantage are unequally distributed, the assertion that genetic factors are of prime importance is an argument for preserving the status quo."[182]

The Roses contend that "the social conditions of western capitalist society of the late 1970s are conducive to the ideology of biologism, a mode of thinking which transfers 'blame' for the inequalities and injustices of the social order and the conflicts which they generate away from the social structure and onto the biology of people and groups oppressed by it."[183] To link race and intelligence is to overlook the institutional reasons for the failure of black children to be educated.

Thomas F. Pettigrew has put forward a related proposition that merits examination: "It can almost be stated as a social psychology law: Historical periods of intergroup threat and tension occasion a rise in charges of innate intellectual inferiority against economically deprived groups."[184] Like the four preceding scholars, Pettigrew links the rise of scientistic racism and the victimization of the poor. While others may specify the late 1970s or the early nineteenth century, Pettigrew does not refer to any particular period. (He made the statement quoted here in the course of a book review.) Yet, a historian could readily check the accuracy of Pettigrew's statement.

The evident failure of the genetic hypothesis to be confirmed or even to be given factual support stimulated research into another biological direction—the possible significance of prenatal and early postnatal forces in shaping apparent IQ differences. Two special emphases emerged—maternal undernutrition and infant malnutrition—but the significance of neither has been definitively established.

Michael J. Begab summarized the general situation:

Of the various factors associated with low birth weight and mental performance malnutrition in the pregnant mother and the young infant may be the most significant and widespread. In the developing countries, 3 percent of the children, or 11 million, suffer from severe calorie deficiencies. Moderate malnutrition embraces another 76 million. The blacks in our urban ghettos, the Indians, other minority groups, and the children of migrant farm workers are part of this population.[185]

Researchers at the University of Minnesota hospitals conducted a seven-year study of the effects of low birth weight, which is found disproportionately often among poor and minority children, on later educational progress. They concluded that low birth weight was associated with "impaired school progress as well as impaired performance on measures of mental development, language development, school readiness, and academic achievement from preschool through the early elementary school years."[186] The sample studied was 96.5 percent white. A predominantly black sample probably would have underscored the same conclusion. A question has been raised about the quality of the control groups used in the Minnesota study.

Jefferson L. Sulzer, in a study of 300 black children attending Head Start programs in New Orleans, found that children with iron-deficient anemia scored lower on IQ tests. Children with a record of past and present malnutrition, Sulzer found, suffered an "intellectual decrement of a generalized nature. . . ."[187] A similar conclusion was reached by the Ross Conference on Pediatric Research, which heard reports on intellectual functioning by iron-deficient children who evidenced "a decreased ability to focus, orient, and sustain interest in a learning task."[188] Chase and Harold P. Martin studied children who had been characterized as malnourished for three and one-half years after their first year of life. Comparing test and control groups, they found that "the intelligence or developmental quotients of the children with greater than 4 months undernutrition were 30 points lower than the control group and 25 points lower than the children who had short periods of undernutrition before diagnosis and intervention."[189]

Reversal of malnutrition effects has been demonstrated repeatedly although not invariably with the same degree of success. The most spectacular case unfortunately has not yet been fully reported, although Begab recently communicated the results based on unpublished reports by Rick Heber and his team at the University of Wisconsin. The Heber group studied a group of black children at the poverty level in Milwaukee. The mothers and children received a very broad span of special educational and social services. After five years, according to Begab, "the experimental children have a mean IQ of 125, the controls, 92. This disparity as well as the levels, have remained fairly constant from three years of age on."[190] Martin also reports smaller-scale successes.[191] Yet, the damage of early malnutrition may be so profound that the original potential of the child is beyond retrieval.[192]

Attempts to conceive of human potential as fixed by genetic inheritance have failed. The main direction of nutritional research findings is in favor of a more open-ended view of human capabilities—intellectual and otherwise. As Lewontin has written: "What we are morally obliged to do is to eliminate blackness per se as a cause of unequal treatment and for that program we have no need of genetics."[193]

Summary

The significance of two and a half centuries of slavery is not that black people are forever and irretrievably maimed by the experience. Rather, slavery deprived four million Americans of an opportunity to share in the benefits of an educational structure which their labor and taxes helped build. After slavery, American society incorporated within itself institutional proscriptions to perpetuate inequality of opportunity. The scope of the deprivation was so extraordinary that mere statistics cannot convey its impact. For example, the ordinary measurement of IQ test scores involves a spread of modest proportions. Differences of 10 or so percent are regarded as significant. But in 1860 the ratio of white to black children in schools was about 27 to 1. The gap was not bridged until a century after *that*. Meanwhile other privileges accrued to whites. It is the institutional, not the genetic, burden of the past that created and maintains the broadest educational inequalities of today.

Intelligence testing in the United States was from its earliest days intertwined with the antiequalitarian doctrines of many of its leading practitioners. This ideology is part of the burden of the past. (It is examined in more detail in following chapters, especially in relation to the role of socioeconomic differences among students.) The rise of worldwide movements for equality has loosened the once secure position of dominance occupied by the IQ test. A half-century ago, the president of Cornell University could say soberly: "We have never had a true democracy, the low level of the intelligence of the people will not permit our having one."[194] Hardly anyone today would treat such an opinion with respect. In the educational world, however, ancient conceptions die hard.

Arguments about the role of heredity are products of environment, not heredity. They will probably continue to be considered until we achieve a society in which race is not a signal for deprivation and discrimination. This would suggest that eventually the argument will not so much be settled as fail to be raised.

Notes

1. A. Irving Hallowell, "Self, Society, and Culture in Phylogenetic Perspective," *Evolution After Darwin*, Vol. 2, *The Evolution of Man* (Chicago, Ill.: University of Chicago Press, 1960). For a summary of Hallowell's thinking, see Meyer Weinberg and Oscar E. Shabat, *Society and Man*, 2d ed. (Englewood Cliffs, N.J.: Prentice-Hall, 1965), pp. 94–102.

2. See Charles Verlinden, *The Beginnings of Modern Colonization*. Trans. by Yvonne Freccero (Ithaca, N.Y.: Cornell University Press, 1970).

3. See Bernard Lewis, *Race and Color in Islam* (New York: Harper & Row, 1971).

4. Winthrop D. Jordan, *White Over Black: American Attitudes Toward the Negro, 1550–1812* (Chapel Hill: University of North Carolina Press, 1968), p. 232.

5. Alexander Crummell, *The Attitude of the American Mind Toward the Negro Intellect*. The American Negro Academy, Occasional Papers, No. 3 (Washington, D.C.: The Academy, 1898) (emphasis in original).

6. Jordan, *White Over Black*, p. 355.

7. Charles S. Johnson, "Mental Measurements of Negro Groups," *Opportunity*, 1 (February 1923), p. 21.

8. *Liberator*, May 3, 1834.

9. Ibid., March 7, 1835.

10. Ibid., February 23, 1844.

11. Ibid., August 21, 1846.

12. Ibid., May 14, 1852.

13. Ibid., October 22, 1852.

14. Ibid., November 26, 1852.

15. Ibid., February 14, 1862.

16. George Ward Stocking, Jr., "American Social Scientists and Race Theory: 1890–1915" (doctoral diss., University of Pennsylvania, 1960), p. 80.

17. J. F. Ade. Ajayi and E. J. Alagoa, "Black Africa: The Historians' Perspective," *Daedalus*, 103 (Spring 1974), p. 127.

18. See Michael Banton, "1960: A Turning Point in the Study of Race Relations," *Daedalus*, 103 (Spring 1974), p. 33.

19. Stocking, "American Social Scientists and Race Theory," p. 498.

20. Quoted in ibid., p. 510.

21. Ibid., p. 21.

22. Franz Boas, *The Mind of Primitive Man*, rev. ed. (New York: Free Press, 1963, orig. 1938; 1st ed., 1911), p. 240.

23. E. A. Ross, "Present Problems of Social Psychology," *American Journal of Sociology*, 10 (1905), pp. 468–69, quoted in Stocking, "American Social Scientists and Race Theory," p. 501.

24. W.E.B. Du Bois, "The Storm and Stress in the Black World," *Dial* (April 16, 1901), p. 264. See also Du Bois, review of A. D. Mayo, *The Mental Capacity of the American Negro*, in *Journal of Philosophy*, 11 (September 24, 1914), pp. 557–58.

25. Edward H. Beardsley, "The American Scientist as a Social Activist: Franz Boas, Burt G. Wheeler, and the Fight for Racial Justice, 1900–1915," *Isis*, 64 (March 1973), p. 60.

26. Boas, *The Mind of Primitive Man*, p. 241.

27. Kenneth M. Ludmerer, *Genetics and American Society: A Historical Appraisal* (Baltimore: Johns Hopkins University Press, 1972), p. 22.

28. Ibid., p. 20.

29. Ibid., p. 25.

30. Jacques Loeb, "Science and Race," *Crisis*, 9 (December 1914), p. 92.

31. Ludmerer, *Genetics and American Society*, p. 42.

32. Quoted in ibid., p. 84.

33. Alfred Binet and Theodore Simon, *The Development of Intelligence in Children (The Binet-Simon Scale)*. Trans. by Elizabeth S. Kite (Vineland, N.J.: Training School at Vineland, 1916), p. 9.

34. Ibid., p. 43.

35. Ibid., p. 239.

36. Ibid., p. 240.

37. Ibid., p. 42.

38. Ibid., p. 281.

39. Ibid., p. 323.

40. Alfred Binet and Theodore Simon, *The Intelligence of the Feeble-Minded*. Trans. by Elizabeth S. Kite (Vineland, N.J.: Training School at Vineland, 1916), p. 87.

41. Read D. Tuddenham, "The Nature and Measurement of Intelligence," p. 488, in Leo Postman (ed.), *Psychology in the Making: Histories of Selected Research Problems* (New York: Knopf, 1962).

42. Binet and Simon, *Development of Intelligence in Children*, p. 301.

43. Quoted in Thomas Pogue Weinland, "A History of the I.Q. in America, 1890–1941" (doctoral diss., Columbia University, 1970), p. 123.

44. Binet and Simon, *Development of Intelligence in Children*, p. 240.

45. For an analysis of the cool reception accorded the psychologists by Army of-

ficers, see Daniel J. Kevles, "Testing the Army's Intelligence: Psychologists and the Military in World War I," *Journal of American History*, 55 (1968), pp. 565–81.

46. Carl C. Brigham, *A Study of American Intelligence* (Princeton, N.J.: Princeton University Press, 1923), pp. 204–5.

47. Ibid., p. 171.

48. Ibid., p. xxi.

49. Ibid., p. 192.

50. Ibid., p. 210.

51. This argument was still being used fifty years later; see Henry E. Garrett, *IQ and Racial Differences* (Cape Canaveral, Fla.: Howard Allen Enterprises, 1973), p. 11. See also, however: J. St. Clair Price, "Negro-White Differences in General Intelligence," *Journal of Negro Education*, 3 (July 1934), pp. 435–37; Russel F. Green, "On the Correlation Between I.Q. and Amount of 'White' Blood," *Proceedings of the Annual Convention of the American Psychological Association*, 7 (1972), Part 1, pp. 285–86; and Christopher Bagley, "IQ and Europid Link Is a Myth," *Times Educational Supplement*, March 8, 1974 (letter). On the problem of arriving at a reliable estimate of intermixture, see T. Edward Reed, "Caucasian Genes in American Negroes," *Science*, 165 (August 22, 1969), pp. 762–68.

52. Henry E. Garrett and M.R.S. Schenck, *Psychological Tests, Methods, and Results* (New York: Harper & Row, 1933), p. 203.

53. Kevles, "Testing the Army's Intelligence," p. 576.

54. See Brigham, *A Study of American Intelligence*, pp. 12–16.

55. Kimball Young, *Mental Differences in Certain Immigrant Groups. Psychological Tests of South Europeans in Typical California Schools Bearing On the Educational Policy and on the Problems of Racial Contacts in This Country*, University of Oregon Publications, No. 11 (Eugene, Oreg.: Oregon University Press, 1922), p. 8.

56. Ibid., p. 60.

57. H. J. Muller, "Mental Traits and Heredity," *Journal of Heredity*, 16 (December 1925), p. 434.

58. Ibid., p. 440.

59. Ibid., p. 443.

60. Herbert B. Alexander, "A Comparison of the Ranks of American States in Army Alpha and in Social-Economic Status," *School and Society*, 16 (September 30, 1922), p. 392.

61. Horace Mann Bond, "What the Army 'Intelligence' Tests Measured," *Opportunity*, 2 (July 1924), p. 202.

62. Horace Mann Bond, "Intelligence Tests and Propaganda," *Crisis*, 28 (June 1924), p. 62.

63. Bond, "What the Army 'Intelligence' Tests Measured," p. 198.

64. Bond, "Intelligence Tests and Propaganda," p. 64.

65. Ludmerer, *Genetics and American Science*, pp. 135–36.

66. Guy Montrose Whipple (ed.), *Intelligence: Its Nature and Nurture. Part I: Comparative and Critical Exposition* (Bloomington, Ill.: Public School Publishing Co., 1940), p. 263.

67. Ibid., p. 260.

68. Charles H. Thompson, "The Conclusion of Scientists Relative to Racial Differences," *Journal of Negro Education*, 3 (July 1934), p. 511 (emphasis in original).

69. Walter F. Dearborn and Howard H. Long, "The Physical and Mental Abil-

ities of the American Negro: A Critical Summary," *Journal of Negro Education*, 3 (July 1934), pp. 544–45.

70. Frank N. Freeman, "The Interpretation of Test Results with Especial Reference to Race Comparisons," *Journal of Negro Education*, 3 (July 1934), p. 522.

71. Howard L. Long, "The Intelligence of Colored Elementary Pupils in Washington, D.C.," *Journal of Negro Education*, 3 (July 1934), p. 222.

72. Joseph Peterson, "Basic Considerations of Methodology in Race Testing," *Journal of Negro Education*, 3 (July 1934), p. 408 (emphasis in original).

73. Matthew T. Downey, *Carl Campbell Brigham* (Princeton, N.J.: Educational Testing Service, 1961), p. 27.

74. Carl C. Brigham, "Intelligence Tests on Immigrant Groups," *Psychological Review*, 37 (January 1930), p. 165.

75. Weinland, "A History of the IQ in America, 1890–1941," p. 242.

76. Brigham, in *A Study of Error* (New York: College Entrance Examination Board, 1932), pp. 248–49, quoted in Downey, *Carl Campbell Brigham*, p. 28.

77. Ibid., p. 30.

78. Franz Boas, "Race and Progress," pp. 11–14, in *Language and Culture* (New York: Macmillan, 1940).

79. Boas, *The Mind of Primitive Man*, pp. 28–29.

80. Ibid., p. 227.

81. Otto Klineberg, *Negro Intelligence and Selective Migration* (New York: Columbia University Press, 1935). See also "Cultural Factors in Intelligence-Test Performance," *Journal of Negro Education*, 3 (July 1934), pp. 478–83.

82. Melville J. Herskovits, "A Critical Discussion of the 'Mulatto Hypothesis,' " *Journal of Negro Education*, 3 (July 1934), pp. 389–402. See also William B. Provine, "Geneticists and the Biology of Race Crossing," *Science*, 182 (November 23, 1973), pp. 790–96.

83. Henry E. Garrett, "Negro-White Differences in Mental Ability in the United States," *Scientific Monthly*, 65 (1947), pp. 329, 333 (emphasis in original).

84. Ernest A. Haggard, "Social Status and Intelligence," *Genetic Psychology Monographs*, 49 (1954), pp. 141–86.

85. James O. Eastland, *The Supreme Court, Segregation, and the South* (Washington, D.C.: U.S. Government Printing Office, 1954), p. 6.

86. W. C. George, *Race, Heredity, and Civilization: Human Progress and the Race Problem*, 4th ed. (London: Britons Publishing Society, 1963; orig. 1961), pp. 30–31.

87. Henry E. Garrett, *Klineberg's Chapter on Race and Psychology: A Review* (reprinted from *The Mankind Quarterly*, 1 (July 1969)).

88. Henry E. Garrett, "The Equalitarian Dogma," *Perspectives in Biology and Medicine*, 4 (1961), pp. 480–84.

89. Henry E. Garrett, "The S.P.S.S.I. and Racial Issues," *American Psychologist*, 17 (May 1962), p. 1 (reprint).

90. Quoted in ibid.

91. Henry E. Garrett, *Desegregation: Fact and Hokum* (Richmond, Va.: Patrick Henry Press, [1962?]), p. 24.

92. *Stell* v. *Board of Education of Savannah*, 220 F. Suppl. 241 (1963).

93. *Evers* v. *Jackson*, 232 F. Suppl. 241 (1964).

94. Henry E. Garrett, "How Classroom Desegregation Will Work," *Citizen*, 10 (October 1965), p. 5.

95. Henry E. Garrett, "How Classroom Desegregation Works," *Citizen*, 10 (February 1966), p. 20.

96. Henry E. Garrett, "Garrett's Stuff," *Integrated Education*, 6 (March–April 1968), pp. 42–43.

97. Henry E. Garrett, testimony in *U.S.* v. *Hinds County School District*, October 8, 1968, page T-415 of court transcript.

98. Garrett, *IQ and Racial Differences* (Cape Canaveral, Fla.: Howard Allen, 1973).

99. Gerald E. McClearn, "The Inheritance of Behavior," p. 210, in Postman, *Psychology in the Making*. See also David Layzer, "Heritability Analyses of I.Q. Scores: Science or Numerology?" *Science*, 183 (March 29, 1974), pp. 1259–66.

100. Ernst W. Caspari, "Behavioral Consequences of Genetic Differences in Man: A Summary," p. 275, in J. N. Spuhler (ed.), *Genetic Diversity and Human Behavior* (Chicago: Aldine, 1967).

101. Theodosius Dobzhansky, "On Types, Genotypes, and the Genetic Diversity in Populations," p. 9, in Spuhler, *Genetic Diversity*.

102. Irving I. Gottesman, "Statement," p. 38 in U.S. Congress, 92d, 2d session, Senate, Select Committee on Equal Educational Opportunity, *Environment, Intelligence, and Scholastic Achievement* (Washington, D.C.: U.S. Government Printing Office, June 1972) (Hereinafter cited as *Environment, Intelligence, and Scholastic Achievement*).

103. See Cyril Burt, "Inheritance of General Intelligence," *American Psychologist* 27 (March 1972), pp. 175–90.

104. Leon J. Kamin, "Heredity, Intelligence, Politics, and Psychology," 1973, unpublished, pp. 11 and 14. See also "Text of Dr. Kamin's Presentation Denying that Proof Exists that IQ Test Scores are Hereditary," *South Today*, 4 (May–June 1973), pp. 1–5.

105. Arthur R. Jensen, "Kinship Correlations Reported by Sir Cyril Burt," *Behavior Genetics*, 4 (March 1974), pp. 1–28.

106. Michael McAskie and Ann M. Clarke, "Parent–Offspring Resemblances in Intelligence: Theories and Evidence," *British Journal of Psychology* (1976), pp. 267–68.

107. Ibid., p. 270.

108. Oliver Gillie, "Did Sir Cyril Burt Fake His Research on Heritability of Intelligence?" *Phi Delta Kappan*, 58 (February 1977), pp. 469–71.

109. A. Halsey (ed.), *Heredity and Environment* (London: Methuen, 1977), pp. 9–10.

110. Michael McAskie, "Carelessness or Fraud in Sir Cyril Burt's Kinship Data?" *American Psychologist* (May 1978), p. 496.

111. Arthur R. Jensen, "Sir Cyril Burt in Perspective," *American Psychologist* (May 1978), p. 502.

112. L. S. Hearnshaw, *Cyril Burt, Psychologist* (Ithaca, N.Y.: Cornell University Press, 1979), p. 318.

113. Arthur R. Jensen, *Bias in Mental Testing* (New York: Free Press, 1980), p. xxxii.

114. Ludmerer, *Genetics and American Science*, p. 138 n. 10.

115. Arthur R. Jensen, "How Much Can We Boost IQ and Scholastic Achievement?" *Harvard Educational Review*, 39 (Winter 1969), pp. 1–123.

116. Ibid., p. 80.

117. Ibid., p. 82.

118. Ibid., p. 95.

119. Ibid., p. 110.

120. Ibid., p. 117.

121. Arthur R. Jensen, "Social Class, Race and Genetics: Implications for Education," *American Educational Research Journal*, 5 (1968), p. 23.

122. Ibid., p. 15.

123. Arthur R. Jensen, *Educational Research*, 10 (November 1967), pp. 4–20, quoted in Philip E. Vernon, *Contemporary Psychology*, 15 (March 1970), pp. 161–62.

124. Arthur R. Jensen, in Martin Deutsch, Irwin Katz, and Arthur R. Jensen (eds.), *Social Class, Race, and Psychological Development* (New York: Holt, Rinehart and Winston, 1968), p. 9.

125. See Arthur R. Jensen, "Statement . . . Before the General Subcommittee on Education, House Education and Labor Committee," *Congressional Record*, July 1, 1970, p. H 6325: "I personally favor racial integration and I hopefully believe it is coming about."

126. Arthur R. Jensen, "On 'Jensenism': A Reply to Critics," *Education Yearbook, 1973–74* (New York: Macmillan, 1973), p. 295.

127. Arthur R. Jensen, "The Differences Are Real," *Psychology Today*, 7 (December 1973), p. 86.

128. Arthur R. Jensen in F. J. Ebling (ed.), *Racial Variation in Man* (London: The Institute of Biology, 1975), p. 106.

129. Arthur R. Jensen, *Bias in Mental Testing* (New York: Free Press, 1980), p. xi.

130. Langdon E. Longstreth, "A Comment on 'Race, IQ, and the Middle Class,' by Trotman: Rampant False Conclusions," *Journal of Educational Psychology*, 70 (1978), footnote, p. 470.

131. H. J. Eysenck, *London Observer*, March 2, 1972 (letter), quoted in Jennie Laishley, "Some Perspectives on Race and Intelligence," *New Community*, 2 (Spring 1973), p. 192.

132. See James F. Crow, "Genetic Theories and Influences: Comments on the Value of Diversity," *Harvard Educational Review*, 39 (Spring 1969), p. 308.

133. Richard J. Herrnstein, *Atlantic Monthly*, 228 (December 1971), p. 110.

134. P. E. Vernon, "Vernon on Jensen," *New Society*, December 14, 1972, p. 645.

135. Theodosius Dobzhansky, *Genetic Diversity and Human Equality* (New York: Basic Books, 1973), p. 20.

136. Walter F. Bodmer, "Biomedical Advances—A Mixed Blessing?" *The Herbert Spencer Lecture* (1973?), typescript, pp. 18–19.

137. L. I. Cavalli-Sforza, "Statement," U.S. Congress, *Environment, Intelligence, and Scholastic Achievement*, p. 3.

138. See Richard C. Lewontin, "Race and Intelligence," *Bulletin of the Atomic Scientists*, 26 (March 1970), pp. 2–8, and "Further Remarks on Race and the Genetics of Intelligence," *Bulletin of the Atomic Scientists*, 26 (May 1970), pp. 23–25; and "Herrnstein's Sleight-of-Hand," *Harvard Crimson*, December 11, 1973: "The methodological problem of estimating the genetic component of the differences between groups in human populations is as yet unsolved and no experiment performed or proposed has ever come close to doing so." See also Jerry Hirsch, "Behavior—

Genetic Analysis and Its Biosocial Consequences," *Seminars in Psychiatry*, 2 (1970), pp. 89–105.

139. M. F. Elias, "Disciplinary Barriers to Progress in Behavior Genetics. Defensive Reactions to Bits and Pieces," *Human Development*, 16 (1973), p. 129.

140. Irving J. Gottesman, "Biology, Social Structure, and Equality," U.S. Congress, *Environment, Intelligence, and Scholastic Achievement*, p. 44. Reference is to Audrey M. Shuey, *The Testing of Negro Intelligence*, 2d ed. (New York: Social Science Press, 1966).

141. "Genetic Differences in Intelligence," *Intellect* (January 1977), p. 215.

142. Ibid.

143. Sandra Scarr and Richard A. Weinberg, "IQ Test Performance of Black Children Adopted by White Families," *American Psychologist* (October 1976), p. 729. An earlier, popularized version of this article is "When Black Children Grow Up in White Homes," by Sandra Scarr-Salapatek and Richard A. Weinberg, *Psychology Today* (December 1975), pp. 80–82. A related article is "Intellectual Similarities within Families of Both Adopted and Biological Children," by Sandra Scarr and Richard A. Weinberg, *Intelligence*, 1 (1977), pp. 170–91, which is criticized in "Critique of Scarr and Weinberg's IQ Adoption Study: Putting the Problem in Perspective," by Robert Plomin, in *Intelligence*, 2 (1978), pp. 74–79.

144. Scarr and Weinberg, "IQ Test Performance of Black Children," p. 735.

145. Ibid., p. 737.

146. Ibid.

147. Ibid., p. 738.

148. Ibid., p. 737.

149. Ibid., p. 738.

150. Chester W. Oden, Jr. and W. Scott MacDonald, "The RIP in Social Scientific Reporting," *American Psychologist* (October 1978), p. 953.

151. Ibid., p. 954.

152. Sandra Scarr and Richard A. Weinberg, "The Rights and Responsibilities of the Social Scientist," *American Psychologist* (October 1978), p. 955.

153. Ibid., p. 956.

154. For a study that examined social class differences in adoption in France, see Michel Schiff and others, "Intellectual Status of Working-Class Children Adopted Early into Upper-Middle-Class Families," *Science*, 200 (June 30, 1978), pp. 1503–4.

155. Frances K. Trotman, "Race, IQ, and the Middle Class," *Journal of Educational Psychology*, 69 (1977), p. 267.

156. Ibid., p. 269.

157. Longstreth, "A Comment on 'Race, IQ, and the Middle Class'," *JEP* 69, pp. 469–72.

158. Joseph L. Wolff, "Utility of Socioeconomic Status as a Control in Racial Comparisons of IQ," *JEP* 69, pp. 473–77.

159. Trotman, "Race, IQ, and Rampant Misrepresentations: A Reply," *JEP* 69, pp. 478–81.

160. Philip V. Tobias, "Brain-size, Grey Matter and Race—Fact or Fiction?" *American Journal of Physical Anthropology*, 32 (1970), p. 22.

161. Ibid.

162. Ibid., p. 4.

163. Ibid., p. 5.

164. Ibid., p. 9.

165. Ibid., p. 13.

166. Ibid., p. 16.

167. Ibid., p. 18.

168. Jonathan Harwood, "The Race-Intelligence Controversy: A Sociological Approach. I. Professional Factors," *Social Studies of Science*, 6 (1976), footnote 3, p. 385.

169. Jonathan Harwood, "The Race-Intelligence Controversy. II. 'External' Factors," *Social Studies of Science*, 7 (1977), p. 2. The work referred to is by Nicholas Pastore, *The Nature-Nurture Controversy*. (New York: King's Crown Press, 1949).

170. Harwood, "The Race-Intelligence Controversy. II. 'External' Factors," pp. 15-16.

171. Ibid., p. 18.

172. Ibid., p. 20.

173. Jane R. Mercer, "Test 'Validity,' 'Bias,' and 'Fairness': An Analysis from the Perspective of the Sociology of Knowledge," *Interchange*, 9 (1978–79), p. 15.

174. Ibid.

175. Ibid., p. 3.

176. Ibid., p. 4.

177. Ibid., p. 5.

178. Ibid., p. 14.

179. See, for example, the criticism of Jensen in Stephen Jay Gould, "Jensen's Last Stand," *New York Review of Books*, May 1, 1980.

180. Mercer, p. 15.

181. Azinna Nwafor, "History and the Intelligence of the Disinherited," *Review of Radical Political Economics* (Fall 1975), p. 43.

182. Barbara Tizard, "The Environment and Intellectual Functions," p. 109, in F. J. Ebling (ed.), *Racial Variation in Man* (London: The Institute of Biology, 1975).

183. Hilary Rose and Steven Rose, "The IQ Myth," *Race and Class* (Summer 1978), p. 74.

184. Thomas F. Pettigrew, "IQs and Uncle Toms," *Commonweal* (October 5, 1973), p. 14.

185. Michael J. Begab, "The Major Dilemma of Mental Retardation: Shall We Prevent It? (Some Social Implications of Research in Mental Retardation)," *American Journal of Mental Deficiency*, 78 (March 1974), p. 525.

186. Rosalyn A. Rubin, Cynthia Rosenblatt, and Bruce Balow, "Psychological and Educational Sequelae of Prematurity," *Pediatrics*, 52 (September 1973), p. 361.

187. Jefferson L. Sulzer, Wesley J. Hansche, and Frederick Koenig, "Nutrition and Behavior in Head Start Children: Results from the Tulane Study," p. 104, in David J. Kallen (ed.), *Nutrition, Development and Social Behavior, Proceedings of the Conference on the Assessment of Tests of Behavior from Studies of Nutrition in the Western Hemisphere* (Washington, D.C.: U.S. Government Printing Office, 1973).

188. Harold P. Martin, "Nutrition: Its Relationship to Children's Physical, Mental, and Emotional Development," *American Journal of Clinical Nutrition*, 26 (July 1973), p. 768.

189. Ibid. See also David Baird Coursin, "Nutrition and Brain Development in Infants," *Merrill-Palmer Quarterly*, 18 (April 1972), pp. 177–202; and Steven Rose,

"Environmental Effects on Brain and Behavior," in Richardson and Spears with Richards (eds.), *Race and Intelligence*, p. 139.

190. Begab, "The Major Dilemma of Mental Retardation," p. 527. For preliminary reports, see Rick Heber and Howard Garber, "An Experiment in the Prevention of Cultural-Familial Mental Retardation," pp. 478–93, in *Environment, Intelligence and Scholastic Achievement*, published by U.S. Congress; *Rehabilitation of Families at Risk of Mental Retardation*, by Rick Heber and others (Madison, Wis.: Rehabilitation Research and Training Center in Mental Retardation, University of Wisconsin, December 1972); and Carol A. Falender and Rick Heber, "Mother-Child Interaction and Participation in a Longitudinal Intervention Program," *Developmental Psychology*, 11 (1975), pp. 830–36. For a more skeptical view of the Heber research, see Ellis B. Page, "Miracle in Milwaukee: Raising the IQ," *Educational Researcher*, 1 (October 1972), pp. 8–10, 15–16.

191. See Martin, "Nutrition," pp. 772–73.

192. See ibid., p. 768. See also Harrison McKay and others, "Improving Cognitive Ability in Chronically Deprived Children," *Science*, 200 (April 21, 1978), pp. 270–78. This study relates to Colombia.

193. Lewontin, "Further Remarks on Race and the Genetics of Intelligence," p. 25. For a positive example of health improvement derived from social measures, see Anita Yanochik-Owen and Morissa White, "Nutrition Surveillance in Arizona: Selected Anthropometric and Laboratory Observations Among Mexican-American Children," *American Journal of Public Health*, 67 (February 1977), pp. 151–54.

194. George B. Cutten, quoted in Weinland, "A History of the IQ in America, 1890–1941," p. 172.

4

Changing Discriminatory Educational Processes

"It is never wise or productive, either for the educational system or the teacher," write Stern and Keislar, "to insist that a program be implemented by someone who is basically antagonistic to it."[1] How does this apply to desegregation programs in American schools? Frequently, the assumption is made that following a court order in a desegregation case the course of events is more or less a technical one, of joining resources and personnel. In fact, however, this is a grand oversimplification. Many of the value conflicts around desegregation do not disappear with the court order. They persist. In other cases, they are resolved creatively. We must examine both kinds of resolutions. In this chapter, we will review studies of school boards and school administrators, the role of teachers, student interracial interaction, and related topics.

In 1976 Rodgers and Bullock, two prominent researchers, reported on their study of 170 black and white school officials in thirty-one Georgia school districts.[2] Actual interviews occurred four or five years earlier. A clear majority (62 percent) expressed continued opposition to desegregation, with only 32 percent saying they favored it. There was a clear racial separation of views; nine out of ten black officials favored desegregation. With reference to this latter finding, the researchers observe, "less universal support might have been expected since in some of the districts black administrators and teachers were demoted and dismissed as a consequence of the elimination of all-black schools."[3]

When asked whether desegregation had harmful or beneficial effects on achievement in the schools, over half (59 percent) of the white officials thought there were harmful effects. Sixty-three percent of the blacks thought the impact had been positive. Responding to a question on the impact of desegregation on race relations, 40 percent of white officials and 79 percent of black officials thought the impact had been positive.

Rodgers and Bullock believe their Georgia sample is typical of the Deep

South. If so, there is reason for concern. The researchers write: "We infer from the persisting white opposition to desegregation that Georgia officials will unilaterally do little to correct second generation desegregation problems."[4] (These include racially discriminatory placements in special education, disciplinary measures, ability grouping, and others.)

Research by Stewart, completed in 1977, supports Rodgers and Bullock's pessimism.[5] Taking southern school districts as a whole, Stewart found that racially discriminatory placements in special education and the disproportionate replacement of black teachers increased during 1968–1974. On the other hand, over a shorter period, 1971–1974, racially discriminatory retentions of pupils and punishments for disciplinary infractions fell.[6] In all four cases, however, the percentage of school districts found to be discriminating was 70 percent or higher; in most cases it was 80 or 90 percent.

Stewart also studied whether the legal agency utilized—HEW, the Department of Justice, or a private lawyer—made any difference in solving second-generation desegregation problems. He found that Justice was comparatively ineffectual in moderating second-generation problems. (These years, it should be remembered, were almost all during the presidencies of Richard Nixon and Gerald Ford, neither of whom was devoted to strict enforcement of civil rights laws.) Thus, Stewart concludes, "blacks will continue to be the victims of discrimination in the desegregated school system of the South for the foreseeable future."[7]

Maldonado and Byrne examined the attitudes of non-Chicano educators in Utah toward Chicano students.[8] The researchers reported in 1978 that, in that state, no Chicanos sit on the state board of education, no local superintendent is a Chicano, only 4 of the state's 637 principals are Chicano, and only two Chicanos are members of the forty local school boards in the state. Chicanos, who make up only 2 percent of certified employees in the state's schools, work in nearly one-third of the districts.

Maldonado and Byrne contacted a random sample of educators in the state. They established a typology of four possible perceptions of Chicano students: oppressed, copers, pathological, and noble poor. The perception of Chicanos as oppressed was based on use of a revolutionary strategy; as copers, on pluralistic strategies such as bilingual-bicultural programs; as pathological, on compensatory education strategies involving elimination of Spanish and other cultural elements; and as the noble poor, based on separatist strategies involving separate schools for Chicanos with Spanish as the medium of instruction. In this schema, educators seem to appraise the noble poor and copers positively and pathologicals and oppressed negatively. Respondents were asked to rank each type from 1 to 4 with 1 as the highest.[9] The findings are given in Table 4.1 which shows that the pathological perspective is by far the most popular among educators.

At the same time, Anglo educators in Utah acknowledge that Chicano parents and leaders reject the pathological perspective. By an analysis of

Table 4.1
Ranking by Educators of Four Perceptions of Chicano Students

Rank	Oppressed	Copers	Pathological	Noble Poor
1	7	32	57	4
2	10	53	28	9
3	49	12	13	26
4	34	2	3	61

subsamples of the educators, Maldonado and Byrne found that while as a whole they favored a pluralistic perspective, this was least true in rural or suburban-rural areas. "It is highly possible," write the researchers, "that for many educators the conception of the child failing because his home and culture fail remains an operational truth. Several years of observation of school people in Utah would seem to support this assertion."[10]

The preceding research suggests strongly that much that does or does not occur in the classroom depends on factors that extend beyond the immediate milieu of the classroom. (Teacher-training institutions totally ignore the implications of this fact when they define field experience solely in terms of activity within a classroom.)

Let us move on now to examine a series of studies of classroom experiences chiefly in desegregated schools.

Classroom Experiences in Desegregated Schools

Birdin questioned 1,250 black and white teachers in twelve Illinois school districts with reference to their apprehensions about teaching in schools predominantly of the opposite race.[11] He found blacks were the more apprehensive on school-related matters while whites were more so on intimate personal relationships such as dating or marrying over racial lines.

Three studies involved Anglo teachers and their interaction with Mexican-American students.

Sayavedra's research focused on five high schools in Laredo, Texas, and environs.[12] Twenty teachers, half of them Anglo and half Chicano, were involved in twenty physical science classes, in each of which there were at least six Anglo or Chicano students. The researcher personally observed every classroom. Overall, both groups of teachers paid more attention to students for whom they held high academic expectations and tended to avoid interaction with students at the low end of the expectation scale. At the same time, Chicano teacher interaction with students was less related to ethnic membership. In other words, Chicano teachers interacted productively with Anglo as well as Chicano students. Chicano teachers also interacted more encouragingly with Chicano students than did the Anglo teachers. Sayavedra comments that "Mexican-American teachers may possibly be trying to encourage Mexican-American pupils to participate and to contribute to the class."[13]

Because most teachers were Anglo and because they tended less than their Chicano peers to interact productively with Chicano students, Sayavedra concludes: "The academic level of teacher-pupil interaction experienced by Mexican-American pupils is inferior to that experienced by Anglo-American pupils even when the teacher and pupils are predominantly Mexican-American."[14] Part of the reason for the latter finding is the tendency noted above of both groups of teachers to skirt interaction with students for whom they have low expectations.

Laosa reported in 1979 on his study of kindergarten and second-grade Anglo and Mexican-American children.[15] He reviewed fourteen classrooms in five Los Angeles area schools, all of which had some form of bilingual interaction, and classified each of the Chicano children as English-dominant or non-English-dominant. Laosa then arranged 153 threesomes, each containing one Anglo, English-dominant; one Mexican-American, English-dominant; and another Mexican-American, non-English-dominant. Members of each threesome were closely matched by sex, occupational status of the head of their household, and reading and mathematics achievement scores. All teachers were Anglos, but each teacher had a Mexican-American aide.

In kindergarten classes, Laosa found, Chicano children experienced fewer "cognitively stimulating interactions" than did Anglo children. Yet, as compared with second graders, kindergarteners "received fewer disapprovals and more nonevaluative academic, or academically related information from teachers than the Anglo children. . . ."[16] Teachers' disapproving behavior toward children was more readily explained by students' language dominance than by ethnic group. Without respect to sex, non-English-dominant Chicano students experienced an increase in teacher disapprovals, from kindergarten to second grade. On the other hand, for English-dominant students, disapprovals fell in the same period. Just as significant is the fact that between kindergarten and second grade, non-English-dominant Chicano students increased their attempts to gain the teacher's attention.

The combination of greater disapproval and less instruction, Laosa declares, can be deadly: "This pernicious process could easily explain, at least partially, the allegations of low self-esteem and lack of motivation in Mexican-American pupils and the observed academic failure for many members of this ethnic group." Laosa also addressed the role of bilingual education in this situation: "The findings indicate that bilingual, bicultural education—as it was implemented in the classrooms observed in this study—is no assurance of educational quality and equality of opportunity for ethnic minority and limited-English speaking students."[17] In fact, very little bilingual instruction went on in these classrooms since none of the teachers was bilingual; only the aides were.

Carter, in research completed in 1976, more or less supported the Laosa study, at least in one important respect.[18] She examined 100 Anglo and Chicano third- and fourth-grade teachers in four schools located in a Texas metropolitan center and in a South Texas town. The teachers listened to tape recordings of children speaking highly accented English as well as virtually unaccented English, and were asked to express an opinion of the child's ability to learn, based wholly on the recording. Anglo teachers were more negative than Chicano teachers but both groups of teachers were negative toward speakers of highly accented English. Teachers' attitudes toward children with accents were unaffected by whether the teacher had studied Spanish.[19]

The Sayavedra, Laosa, and Carter studies lend support to earlier findings that stressed the fundamental inequality of learning conditions for Mexican-American children.[20]

Daniels studied professional staff views at the Ribault Senior High School and its eleven feeder schools in Jacksonville, Florida.[21] The school had been desegregated by court order in 1971. Seventy staff members were interviewed three years after this date. During 1971–1972, the school had been closed three times because of student violence. Now, however, teachers in the Ribault elementary feeders agreed that student interaction was more positive than in 1971. Among sixth graders, numerous teacher reports stressed more cohesive and congenial relationships among black and white boys than among girls.

Faculty relations improved greatly:

Several teachers on one faculty reported that prior to this study it was understood that black and white teachers did not communicate during school hours. If they wanted to make plans involving activities for students, they had to do it over the telephone in the afternoons or sneak and do it on school time. If a white teacher was seen communicating with a black teacher, then the white teacher was treated in the same negative manner by the principal, as the black teacher.[22]

In another school, teachers sat separately by race during staff meetings on desegregation in 1972.

White student acceptance of black teachers had improved markedly. In general, teachers were said to be more empathic with students, but the situation varied from one feeder school to another. In one, School L, student hostility was said to have increased over 1971. In School F, on the other hand, relations had greatly improved.

Teachers attributed much of the overall improvement in Ribault to inservice programs. Unfortunately, Daniels does not describe these programs.[23]

Espinosa investigated what we may call the role of paternalism in teacher-minority student relationships as demonstrated in San Francisco high schools.[24] He sought to understand the continued failure of poorly performing minority students in high school. What were the dynamics of the process as they affected student-teacher relations? Espinosa analyzed the experience of 770 students in eight high schools; he used three suburban schools and one school of technology as controls. One thing became clear very soon. Minority students who were performing poorly nevertheless believed they were putting out much effort; actually, they were not. What then led them to believe otherwise? Espinosa replies that "their differences in effort and achievement are perpetuated by teacher behavior and academic standards."[25]

What led Chicano and black students to overrate their academic effort and how did teachers encourage such misperceptions? These students spent the least time—of all ethnic groups—on homework. They achieved at distinctly lower rates than did Anglo and Asian students, for example. They also indulged in widespread cutting of classes and were frequently absent from school without excuses. At the same time, teachers were warm and informal with them, praising them frequently. Students interpreted such personal warmth as friendliness and as a positive evaluation of their academic efforts.

The teachers, for their part, saw the matter differently. They expected little of the lower-achieving Chicano and black students and graded them by low academic standards. Thus, observed Espinosa, "students who are low in verbal and math skills as they enter high school can get better grades without improving their skills."[26] Teachers substitute personal warmth for challenging academic standards. Espinosa is severe in his conclusion:

These schools may be viewed as supporting an elaborate custodial system which cools-out students. Supportive teacher control mechanisms, such as warmth, tend to be a successful way of not only deceiving students about their performance but keeping students in school.[27]

Along with other institutions, the school thus joins in the devaluation of minority achievement in a process of its own creation.

Gerald Adams studied the role of race and physical attractiveness in teacher-student relations in twenty-five preschools in four states.[28] Adams presented 240 teachers with photographs of children of a high or low degree of attractiveness. Teachers were then asked to judge the intelligence and academic achievement of each child pictured. One hundred twenty-eight of the teachers were white and one hundred twelve were black.

In general, the findings were as follows:

Preschool teachers judged white children as more intelligent than black children, physically attractive children more intelligent than less attractive youth, with white teachers predicting higher intelligence levels than black preschool teachers. . . . Academic achievement was expected by preschool teachers to be higher for white children than for black children, white teachers also judged higher achievement for physically attractive in comparison to unattractive children.[29]

Thus, whiteness and attractiveness are the most highly valued characteristics. The highest academic achievement was predicted for physically attractive white males, the lowest for the least attractive black females.

Black and white teachers did not have significantly different views. This
led Adams to write: "[If] the concept 'black is beautiful' is becoming more
evident, the black preschool teachers revealed few signs of it." The mere
presence of black teachers as presumed models for the black children was of
little, if any, help. "It seems reasonable to suggest," Adams concludes,
"that all the 'modeling' effects in the world will have little or no positive
effect upon the child's self-attitude, racial awareness, or personality development unless the teacher also holds strong and positive expectations for
the child's potential."[30]

Marwit and colleagues also examined the influence of attractiveness and
race upon 137 teachers and 60 student-teachers in St. Louis.[31] The former
were found to be influenced by a child's attractiveness but not by the child's
race. Student-teachers, on the other hand, were more negatively influenced
by black children's behavior after their practice teaching than before.

Gene Piche and others analyzed the role of nonstandard black dialect in
teacher-student interaction in a novel way.[32] Fifty white teachers and fifty
white preservice teachers read two compositions which were identical in
content and vocabulary except for the presence in one of certain black dialect expressions. The researchers posed two problems: (1) Could the readers
infer the racial identity of the writer, and (2) Is the teacher influenced by
that knowledge in making qualitative judgments of the composition?

Teachers were able to identify the racially "white" or standard English
versions but not the race of the writer of the nonstandard version. At the
same time, teachers recognized the nonstandard version from the black dialect content. Further, these "black" compositions tended to be rated poorer
in quality. "A general ethnocentric bias exists which affects teachers' judgments of the quality of students' written composition," write the researchers, "but . . . it bears no close relations to specific linguistic features of
such writing."[33]

This distinction is somewhat difficult to follow. Piche and colleagues are
acknowledging that teachers' expectations may affect children's achievement or at least the teacher's evaluation of achievement. They question,
however, whether the black dialectal expressions lead directly to teacher discrimination. The researchers seem to be saying that the use of Black English
does not invariably result in alienating teachers, causing them to be prejudicial to the Black English writers. Instead, they attribute the teacher prejudice to "a general ethnocentric bias." This may be a distinction without
difference.

A somewhat related study by Thomas Pietras and Rose Lamb, conducted
during 1973–1974, perhaps in Ann Arbor, Michigan, dealt with thirty teachers
of black children attending four all-black schools and one heavily white
school.[34] The investigators found that in-service work with these teachers on

curricular and other problems seemed to be more beneficial than undergraduate and/or graduate level course work.

Joyce Riley examined the role of black teachers in the political socialization of black elementary students.[35] By political socialization, Riley meant
citizenship training. Fifty teachers of K-6 black students in Cleveland, Philadelphia, Newburgh, and Poughkeepsie were interviewed. Riley points out
a fact that is rarely highlighted: while black teachers make up only one-
twelfth of all teachers, they teach about three-quarters of all black elementary students in the country. (This is because of the continuing segregation
of many black children, especially in large city schools.)

While "a large majority" of these black teachers valued Afro-American
history highly, fewer than half dealt with it "frequently" in the curriculum.
Indeed, noted Riley, "the teachers . . . tended to stay away from issues of
controversy in the classroom. . . ." Most, as she notes, taught in predominantly black schools with black teachers and a black principal. "A large
proportion of teachers who 'frequently' included issues of controversy in
the classroom curriculum," observes Riley, "taught in . . . minority black
[schools]."[36] The socially quiescent approach of Riley's sample extended
to the philosophy of education as well. Thus, she reports: "Fifty-six percent . . . of all teachers sampled accepted the 'victim' hypothesis. That
is, they believed that learning problems of black youngsters are rooted in
the home environment rather than the school system."[37] Judging from
Riley's findings in schools in four cities, the Afro-American teacher of
black children in mainly black schools was socializing the children to play
roles not greatly different from those taught them in other American schools.

Valora Washington probed the meaning of teacher racial attitudes for effective instruction.[38] Studying ten second-grade classrooms in Indianapolis,
she found both white and black teachers expressed prodesegregation sentiments, with those of the latter being stronger than those of the former.
After four visits to each of the ten classrooms, Washington found that, on
the whole, both black and white teachers were disproportionately negative
in characterizing black children; whites more so than blacks. Teacher attitudes toward desegregation, however, seemed to make a difference. Black
teachers most favorable to desegregation tended to perceive black children
most positively. Conversely, white teachers least favorable to desegregation
were slightly unfavorable to black children.

But Washington was not conducting a simple attitude study or a public
opinion poll. She went beyond that and sought to determine the classroom
consequences of teacher attitudes. Unexpectedly, she found that attitudes
and practices were not always congruent with each other. Black teachers
who strongly favored desegregation, for example, were found "more favorable in their instructional strategies toward white children than were white
teachers."[39] One white teacher—called Mrs. Q by Washington—illustrated
another contradiction: "While Mrs. Q. showed unfavorable attitudes
toward ethnicity, and unfavorable perceptions of black children, her behav-

ior toward black children in her classrooms was positive/slightly favorable.''[40] How did Washington account for this kind of finding?

"Teachers," declares Washington, "appear to recognize that they have negative attitudes, yet when social pressure for a positive posture is asserted, this may lead to behavior which overcompensates for negative attitudes.''[41] Such an interpretation is in line with recent thinking in the field of human relations. There is less emphasis on creating "right attitudes" and more on creating opportunities for changed behavior. Over time, it is hoped, repeated "right behavior" will transform less favorable attitudes into more wholesome ones. The relationship between attitudes and actions is far more complex than suggested by this shuttling from one to the other.

Most crucial, perhaps, is the need to explore the nature of Washington's "social pressure for a positive posture." What are the social forces that create new norms and values that affect the reconstruction of individual attitudes and behavior? How may these be encompassed in in-service programs for teachers in schools undergoing desegregation? More than fifteen years ago Francis Keppel, then U.S. Commissioner of Education, exclaimed, "Thank God for the civil rights movement.''[42] He meant that the movement was helping to revolutionize education by placing new demands and approaches before the country. This is one form of "social pressure for a positive posture" by teachers.

Dolores Mathis studied twenty third- and fourth-grade classrooms in five southeastern schools—four suburban, one rural—to examine differences in teacher interactions with students of different races.[43] She found:

> Nearly half of all the black students in the classrooms under study were perceived by their teachers as severe disciplinary problems. . . . On the majority of the measures of verbal interaction between teacher and student there were gross disparities in favor of the white student. . . . Black teachers showed less partiality than white teachers to both ethnic student groups. . . . Black students fare better with black teachers. . . . White students received an overwhelming amount of positive teacher time, as well as interaction.[44]

Mathis added a startling bit of documentation: "In one class, the teacher at the end of the day passed out treats to her class which consisted of peppermint candy and cookies. The six black students were allowed one treat; whereas, the twenty white students were given three treats each.''[45] Except for this amazing example, Mathis's findings are unexceptional in the literature.

Peter Peretti analyzed the effects of teacher attitudes on the emergence of discipline problems in three desegregated Evanston, Illinois, schools.[46] His central finding was that "teachers with a positive attitude toward busing for integration did have fewer discipline problems and required fewer discipline measures in their classrooms as compared to teachers with a negative attitude." Further, interracial interaction among students grew friendlier in those classrooms whose teachers had favorable attitudes toward the desegregation program. Just how teachers communicated their sentiments about desegregation to their students was not analyzed in detail but Peretti observed that "students tend to know what the teacher thinks about their social climate. . . ."[47] The Peretti piece is not rich in detail so it is difficult to appraise. On the other hand, it is consistent with a fair amount of the material in the literature.

A study in England by Kevin Marjoribanks is suggestive.[48] He found that "modest" changes in student achievement were associated with changes in teacher perceptions of student behavior, at any given level of student intelligence and social environment. Marjoribanks also reported that "at each level of teacher perceptions, increases in intelligence and social environment scores are related to sizable increments in academic achievement." He concluded that "if the children came from a deprived social environment or had a low level of intelligence and were perceived by teachers as having unfavorable school related behavior, then they suffered a compounded deprivation in relation to achievement."[49] On the other hand, he reported, they overcame, in part, the disabilities of their environment and low IQ test scores if teachers perceived them favorably.

We now shift our perspective to other vantage points from which to view equity problems in the operation of desegregated schools. Whenever possible, we will examine schoolwide rather than individual teacher-student relationships.

Equity Problems in Desegregated Schools

George James Hagerty II studied a desegregated school in what he calls "Midwest City," during 1976-1977.[50] The details suggest strongly that the city is Boston—which is west of the Atlantic!—and that the institution is South Boston High School or Hyde Park High School. Much of the work is a day-by-day account of events during the author's year there. It is important to acknowledge here that the incidence of violence in the school had multiplied to an almost unique degree. At the same time, Hagerty reported that "learning was proceeding." This held true, he observed, despite the school's "tension-filled atmosphere."

Prior to desegregation, initiated in 1974, the school had been virtually all-white, attended mainly by lower-class children, few of whom went on to college. At that time, the level of academic achievement was comparatively low and, according to Hagerty, "no true reading program had been established." The desegregation court order directed that remedial tutoring be instituted; curriculum reform also began. In 1976, when Hagerty arrived at the school, nine out of ten entering freshmen read below grade level; one-tenth read only at second-grade level. The benevolence that resulted in curriculum reform and reading instruction did not infuse all aspects of the school; suspensions of blacks outnumbered those of whites by a ratio of 2.5 to 1.0.[51] (Five years after Hagerty completed his study, relative academic achievement at South Boston had risen so much that its reading scores ranked first among the city's nonexamination high schools.)[52]

Hagerty studied the school during its third year of desegregation. Aside from instructional improvements, he reported "the initiation of a general community acceptance of desegregation."[53] (Five years later, however, little positive support for desegregation could be found among whites living in the vicinity of South Boston. On the other hand, overt violence in school and neighborhood has practically disappeared.) Inside the school, Hagerty explained, black and white students who had known each other before desegregation—there could not have been many of these—communicated extensively, except during disturbances. White and black students who were new to each other communicated mainly within the formal confines of classroom routine. Throughout the first two years of desegregation, black and white students never sat at the same lunchroom tables, but during 1976–1977 they began to share tables for the first time.

Hagerty's is a worm's-eye view of a tumultuous episode in American education. Referring to desegregation, he asserted that "the value of this social change is its tendency to reawaken and refresh declining institutions" such as the school under study.[54] But the "reawakening" occurred only under an extraordinary court order that included, for a time, the imposition of a court-ordered receivership. A detailed history of this school's desegregation would undoubtedly uncover numerous other sources of change. These include the role of organized parents, the growing unacceptability of violence in school affairs, the deliberate use of differences over school desegregation for political advantage, and more.

Jean Ann Linney investigated school desegregation in Danville, Illinois, a town of about 40,000 people.[55] The desegregation plan provided for busing blacks to formerly white schools, but whites were not to be bused in return. In the Fall of 1974, the plan was implemented. Linney collected data on 343 students for the two years preceding desegregation and for two years after.

Unlike in Hagerty's school, apparently there were no changes in curriculum and instructional practices in the Danville schools. Achievement gaps between white and black children persisted through the two years of desegregation. Linney also found that bused black children were relatively isolated and friendless in the desegregated school, in contrast with the situation in their previous school. On the other hand, Linney found that black children attending a neighborhood desegregated school did gain in academic achievement and social acceptability. Apparently, this was not due to socioeconomic similarity with their white classmates. (Linney has written that in Danville "there is no identifiable pattern of assignment based on socioeconomic levels as is often common.")[56] Neither Hagerty nor Linney studied systematically the role of teachers in effective change.

As for the existence of discriminatory treatment of students, Linney wrote in one place that "there is some suggestion that after the desegregation black children are being placed in EMH [educable mentally handicapped] classes at a rate different from that prior to desegregation." But in another place she observed: "The appropriate data are not available to determine the extent to which special education placements for black students have increased following the desegregation, or if in fact they have definitely increased at all."[57]

Joseph Gestaut presented another view of the actualities of desegregation in his study of extracurricular activities in Arkansas high schools during the 1970–1971 school year.[58] He chose forty-nine predominantly white high schools and examined the student yearbooks for those schools. He found 86 percent of black students underrepresented in extracurricular activities and only 14 percent overrepresented. The area of greatest black overrepresentation was in sports and underrepresentation was in membership in scholastic honor organizations. He measured over- and underrepresentation in relation to enrollment in the school. Table 4.2 summarizes Gestaut's findings.[59]

Of the forty-nine schools surveyed by Gestaut, black students underparticipated in forty-two. Gestaut views this finding as an indication that "only token integration was implemented in most instances."[60]

Vera Wilson also studied extracurricular activities in five high schools, in her case in Baltimore during 1977.[61] The schools ranged from 30 percent to 70 percent black. Wilson found racially disproportionate enrollment patterns in each of the schools; in most instances, blacks were disproportionately less enrolled in honors groups while whites were disproportionately more enrolled in honors and service groups. In music and fine arts groups black membership was disproportionately high. Whites, on the other hand, participated less in school cultural events but more in community and church groups.

Wilson reported that "in one majority white high school, an increase above 50 percent black membership in a co-curricular club or activity resulted in an exodus of white members." While she did not indicate that this was always true, nevertheless Wilson wrote that the racial pattern of extracurricular activities attested to the existence of parallel social systems in the schools. "To augment separate or parallel social systems," Wilson concluded, "breeds racism."[62]

Surprisingly few desegregation studies examine actual classroom behavior. Researchers prefer to administer questionnaires or other instruments at two time points and record any difference. The difference, they assume, is attributable to desegregation, provided certain statistical precautions have been taken. Terrence Scout, however, chose to test the theory—propounded principally by Elizabeth Cohen and discussed below on p. 107—that majority-white acceptance of minority classmates will develop more readily if the two groups cooperate on common tasks.[63] Competition within the work groups is expected to recede as all cooperate. The theory is important be-

Table 4.2
Under- and Overrepresentation of Black Students in Extracurricular Activities
in Arkansas High Schools, 1970–1971, by Area

Area	% Under-represented	% Over-represented
Athletics:		
Sports Groups	55	45
Athletic Social Group	68	32
Music:		
Vocal	81	19
Instrumental	—	—
Cooperatively Sponsored	63	37
Subject	69	11
Advisory Groups	92	8
Service:		
Pep	88	12
Service	50	20
Honor and Awards:		
Honor	100	0
Individual Awards	84	16
Special Interest	78	22
Average %	86	14

cause it points to a feature of school organization that might need to be changed to facilitate integration, a step beyond desegregation.

Scout studied 372 Mexican-American ninth graders in the Riverside-San Bernardino, California, area. They were located in two schools: one experimental, in which cooperative, interethnic work teams were used; and one control, in which traditional organization prevailed. The former group had 161 students, the latter, 211.

The results were disappointing. On the positive side, Mexican-American males in the cooperative work teams grew more positive in their perceptions of Anglo males. But the opposite was true for Mexican-American females; they grew *less* positive over time. Indeed, female Mexican Americans in the comparison group grew even more negative than those in the experimental group. Grouping male and female Mexican Americans together within the experimental sample, they "report a decrease in their mean number of associates who are Anglo, while the comparison group reports an increase." White students in the experimental group did not show an increase in positive perceptions of Mexican-American students. Scout concluded that the Cohen theory is "simply . . . not practical on a large scale at this time."[64] The question is: did Scout in fact demonstrate this? It is doubtful that he did.

For one thing, the Cohen theory, called the theory of "interracial interaction disability," depends upon minority children being taught some knowledge which they then teach to white children. Presumably, the latter thus have a chance to view minority children in a new, socially valued role. It is not known to what degree Scout implemented such a procedure. Further, Scout himself notes some methodological weaknesses in his own study. For example, subjects were not randomly chosen nor were subjects in the two groups matched. The Anglos had a higher socioeconomic status than the Mexican Americans, and Anglos in the comparison group exceeded the status of those in the experimental group. Mexican Americans in both groups had a comparable status. Scout also reports that pretests were given "after the students had already been exposed to the treatment for about two months."[65] Thus, the absence of the hoped-for experimental effect may be a consequence of failing to administer a pretest before the experimental treatment—that is, cooperative work groups and the like—began.

There is another problem with Scout's research design. He did not study the possible effects of teachers on interethnic student attitudes. Yet, we know from earlier material relating to the Riverside schools that teacher attitudes underwent a long period of change, ranging from fear and rejection of minority children to more considerate and cooperative relations.[66] Teacher preference for Anglo children could easily help separate them from Mexican-American children and engender a mutual coolness between the groups.

Two studies report findings that somewhat mute other findings of teacher discrimination. Jeremy Lietz studied the frequency with which elementary students in a single school during 1972–1974—in Milwaukee?—were reported to the school office for misbehavior.[67] Twenty-nine percent of black students, 21 percent of white, and 12 percent of Spanish-surnamed students were "reported." The rate at which teachers reported students varied by race. The average number of referrals per teacher was as follows: white, 2.12; Spanish-surnamed, 1.72; and black, .92. Lietz found, however, that "teachers do not report disproportionately more than other-ethnic students. . . ."[68]

Hillman and Davenport studied teacher-student interracial interaction in Detroit during 1976.[69] Fifteen hundred teachers from eighty schools, K-12, attended one weekend workshop in human relations. Observers then sat in the classrooms of 306 of these teachers to analyze possible discrimination against black students. The researchers found a mixed picture rather than a clear one. White teachers of black students seemed to take special pains to get the lesson across to them. Hillman and Davenport are cautious in their conclusion. They raise the possibility that white teachers were straining to "make the patterns appear to be equal,"[70] or that the patterns are in fact equal. Another possibility the authors did not mention is that the subjects of the study are not at all typical since they were drawn from a group of teachers who had volunteered to attend an in-service workshop. Among classroom teachers, such behavior is comparatively rare. In a real sense the teachers in the sample were a self-selected group and thus oriented against discrimination in the classroom.

Desegregation research often proceeds, as does much of educational research, as though classrooms and schools were self-regulating mechanisms, subject principally to considerations of efficiency and technical proficiency. Thus, when desegregation is ordered, it is assumed that the school and its personnel will try their utmost to make a success of it. Yet, as we have seen in this chapter, the empirical realities are frequently quite different.

School board members and administrative officials may tend to resist implementation of desegregation. The Rodgers, Bullock, and Stewart studies underscore the real possibility of the growth of, rather than the redirection of, racial discrimination under desegregation. Federal regulatory agencies may fail in their duty of enforcing court orders and statutes, to the detriment of desegregation; in this way, school resistance is encouraged.

Research by Sayavedra, Laosa, and Carter underscores the continuing failure of many American schools to accord equal education to Hispanic children. That the studies were made in Texas and California, the traditional residence of most Chicanos, attests to the depth of the deprivation. Espinosa's analysis of classroom paternalism, seldom recognized as such, adds to the documentation of the school as an engine of deprivation for minority youth.

Adams, Marwit and colleagues, and Pietras and Lamb explored the educational destructiveness of white standards of physical attractiveness and spoken dialect. A striking finding by Adams concerned discrimination against black children by black teachers. Riley observed a similar phenomenon, reporting that black teachers were socializing black students to a subordinate social status. Washington made the point that black teachers favorable to desegregation perceived black children most favorably.

Hagerty's study made evident that a desegregated school under virtual siege can manage to operate and even improve its educational offering. A federal court provided support. Dedicated school leadership was especially critical in whatever success was achieved. In the Danville schools, Linney records the academic and social gains of black children attending a desegregated neighborhood school and, contrariwise, the penalties of black children attending, via buses, a more distant desegregated school. The precise reasons for both outcomes are obscure.

Researchers have also examined extracurricular activities for their contribution to desegregation. Distinct racial patterns emerged in the two studies reviewed here, but not uniformly. It is surprising that so few studies have been made of this area of student activity.

Perhaps the most significant aspect of this chapter is that nearly every action discussed in it was under the control of the school or school system in which it occurred. Neither fate nor history determined the action taken. The course of desegregation (or any major educational change, for that matter) depends greatly on the educational leadership that is brought to bear. Continuing patterns of discrimination are subject to administrative changes, should the school authorities wish to make them.

Notes

1. Carolyn Stern and Evan Keislar, "Teacher Attitudes and Attitude Change: A Research Review," *Journal of Research and Development in Education*, 10 (1977), p. 75.

2. Harrell R. Rodgers, Jr. and Charles S. Bullock, III, "The Impact of School Desegregation," *Integrateducation* (April 1976).

3. Ibid., p. 33.

4. Ibid., p. 34.

5. Joseph E. Stewart, *Second Generation Discrimination: Unequal Educational Opportunity in Desegregated Southern Schools* (doctoral diss., University of Houston, 1977). (University Microfilms Order No. 77-29,685.)

6. Ibid., p. 56.

7. Ibid., pp. 112-14.

8. Lionel A. Maldonado and David R. Byrne, *The Social Ecology of Chicanos in Utah* (Iowa City, Iowa: Iowa Urban Community Research Center, 1978).

9. Ibid., p. 38.

10. Ibid., p. 39.

11. Vinston E. Birdin, "A Study of Selected Apprehensions of Teachers Working in Schools Predominantly of the Opposite Race" (doctoral diss., Virginia Polytechnic and State University, 1978), p. 96.

12. Leo Sayavedra, *Teacher Differential Expectations and Interaction with Mexican American and Anglo American Secondary Physical Science Students* (doctoral diss., University of Texas, 1976). (University Microfilms Order No. 77-3978.)

13. Ibid., p. 103.

14. Ibid., pp. 113-14.

15. Luis M. Laosa, "Inequality in the Classroom: Observational Research on Teacher Student Interactions," *Aztlan*, 8 (1979).

16. Ibid., p. 60.

17. Ibid., p. 62 for both questions in this paragraph.

18. Ruth Barrera Carter, "A Study of Attitudes: Mexican American and Anglo American Elementary Teachers' Judgment of Mexican American Bilingual Children's Speech" (doctoral diss., University of Houston, 1976).

19. Ibid., pp. 66, 67, 74.

20. See Meyer Weinberg, *Minority Students: A Research Appraisal* (Washington, D.C.: U.S. Government Printing Office, 1977), pp. 286-98.

21. Lorraine H. Daniels, *Changes in Opinions of Professional Staff in Schools*

Experiencing Rapid Integration (doctoral diss., University of Florida, 1974). (University Microfilms Order No. 76-16,370.)

22. Ibid., p. 37.

23. Another study of Ribault is by Alphonso Scurry, *The Interrelationships Among Disruptive Behavior and Student Perceptions of Alienation and Internal-External Control in Black High School Seniors* (doctoral diss., Florida State University, 1976). (University Microfilms Order No. 76-28,639.) The disruptive group was found to be more alienated while no differences were found on internal-external control.

24. Ruben W. Espinosa, *The Impact of Evaluation Processes Upon Student Effort in Ethnic Groups which Vary in Academic Preparation* (doctoral diss., Stanford University, 1975). (University Microfilms Order No. 75-25,521.)

25. Ibid., p. 41.

26. Ibid., p. 93.

27. Ibid., p. 97.

28. Gerald R. Adams, "Racial Membership and Physical Attractiveness Effects on Preschool Teachers' Expectations," *Child Study Journal*, 8 (1978).

29. Ibid., p. 33.

30. Ibid., pp. 38, 39.

31. Karen L. Marwit and others, "Effects of Student Race and Physical Attractiveness on Teachers' Judgments of Transgressions," *Journal of Educational Psychology* 70 (December 1978), pp. 911-15.

32. Gene L. Piche and others, "Teachers' Subjective Evaluations of Standard and Black Non-Standard English Composition: A Study of Written Language and Attitudes," *Research in the Teaching of English*, 12 (May 1978), pp. 107-118.

33. Ibid., pp. 116-17.

34. Thomas Pietras and Rose Lamb, "Attitudes of Selected Elementary Teachers toward Non-Standard Black Dialects," *Journal of Educational Research*, p. 296.

35. Joyce B. Riley, *Political Socialization in the Elementary School: The Role of the Afro-American Teacher* (doctoral diss., University of Illinois, 1975).

36. Ibid., pp. 127, 131.

37. Ibid., p. 120.

38. Valora Washington, *Desegregation Attitudes, Perceptions, and Classroom Behavior of Black and White Teachers of Second Grade: Group Profiles and Interrelationships in Integrated Settings* (doctoral diss., Indiana University, 1978). (University Microfilms Order No. 7821776.)

39. Ibid., p. 167.

40. Ibid., p. 142.

41. Ibid., p. 175.

42. Francis Keppel, "Thank God for the Civil Rights Movement," *Integrated Education*, 2 (April-May 1964), p. 10.

43. Dolores W. Mathis, *Differences in Teacher Interaction with Afro-American and Anglo-American Students in the Same Classroom* (doctoral diss., University of Michigan, 1975). (University Microfilms Order No. 75-29,283.)

44. Ibid., pp. 70-71, 80.

45. Ibid., p. 83.

46. Peter O. Peretti, "Effects of Teachers' Attitudes on Discipline Problems in Schools Recently Desegregated," *Education*, 97 (Winter 1976) pp. 136-40.

47. Ibid., p. 139 for both quotations in this paragraph.

48. Kevin Majoribanks, "Teacher Perceptions of Student Behavior, Social Behavior, Social Environment, and Cognitive Performance," *Journal of Genetic Psychology*, 133 (December 1978), pp. 217-28.

49. Ibid., p. 226.

50. George James Hagerty, II, *Desegregation in Midwest City: A Qualitative Study of an Urban, Comprehensive High School and Its Interaction with Community Agencies* (doctoral diss., Harvard University, 1978), p. 71. (University Microfilms Order No. 7823677.)

51. Ibid., pp. 71, 98, 111.

52. See Geraldine Kozberg and Jerome Winegar, "The South Boston Story: Implications for Secondary Schools," *Phi Delta Kappan* (April 1981), pp. 565-769.

53. Hagerty, *Desegregation in Midwest City*, p. 76.

54. Ibid., p. 163.

55. Jean Ann Linney, *A Multivariate, Multilevel Analysis of a Midwestern City's Court Ordered Desegregation* (doctoral diss., University of Illinois, 1978). (University Microfilms Order No. 7820994.)

56. Ibid., p. 64.

57. Ibid., pp. 143, 152.

58. Joseph P. Gestaut, *A Survey of Student Participation in Extracurricular Activities in Integrated High Schools of Arkansas as Depicted by Yearbooks* (doctoral diss., University of Arkansas, 1974). (University Microfilms Order No. 74-28063.)

59. Ibid., p. 56.

60. Ibid., p. 121.

61. Vera I. Wilson, *The Relationship Between Racial Composition of Desegregated High Schools and Membership in Co-curricular Programs in Baltimore City* (doctoral diss., Temple University, 1978). (University Microfilms Order No. 7817420.)

62. Ibid., pp. 32, 97.

63. Terrence M. Scout, *School Desegregation to Integration Through Changes in Social Structure* (doctoral diss., University of California, Riverside, 1976). (University Microfilms Order No. 76-28,080).

64. Ibid., pp. 21, 95.

65. Ibid., p. 71.

66. See Meyer Weinberg, *Minority Students: A Research Appraisal* (Washington, D.C.: U.S. Government Printing Office, 1977), pp. 233-34. See also Joan A. W. Linsenmeier and Paul M. Wortman, "The Riverside School Study of Desegregation: A Re-examination," *Research Review of Equal Education*, 2 (Spring 1978), entire issue, esp. pp. 32-34.

67. Jeremy J. Lietz, "School Deportment and Student Teacher Sex and Ethnicity," *Psychology in the Schools*, 14 (January 1977), p. 73.

68. Ibid., p. 75.

69. Stephen B. Hillman and C. Gregory Davenport, "Teacher-Student Interactions in Desegregated Schools," *Journal of Educational Psychology*, 70 (1978).

70. Ibid., p. 551.

5

Education in Black Schools

The question of what preconditions favor the development of minority achievement in the schools is enveloped in a mist of speculation and a narrow range of inquiries. Two unresolved—and infrequently posed—queries about this problem have begun to be raised insistently in recent years. One is whether the all-black or predominantly black school can be a favorable setting for black achievement. The other has to do with the degree to which material equality exists between individual schools in the same school system. Neither question has attracted many researchers. This chapter is devoted to an examination of whatever evidence is available in the research literature on the first query. The second one is examined in the following chapter.

In recent years the question has been raised whether schools that are all-black can also be good schools. Frequently, the question arises in the context of desegregation. What, it is asked, would be the educational consequence of planning for predominantly black schools as part of a desegregation program? Can children in such schools be educated or are they doomed because their schools are all-black? If the latter, does this mean a high-level education for blacks was impossible during the days of forced segregation? Correspondingly, how was it possible for black professionals to be educated in all-black schools? If blackness is no bar to educational excellence, why not ignore desegregation and concentrate on improving instruction? In the light of such questions, it is no wonder Ronald D. Henderson recently declared it "essential that effective education in predominantly black schools be identified and systematically examined."[1]

One concern embodied in these queries comes from the obvious fact that half the country's black—and an increasing proportion of Hispanic—children continue to attend segregated schools. Another factor is the failure of some, but by no means most, desegregated schools to facilitate black academic achievement. In addition, some few black groups prefer, as a matter of choice, to use black schools. Finally, many whites encourage this preference as a way to avoid the possibility of their own or of other white children attending schools with blacks or as an expression of their own ideology.

Two central issues are involved. One is whether black children are intellectually capable of learning satisfactorily. This question must be answered in the affirmative since, as reviewed in Chapter 3, no genetic evidence has ever been produced to the contrary. The second question must be divided into two parts: Why have so many black schools failed to educate their students adequately? And under what conditions have black schools succeeded in educating them?

Before addressing the question of why black schools often fail, it should be acknowledged that many predominantly white schools fail their students, especially if the latter's parents are poor and powerless. The problem of failing schools is thus not entirely racial. In a racist system, however, race accentuates the failure.

What has been the historic record of black schools? During many of the slightly more than ten decades since public schooling became freely available to black children, their schools were planned to be inferior. The principal means was discriminatory funding; sometimes a white child received as much as twenty times more than a black child. Teachers were less trained, buildings were barely sufficient, the school year was shorter, and supplies and materials virtually unavailable. The curriculum was deliberately kept narrow and impoverished. At times, no schooling at all was available to black children. After 1899, for example, when the U.S. Supreme Court in effect permitted authorities in Augusta, Georgia, to close down the only public high school for blacks in town, another was not built until 1937.[2] (Meanwhile, the white high school continued in operation.)

Schooling for the majority of black children improved most after World War I, when a large black migration northward occurred. Even then, schooling for blacks in the North was rarely without discrimination and deprivation.

Yet, even in the South elements of excellence did express themselves in black education. Unfortunately, there is no way to obtain any systematic data for black schools in general. We must use whatever fragmentary evidence is available.

Horace Mann Bond, in his final work published before his death, dealt with one aspect of this problem. Through this work, we learn about some outstanding black schools in the South, especially during the late nineteenth and early twentieth centuries. Bond was concerned with discovering the family and school backgrounds of black scholars, whom he defined as persons who had received academic doctorates, not degrees in medicine or dentistry.

In almost every case, Bond found that the scholars were descended from persons who had been free before the Civil War or who had become literate while enslaved. After the war, many children of both groups entered colleges organized by northern missionaries as well as by southern black denominations. Bond observed that few enrollees completed a collegiate curriculum:

> For every "college" student actually graduated, these schools gave a thorough elementary and secondary education to scores of students who in their turn passed on, through family and friends, their knowledge of the fundamentals and their acquired habits and discipline. Their children and grandchildren did not have to start from scratch, in an illiterate home and a wretched school or in no school at all. . . . These institutions provided for Southern Negroes some of the most effective educational institutions the world has ever known. The Negro scholars today are, for the most part, the children and grandchildren of persons who received their education in these institutions.[3]

In these mission schools, life was a rounded whole. Students and staff studied, prayed, ate, and relaxed together. Bond held that one of these, the Lincoln Normal and Industrial School in Marion, Alabama, was "the best predominantly Negro secondary school this country has known."[4] Teachers in mission high schools, according to Bond, were "zealous in directing their graduates onward and upward."[5]

Four common denominators among the families who produced most of the country's black scholars were (1) at least three generations of literacy; (2) enough income to finance private schooling; (3) access to excellent schools; and (4) extraordinary motivation.[6] Family influence was fundamental; the quality of the school came second.

Bond insists that black public schools in the South, from Emancipation until the 1940s, "were of a disgracefully inadequate and ineffective kind."[7] Black scholars did not emerge from such limited circumstances. In the large-city black high school, both North and South, wrote Bond, conditions were not conducive to the development of black scholarship. When formerly private schools came under government control, enrollments expanded and a changed "pitch and tempo of motivation" was evident.[8]

A rarified sample of black families produced the black scholars. According to Bond's calculations the families of black scholars made up only about one-hundredth of one percent of all black families in the United States. Using 1966 figures, he counted 5,200 scholars, physicians, dentists, and lawyers and 4,250,000 families. (While he did not give corresponding figures for whites, they must have been significantly larger.) "The gestating scholar," Bond wrote, "requires the advantages of an excellent education all along the line: elementary school, secondary school, college, and university. This advantage few Negroes had, hence, few scholars."[9]

The 609 blacks who received their academic doctorates between 1957 and 1962 attended 360 high schools. The seven high schools listed below produced the largest number of doctorates during that period:[10]

16 Dunbar, Washington, D.C.
9 Douglass, Baltimore, Maryland

9 McDonogh, New Orleans, Louisiana
8 Lincoln, Kansas City, Missouri
8 Washington, Atlanta, Georgia
7 Tuskegee Institute H.S., Tuskegee, Alabama
7 Anderson, Austin, Texas

Bond characterized these institutions as having been "the principal college preparatory high schools for Negroes, enrolling numbers of children of middle class, professional, and semi-professional occupations."[11]

In another place, Bond listed the black high schools with the highest doctorate productivity rates. Elsewhere in his book, he compared the number of doctorates produced during 1957–1962 with the number of 1952 graduates of each high school. The seven with the highest productivity rates follow:

Table 5.1
Black High Schools With Highest Doctorate Productivity Rates, 1957–1962

	Number of doctorates 1957–1962	Number of graduates	Ratio of graduates to doctorates
Wayne County Training Jesup, Georgia	3	14	4.7:1
Douglass Bristol, Virginia	2	15	7.5:1
Dunbar Okmulgee, Oklahoma	3	23	7.6:1
Langston Johnson City, Tennessee	2	18	9.0:1
J. C. Corbin Pine Bluff, Arkansas	3	28	9.3:1
Douglass Key West, Florida	2	21	10.5:1
State St. Bowling Green, Kentucky	3	32	10.6:1
Average	2.6	25.2	9.9:1

Similar ratios for the seven high schools listed earlier follow:

Table 5.2
Black High Schools Producing Most Doctorates, 1957–1962

	Doctorates	Graduates	Ratio
Dunbar	16	503	31.4:1
Douglass	9	561	62.3:1
McDonogh	9	190	21.1:1
Lincoln	8	184	23.0:1
Washington	8	351	43.8:1
Tuskegee Institute H.S.	7	95	13.5:1
Anderson	7	129	18.6:1
Average	9.1	288	30.5:1

Whenever he had information, Bond characterized each school or its setting. Bristol, Virginia, the home of Douglass High School, was "a city with a tradition of educated pastors, the production of scholars." Okmulgee, Oklahoma, he described as "a small city; Negro families generally in good financial circumstances; long line of able teachers and principals." Of Corbin High School in Arkansas, he noted that "the state college for Negroes sent its faculty children to this school." Bond points to West Indian immigrants concentrated in Key West as one possible reason for the preeminence of Douglass High School there. He describes Bowling Green, Kentucky, location of the State Street High School, as follows: "City population includes number of 'old,' stable families; long tradition of college attendance, especially at excellent colleges not far distant." Lincoln High School in Kansas City, Missouri, gave rise to this observation: "This school had a long tradition of excellence in the latter years of the 19th Century when salaries were relatively high for Negro teachers, and high school attendance for Negroes was limited to the topmost social classes." He adds: "Lincoln in Kansas City, Kansas, . . . Sumner in St. Louis, Missouri, and Kansas City, Kansas, were similar to Dunbar, in Washington, in type of faculty, program, and goals."[12]

Clearly, small, private schools attended primarily by children of better-off families had long provided the best instruction for blacks in the South. By the 1930s, this had begun to change. As private schools closed or merged into public ones, they lost their character as elite schools. By the 1950s few such schools, especially those in large cities, offered effective education.

To be sure, schools may provide a high level of education even if they never produce a single student who later earns a doctorate. But lacking empirical descriptions or even references to any such schools, we are left with the schools Bond studied. Presumably, the somewhat privileged families who enrolled their children in the best of them were quite capable of evaluating their excellence. We may take their word for it. Few poor black children, however, benefitted fully from these schools, although there were some exceptions. In discussing Philadelphia, Bond writes that "an examination system channeled some ghetto children into the city's selective high school, Central. . . ."[13]

Thus, Bond's study does not lend support to the theory that black children gained a high-quality education in segregated black schools. Undoubtedly, a very tiny minority of students did. But the fact that there were so few of them was as much a product of racism as was the exclusion of the great majority of black children from the same opportunity.

Only one historically black secondary school has been studied in detail. Besides an informal history written by a retired principal of Dunbar High School in Washington, D.C., there are two contemporary analyses: one by Jervis Anderson, biographer of A. Phillip Randolph, and the other by Thomas Sowell, an economist.

Before discussing Anderson's and Sowell's work, several shortcomings in their analyses must be noted. The most serious is the isolated manner in which they treat Dunbar. They pay no attention, for example, to other high-quality black schools that existed before or at the same time as Dunbar although, as Bond pointed out, there were a number of these in the South. Dunbar's record of production of doctorates, at least in the 1950s, was not highly distinguished. (Earlier, it had probably been.) As a consequence, both Anderson and Sowell exaggerate Dunbar's later national ranking. In Bond's view, Dunbar was not the best black high school.

In his study, Anderson quickly sets the scene:

Not long after it was founded, in 1870, it became the academy of Washington's black well-to-do. . . . It wasn't only the children of such families who attended Dunbar. . . . But if Dunbar did not exclude the children of the working class, its standards were so high that only the brightest students could meet them. And, especially after 1900, a disproportionate number of such students came from the homes of doctors, lawyers, teachers, and government officials.[14]

Sowell also asserts that "the history and traditions of the school were to a large extent shaped by members of a few prominent families in Washington's Negro community."[15]

Ernest McKinney, who graduated from Dunbar in 1905, recalled another factor—skin color—that plagued the black community:

In those days, a black-skinned girl couldn't get a job in a Negro lawyer's office. You found some of these same color distinctions at the M Street School [until 1916 this was the name of Dunbar]. It may not have prevented you from getting a good education, but you couldn't help noticing that it was a factor in the students' general behavior.[16]

Dunbar's reputation for what Anderson calls "light-skinned, middle-class snobbery" grew, especially after 1916.

Sowell and Anderson agree on Dunbar's intellectual preeminence. It had the pick of well-educated black teachers who, fresh from Harvard, Amherst, and the like, were turned away from employment in white schools and colleges. Paid relatively good salaries equal to those of white teachers, Dunbar's teachers were of a highly trained level, more so, no doubt, than white high school teachers in the area. Also, Dunbar drew its students from a very broad region, even from Maryland and Virginia. In fact, few Dunbar students lived in the very poor area surrounding the school.

Sowell identified three special features that seemed to account for Dunbar's academic success:

(1) the motivational element associated with self-selection for such a school; (2) the benefits of mutual association of high-quality students and teachers attracted to teaching such students; (3) the school tradition, including distinguished alumni who were constantly being held up as examples to the students.[17]

That success, however, seemed to peak some time before 1938; after that Dunbar was on the downgrade.[18]

It is the downgrade period that Sowell studied carefully, although he does not make this clear enough:

A study of class records for the period 1938-1955 . . . confirms that most Dunbar students' parents were not middle-class professionals. Among those students whose parents' occupations could be identified and categorized, the largest single category was consistently "unskilled and semi-skilled," and the median job index was at about the level of a white-collar worker.[19]

During the years Sowell studied the school, Dunbar enrolled about one-third of all black high school students in the District of Columbia, and professionals among Dunbar parents never represented more than 10 percent of its enrollment. The fact that high school attendance at this time was far from universal, either in Washington or the country at large, lessens the significance of this figure. In other words, Dunbar served a significant minority of a moderate-sized group.

What, then, is the meaning of Dunbar in terms of first-rate education for black youth? Anderson seems to tend toward the evaluation of psychologist Kenneth B. Clark:

Dunbar was, in effect, a "white" school in a segregated system. . . . Dunbar is the only example in our history of a separate black school that was able, somehow, to be equal. But this was possible only because of the class distinctions among blacks. . . . The Dunbar phenomenon was atypical. It reflected variables that came together at a particular time and place, and that are not likely to be duplicated. It could scarcely have existed in any other part of the country.[20]

In fact, it did exist elsewhere, as we have seen. But wherever it did so, the broad reasons were the same: social class advantages for a relative few. Bond would add: and family networks. Sowell, too, acknowledges the fundamental role of class but he stresses equally a determination by individuals to strive for academic success. (Sowell's account of his own struggles for an education throws a light on this emphasis.)[21]

Sowell also addresses the issue of Dunbar's racial composition:

> The Dunbar experiment is by no means an argument for either externally imposed segregation or self-imposed separation—and in fact the school fought against both these ideas. The founders of the school first tried to secure equal access to all public schools for all students, and only when this failed did they set about producing the best school they could for black youth.[22]

The same could have been said for many of the institutions evolving out of the black community. The historically black colleges are an excellent example.

Anderson declares that Dunbar is now one of the worst high schools in the District. The percentage of students going on to college has fallen from 80 to 30.[23] While desegregation in the District from 1955 on was more a public relations slogan than a daily reality, it did result in the geographic zoning of Dunbar, as it did for other schools. As a result, many more very poor black children, with an inadequate elementary school preparation, entered Dunbar from the vicinity of the school. In other words, Dunbar became just another large-city black high school. The former select faculty transferred or retired early. One may guess that the school found it increasingly difficult to receive adequate funding. Dunbar was never desegregated, nor is it today. Not the racial composition, but the social circumstances of the school, which had already changed noticeably by the 1940s, continued to change. Events of the next decade simply hastened the outcome.

The historical Dunbar became an incongruity in a largely black city such as Washington. As the inadequacy of education for many thousands of District children stirred sentiments and organizational forms of protest, the fact that some few black students were educated satisfactorily was of diminishing importance. The greater challenge by far was to develop that kind of educational structure for the thousands.

Can modern urban schools educate black and other poor children? Are there any examples of such schools? If so, what can we learn from them?

In 1974, a group led by Ronald P. Edmonds undertook just such an inquiry. Thus far, they have issued no overall, detailed report. Let us review the ideas behind this research before proceeding to examine any of its details.

The greatest obstacle the project has had to overcome is the orthodox belief among many educators that poor children are less capable of learning than are nonpoor children. A truly effective school, writes Edmonds, is "one in which the children of the poor are at least as well-prepared in basic school skills as the children of the middle class."[24] His thesis (expressed elsewhere in a study of twenty Detroit schools) is "that all children, excepting only those of certifiable handicap, are eminently educable, and [that] the behavior of the school is critical in determining the quality of that education."[25] An effective school, then, is one in which poor children achieve at the same minimal level expected of children of middle-class families.

Are there any such schools?

The twenty schools Edmonds and two colleagues studied in Detroit in 1974 were attended by children residing in the city's Model Cities Neighborhood. They found eight schools which scored at or above the city mean in math, nine in reading, and five in both.[26] Two of the schools enrolled students of comparable socioeconomic status (SES). One scored four months above the city mean in reading and math while the other was three months below the city mean in reading and 1.5 months below in math. Edmonds concludes that "in and of itself, pupil family background neither causes nor precludes elementary school instructional effectiveness."[27]

Edmonds and John R. Frederiksen reviewed scores from sixth-grade students in northern elementary schools. These were taken from the 1966 Coleman Report. They found fifty-five schools attended by the poor which could be classified "effective." (Those scoring above the 75th percentile were "effective" and those below the 75th were "ineffective.") Coleman had found student reading achievement to be highly correlated with teachers' verbal ability. Edmonds and Frederiksen, however, arrived at a different finding: "The verbal ability of a teacher is not related to the verbal achievement of poor black children, although it is associated with high achievement for white children and to a lesser extent for middle class black children."[28] Another of their findings was, perhaps, even less expected: "The schools in our sample that are effective in teaching poor children tend to have teachers who have been assigned to their school, while the less effective schools have teachers who have chosen to work in their school."[29]

This latter finding is surprising since it clashes with a widely held view that low-achieving schools should take special measures to attract teachers. Los Angeles, for example, has adopted a pay schedule that awards a bonus to such teachers. Edmonds and Frederiksen state their finding without interpretation. One still has to inquire if it simply expresses the known fact that more effective teachers are assigned to the more effective students while students in less effective schools have to make do with whatever teachers they can get. It has long been a conviction in poor and minority areas of large cities that schools in these areas frequently attract teachers who had failed elsewhere in the city.

Another finding of interest drawn from the Coleman data by Edmonds and Frederiksen relates to teacher attitudes about compensatory education: "Teachers in the more effective schools do not agree that 'culturally disadvantaged' children benefit from programs of compensatory education, but hold conversely that a common standard of instruction can be applied to all.''[30] This implies that teacher expectations play a role in facilitating student achievement. It rejects the extremely widespread sentiment among many teachers and administrators that less must be expected of poor and minority children.

Edmonds's study of Detroit was published in 1974; the analysis of the Coleman Report that he and Frederiksen made involved 1965 data. In 1977, Edmonds reported that he and his colleagues were gathering data on 70,000 children in Detroit and Lansing. Two years later, he wrote that five schools in Lansing had been found in which academic achievement of poor children seemed independent of pupil social class, but he provided few details.[31]

Nevertheless, the conclusions Edmonds arrived at are provocative. One feature of whatever effective schools he has found is crucial: "What effective schools share is a climate in which it is incumbent on all personnel to be instructionally effective for all pupils." Further:

One of the most tangible and indispensable characteristics of effective schools is strong administrative leadership, without which the disparate elements of good schooling can be neither brought together nor kept together. . . . The school's atmosphere is orderly without being rigid, quiet without being oppressive, and generally conducive to the instructional business at hand. Effective schools get that way partly by making it clear that pupil acquisition of basic school skills takes precedence over all other school activities.[32]

Since Edmonds has published few details of his research, it is not possible yet to ascertain on what data his conclusions rest.

Edmonds goes beyond pedagogy to policy: "Schools teach those they think they must and when they think they needn't they don't. . . . There has never been a time in the life of the American public school when we have not known all that we needed to teach all those that we chose to teach."[33] Clearly, Edmonds charges much of the inadequacy of schools attended by poor and minority students to a deliberate decision by those who control the schools not to educate these children. The failure is not due to the lack of technical knowledge by educators. Nor is it explained by any inherent shortcomings of the students or their families. Ultimately, Edmonds concludes, the problem is political. "If you genuinely seek the means to educational equity for all our people," he writes, "you must encourage parent attention to politics as the greatest instrument of instructional reform extant."[34]

Since Edmonds is studying many all-black schools, the question arises as to how his work bears on desegregation. Does he see the issue of effective schools as a contradiction to desegregation? Or, as a substitute for it? His answer is clear: "My unstinting opposition to segregation compels me to continue to support court-ordered desegregation."[35] Yet, he adds, one must seek educational improvement even under conditions of segregation, whatever the ultimate prospect for desegregation.

Thus far, it is difficult to appraise the body of Edmonds's work. While its theoretical approach and political framework are clear, the precise factual underpinnings of both remain unclear. Also, the import of the research for the issue of black schools is somewhat doubtful since the inquiry seems more concerned with class than race. (This is not to say the two can be easily distinguished.)

Van M. Christopher studied the organizational climate of what he describes as an "inner-city school" in Los Angeles for ten months during 1973–1974. One of his findings coincides with that of Edmonds and Frederiksen. "Rather than cajoling or forcing teachers to work in ghetto schools," he writes, "we should screen candidates who volunteer."[36] During the course of his observations, Christopher found that some teachers were alienated from the community. A number of the students seemed to "elicit from many teachers scorn, resentment, antagonism, and worst of all, fear."[37] Interestingly, it was shortly after Christopher completed his work that the Los Angeles schools began to pay a bonus to certain teachers as described above. Nevertheless, his research adds a bit of positive documentation to Edmonds's work.

During the past several years, some writers have pointed to specific black schools as effective. Mary Rhodes Hoover, for example, listed fifteen such schools.[38] These follow, with an indication, noted by Hoover, of who nominated each as effective. She defines as "effective" schools in which students read at grade level or above.

Private schools:	Nominated by:
Nairobi Day School, E. Palo Alto, California	*N.Y. Times, Ebony*
Freedom Library Day School, Philadelphia, Pennsylvania	O. Lindenmeyer, *Black History: Lost Stolen or Strayed* (1970)
Holy Angels Catholic School, Chicago, Illinois	*Wall Street Journal*
University of Islam-Temple No. 4, Washington, D.C.	*Newsweek*

Public schools:	
Woodland School, Kansas City, Missouri	Weber; Thomas paper
Hill School, Philadelphia, Pennsylvania	No entry
P.S. 234, Bronx, New York City	*Newsweek*
New York School A, New York City	N.Y. State Dept. of Ed.

Howard D. Woodson, Washington, D.C.	*Newsweek*
Windsor Hills, Los Angeles, California	*Newsweek*
Grant Elementary, Chicago, Illinois	*Time*
Roth Elementary, Cleveland, Ohio	*Newsweek*
Martin Luther King, New Haven, Connecticut	*Time*
Longstreth School, Philadelphia, Pennsylvania	No entry
Henry School, Philadelphia, Pennsylvania	No entry

Since specific issue and page references are not given for most of the nominators, it is not possible to examine the precise basis for the nominations. We can make several observations, however. For one thing, private schools are selective and are not obliged to accept all applicants. Thus, their enrollment is far from typical. One, at least, of the public schools—Windsor Hills—is a middle-class school and has no relevance to the issue of educating poor students.[39] In addition, some of the others may have entrance requirements which filter out low-scoring students. This is far from unusual in a number of high-scoring minority schools. Finally, we do not know the period during which the schools' test scores were high. Frequently, scores fluctuate from one year to another. All in all, much more evidence is needed before the schools listed by Hoover can be accepted as schools which offer a high level of instruction to poor black students.

Articles have begun to appear in popular magazines discussing black schools which provide quality education. Mark Frazier names four schools, only one of which is a public institution. This is P.S. 91 in Brooklyn, described as having "experienced a shift in student composition from majority white to overwhelmingly black and Hispanic over the past 15 years."[40] He notes that during these years test scores rose above national norms. He presents no additional data other than a statement that the scores rose "because of steps taken by the school's dedicated administrators and teachers."[41]

During the same month, *Ebony* magazine reported on the High School for Engineering Professions (HSEP), part of the Booker T. Washington High School in Houston. HSEP enrolls 325 students, or nearly a quarter of the high school's total student body, and is financed by large corporations. In 1975, when it began, 87 percent of its students were black. The account refers to "the battery of tests required for admittance into the program."[42] Thus, enrollees are a highly selected group.

To repeat, no genetic evidence has ever been produced to show that black children are intellectually incapable of mastering school learning tasks. Yet, some educators continue to treat the subject as though it were still an open question. Franklyn D. Wesley, principal of Houston's Booker T. Washington High School, has said of the High School for Engineering Professions: "All across the country there is the myth that Black schools have inferior education. Black youngsters can learn and Black schools *can* learn and Black schools *can* provide quality education."[43]

Historical and other evidence demonstrates that both parts of Wesley's statement are correct, and that truth has been established repeatedly. The question today is whether poor children in any nonselective all-black public schools are receiving a first-rate education. Up until now, there have been few examples. Under the intense religious-communal conditions Bond describes, the southern mission schools, to a limited degree, achieved such a goal. Since then, nearly all examples have been the product of fortuitous combinations of gifted leadership, inspired teaching, extraordinary motivation, social class advantage, and/or selection processes. But evidence of systematic provision of equal education to children of poor families is missing.

Although Edmonds's approach has yet to yield substantial results, it seems promising; but the method by which he defines instructional effectiveness casts doubt on the project. In the Detroit study, less than one grade level separated effective from ineffective schools on the reading criterion. The greater number of poor black children in urban schools, however, probably attend schools in which the grade-level lag is nearer to two years; many exceed that. School mean reading scores in New York, Chicago, and Los Angeles yield numerous examples of this type of lag. Thus a question can be raised as to how representative Edmonds's Detroit sample actually is. Recently, it was announced that he is heading the School Improvement Program in New York City, embracing twenty-four inner city schools, to test his approach further.[44] Results of his work there may be significant.

Notes

1. Ronald D. Henderson, "Input to Education Decision-Makers: A Missing Perspective," *Journal of Negro Education*, 48 (1979), pp. 214–15.

2. June O. Patton, "The Black Community of Augusta and the Struggle for Ware High School 1880–1899," in Vincent P. Franklin and James D. Anderson (eds.), *New Perspective in Black Educational History* (Boston: Hall, 1978). Reference is to *Cumming* v. *County Board of Education*, 175 U.S. 545 (1899).

3. Horace Mann Bond, *Black American Scholars: A Study of Their Beginnings* (Detroit: Balamp Publishing, 1972), pp. 23–24.

4. Ibid., p. 42.

5. Ibid., p. 65.

6. Ibid., pp. 56–57.

7. Ibid., p. 29.

8. Ibid., p. 65.

9. Ibid., p. 30.

10. Ibid., p. 25.

11. Ibid.

12. Ibid.

13. Ibid., p. 114.

14. Jervis Anderson, "A Very Special Monument," *New Yorker*, March 28, 1978, p. 96.

15. Thomas Sowell, "Black Excellence—The Case of Dunbar High School," *Public Interest* (Spring 1974), p. 12.

16. Quoted in Anderson, p. 104. See also letter from the *Washington Post* quoted on this point, ibid.

17. Sowell, p. 9.

18. Ibid.

19. Ibid., p. 11.

20. Quoted in Anderson, p. 108.

21. Thomas Sowell, *Black Education: Myths and Tragedies* (N.Y.: McKay, 1972), pp. 26–27.

22. Sowell, "Black Excellence," p. 16.

23. Anderson, p. 108.

24. Ronald R. Edmonds, "Some Schools Work and More Can," *Social Policy*, (March–April 1979), p. 28.

25. Ronald R. Edmonds and others, *Search for Effective Schools: The Identification and Analysis of City Schools that are Instructionally Effective for Poor Children*, 1977, p. 4. (ERIC ED 142 610.)

26. Ibid., p. 5.

27. Ibid.

28. Ronald R. Edmonds and John R. Frederiksen, *Search for Effective Schools: The Identification and Analysis of City Schools that are Instructionally Effective for Poor Children*, 1979, p. 39. (ERIC ED 170 396.)

29. Ibid., p. 40.

30. Ibid.

31. Ron Edmonds, *A Discussion of the Literature and Issues Related to Effective Schooling*, 1979, p. 34. (ERIC ED 170 394.)

32. Edmonds, "Some Schools Work and More Can," p. 32.

33. Ibid.

34. Edmonds, *A Discussion of the Literature and Issues Related to Effective Schooling*, p. 37.

35. Edmonds and others, *Search for Effective Schools*, p. 1. (ERIC ED 142 610.)

36. Van M. Christopher, *The Organizational Climate of an Inner-City Secondary School* (doctoral diss., Claremont Graduate School, 1975), p. 59.

37. Ibid., p. 60.

38. Mary Rhodes Hoover, "Characteristics of Black Schools at Grade Level: A Description," *Reading Teacher* (April 1978), p. 760.

39. In the original listing by Hoover, Windsor Hills is placed erroneously in Chicago. For an account of this school, see Olive Walker, "The Windsor Hills Story," *Integrated Education*, 8 (May–June 1970), pp. 4–9.

40. Mark Frazier, "Inner-City Schools That Work," *Reader's Digest*, 116 (June 1980), p. 25.

41. Ibid., p. 26.

42. "Tomorrow's School Today," *Ebony*, 35 (June 1980), p. 80.

43. Ibid., p. 78.

44. Dena Kleiman, "City Aiming to Upgrade Schools—Not the System," *New York Times*, June 28, 1980.

6

Intradistrict Inequalities

How well a child is educated depends, in part, on the educational resources the child commands.[1] These include teachers, supplies, books, equipment, buildings—in fact, anything useful in the instruction of students. While some resources are "free" to the student (such as his family's encouragement) most others "cost" the community or that part of it which pays taxes.

How equitably are those resources distributed among the children who need them? To answer this question we must examine actual patterns of resource use, but such research is rare. The vast majority of research studies in educational finance are several removes from classroom realities. As long as this is true, the subject of resources will continue to be unexplored.

The 40 million or so public school students in the United States are supported by a total of some $80 billion in current expenditures. This stream of resources is fed by several tributaries. The federal government contributes about 8 percent, state governments about 44 percent, and localities 48 percent. Except for a few specific programs, federal authorities do not even attempt to determine whether most school children are equitably served. State governments have certain statutory obligations to check on local compliance with legal requirements, but much of this supervision is perfunctory. Inside the individual school districts almost nothing is known of how equitably resources are distributed among schools.

For the past decade or so, to many observers or scholars, the topic of educational finance has come to mean reform of the property tax system. Proponents of this reform claimed its goal was a more just distribution of resources among school districts. Since they express no interest in equality of resources among schools, they continue to change the taxing system rather than the resources of individual schools or classrooms.

Unless tax reformers concern themselves with the individual school, they lack any means of discerning the educational impact of tax reforms. As a result, it will be merely tax rates that are reformed. A more uniform system of tax rates among school districts in a state is laudable, but it has no necessary effect on educational equity. If, for example, a school district receives additional money as a result of tax reform, there is no guarantee the funds will be any more equitably distributed within the district. This is true for every known interdistrict tax reform approach.

Children, after all, attend single schools, not districts. If a change in district financing occurs, it may or may not affect educational expenditures at the local level. It could more adequately fund a basically unjust system of allocating resources among schools in a district. Or, it may simply maintain the system's injustices at a higher dollar level. Or, it could provide an extra fund for compensatory education of the poorest children in the system. What is dismaying in the educational finance literature is the failure of virtually all researchers to consider the interrelation of interdistrict and intradistrict finances.

Children attend single schools. Researchers on educational finance, however, prefer to study whole school districts or entire states. Is this sound? Essentially, to ignore individual schools is to assume that no significant differences exist among schools in a single school district. In a homogeneous community, this is conceivably true. But no urban community is homogeneous. Differences of income, wealth, power, status, and race overwhelmingly characterize American cities. The schools are not immune to these forces. A walk through any city shows as much. Aside from a common architectural model, the schools embody very different educational realities.

Despite a surfeit of discussion of equality in the educational literature, few researchers have actually studied the subject at the local level, where schooling inequality is plainest. And in the field of educational finance, scholars have been so absorbed at the district level that they have all but ignored the local level. Reform of school financing has now been equated with educational equality. Through action of state courts and legislatures, fiscal equity is to be transformed into classroom equality. Yet, no evidence is available to test this expectation. Do children attending schools in districts and states where there has been fiscal reform experience greater educational equality as a result of the changes? An early study by Rand of reform experience in five states found that "the reform movement's victories have proved somewhat hollow."[2] Instead of greater fiscal equity among districts, the study reported, "reform has favored districts serving higher-income populations relative to districts serving lower-income populations."[3] Rand, however, did not investigate the classroom consequences of fiscal reform. Very likely there were none. Originally, fiscal reform was declared to be a way of delivering greater resources to children who were especially disadvantaged. Neither Rand nor the field in general has inquired about this outcome.

Exclusive concerns with district and state dimensions mirror managerial concerns more than anything else. Central school administrators search for ways to increase the flow of funds into their districts. At the same time, details of the distribution of funds in individual schools within the district are guarded and unavailable to the public or researchers. Consequently, certain subjects are unavailable and even ignored for purposes of research. The researchers, then, adjust research perspectives to actual opportunities to gather data. When large enrollments of poor and minority children are involved, public records of actual expenditures on a school-by-school basis are especially rare.

In extensive discussions with many active minority citizens over the years, the stress is on the inadequate resources at schools attended by their children; they cite endless examples. In one city after another, many reliable observers of local school scenes report the same experience. Less frequently, however, do they offer examples of inequality. In large part, this is a result of segregation. Relatively few minority persons have attended non-segregated schools, which, of course, also represent a wide range of class-related resources. Since passage of the Civil Rights Act of 1964, school authorities have become increasingly concerned about the legal liability of school districts for these school-by-school inequalities. Undoubtedly, this factor was extremely important in the almost unprecedented refusal in 1965 of Chicago and other large cities to participate in the congressionally mandated Equal Educational Opportunities Survey (the Coleman Report). Even though individual districts were not identified in the study, federal authorities permitted this defiance to stand.

Deliberate shortchanging of black children was a nationwide pattern before and after the Civil War. Blacks more or less paid for their own schooling. Where the political structure permitted, state appropriations for black children were systematically raided for the benefit of white schools in the same district. In northern cities such as Newark, when blacks made up only a tiny part of the city's enrollment, segregation was enforced even if it temporarily required larger per-pupil expenditures. In Chicago, between 1910 and 1940, the gap between expenditures for black and white schools grew as the numbers of blacks in the city increased. This pattern persisted into the 1960s.[4] Before 1954, in legally segregated systems such as Washington, D.C., intradistrict inequalities were frequently fostered.[5]

Nearly all the above-mentioned instances principally concerned racial discrimination. It was not until 1961 that the first full-scale study was made of intradistrict inequalities which were not basically racial in nature. This was Sexton's analysis of Detroit, a city whose population a year earlier was 28.9 percent black. She found a systematic bias in the distribution of school resources and expenditures to schools attended by low-income children, white and black. She summarized:

A typical upper-income child . . . goes to a school that is safer, more suitable and adequate for his needs, more attractive inside and out, with much better facilities in most subjects, including science, music, art, and library, and also with better lighting, lavatory, and other health facilities than the school attended by the average lower-income child.[6]

The schools for poor children also had significantly greater numbers of less-trained and inexperienced teachers.

Kenneth B. Clark hailed Sexton's findings as erasing "any reasonable doubt that our public school system has rejected its role of facilitating social mobility and has become in fact an instrument of social and economic class distinctions in American society."[7] Other educational researchers ignored the Sexton book. Jesse Burkhead and associates, in a book published three years after Sexton's, did not even discuss her evidence or conclusions. Instead, they were impressed by variability among schools in similar neighborhoods rather than by the variability of poor and rich schools:

There are very often sharp differences in the quality of education in communities that seem to have the same general socioeconomic characteristics. . . . Striking differences will be found among schools in the slum areas of large cities and among neighborhoods that seem to be similar.[8]

The authors ignored class-based differences.

In 1969, eight years after publication of the Sexton book, a book on school financing, *The Economics and Financing of Education*, by Johns and Morphet, was published. In it they referred more than once to equality of educational opportunity but they treated inequalities operating to the detriment of poor children as not especially objectionable: "The educational opportunities available may be reasonably adequate or quite inadequate, but inequities usually have not been particularly obvious, except in the poverty or ghetto areas."[9] They offered no references at this point, but discussed the subject again on the same page:

However, there are variations in most school systems. . . . Some children may have to attend in antiquated buildings or in schools to which frequently the less competent principals, teachers, and noncertified personnel have been assigned. In many systems, most of these are schools in underprivileged areas.[10]

They gave no indication as to the absolute or relative frequency of such variations, nor did they discuss remedies for intradistrict inequalities in the remainder of the chapter in which remedies for interdistrict inequalities were described.

In other quarters, Sexton's research was welcomed, although only as subsidiary to some other concern. In 1968, for example, Wise's *Rich Schools, Poor Schools* was published. This pioneer work tried to formulate a constitutional theory whereby interdistrict inequalities might be held in violation of the Fourteenth Amendment. He noted: "The present study is not concerned with the problem of variation in expenditures among schools within a single district. That problem has received the attention of others."[11] Only Sexton was cited in a footnote at this point.

Thus, during the eight years following publication of Sexton's work, specialists in the field of educational finance had paid it little heed. The historical literature of educational finance is almost devoid of references to the fiscal realities of intradistrict educational inequality.

A sobering implication of this traditional inattention to or slurring of intradistrict inequalities is that virtually all present-day school administrators, government policymakers, and researchers were nurtured at the same fount of formal ignorance. Only the rarest exception could be found until the 1970s.

Did the situation change any during the past decade?

The literature reflects a somewhat heightened awareness of the problem. Michelson writes that "large inequalities occur within as well as between districts, and . . . these inequalities are derived from the political process which favors wealth and whiteness."[12] This observation is weakened by an earlier comment of Michelson's: "As long as 'ruling class' children do not attend local schools, the system need not favor those middle-class children who do."[13] (What, however, if the middle class is itself one of the social groupings on whose rule the polity rests?) Michelson cited the unequal distribution of per-pupil teacher costs in Detroit during 1970:[14]

Schools	Percentage of Black Students		
	0–10	10–90	90–100
K-6	$432	$374	$380
With K–7, K–8, or grades 6–9	$415	$391	$368

Children in the K–6 schools that were almost all-black received 13.7 percent less than children in the nearly all-white schools; children in the other schools lagged by 12.8 percent.

In 1971, *Schools and Inequality*, by Guthrie, Kleindorfer, Levin, and Stout, was published.[15] It is the best example of school finance research embracing the three levels of the flow of resources: interdistrict, school-by-school, and within classrooms. On all three levels the researchers found resource inequalities related to race and socioeconomic status: "Individual schools that enroll large numbers of poor children tend to provide fewer and lower-quality services than schools that enroll small numbers of poor children."[16] Within single schools, "inequities among individual students exist to the effect that poor children are provided with lower-quality services than wealthy children, almost regardless of the school districts in which they live, or the schools that they attend."[17] They found entire school districts that reflected socioeconomic status and thus differential educational opportunity. The Guthrie group's study concerns Michigan, but it surveyed the entire literature of the subject with great care. Unfortunately, their work did not influence much further research in the field, which still suffers from a narrowness of conception, especially with regard to the levels of resources.

In comparing intradistrict with interdistrict inequalities, Grubb and

Michelson formulated an important distinction: "Whereas inter-district and inter-state inequities arise from reliance on local financing and the market forces which tend to create homogeneous communities, inter-school inequities within districts must be due to deliberate policies of resource allocation."[18] Further on they conclude: "It is clear . . . that considerable intra-district differentials exist, and that some (though not all) of them are discriminatory, the results of political processes which favor wealth and whiteness."[19] Since single schools are not financed by separate taxes, financial diffferences between them cannot be accounted for by forces similar to those that operate between entire districts.

Henry M. Levin, who has the same general orientation as Michelson and Grubb, has discussed the issue more systematically:

> Those city schools with heavy concentrations of lower-class and non-white enrollments appear to have been discriminated against for years in the allocation of resources. School systems can get away with this kind of discrimination because the conventional school accounting systems do not report expenditures on a school-by-school basis. Furthermore, few school superintendents and other high officials will admit that such disparities exist since to do so would be politically dangerous. . . .[20]

The acerbity of his criticism is matched by the specificity of his analysis. Few other writers have gotten down to such critical details as an accounting system.

Levin makes an important contribution to the discussion by questioning a principal technique used by just about every investigator of intradistrict inequalities:

> Comparing dollar inputs between schools attended by minority students and those attended by middle-class whites is an erroneous way of measuring school resource endowments between races. To the degree that money is spent in both cases on teachers, curriculum, and other inputs that are more effective for white children than for black or Spanish-speaking students, dollar expenditures tend to overstate vastly the relative resources available to the latter group. Rather, the nominal resources devoted to the two groups of schools must be weighted by their effectiveness to ascertain their true values.[21]

The statement's cogency lies in its insistence that educational effectiveness rather than the magnitude of expenditures must be the criterion for evaluating intradistrict inequalities. Essentially, Levin is pointing out that one hundred dollars worth of ineffective education is not equal to a similar expenditure on effective education. By treating them as equal, the educational productivity of the money is greatly exaggerated. Or more to the point, the magnitude of the educational inequality is greatly understated.

To ensure equity for inner-city schools, concludes Levin, the reporting of school-by-school budgetary requirements and expenditures must be mandatory. In addition, he calls for linking reward structures to educational effectiveness either through market alternatives such as vouchers or through political incentives such as decentralized schools.

A small group of researchers has investigated actual cases of intradistrict inequalities.

Ralph Andrew and Robert J. Goettel studied 120 elementary, junior high, and senior high schools in Rochester, Syracuse, and Community District No. 2 in New York City. They began with an observation that deserves to be a postulate in the field: "The extent and impact of educational services can only be determined by understanding patterns of resource distribution to administrative units below that of the school district."[22] The researchers sought to discover whether funds flowed to those schools with the greatest educational needs and distinguished between state and local funds, on the one hand, and federal funds—usually compensatory—on the other.

Andrew and Goettel found that "total resources from all sources of funding, both dollars and staff, are generally distributed according to educational need, but the pattern in the three cities is uneven."[23] They also found that "in all three cities schools with the smallest proportion of disadvantaged pupils consistently receive more dollars per pupil from local tax levy and general state funds than do those with higher proportions."[24] With reference to the number of staff per 1,000 students, however, there is a reversal of this pattern. A third finding was that "teachers in schools that have high levels of reading disadvantagement are consistently younger and less experienced and few[er] have attained tenure than teachers in schools with higher levels of student achievement."[25] The researchers stressed, as did Levin a year before, the need for school-by-school budgeting and accounting. They noted that "without direction from the state . . . few school districts will take the initiative. . . ."[26]

John D. Owen contributed two pieces of research to the discussion. In an article published in 1972, he reported his findings in a study of nine cities. "There is a significant tendency," he wrote, "for higher quality educational resources to be assigned to middle-class white neighborhoods."[27] Between race and class, which was more important in triggering a maldistribution of resources? Owen replies that "the influence of racial composition of the school appears to be somewhat greater than that of neighborhood income."[28] Finally, he found that the school districts, all of which distributed teacher resources unequally, did the same with physical resources. This practice was the same as that revealed by Sexton in Detroit.

In his book, published two years later, Owen explored the subject in greater detail and drew certain conclusions about more general issues. For example, a 1 percent increase in neighborhood income was found to be associated with a 0.1 percent increase in the verbal ability of teachers and a 0.43 percent increase in salary expenditures.[29] Owen's treatment of the general issue is of particular interest.

He writes that "the large center-city school system provides a good example of the way in which bureaucratic structures are used to undermine a manifest commitment to equality.''[30] Interpreting school board teacher assignment policies that led to an unequal distribution of teacher resources, Owen comments that ''the extent to which the school systems systematically assign their white teachers to their white students is a useful index of the degree to which they are actually bowing to the preferences of white parents for white teachers and of white teachers for white students.''[31] He relates inequality of resources not only to the middle-class bias of school systems but also to ''the well-established, 'normal' customs and traditions that underlie discrimination in the allocation of resources in large city school systems.''[32] In the context of expanding equality during the past years, Owen insists that ''the very considerable gains in equalizing educational opportunities for the black minority appear especially dependent on federal intervention to check the racist, or at least inegalitarian, tendencies of the state and local system.''[33]

It is rather startling to encounter in Owen's book a topic which had been discussed eighty-two years earlier—namely to what extent did blacks pay for their own public schooling? Referring to an average expenditure of $900 per child in 1969, Owen writes:

Since the primary basis for educational expenditures is regressive local taxes . . . blacks pay a significant proportion of this cost despite their low income. Hence the gap between actual state expenditures on a black child and black school taxes paid per black child is probably much less than $900.[34]

Perhaps more striking than this or that dollar figure is the apparent need to repeat the earlier contention so many years later.

Anita A. Summers and Barbara L. Wolfe studied intradistrict inequalities within Philadelphia. In elementary and junior high schools enrolling more blacks and poor students, teachers were less well qualified in terms of the quality of their undergraduate education as well as in other measures, and principals were less experienced. Schools at all levels which enrolled many low-income students had the highest number of teacher vacancies.[35] Interestingly, they found that ''in elementary schools, low-achieving students did best with relatively new teachers.''[36] The researchers did not indicate whether such students were more likely to be found in poor or more well-to-do schools. Summers and Wolfe were less interested in resource differences as such than in the educational effectiveness of the resources.

Frank Levy and his colleagues studied the distribution of resources among the sixty-three elementary schools of Oakland, California. As expected, they found that in the years before 1970–1971 ''the well-paid teachers [were] concentrated in the upper-income, white schools.''[37] During 1970, a new superintendent, black educator Marcus Foster, was employed. He set out to rectify the imbalance in per-pupil teacher expenditures. Local and state funds were reallocated in favor of black schools, as follows:

District Personnel Salary Dollars Per Student

Year	White Schools	Black Schools
1969–1970	370	350
1970–1971	416	466

Actually, teaching positions were equalized with local funds and outside, compensatory funds were used to give the black schools an unaccustomed edge. (The Foster experiment ended tragically when he was murdered by the Symbionese Liberation Army.)

Betsy Levin and colleagues examined intradistrict inequalities in two districts in California and five in Michigan. They summarized their findings:

District discretionary funds are usually concentrated in the schools of higher income and low minority populations, while state and federal compensatory funds are directed to low income high minority schools. District discretionary funds and compensatory monies, in some cases, were found to complement each other; that is, total expenditures for the lowest income, high minority schools and the highest income, white schools are almost equal. . . . Even though rich and poor schools may receive equal dollars, these funds buy different types of teachers in terms of education and experience levels.[38]

The findings varied, of course, from district to district.

On the whole, funds designated as compensatory were not used for this purpose. If they had been, every disadvantaged school would have had greater per-pupil expenditures than nondisadvantaged schools. Compensatory funds theoretically are designed as an "add-on" to per-pupil expenditures from regular funds that are presumably equal in all schools. "In nearly all of the districts studied," the Levin group reported, "compensatory funds are used to supplant district discretionary expenditures."[39] In other words, compensatory funds designated for schools attended by poor children are converted into a substitute for regular funds, while a portion of regular funds becomes an add-on for the benefit of schools attended by affluent students.

In 1972, the official Fleischmann Commission issued a report on the quality, cost, and financing of elementary and secondary schools in New York State. While it found sizable inequalities between school districts, it rejected any claims of extreme inequality within the cities. With respect to New York City, for example, it stated: "There is no evidence of gross inequities such as occur between two districts of unequal wealth. . . . The facts of *Hobson* v. *Hansen* do not hold true for New York City."[40] On the other hand, the Commission acknowledged, "There is a noticeable difference between the kinds of services purchased for students from minority-ethnic or low-income backgrounds and those purchased for more middle-class white students."[41] Evidently, the commission did not consider it a gross intradistrict inequity that similar amounts of money purchased unequal amounts of resources.

In 1973, Paul Ritterband, in a study of primary schools in New York City, found a high concentration of inexperienced teachers in nonwhite schools.[42] He asserted that the school district's policy of reducing class size in some such schools did not compensate for the lack of experience. (What appeared to Ritterband as an inequity was permissible under 1970 standards of comparability under Title I.) Two of Ritterband's specific findings are of interest: (1) "together mean teacher salary and pupil teacher ratio account for 52 percent of variation in per pupil expenditures," and (2) "the cost increment per percentage point increase of black children is four times that for Puerto Rican children. The pupil-teacher ratio is lower for blacks than it is for Puerto Ricans while the mean teacher salary is lower for Puerto Ricans than it is for blacks."[43] Clearly, the comparative disadvantage of Puerto Rican children in the city's primary schools is enormous, but even those used as the standard of comparison, black children, are themselves at a disadvantage.

In 1977, the Office for Civil Rights (OCR) of the U.S. Department of Health, Education, and Welfare completed its New York City study, the most detailed and largest-scale investigation of intradistrict inequalities in a single city yet made in the United States.[44] The study began in June, 1973, and was for all practical purposes finished early in 1977.

The director of the study summarized its findings:

> Minorities are receiving lower amounts of local resources for basic education, in poorer quality facilities which have a more limited range of curricula. . . . Minorities are . . . given unequal educational services. . . . Minority and female students in junior high/intermediate and high schools are channelled to less desirable and more restrictive academic, vocational and special programs and are provided with less effective counseling services.[45]

At this point we will use illustrative examples from the OCR study to document some of the findings.

The condition of facilities and equipment in the city schools during 1975–1976 varied directly with the percentage of minority students enrolled. Here are figures showing the percentage of facilities and equipment rated "excellent" in schools with different proportions of minority students:

Facility/Equipment	Percentage Minority:	
	1–10%	*91–100%*
Heating	33	21
Audio-visual equipment	39	16
Textbooks	45	17

Lighting	53	28
Regular classrooms	45	19
Classroom furniture	24	9
Library books	49	28
Science laboratories	13	6

Source: OCR Study, Appendix C

The ratio of guidance counselors varied the same way. The counselor-student ratio in nonminority schools was 1:741, while it was 1:1,050 in minority schools.[46]

Attrition rates in city high schools, as measured by passage from the tenth to the eleventh grade, varied as follows:

Students	**Percentage**
Total students	21.4
Black students	25.7
Spanish-surnamed students	34.2
Other (i.e., white) students	9.1

Source: OCR Study, Appendix N

Asian and white students attended special admissions academic high schools in disproportionately large numbers; black and Hispanic students attended at low rates.[47] Disciplinary practices were discriminatory against minority students. In October, 1977, OCR communicated a new set of charges to the New York City school district. These included several that dealt with intra-district inequalities. For one thing, language-handicapped students were being deprived of an opportunity "to obtain the education generally obtained by other students in the system." Nearly 11,000 Hispanic elementary students with severe English-speaking difficulties—as well as approximately 17,000 more with less severe difficulties—were in schools lacking "Spanish-fluent staff providing guidance services."[48] There was a similar lack of Spanish-speaking personnel in disciplinary or guidance activities. In District 3, three schools enrolled 3,786 students whose first language was Spanish but there were no discipline or guidance personnel who spoke Spanish.[49] In one district with ten bilingual psychologists and 54,139 Spanish-dominant speakers, the ratio was 5,414:1. This far exceeded the number of English-speaking children guided or counseled by each English-speaking counselor.

According to OCR's January, 1977, charges, "as the percentage of minority students attending a school increases, so does the prospect of poor lighting, unsanitary conditions and infestation by vermin."[50] High schools received 15 percent more money per pupil when they enrolled substantial numbers of nonminority students than when they enrolled most minority students.[51] OCR also found that "the size of reading and math instructional groups increases as the percentage of minority student enrollment increases."[52]

OCR studied per-pupil expenditures on a classroom basis as well as on the more customary school basis. Teachers in minority schools were less experienced, lower paid, and had fewer advanced degrees. The same pattern prevailed even within single schools. In other words, "individual classes which have higher percentages of minority students are often taught by teachers with less experience and lower educational qualifications than classes which have higher percentages of nonminority students."[53] This finding is based on data from schools in six community districts.

OCR charged that the school district was violating Title I rules. Federal funds were being diverted in two ways, according to the agency:

(1) The funds are used for the provision of regular instruction programs, rather than supplementary programs, and (2) while the funds are used to provide instructional services in predominantly minority schools, these same instructional services are provided in predominantly nonminority schools from local tax revenues and are, therefore, not supplementary.[54]

OCR added that "in the predominantly minority academic high schools the school system clearly appears to substitute dollars for local tax revenues in providing instruction."[55]

OCR made many other findings that are related indirectly to intradistrict inequalities. Minority students were overrepresented in mental disability classes and were three times as likely to be disciplined as were nonminority students. In over 200 elementary schools, 430 classrooms were segregated. In nearly 150 elementary schools, ability grouping resulted in racially identifiable instructional settings. Language-assessment techniques were inadequate. Meetings with parents were three times more likely to be called by guidance counselors in nonminority schools as in minority schools. While nearly half the counselors in nonminority schools sent special material to parents, none in minority schools did. Nonminority students received far better preparation for entrance exams to special admission high schools. Many instances of sex discrimination were found in the schools.

Clearly, the Fleischmann Report had erred in 1972 when it denied *Hobson*-type intradistrict inequalities were present in New York City. The OCR data, developed independently from basic records supplied by school authorities, document not only *Hobson*-type conditions but resemble some of the disparities found in the District of Columbia by the Strayer inquiry of 1949, five years before *Brown*.

OCR had communicated its findings to the city district two days before President Carter took office in January, 1977. In October, 1977, OCR notified the school board that the January letter had been "withdrawn for further consideration."[56] At the same time, OCR reserved the right to raise in the future the issues discussed in January, 1977, and it did not repudiate the statistics of January, 1977.

The OCR study established the existence of a general pattern of intradistrict inequality within New York City. Curiously, the city's financial stringency led to an easing of inequality in per-pupil expenditures for teachers. Teachers laid off tended to be those with the least seniority and experience, and there was a redistribution of the remaining teachers who had greater seniority. In this way, economic equality gained while economic sufficiency lost ground. In Washington, D.C., however, equalization due to the *Hobson* decrees had been accomplished without such a penalty.

Baron, in his study of school spending in Chicago during 1961–1966, found that by the end of the period city schools were using Title I funds to supplant local and state funds.[57] Schools attended principally by educationally disadvantaged children were thereby deprived of compensatory education since the target schools did not receive the "extra" funds.

In 1973, after years of pressure, the Illinois state legislature passed a program for state-financed compensatory education. A new "resource equalization formula" contained a weighting factor dependent on the number of disadvantaged children in the district. The law required each recipient district to submit a plan to the state indicating how the funds were to be used "for the improvement of instruction."

Three years later, Sharon Gelder, an alert education editor for the *Chicago Reporter*, found to her surprise that (1) the state had failed to formulate guidelines for the law, as was required by the legislation; (2) Chicago had not submitted a plan; and (3) the Chicago school board placed the "compensatory" funds in general financial accounts to be spent in all schools, disadvantaged and advantaged alike.[58] Since the historic pattern in Chicago has been to allocate higher per-pupil expenditures to schools attended by middle-class students, the school board used the new funds to further widen the gap between disadvantaged and advantaged schools.[59] Some three months later, the state education department released interim guidelines. In mid-December, 1976, a lawsuit was filed by Operation PUSH against the school board requesting that special state funds be spent only on disadvantaged students.[60]

Superintendent Joseph Hannon acknowledged the use of special funds for advantaged students and cautioned against a too-abrupt change in this policy. In a projection published a day after the above-mentioned lawsuit was filed, Hannon said that sudden withdrawal of special funds from one predominantly white and largely middle-class district would result in an average class size of 80.4 in that district. Late in January, 1977, in the face of rising criticism, the board met in executive session and decided to allocate all funds earmarked for disadvantaged students to such students within three years. But at no time thereafter, in an open meeting, did the board acknowledge having made such a decision.

During Spring, 1977, the Chicago Urban League published an analysis of the misuse of state compensatory funds. Superintendent Hannon was accused of exploiting rather than violating the law. The League pointed out that nearly $225 million in compensatory funds were available to the district, as follows:

Title I	$ 51,000,000
State funds for the disadvantaged	173,000,000
Total	$224,000,000

From state funds alone, $815 "extra" was theoretically available for each pupil classified as disadvantaged. About three out of every ten students were so classified, yet they were not receiving their allotments.

The League compared alternative remedies, especially reassigning teachers and lowering class size, and found the latter preferable. Of reassigning teachers, the League noted: "That method of redistribution would be intolerable, not only for its effects upon losing schools, but also for the reason that by itself it is non-programmatic and nothing more than a way of carrying money from one place to another."[61] The League contended that after lowering class size in schools enrolling large numbers of disadvantaged pupils, no class in any school would be larger than thirty-six pupils. The school board continued to resist a resolution of the matter.

In March, 1977, the Illinois Board of Education issued its final version of regulations governing the use of special state funds for the disadvantaged. While the rules clearly directed that disadvantaged children benefit from the funds, nondisadvantaged children were not flatly excluded from its benefits. Black legislators tried in vain to extract a legislative declaration directing that all the special funds be utilized for poor children only. During July and August, lawyers representing plaintiffs in the PUSH lawsuit against the Chicago school board could not convince the board to discuss its off-the-record decision of January with them.

Black legislators renewed their campaign in the state legislature when they introduced H. B. 2619 in February, 1978. The compromise measure required that only 55 percent of the special funds be spent on disadvantaged children. The school board would be given until September, 1982, to implement the law fully. In June, the bill passed and was signed into law. Some critics objected that much of the basic inequity remained, but an Urban League spokesperson commented: "A proportion of the other 45 percent was going to overall administrative overhead or for existing programs for the disadvantaged . . . so it is not as if the funds were lost to poor and black schools."[62]

Viewed in the context of traditional Chicago politics, passage of H. B. 2619 ranked as a constructive compromise. Yet, it also embodied a standard of apportionment that cast serious doubt on the concept of compensatory education. Under federal Title I comparability standards, H. B. 2619 would not have been acceptable.

That reform comes hard in Chicago was underscored as the August 15, 1979, deadline for school board submission of a plan indicating how $196 million in special funds for disadvantaged students would be spent arrived and departed without such a plan. Actually, the superintendent sent a plan to the state without seeking prior school board approval of it. The board later voted to rescind the plan in mid-September, 1979. A black board member who moved the action complained that she was unable to learn from the superintendent, according to one account, "what children from poor families are getting new education programs they did not receive last year, in what schools the new programs are planned, and how the spending would be monitored."[63] Soon thereafter, a majority of the board approved the superintendent's plan.

Intradistrict inequalities are a fact of life in American public schools. Historically, their existence is extensively documented especially with respect to race, but such racial inequalities are by no means unknown today. Yet, educational researchers and reformers alike have all but ignored the reality of intradistrict inequalities. Even researchers who seem aware of the problem and affirm its importance very often do not view it as weighty enough to engage their personal research energies.

Yet, researchers in educational finance who fail to incorporate the intradistrict dimension into their analysis give up an important means of ascertaining the educational significance of changes in state financing systems. One reason for their failure is the overreliance of many researchers on national and regional aggregated statistics in their analyses. Individual school data are lost in the shuffle, even if the research purportedly is concerned with educational equality. Neither the authors of the Coleman Report, for example, nor its critics are able to tell us much that is helpful about school-by-school material inequalities since single schools are excluded from their analysis.

The point is not to drop interdistrict analysis in favor of intradistrict research. Rather, the goal should be to study the entire stream of resources travelling to the student rather than only one element, usually the interdistrict element. Unless both elements are joined in a single analysis, the public will continue to invest vast funds in a process without knowing its culmination. School systems are virtually free of external checks on the final disposition of enormous tax funds, a prerogative school boards and superintendents guard most jealously. Attempts to elicit detailed school-by-school expenditure data from school systems are resisted and the national research community has not seen fit to challenge this stance. Instead, it tends to tailor its research formulations to the political realities of fiscal secrecy.

Many researchers totally ignore the civil rights interest in educational finance. Typical research reports by experts on educational finance do not present the viewpoints and findings of poor and minority parents and representatives. Yet, extensive empirical observations by civil rights sources are readily available. They are ignored, for the most part, much as one might expect if school system authorities were doing the research. Much of the evidence of intradistrict inequalities which courts have found to be well established was available from civil rights sources long before. Researchers ignored this evidence and, by and large, they continue to do so. There is a great gap between court evidence of intradistrict inequalities and researchers' recognition of such evidence.

Future research on intradistrict inequalities depends crucially on the quality and availability of school and classroom financial data. Many large school systems lack the fundamentals of cost data. Until, for example, a court-appointed financial expert searched the records of the Cleveland, Ohio, school district, the district was considered exceptionally businesslike. The opposite was nearer the truth, as the expert—a tax lawyer by training—found to his dismay.[64] When the New York City school district received the November, 1976, charges from OCR, it was not able to evaluate these until a small internal staff devised an appropriate system of records and data. Thereupon, the school board decided not to challenge the accuracy of the OCR charges.[65]

Many central school administrators are reluctant to publicize per-pupil expenditures because of possible community repercussions. Others express an almost proprietary interest in keeping the figures confidential, as a private business person might more appropriately do. Possibly, financial data about the daily operations of public schools are less public than data about any other level of government. Civil rights groups and other civic groups do not represent the public in seeking cost data. Levin has suggested that school districts be required to publish separate cost data for each school in the district.[66] While such a step is technologically feasible in school districts such as Chicago which record per-school expenditures internally, there seems little prospect that it will be implemented. Pressure groups representing school boards and local and state superintendents may be expected to oppose such an innovation.

Two significant sources of data still lie untapped. One is the findings of OCR compliance reviews such as the one reported above for New York City. Such reviews have been made for Chicago, Los Angeles, Houston, and Philadelphia. Records of the HEW Audit Agency also include extensive documentation on intradistrict inequalities related to violations of Title I regulations. These two sets of data are almost unique in American education.

Does desegregation eliminate intradistrict inequalities? In part, yes, because gross inequalities on a school-by-school basis are less likely on a racial basis in desegregated schools. At the same time, many class-based inequalities may continue. More important, however, are per-pupil inequalities based on classroom-to-classroom inequalities. The OCR data on New York City, it will be recalled, revealed such inequalities. Ability grouping and tracking and teacher-transfer rules are the principal mechanisms for perpetuating intraschool inequalities. As desegregation spreads, the absence of research on classroom inequalities becomes more regrettable.

Financial equity is a critical component of equal education. Like other forms of equity in our society, it, too, is subject to constraints of race and class. We must study the broad range of levels on which public funds are managed and allocated to understand failures to provide financial equity. Only then can we build up a reliable body of knowledge of financial equity in the schools.

Notes

1. This chapter consists of extracts from Meyer Weinberg, "Intradistrict Inequalities, I and II," *Research Review of Equal Education*, 3 (Winter and Spring 1979), pp. 3–5, 10–18 (I); and 14–21, 40–42 (II).

2. Stephen J. Carroll with the assistance of Millicent Cox and William Lisowski, *The Search for Equity in School Finance: Results from Five States* (Santa Monica, Calif.: Rand, March 1979), p. 173.

3. Ibid., p. 174.

4. Harold Baron, "Race and Status in School Spending: Chicago, 1961–1966," *Journal of Human Resources*, 6 (1971), pp. 3–24. Cf. Jesse Burkhead with Thomas G. Fox and John W. Holland, *Input and Output in Large-City High Schools* (Syracuse, N.Y.: Syracuse University Press, 1967).

5. See George Strayer, *The Report of a Survey of the Public Schools of the District of Columbia* (Washington, D.C.: U.S. Government Printing Office, 1949).

6. Patricia Cayo Sexton, *Education and Income Inequalities in Our Public Schools* (New York: Viking Press, 1961), p. 132.

7. Kenneth B. Clark in ibid., pp. viii–ix.

8. Jesse Burkhead with others, *Public School Finance, Economics and Politics* (Syracuse, N.Y.: Syracuse University Press, 1964), p. 86.

9. Roe L. Johns and Edgar L. Morphet, *The Economics and Financing of Education. A Systems Approach* (Englewood Cliffs, N.J.: Prentice-Hall, 1969), p. 171.

10. Ibid., pp. 171–72.

11. Arthur Wise, *Rich Schools, Poor Schools* (Chicago: University of Chicago Press, 1968), p. 163.

12. Stephan Michelson, "The Political Economy of Public School Finance," in Martin Carnoy (ed.), *Schooling in a Corporate Society* (New York: McKay, 1972), p. 172.

13. Ibid., p. 169.

14. Ibid., p. 161.

15. James W. Guthrie, George B. Kleindorfer, Henry M. Levin, and Robert T. Stout, *Schools and Inequality* (Cambridge, Mass.: MIT Press, 1971), p. 55.

16. Ibid.

17. Ibid.

18. W. Norton Grubb and Stephan Michelson, *States and Schools: The Political*

Economy of Public School Financing (Lexington, Mass.: Lexington Books, 1974), p. 61.

19. Ibid., p. 66.

20. Henry M. Levin, "Financing Education for the Urban Disadvantaged," pp. 8-9, in Sterling M. McMurrin (ed.), *Resources for Urban Schools: Better Use and Balance* (New York: Committee for Economic Development, 1971).

21. Ibid., p. 11-12.

22. Ralph Andrew and Robert J. Goettel, "School-by-School Resource Allocation and Educational Need in Three Urban Districts," in Joel S. Berke and others (eds.), *Financing Equal Educational Opportunity: Alternatives for State Finance* (Berkeley, Calif.: McCutchan, 1972), p. 143.

23. Ibid.

24. Ibid., p. 148.

25. Ibid.

26. Ibid., p. 166.

27. John D. Owen, "The Distribution of Educational Resources in Large American Cities," *Journal of Human Resources*, 7 (Winter 1972), p. 27.

28. Ibid., p. 34.

29. John D. Owen, *School Inequality and the Welfare State* (Baltimore: Johns Hopkins University Press, 1974), pp. 20-21.

30. Ibid., p. 14.

31. Ibid., p. 23.

32. Ibid., p. 27.

33. Ibid., p. 147.

34. Ibid., p. 89.

35. Anita A. Summers and Barbara L. Wolfe, "Intradistrict Distribution of School Inputs to the Disadvantaged: Evidence for the Courts," *Journal of Human Resources*, 11 (Summer 1976), p. 339.

36. Anita A. Summers, "Can Schools Make a Difference?" in Ruth W. Wooding (ed.), *Critical Issues in Education* (Athens, Ga: Institute of Government, University of Georgia, 1978), p. 51.

37. Frank Levy and others, *Urban Outcomes, Schools, Streets, and Libraries* (Berkeley: University of California Press, 1974), p. 78.

38. Betsy Levin and others, *Public School Finance: Present Disparities and Fiscal Alternatives*, I (Washington, D.C.: President's Commission on School Finance, January 1972), pp. 273-75.

39. Ibid., p. 304.

40. *Report of the New York State Commission on the Quality, Cost and Financing of Elementary and Secondary Education*, Vol. 3 (Albany: The Commission, 1972), p. 12B1.

41. Ibid.

42. Paul Ritterband, "Race, Resources and Achievement," *Sociology of Education*, 46 (Spring 1973).

43. Ibid., pp. 164-67.

44. For background of this study, see Martin H. Gerry, "The HEW Review of Educational Services to NY's Minority Children," *Integrateducation*, 13 (May–June 1975), pp. 160-65.

45. Statement by Martin H. Gerry, Director of OCR, January 18, 1977, p. 1.

46. Ibid., Appendix K.

47. Ibid., Appendix O.

48. William Valentine, OCR acting regional director, Region II, to Chancellor Irving Anker, October 4, 1977, p. 6.

49. Ibid., p. 7.

50. Martin H. Gerry to Chancellor Irving Anker, January 18, 1977, Appendix C.

51. Ibid., p. 5.

52. Ibid., p. 6.

53. Ibid., p. 8.

54. Ibid., p. 9.

55. Ibid.

56. Valentine to Anker, October 10, 1977, p. 2.

57. Harold Baron, "Race and Status in School Spending: Chicago, 1961–1966," *Journal of Human Resources*, 6 (1971), p. 15.

58. Sharon B. Gelder, "Reading Scores Per Pupil Expenditures—Higher in White than Black Chicago Schools," *Chicago Reporter*, August 1976.

59. See Jesse Burkhead and others, *Input and Output in Large-City High Schools* (Syracuse, N.Y.: Syracuse University Press, 1967), p. 92.

60. The suit, filed December 14, 1976, and sponsored by Operation PUSH, was headed by Rev. Jesse Jackson.

61. Roger Fox and Bernard Lacour, *The Issue of Resource Equalization: Funding the Education of Economically Disadvantaged Children* (Chicago: Chicago Urban League, Spring 1977), p. 42.

62. *Chicago Urban League Newsletter*, Fall 1978, p. 6.

63. Ms. Carey Preston, School Board Vice President.

64. *Reed* v. *Rhodes*, C73-1300, February 6, 1978, p. 48. See also David L. Parham, *The Cleveland School Desegregation Decision* (Cleveland: Greater Cleveland Project Resource Center, December 23, 1977).

65. *Response of the Board of Education of the City of New York to the November 9, 1976 Letter from the Office of Civil Rights, United States Department of Health, Education, and Welfare*, April 22, 1977.

66. Henry M. Levin, "Financing Education for the Urban Disadvantaged," in Sterling M. McMurrin (ed.), *Resources for Urban Schools: Better Use and Balance* (New York: Committee for Economic Development, 1971), p. 16.

7

Desegregation and Academic Achievement

Much has been written concerning the effects of desegregation. In nearly all these studies, however, no distinctions are made among various kinds of effects. As a result, the literature of the subject is confusing. Instead of asking whether desegregation has *an* effect *or* affects this or that, we should ask how different *kinds* of desegregation effects are manifested. Conceivably, a specific desegregation experience could be effective in one way and less effective or even ineffective in others.

Desegregation effects can be expressed on three levels: policy, mechanical, and instructional.

Policy effects are those changes induced by managerial decisions to alter the goals of the school system and to reallocate resources accordingly. They affect organizational units rather than individual students. Nonetheless, they may be of crucial importance. A decision to pair a severely short-changed minority school with a well-endowed majority school sets the scene for more equal and more productive education. But the decision to pair, while critical for further progress, is insufficient to produce actual educational change for individual students. Policies are only that—policies. They remain to be translated into action. Without the new policies, however, little more can happen.

Mechanical effects are changes in general housekeeping routines and in the physical flow of students into, through, and out of a school. Such processes have only an incidental relationship to a school's educational function. Yet, they may come to be perceived as major elements in the desegregation process because of their physical prominence. Busing is a prime example. Strictly speaking, its only effect can be to transport children from one place to another. Aside from that, busing can neither be assigned nor be expected to discharge an educational function. Educational research has never found educational achievement dependent upon the particular mode of student transportation to and from school—whether a student walks or rides has no effect on that student's learning. Consequently, it is improper to attribute any educational effect to busing—or walking, for that matter. Issues of distance, health, and comfort apply to all modes of transportation.

Instructional effects are changes in the educational effectiveness of a school in terms of individual students. These effects may be linked to changes in the climate of the school, including high expectations and goals for all the children in a school. They may be facilitated by reorganization of curriculum and of modes of student-teacher relationships; increased use of cooperative modes of learning; improvement of textual materials; creation of an atmosphere of mutual respect and regard for all members of the school community; and, not least, employment of a firm central administrative policy of support.

Extremely few studies have been made of the policy effects of desegregation. On the other hand, numerous studies utilize the word "busing" in their titles without, in fact, measuring busing as such. The authors of these studies make the mistake of using the word as a synonym for desegregation. This, of course, is a mistake. If researchers wish to study busing and achievement, they must compare relative achievement under various modes of transportation, including busing. Such studies have not been made; thus, mechanical effects of desegregation are irrelevant to academic achievement, given present knowledge.

The great mass of studies of instructional effects of desegregation relate to the narrowest aspect of the subject—namely, achievement test scores. Little if any attention is paid to the classroom dynamics behind the scores, to the bearing of curriculum on them, to the organization of student learning modes, or to the possible effects of school or school system policies.

Before the 1950s, educators were not interested in studying how racial segregation affected academic achievement. For one thing, the answer seemed obvious. Boards of education made few attempts to maximize the academic achievement of minority children. Moreover, in such school systems funds intended for the use of minority children were frequently diverted for use in white schools, to the detriment of minority achievement. None of the national organizations of school board members, administrators, teachers, or educational researchers protested against such practices. University schools or departments of education were silent, as well.

The 1954 *Brown* decision and the rising civil rights movement changed this. Civil rights advocates demanded that minority children be educated to an acceptable standard. The abolition of segregation was thus linked with an anticipated rise in educational achievement. Some even thought the former would automatically produce the latter. Behind this reasoning lay a conviction that school personnel were neutral specialists, just as capable and ready to educate as to exclude minority students. As segregation gave way to desegregation, these observers expected that antagonistic attitudes as well as material inequalities would give way, and that minority achievement would prosper.

Progress came slowly, even though parents of poor and minority children expressed deep concern for improving their children's education. In one city after another, the civil rights movement called upon school boards to publish school-by-school achievement scores so that weak spots could be identified and concerted measures undertaken to eliminate deficiencies. Boards of education, however, resisted such demands. Even in cities in which scores were published, they were treated as isolated signposts rather than as distress signals.

In the face of reluctance of school boards to act, the question arose whether achievement in desegregated schools was any different than that in segregated schools. Ideological opponents of desegregation were certain achievement would decline in the newly desegregated schools. Academic skeptics, unused to analyzing racial factors in education, failed to see their possible relevance in the present case. And proponents of desegregation hoped for the best without much evidence or assurance of success.

During the first decade after *Brown*, few schools in the South were desegregated beyond a token basis. In the North, *Brown* brought no changes, at first. There were, therefore, few cases of actual desegregation. Persons seeking overall views of the effects of desegregation on achievement looked in vain for studies.

Between 1964 and 1970, Weinberg wrote the first three works devoted exclusively to desegregation effects. In a pamphlet written in 1964, he surveyed whatever scrappy evidence existed.[1] He examined the few dissertations available, the testimony of superintendents, and statements of various firsthand observers. He concluded that desegregation seemed to improve the achievement of black children without adversely affecting that of white children. In a book published in 1968, Weinberg included an entire chapter on the subject.[2] This time he reported, in far greater detail, on more formal research and utilized fewer anecdotal reports. His conclusion remained essentially unchanged. Two years later, in 1970, a new edition of the book contained an expanded chapter on the subject, once more repeating the earlier conclusions.

That same year, 1970, Nancy St. John published a lengthy article which reviewed studies of desegregation and achievement.[3] She criticized many of the studies as methodologically weak, a point that Weinberg had not emphasized. A number of studies, for example, did not take socioeconomic conditions into account; others did not have adequate control of factors under study; still others lacked a pretest and thus might have confounded a condition existing before desegregation with an effect of the desegregation process itself. Desegregation and achievement were the central concern of a book published by St. John in 1975.[4] This work dealt less with methodological shortcomings of studies. A critical aspect of her views, however, was her conviction that studies on the subject showed only that desegregation was an indeterminate process. Whether desegregation aided achievement or not depended on other factors, including the contribution of the teacher.

In 1977, Weinberg published a new book which included a comprehensive examination of evidence bearing on desegregation and achievement.[5] In it he reported on evidence of all sorts, including studies in which desegregation was found not to encourage higher achievement. Again, he concluded that desegregation helped minority achievement in more cases than not.

Overall, both St. John and Weinberg pretty much took the evidence as it was, trimmed off the most obvious shortcomings, and drew cautious conclusions. St. John tended to be somewhat more skeptical, while Weinberg placed more emphasis on empirical and historical evidence and more positive results. Indeed, writers in the field who favored one or the other emphasis tended to cite only the studies which they found acceptable, ignoring the others. The resulting distortion was unfortunate.

During 1977–1978, there were new advances in the evaluation of desegregation research and the effort became more systematized. For another, instead of continuing to make the same old queries, researchers asked new questions of the data.

In 1978, Ronald A. Krol sallied forth onto the rare heights of meta analysis, a term meaning the process of analyzing analyses.[6] His central interest was to settle, if possible, the debate about the effects of desegregation on academic achievement. He derived his hypotheses explicitly from the St. John and Weinberg books, although unlike these two authors, he established precise rules for admitting evidence. He located 129 analyses that satisfied the six criteria he set up. A study had to be of a before-after kind. Change in achievement could only be measured in comparison with an earlier point. Achievement had to be measured quantitatively; otherwise, exact determinations of effect-size could not be made. Certain statistical information had to be provided in the study. This included the number of students and the extent of variation in scores within the population studied. Studies using only measures of attitudes, whether those of teachers or students, were excluded. Studies that measured a situation only once ("cross-sectional") were not considered. Krol pointed out that many such studies analyzed the effect of different racial composition ratios on achievement at one time rather than the effects of a change from segregation to desegregation over a period of time. Studies seeking to ascertain the effect of desegregation on I.Q. scores were rejected since Krol deemed I.Q. and achievement to be different concepts.

A total of 129 analyses performed in fifty-five separate studies remained. What did these analyses reveal?

For seventy-one studies, reported Krol, "the mean of the experimental group [the desegregated group] exceeded the mean of the control group by 0.16 standard deviations."[7] In only ten out of seventy-one cases did the experimental group score less than the control group. Krol also tested whether the positive achievement effect of desegregation was greater for younger than for older children. It was not.[8] He found differences between average achievement in mathematics and reading and length of exposure to desegregation made no difference for achievement.[9]

Krol thus detected "slightly positive" effects on achievement. He noted that less rigorous techniques of analysis yielded more or less the same conclusion. One such technique—which Krol calls "voting"—was employed by Weinberg when he observed that more times than not, desegregation affected minority achievement positively.[10] At the same time, Krol also reported: "Studies which were considered to be of a weaker design (no control group) did have a greater effect size than those studies which were considered to be stronger (with control group)."[11] Krol, however, rejects the possibility of drawing a negative conclusion from the studies he analyzed: "One cannot say based on this study that desegregation produces harmful effects."[12]

Krol is not an admirer of the desegregation studies he reviewed. None, he declares, is an exemplary study; at best, they are mediocre. What is more, they are indefinite as to the kind of experimental or other "treatment" going on in the classroom as a result of desegregation. "The treatment for all the studies in the meta analysis," writes Krol, "is simply the act of placing the minority children in a predominantly white school."[13] He notes: "None of the researchers attempted to find out the atmosphere inside these schools, or if the children were actually placed in integrated classes within the desegregated school."[14]

Evidence from other quarters suggests that minority children in formally desegregated schools frequently find themselves in segregated classes. They are thus deprived of any positive achievement effect. Conceivably, more adequate enforcement or legal desegregation requirements might yield greater achievement. The reluctance of desegregation researchers to investigate classroom dynamics has been noted for more than a decade.[15] Sponsors of research, however, continue to ignore this glaring weakness.

In 1978, Robert L. Crain and Rita E. Mahard published an analysis of desegregation and academic achievement.[16] These investigators broke new ground by asking novel questions, far beyond a simple one about the existence of overall test-score differences between students attending desegregated or segregated schools.

Does educational success depend on region? Nearly two-thirds of fifteen studies of students in the South showed positive gains for black students while only slightly over a third of twenty-six studies of northern students showed such a gain.[17] Is desegregation at an earlier age better? Crain and Mahard found the answer "clear and unmistakable": the earlier the grade at which desegregation occurs, the more positive the impact on achievement.[18] Do desegregation effects vary by curriculum? The quantitative evidence is not at all clear-cut but Crain and Mahard believe that, in many cases, desegregated black children learn more because they are using a better curriculum rather than from increased racial interaction.[19]

Are voluntary or mandatory desegregation plans more effective in stimulating black learning? "On the whole," the researchers report, "the evidence suggests that there is a significant correlation between mandatory assignment and positive achievement outcomes."[20] Crain and Mahard cautioned their readers against hastening to apply this somewhat unexpected finding. (Their caution turned out to be well-taken. Two years later, in mid-1980, when they analyzed more studies, they found no achievement advantage for either mandatory or voluntary desegregation.)

All in all, Crain and Mahard maintain that desegregation has a positive effect on black academic achievement. But not always. The effect depends on what actually goes on in the classroom:

> Desegregation sometimes results in better curricula or facilities; it often results in blacks having better trained or more cognitively skilled teachers; it is frequently accompanied by a major effort to upgrade the quality of education; and it almost always results in socioeconomic desegregation. When desegregation is accompanied by all of these factors, it should not be surprising that there are immediate achievement gains half to two-thirds of the time.[21]

They estimate the average achievement gain of blacks during the first one or two years of desegregation as about one-half of a grade equivalent.[22]

In 1977, Laurence and Gifford Bradley conducted a study which paralleled that of Crain and Mahard.[23] They sought to discover whether existing studies established a positive achievement effect for desegregation. The Bradleys and Crain and Mahard completed their studies at about the same time although publication was delayed for a year in the latter case. Apparently neither pair knew of the other's study.

The Bradleys asked whether open enrollment—choice of school by individual students regardless of residence—encouraged black academic achievement growth. All four studies of this technique reported a positive achievement effect. While, according to the Bradleys, two of the studies had grave methodological weaknesses, the other two were more sophisticated. One might conclude, even if the Bradleys did not do so in so many words, that studies of open enrollment supported a positive achievement effect.[24]

The Bradleys then examined the evidence bearing on central schools as a desegregation device. These are schools to which students are assigned after their own schools have been closed, the better to achieve a desirable racial mixture. "All of the Central Schools investigations reported increased black achievement following desegregation," wrote the Bradleys.[25] They described some of these studies, however, as methodologically weak.

A number of researchers have studied school closings and dispersal of students throughout a city. Their findings are mixed and, the Bradleys asserted, the studies are so weak methodologically that no firm conclusions can be fairly drawn.[26]

There are numerous studies of the effects of desegregation plans implemented by busing but the Bradleys did not reach a definite conclusion on them. Discussing the well-known Pettigrew-Armor debate on the subject, however, they declared: "Armor's conclusion that busing is an ineffective intervention must be considered tenuous."[27]

The Bradleys examined a single experimental study by Frary and Goolsby in Gulfport, Mississippi. They found what the Bradleys agreed was "relatively strong evidence that desegregation may have beneficial effects on black student achievement."[28]

Throughout, the Bradleys stressed heavily the presence of methodological weakness in practically all desegregation studies. They considered most of these weaknesses serious but not fatal. We are thus left with imperfect evidence. Some of the weaknesses are comparisons without an adequate control group; as a result, an achievement change in a desegregated school may also have happened in a segregated school. In that case, a factor common to both schools may be the formative factor. In other studies, no predesegregation test was given, thus making it impossible to gauge the significance of a test score obtained at the end of a study period. (It should be noted that these two methodological weaknesses were of no importance in Krol's study since he omitted desegregation studies lacking controls and pretest scores.)

It is of some interest to examine how different researchers evaluate the methodological soundness of a specific study. For example, Crain and Mahard say that the Zdep study has a "carefully executed research design,"[29] but they as well as the Bradleys note a weakness. Some black children were bused from their all-black school to attend suburban schools while their peers remained in the all-black city school. After nearly a whole school year, the bused children recorded far larger achievement gains. While the magnitude of the gain is impressive and seems attributable to attendance at a desegregated school, it is also possible that the outcome can be explained, to a degree, by quality differences between suburban and city schools. Crain and Mahard observe that these differences "might explain a portion of the very large increase in achievement," while the Bradleys say that the differences "severely weaken" Zdep's results.[30]

Another example is a study by Lawrence G. Felice in Waco, Texas, which, according to the author, showed a negative desegregation effect on achievement. Crain and Mahard criticized the small size of Felice's sample and stated that he had failed to match his treatment and control groups on age, grade, and sex.[31] (Both were matched for previous achievement levels.) The Bradleys also commented on the size of the samples. They pointed out that many of the subjects dropped out of the study, thus strengthening their contention that "there may have been some systematic differences between the experimental and control subjects that might have biased the results." For these and other reasons the Bradleys wrote that "Felice's conclusions must be considered to be questionable."[32] Crain and Mahard, however, left the issue rather open-ended.

In general, Crain and Mahard seemed less definitive in accepting or rejecting a study. The Bradleys, on the other hand, were much readier to reject a study on the basis of methodological weaknesses. In addition, it appeared that neither pair of researchers was swayed excessively by their value positions. Both succeeded in being objective, although with varying emphases.

The preceding analyses of analyses agree, with qualifications, that desegregation has a positive effect on black achievement.

Single studies continue to be published (whether or not they were included in a meta analysis) and several are of special interest.

The first study was conducted by the Systems Development Corporation (SDC) and is an evaluation of the federal Emergency School Aid Act (ESAA). Under the law, federal funds were provided to help school districts carry out a desegregation plan (the Basic program) or to help predominantly minority districts improve the quality of their educational services (the Pilot program). The research problem is to discover whether the federal dollars were educationally effective. A three-year research period was established, from 1973–1974 to 1975–1976.

The study was plagued by a fatal weakness not of its own making. Schools receiving ESAA funds were matched with comparable schools in the same district which did not receive such funds. Presumably, if the ESAA grants were sizable enough, certain features would emerge that favored the ESAA schools over the non-ESAA schools. In fact, however, the non-ESAA schools "tended not only to have nearly as much money as the . . . ESAA schools, but also to spend that money for similar kinds of program activities." It also developed that neither group of schools followed any really innovative techniques or programs.[33] In effect, two groups of similar schools were being tested for differences.

The evaluation was, however, far from a complete loss. A comparison of Basic and Pilot schools, and an in-depth study of thirty elementary and high schools, resulted in important findings. SDC also tried to ascertain what practices improved academic achievement in either ESAA schools or non-ESAA schools.

The researchers found that achievement scores of individual students who had been in a Pilot school over two years underwent "considerable growth."[34] Comparable students in Basic schools exhibited "a consistent pattern of positive differences. . . ." This did not happen in Basic high schools, but, in the tenth and eleventh grades in these schools it was found that "larger reading gains were made by students in districts that undertook more activities designed to facilitate and support school desegregation.[35] Presumably, such an atmosphere encouraged minority children to learn more readily. When individual students were grouped by schools and studied over two years, another achievement-related finding emerged. "The strongest relationship in these data was between the teacher's expectations for the student . . . and the reading outcome. . . ."[36] The SDC researchers emphasize that no significant achievement differences were found between ESAA and non-ESAA schools as such.

At least as significant as the main study was an in-depth study that was also made of twenty-four elementary schools. Fifteen were "successful," that is, at least two grades in each school recorded a rise in national percentile ranks in reading or mathematics. Nine were "unsuccessful." Observers visited each of the schools for a period of two weeks; they sat in individual classrooms and interviewed teachers and administrators.

In the in-depth study, reading and mathematics scores were maximized by the use of paid parent aides in the classroom; the utilization of behavioral or other objectives in classroom instruction; and allocation of major resources per pupil to employ remedial specialists in the classroom. "The importance of this study's findings," according to Jean Wellisch, "lies in the fact that school program characteristics do appear to make a difference in student achievement."[37] If so, improvements in achievement are well within the realm of all schools.

It was found that ESAA expenditures for elementary schools in the Basic sample during the three years of the study helped produce a positive effect on achievement both for reading and arithmetic.[38] A second in-depth study reaffirmed the importance of teacher planning for achievement. It failed, however, to replicate the earlier in-depth study's finding that the presence of paid parent aides helped increase achievement.

The Educational Testing Service (ETS) undertook a second major desegregation study. It covered about 200 elementary and high schools. A survey in 1974 was repeated on a smaller scale the following year. Site visits were made to forty-eight schools the earlier year and to forty-three of these schools the next year. Fifth and tenth graders were tested; teachers, principals, and counselors filled out questionnaires; some were interviewed during site visits.

The three-year-long ETS study is preeminently practical. It is concerned with learning how to foster effective desegregation and integration rather than spinning on about the pros and cons of integration and segregation. Specifically, the researchers sought out specific school conditions that were demonstrably effective. They then asked school personnel in those real situations to suggest to others how integration might best be carried out.

Since so very few applied studies in integration have been made—itself a topic worth studying!—scholars must take care in evaluating such studies. Unlike most theoretical inquiries, the ETS project did not analyze a broad range of experiences of integration. Instead, it compared in great detail very successful instances of integration with ones that had been moderately successful. So unaccustomed are we to such studies that they are sometimes termed "biased" because they do not discuss the "failures." (Such was the hostile reception by some to a recent report by the U.S. Commission on Civil Rights which sought to demonstrate that desegregation was feasible and selected actual cases to test the proposition. The goal was practical— that is, to show that desegregation "worked." Their findings can be refuted only by demonstrating that the specific cases the Commission chose do not, in fact, illustrate what they are alleged to illustrate.)

The ETS study measured successful integration in terms of academic achievement and race relations. School practices that encouraged good race relations were found to be related to conditions which fostered academic growth. Where blacks were learning, so were whites, especially in elementary schools. In high schools, "achievement is significantly related to perception of school fairness."[39]

The ETS researchers did not identify any school factor that, of itself, was directly related to achievement differences. Instead, various school factors, interacting with one another, significantly affected achievement. (A number of these interactions touch on material discussed under separate headings, so they are discussed under those headings.) Especially in an applied study, the way a practice is implemented can be at least as important as which practice is implemented.[40]

Christopher Jencks and Marsha Brown carried out a small research study which, unlike the ETS approach, measured only the effect of the racial composition of schools upon academic achievement. Using data gathered in 1965 from 359 northern elementary schools and 154 northern high schools for the Coleman Report, the researchers concluded that "racially balanced elementary schools may have modest positive effects on both black and white test scores." Most specifically:

On the average attending a predominantly white elementary school boosted a black student's test scores by 0.215 standard deviations. If all blacks gained this much relative to white norms between first and sixth grades, the test score gap between blacks and whites would fall by 21 percent.[41]

Proponents of desegregation might welcome this finding but they could not be greatly helped by it. The research did not specify any factors originating in the schools that might account for the finding. There was no discussion of teaching strategies, school or classroom climates, or any of a myriad of factors that might be at work. The study's finding can only serve as the beginning of an inquiry rather than as a conclusion. It should be kept in mind that the Jencks-Brown data do not illustrate the desegregation process; they were collected at one time, nearly twenty years ago.

The National Assessment of Education Progress (NAEP) used a similar approach in its study of changes in science achievement and found that in the Southeast, the country's most desegregated area, nine-year-old black students' science achievement improved in 1972–1973 over 1969–1970. The following table is a compilation of the changes, by race and region, for these years:
Southeastern blacks as a whole fared considerably better than their northern peers, who registered comparatively large declines.

NAEP also studied achievement changes in relation to school racial composition. As the table indicates, black seventeen-year-olds in the Southeast dropped in achievement but those who attended schools that were 10 percent to 39 percent white showed a gain rather than a drop.[43] Nine-year-old blacks in the North dropped 3.5 percent, as the table shows. On the other hand, those attending up to 2.5 percent white schools in 1972–1973 gained 2.5 percentage points over 1969–1970.[44]

Table 7.1
Differences in Science Achievement: Race, Age, and Region 1969-1970 to 1972-1973
(in percentages)

Region	Blacks	Whites
Southeast		
9 years	+ 2.8	-1.6
13 years	-1.1	-1.2
17 years	-1.2	-1.2
Northeast, Central, Western		
9 years	-3.5	-1.3
13 years	-5.1	-1.8
17 years	-2.5	-3.0

Source: NAEP, *Science Achievement.*[42]

The NAEP survey will reassure those who feared desegregation in the South would bring about a fall in academic achievement. It is not possible, however, to ascribe the southern nine-year-olds' gain to desegregation. Since desegregation brought an improvement in the material quality of black education in the South and compensatory education has made headway there, it is at least plausible to give part of the credit for science-knowledge improvement to desegregation. On the other hand, as in the case of the Jencks-Brown study, one does not know just what specific factors might have been operative to have produced the improvement. Clearly, it could not have been merely changes in racial ratios.

"The pressing need now," writes Nancy St. John, "is to discover the school conditions under which the benefits of mixed schooling are maximized and its hardships minimized."[45] Preoccupation with racial ratios alone does not seem an efficient way of getting at those "school conditions" to which St. John refers.

David R. Anderson conducted a study of two imperfectly matched schools in Daytona Beach, Florida. In June, 1969, an all-black high school was phased out; students were sent to one of two predominantly white schools in which they made up about one-fifth of enrollment. A sample of the newly desegregated black students in 1969-1970 was compared with a sample of black students who had attended the still-segregated school a year earlier.

After the first year, desegregated students earned lower grade averages on the whole.[46] Anderson held that the difference with the previous year was not absolute; that is, he implied that there were higher academic standards in the desegregated school. Thus, even those black students whose grades slumped were not learning less than previously. No precise achievement scores are presented by Anderson.

Between the sexes, black males suffered most of the grade deficit. Females from upper socioeconomic levels did experience a drop in the percentage of

"B" grades earned. Unlike males, however, black females did not receive any more failing grades.

Edward Shutman studied schools in a California district—perhaps Pasadena—which had been desegregated for three years. There were almost equal proportions of blacks and Anglos adding up to 80 percent of the students; the remaining 20 percent were Hispanics. Black children were generally bused to school while Anglos attended neighborhood schools. Shutman found that "the longer the time of desegregation of a school district the higher was the average level of reading performance of Negro pupils at the end of the first grade."[47] Somewhat along the line of Anderson's findings, Shutman reported that "at the end of the second grade, in designated schools, Negro girls tended to be more successful readers than Negro boys."[48]

The Shutman study is difficult to evaluate since its focus is the school district rather than individual schools.

One of the most valuable studies was completed in 1974, but it is not included in the meta analyses discussed here.[49] Donald R. Taylor studied desegregation effects in Hillsborough County (Tampa), Florida. First, he located all black and white students in the county who had attended segregated schools for the first three grades, beginning in 1968–1969, and who had then attended desegregated schools for grades four to five. Second, he drew random samples from the two racial groups: 220 blacks from ten schools and 780 whites from fifty-one schools. Third, he stratified all 1,000 students into three socioeconomic groups. His central interest was the intellectual development of children under desegregation. Fortunately, the same measure of IQ—the Otis-Lennon instrument—had been used throughout the five years Taylor studied.

It should be noted that the socioeconomic distribution of black and white students was not comparable.

Table 7.2
Socioeconomic Distribution of Fourth and Fifth Grade Students in Desegregated Schools in Hillsborough County, Florida[50]

Socioeconomic Group	Blacks		Whites	
	Number	*Percent*	*Number*	*Percent*
Upper	0	0.0	20	2.6
Middle	44	20.0	549	70.4
Lower	176	80.0	211	27.0
Total	220	100.0	780	100.0

Source: Taylor, *A Longitudinal Comparison.*

At the same time, such inconsistency is not at all atypical in southern communities.

Taylor found that black students in desegregated schools increased their IQ scores by an average of 6.5 points; those from poorer families did somewhat better than those from middle-income families.[51] White students gained about 4.2 IQ points over the same period. The greatest white gains were recorded by the financially poorest students although, as in the case of black students, whites from middle-class groups also did well.[52]

Taylor wondered whether black children who attended all-black schools for the entire five years achieved comparably. Although he gathered no specific data, he discovered a 1967 study of "ghetto blacks" in Hillsborough County, covering grades one to six, which showed a reduction in reading and arithmetic scores over the six years. Taylor concluded: "It is highly unlikely that blacks as a group attending ghetto black schools have made significant gains in their intellectual development in the past."[53]

Perhaps Taylor's most noteworthy finding was the superior achievement gain of lower-class blacks and whites over that of middle-class students. This issue of differential social class gains among desegregated black students has attracted much debate in recent years but few hard data are available. Taylor's finding contradicted much traditional thinking and deserves further study. The achievement increase for both black and white middle-class students was also of interest because, in most studies, the rate of learning for middle-class children remained unchanged during desegregation.

Taylor offered few explanations for his findings. To account for the significant gains among poor blacks and whites, however, he stressed that these are precisely the students who constituted the target groups for extensive compensatory education. If so, the project was a happy conjunction of policy and pedagogy. Desegregation created the setting for more productive learning while classroom organization was altered to engender such learning.

Annie D. Smith studied relative performance of 1,416 twelfth graders in two Florida counties as indicated by their scores on a statewide achievement test. In 1962, when they began elementary school, all students had attended segregated schools. It was not until 1973 that they attended desegregated schools. Students in the latter attended either of two high schools, in which blacks made up about one-fifth of the enrollment. In general, desegregated black children achieved at a significantly higher level than their segregated peers.[54] Scores were similarly higher for desegregated black students in urban schools than in rural schools. Curiously, on social science and natural science tests, all groups—black and white, rural and urban—did better in segregated classrooms than in desegregated classrooms. This finding is most unusual.

It is difficult to know how to interpret Smith's study because she gives very little information regarding the students attending segregated schools. No data are available about matching between students and schools in both segregated and desegregated conditions.

Dora C. Baltzell analyzed desegregation effects in Duval County (Jacksonville), Florida schools. In a two-year study of 444 students who entered fourth grade in 1972, she found that blacks made significant gains in reading and arithmetic during the first year and in arithmetic during the second. Contrary to virtually all other segregation studies, however, white achievement in arithmetic was found to have declined. Apparently at a loss to explain any of the study's outcomes, Baltzell asked wonderingly: "Can it indeed be that academic performance is so delicate that a simple change in classroom peer composition or a short-lived systematic disruption, however traumatic, alone sends test scores plummeting and rising so dramatically?"[55] Based on a mass of evidence derived from other studies, the reply would be in the negative. Baltzell, however, did not probe into distinctive city, school, or classroom effects that might have helped to produce the disparate findings in her study.

In a study in Dallas, Kenneth D. Thomas analyzed desegregation effects implemented by one-way busing of minority children to one Anglo school and to four predominantly minority schools. The bused fourth and fifth graders, who attended their new schools during 1976–1977, were compared with similar students who remained in their segregated schools. Unfortunately, little real desegregation occurred in this project since minority children were, in effect, being sent from segregated schools to still predominantly minority schools. Whatever changes in achievement occurred could have been caused by many other factors. In any case, as might have been expected, the results were mixed and fragmentary.[56]

Alton B. Smith studied the effects on achievement of pairing two formerly mainly white elementary schools in the Oklahoma City area town of Shawnee. While white students outscored minority—black and Indian—students, the latter did, according to Smith, narrow the achievement gap between themselves and nonminority students.[57] The study, however, does not adequately document this finding.

In 1973, the Atlanta school desegregation case was settled. Part of the agreement required the pairing of heavily black and poor Hill Elementary with white and middle-class Morningside Elementary. The former school was to have grades one through three and the latter, grades four through six. When the pairing was implemented, two-thirds of the white parents in the Morningside neighborhood withdrew their children and enrolled them in private schools. The court order had set a three-year trial period for the pairing. At the end of the period, white parents requested an extension of time and the court granted the request. White enrollment in the two schools had increased during the course of the trial period.

Paula C. Calhoun, who became principal of the Hill School in 1976, undertook a study of the pairing. She found black students especially benefitted from attending the first three grades in the Hill school:

The black students . . . had had . . . a protective nurturing environment during the first few years of their education. They had had an opportunity on their own home ground to become acquainted with the white students. By the time that they entered

. . . Morningside three years later, they had already had time to develop associations with the white children.[58]

In Hill, most of the teachers were black and highly experienced.

When the pairing began, the Hill students' achievement level was equal to that of the city schools as a whole. By 1976 their average had risen eight points while that of the whites rose two points, thus narrowing the gap between the two groups. Calhoun notes the role in this of the "middle-class black teachers . . . who were success oriented and related exceptionally well with the white parents."[59]

Calhoun's study exemplifies the virtues of a delimited empirical approach. Unlike most other desegregation studies, this one examines the subject in a community setting and takes account of some dynamics of achievement change.

Phillips and Bianchi traced the effect on achievement of closing an impacted black school and transferring its 353 students to two predominantly white, middle-class schools in a Nevada city. For purposes of comparison, they used a fairly matched all-black school as a control. While this school received special compensatory expenditures the two mainly white ones did not. After seven months, the transferred black students outstripped the segregated black students in two of three reading areas tested, but after two years there was no difference.[60] (IQ scores of the desegregated students rose over two years while they fell for segregated students.) Phillips and Bianchi guessed that the seven-month superiority would have held over two years if the white students had been higher achievers.

Elmer A. Lemke studied desegregation in Peoria, Illinois. In a somewhat unusual procedure, he used students in five types of schools:

(1) White residents in segregated black schools

(2) Bused white students in integrated and segregated white schools

(3) Black residents in segregated black neighborhood schools

(4) Bused black students in integrated schools

(5) Bused black students in segregated white schools

Blacks who were bused out of segregated black schools to heavily white schools tended to achieve at a higher level than did blacks who were bused out of similar schools to schools that were less overwhelmingly white. White residents in predominantly black neighborhood schools achieved at a higher level than black residents in the same school. (This finding contradicts one of the least-examined findings of the 1966 Coleman Report.)[61] Lemke speculated that black achievement in Peoria's desegregated schools would have risen more if white students in those schools had been higher achievers themselves.

In addition, Lemke regards language as an important element in the relationships between the varying achievements of the two racial groups. He writes: "Since white students who attend black schools are influenced by the language of the black culture—the language not stressed in the achievement test—they tend to score lower than do whites who are bused to integrated and segregated white schools."[62] Actually, the little evidence there is on this subject contradicts Lemke. White children in a Washington, D.C., school which was 85 percent black was indeed familiar with "Black English," but they easily switched from it to Standard English.[63] Evidence also suggests black children go through the reverse process just as readily.

Schellenberg and Halteman studied the achievement effects of desegregation in Grand Rapids, Michigan. After matching sixty-eight pairs of inner-city elementary students, the researchers analyzed the test scores over a period of two years. There were no achievement differences in reading or arithmetic between bused and nonbused minority children.[64] Sheehan and Marcus found the same to be true over a period of seven months in a group of desegregated schools in Dallas.[65] In both studies, minority children were bused to Anglo schools; apparently, no Anglo children were bused from their neighborhood schools.

Maurice J. Eash and Sue Pinzur Rasher conducted a four-year evaluation of mandatory desegregation in a suburb of Chicago called "Forrestville," which may in fact be Park Forest, Illinois. The researchers conducted a broad-scale study, going far beyond achievement test scores.

During the first two years, scores rose for both blacks and whites. "Of particular significance," wrote the researchers, "was the finding that some black children were doing especially well in a few schools and poorly in other schools."[66] This signal alerted the central administration to concentrate on improving instructional practices in certain schools. The efforts succeeded: "Where an inservice program in mathematics had been held at one grade level significant increases in achievement were registered by these classes."[67] Achievement in general continued to rise into the fourth year but this was especially so when steps were taken to improve instructional practices.

When they probed further, Eash and Rasher found that "achievement differences between black and white students are largely attributable to the amount of home support a child receives: the more support, the greater the achievement."[68] School authorities stepped up efforts to engage parents to a greater extent in the education of their children.

Observers followed instructional practices in classrooms during the third year of the study. A wide variety of problems became evident, ranging from outright incompetence—three such teachers resigned—to lack of understanding of individualized instruction, to an inability to use instructional materials. In-service training on a considerable scale was initiated.

Eash and Rasher wrote of an across-the-board resolve in Forrestville to "make it work" as a major reason for the productiveness of desegregation there. In a simple, sensible statement the researchers stressed that "the problems encountered in improving achievement under desegregation are conventional instructional problems."[69] Clearly, if we do not grapple with those problems, desegregation will not have accomplished anything. At best, desegregation facilitated educational change. Achieving the actual change was a task for the school.

In the world outside the arid precincts of academic research, the issue of desegregation and academic achievement has been prominent in policy debates. Two dominant viewpoints have emerged in recent years. The first is "Desegregate and the rest will follow." The second, "Forget segregation and concentrate on quality education." Stated this way, neither is sufficient.

The emphasis on desegregation stemmed solely from several sources. Given the history of official segregation both in the South and North, the opening of schools to all was an indispensable goal of civil rights forces. "Segregation is a denial of the equal protection of the laws," declared the U.S. Supreme Court in 1954.[70] It followed logically that ending segregation would restore equal protection. Little or no attention was paid to what was to happen in the desegregated schools. Instructing lower federal courts on how to manage desegregation, the Supreme Court in 1955 had declared that "school authorities have the primary responsibility for elucidating, assessing, and solving these varied local school problems arising out of desegregation."[71] Civil rights leaders were willing to leave the actual operation of desegregated schools in the hands of school authorities. In part, this reflected a confidence in the professional integrity of educators; besides, civil rights advocates had few ideas of how to operate a school, desegregated or otherwise. Thus, history, hope, and lack of expertise led to a concern with merely opening the school doors. Good or better education, it was presumed, would follow.

Exclusive concern with quality education, on the other hand, arose from other sources. Racial concentration, whether official or unofficial, was interpreted as a neutral factor in learning. In part, this was a tactical view. Since actual desegregation proceeded very slowly in the first years after 1954, and even up to today—especially in the North—some exponents of quality education advocated educational improvement for minority children wherever they were. This approach was based on a faulty perception of governmental and school authorities as beneficent. Its adherents assumed that these authorities feared racial desegregation so intensely that they would gladly exchange equal sharing of resources for maintaining segregation. In general, they also assumed that segregation might have a nurturing effect on the black child's development or that any damage caused by segregation was minimal. Its supporters also contended that actual learning gains under desegregation were nonexistent or negligible in any case.

Neither of these two major approaches is itself capable of providing every child with a first-rate education.

A racist school system resists both views. The greatest educational inequalities coexist with the highest degree of segregation. Indeed, the fundamental motivation of segregation is to facilitate unequal education—privileges for some and deprivation for the others. Unquestionably, some children learn effectively under segregation. These tend to be the more gifted children. The remainder have to make do as best they can. It is idle to imagine that racist school systems stand to remedy this shortcoming on any significant scale.

The trouble with the exclusive-desegregation school of thought is not the support of desegregation itself or its exclusivity. Throughout the South, and increasingly in the North, the daily reality of desegregation disclosed at least two kinds of shortcomings. These were the so-called second-generation desegregation problems and the persistence of achievement gaps between black and white children. We have begun to deal with the former but the latter are all but ignored.

Many second-generation problems are educational in nature, and desegregation advocates did not anticipate them sufficiently. Such problems include discriminatory disciplinary techniques, ability grouping, and tracking systems that recreate segregated classrooms in formally desegregated schools, exclusionary practices in extracurricular activities, and teacher and staff prejudice. Such practices are not typical of all or even of most desegregated schools, but, where they exist, they interfere seriously with the educational progress of children and make a mockery of the United States Constitution.

Strong advocates of desegregation generally do not address the persistent academic achievement gap between black and white children in desegregated schools. The second-generation problems just discussed help maintain this gap: children must be *put* down before they can be *kept* down. The second-generation practices do both quite efficiently. They also lessen the support of black parents for desegregation if their children attend desegregated schools but still do not have equal educational opportunity. Where black achievement has increased, black parents are the strongest proponents of desegregation; this is the case with most desegregated schools. It is unrealistic, however, to expect enthusiasm from them in the face of continued academic failure.

So, it is difficult to understand the statement frequently made by some desegregation advocates that their support for desegregation does not depend on any achievement benefit. They regard desegregation principally as an adventure in intergroup enlightenment rather than as a means of facilitating equal education. To be sure, getting along with others, especially if they are of a different race, must be a high priority in the schools, let alone in the society as a whole. But black parents are already rather expert in such relationships. What their children lack especially is accomplishment in the more academic aspects of education.

The attainment of a first-rate education for all children, then, cannot rest on either the exclusive-desegregation or the quality-education viewpoint.

They must be merged into a broad movement that can eliminate the racism of systematically unequal education and its main structural support—segregation. In other words, the same forces oppose both equal quality education and desegregation. Unless a school system is desegregated, it cannot undertake to educate all the children equally.

Desegregation, thus, has two interrelated purposes: to discharge a constitutional obligation to eliminate unlawful segregation, and to stimulate the school system to practice equal education. Systems in which schools remain segregated lack any incentive to abolish unequal educational practices. In the largest cities of the country, which enroll a sizable proportion of all black students, disparities between black and white are common, as we saw in the preceding chapter. The single most valuable educational resource in these communities, the supply of experienced teachers, is very unequally distributed in favor of white middle-class schools. It is inconceivable that a redistribution of such teachers will occur short of a legal desegregation order. Nor has any school system volunteered such action in the interest of quality education. But a fairer use of experienced teachers would boost authentic quality education for all children.

The attainment of high-quality education for all requires far more than a declaration of lofty intentions. Unless new and plentiful resources are made available to children in hitherto shortchanged schools, quality education will remain a mere slogan.

Some Current Issues

Let us review several important questions that arise repeatedly in current debates about desegregation and achievement.

1. Do blacks have to sit next to whites in order to learn?

Of course not. Even in the poorest all-black school there are children whose academic record is exemplary. They are fully as talented as any white child and perform adequately by any standard. Many prominent black leaders attended all-black schools throughout their entire academic careers. Yet, their experience hardly supports the viewpoint that, for the mass of black students, desegregation is not a prerequisite for high-quality education.

The question does not revolve around a relative few talented students who would make it on their own in any setting. The problem is with the majority of other children who need a great deal of help. Chances are they will not get this help in a segregated school. Educational researchers have found repeatedly that an all-black school, especially if it is one attended by poor black children, is characterized by low staff and teacher expectations for student achievement, exceedingly easy grading standards, and a general atmosphere of educational defeat. Some children will escape these influences. Unfortunately, most will not. It is these latter children who stand to profit most from a constructively desegregated school.

Numerous public opinion polls attest to the fact that black parents understand this. The polls show again and again that the chief reason parents desire desegregation is that they believe that their children's achievement will improve in a desegregated school.[72]

2. Why can't we spend money on improving education instead of on busing?

People who believe that great sums of money are being spent on busing children for purposes of desegregation frequently ask this question. Actually the cost of busing children to new schools as a result of court-ordered plans averages between 2 percent and 3 percent of a school district's budget.[73]

Two points may be made about this expenditure. One is that it is necessary because the school board was found guilty of unconstitutionally depriving children of their right to equal educational opportunity. No expenditure for busing would be needed if housing were not segregated. (In fact, in growing numbers of cases, courts exempt from busing those neighborhoods in which integrated housing is widespread.) Since constitutional requirements must be honored, however, some busing has been found to be necessary in many school desegregation cases.

Another point is that the busing cost is quite minimal. The money involved could not improve education significantly if it were distributed equally among all students. (Keep in mind that the school board that deliberately segregated children usually also shortchanged the same children. Thus, it was not in the habit of spreading expenditures evenly among all students.)

Educational quality is not lagging in our schools because the needed funds are tied up in desegregation expenses. Indeed, many of the most backward schools are also the most segregated. Segregation does not produce more money for those children who need it most. The reverse would be nearer the truth: segregation compounds the inequality while desegregation is an effort to reduce it.

3. Isn't quality education more important than desegregation?

Only if high-quality education can be obtained under segregation. The evidence of American history is strongly against that possibility.

Take Washington, D.C. Before 1954, when that city's schools were legally segregated, children in the white schools received a fair education. The school system did not want to know how deficient the education of black children was. They were not even given standard achievement tests. When the schools were desegregated in accordance with the Supreme Court's order, all children were tested. Not unexpectedly, the test scores of black students were found to be quite low, and somewhat illogically critics attributed the low scores to desegregation. To be sure, when these scores were averaged with those of the higher-achieving whites, the general scholastic average fell, compared with the predesegregation average. The critics neglected to observe, however, that the pre-1954 average did not include the scores of black children, who were not tested.

Desegregation uncovers but does not create educational problems. Under desegregation, our educational problems can be examined in broad daylight. When these problems remained in the shadows of segregation, nothing was done, or ever would be done, about them.

To tell the truth, nothing much may be done under desegregation. But research tells us that this does not have to be. Every desegregated school that succeeds is a further demonstration that high-quality education is feasible for every child and not just for a chosen few.

We should be careful to avoid thinking that segregation is harmful only to minority children. Many white children, poor ones especially, are denied a high-quality education. Simply going to school with children of their own race is not necessarily conducive to high-quality education. High dropout rates for poor white children in the great cities should be sufficient evidence of that.

Equally important, segregation is not the explanation for the higher achievement of more privileged white children. Usually very few of these higher-achieving children attend schools with black children. Interestingly enough, when they do so, in newly desegregated schools, their academic achievement does not suffer. In other words, they learn as much in desegregated schools as in segregated (white) schools. It turns out, therefore, that for whites to attend schools with other whites does not increase their high academic achievement.

Many white parents will wonder why, then, achievement scores are generally higher in white schools than in black schools. It is not the racial differences but more likely the different attitudes of the school administration and staff that account for much of the difference. Middle-class schools, whether black or white, more easily command the dedication and hard work of principals, teachers, and school boards. The goal of a truly integrated school is to command the same outcomes for poor and minority children. A climate of universal educational accomplishment is unlikely to develop systematically in segregated schools.

4. What is quality education?

Quality education is the education that prepares children to make their own way, as life's challenges arise. Unless the child is literate and numerate, however, it is a play on words to speak of an *educated* child.

A school system that has grown to accept semi-literacy even among adolescents probably also sloughs away many more goals of education. Low reading scores are frequently educational epitaphs rather than signposts for improvement. "Here lies the non-reader," the scores announce. Many well-meaning persons contend that "there's more to quality education than reading, writing, and figuring." Quite so. But whatever else there is lies beyond the reach of children unable to read, write, or cipher. Low reading scores are deadly serious affairs and should not be dismissed as "merely" this or that.

Poor parents, both black and white, are often only too willing to settle for proficiency in these basic skills. This is not necessarily because they are ignorant of the broader aspects of education. Rather, their attitude reflects a realistic response to the frequent failure of the schools to provide their children with the most elementary skills. They know the crucial role of literacy and numerical skills in our urban industrial civilization. These are survival skills and constitute, in that context, "quality education." When minority children in desegregated schools improve their mastery of these survival skills, parents naturally welcome the development.

A school system that lacked concern for poor and minority children before desegregation often continues to do so after desegregation. Such examples are by no means unknown. For others, desegregation can become an opportunity for new educational adventures. Gary Orfield points out how desegregation can loosen the rigidity which characterizes many schools and which interferes with new educational approaches:

One of the things it does in many school systems, especially now that you are getting new input of teaching facility into the schools' very rigid procedure, is break up that rigidity. By the time you desegregate students, you also desegregate faculty. In many cases you create new schools where neither the students nor the faculty have been there as a block before, where everything isn't settled, where there's an opportunity to change.[74]

This very openness of newly desegregated schools may be part of the reason why the academic achievement of minority students tend to rise in such schools where teachers are freer to innovate. Although there are no statistical data available to demonstrate it, probably teachers in desegregated schools are more involved in rethinking procedures and models than are teachers in segregated schools.

But high-quality education is by no means inevitable in desegregated schools. Nor is it in other kinds of schools. Whatever academic gains minority children have recorded in desegregated schools usually outstrip those recorded in most compensatory education projects where minority children remain together, typically in a racially isolated school. And desegregation is far less expensive on a per-student basis. Yet, neither the tiny gains under segregated compensatory education nor the more substantial gains under desegregation are complete solutions to the problems of unequal education. To be practical, however, we should select the process that is more promising under actual classroom conditions.

The greatest promise of non-segregated schools is that they may lead to educational gains for all children. The new learning spirit that many desegregated schools exemplify can help revive urban schools as educating institutions. Fewer middle-class people, white and black, would leave the city if the schools were more adequate. In this sense, desegregation could lead to less rather than more "white flight." The entire metropolitan area would benefit from such a development.

Given the narrow frame of much desegregation research, it is fair to conclude that desegregation generally leads to enhanced academic achievement,
as measured by standardized tests. Yet, researchers have virtually ignored
the task of exploring the reasons for this positive trend.

The Bradleys have stated well the most serious problem: "Very few investigators of school desegregation are aware of what work has been performed by others in the area."[75] Since work in the field is readily available,
and in English, it is difficult to understand why funding agencies, research
directors, graduate school professors, and editors of learned journals have
permitted this state of mutual ignorance to flourish for so long.

Notes

1. Meyer Weinberg, *Research on School Desegregation: Review and Prospect*
(Chicago: Integrated Education Associates, 1965).

2. Meyer Weinberg, *Desegregation Research: An Appraisal* (Bloomington Ind.:
Phi Delta Kappa, 1968). Second edition, 1970.

3. Nancy H. St. John, "Desegregation and Minority Group Performance," *Review of Educational Research*, 40 (February 1970), pp. 111-33.

4. Nancy H. St. John, *School Desegregation Outcomes for Children* (New York:
Wiley, 1975).

5. Meyer Weinberg, *Minority Students: A Research Appraisal* (Washington,
D.C.: U.S. Government Printing Office, 1977).

6. Ronald A. Krol, *A Meta Analysis of Comparative Research on the Effects of
Desegregation on Academic Achievement* (doctoral diss., Western Michigan University, 1978). (University Microfilms Order No. 7907962.)

7. Ibid., p. 105.

8. Ibid., p. 108.

9. Ibid., p. 113.

10. Weinberg, *Minority Students*, p. 122.

11. Krol, *A Meta Analysis*, p. 117.

12. Ibid., p. 124.

13. Ibid., p. 136.

14. Ibid.

15. Weinberg, *Minority Students*, p. 328.

16. Robert L. Crain and Rita E. Mahard, "Desegregation and Black Achievement: A Review of the Research," *Law and Contemporary Problems*, 42 (Summer
1978), pp. 17-56.

17. Ibid., p. 31.

18. Ibid., p. 34.

19. Ibid., p. 39.

20. Ibid., p. 45.

21. Ibid., p. 39.

22. Ibid., p. 48.

23. Laurence A. Bradley and Gifford W. Bradley, "The Academic Achievement
of Black Students in Desegregated Schools: A Critical Review," *Review of Educational Research*, 47 (Summer 1977), p. 419.

24. Ibid.

25. Ibid, p. 425.

26. Ibid.

27. Ibid., p. 442.

28. Ibid., p. 443.

29. Crain and Mahard, "Desegregation and Black Achievement," p. 29. The study is Stanley M. Zdep, "Educating Disadvantaged Urban Children in Suburban Schools: An Evaluation," *Journal of Applied Social Psychology*, 1 (1971), pp. 173-78.

30. See Crain and Mahard, "Desegregation and Black Achievement," p. 42, and Bradley and Bradley, "The Academic Achievement of Black Students in Desegregated Schools," p. 438.

31. Crain and Mahard, "Desegregation and Black Achievement," p. 32.

32. Bradley and Bradley, "The Academic Achievement of Black Students in Desegregated Schools," p. 438.

33. John E. Coulson and others, *The First Year of Emergency School Aid Act (ESAA) Implementation* (Santa Monica, Calif.: System Development Corporation, September 15, 1970), p. viii-1.

34. John E. Coulson and others, *The Second Year of Emergency School Aid Act (ESAA) Implementation* (Santa Monica, Calif.: System Development Corporation, July 1976), p. ix-14.

35. Ibid., p. x-15.

36. Ibid., p. x-36.

37. Jean B. Wellisch and others, *An In-Depth Study of Emergency School Aid Act (ESAA) Schools: 1974-1975* (Santa Monica, Calif.: System Development Corporation, July 1976), p. 12.

38. John E. Coulson and others, *The Third Year of Emergency School Aid Act (ESAA) Implementation* (Santa Monica, Calif.: System Development Corporation, March 1977), p. vi-8.

39. Garlie A. Forehand and others, *Conditions and Processes of Effective School Desegregation* (Princeton, N.J.: Educational Testing Service, July 1976), p. 39.

40. See the good advice in Daniel F. Luecke and Noel F. McGinn, "Regression Analyses and Education Production Functions: Can They Be Trusted?" *Harvard Educational Review*, 45 (August 1975), pp. 347-48.

41. Christopher Jencks and Marsha Brown, "The Effects of Desegregation on Student Achievement: Some New Evidence From the Equality of Educational Opportunity Survey," *Sociology of Education*, 48 (Winter 1975), pp. 136-37.

42. National Assessment of Educational Progress, *Science Achievement: Racial and Regional Trends, 1969-73* (Denver: Educational Commission of the States, March 1976), p. 5.

43. Ibid., p. 21.

44. Ibid.

45. St. John, *School Desegregation Outcome for Children*, p. 122.

46. David Ross Anderson, *The Effects of First Year Desegregation on the Year-End Grade Average, Absentee-Dropout Rate, and Discipline Problems of a Group of Eleventh Grade Black Pupils* (doctoral diss., University of Florida, 1973), p. 115. (University Microfilms Order No. 74-9572.)

47. Edward Shutman, *The Relationship of Desegregation and of Consistent Attendance to Reading Achievement of Primary-Grade Negro Pupils* (doctoral diss., University of Southern California, 1974), p. 68.

48. Ibid.

49. Krol lists the Taylor work but omits it from his study since Taylor used IQ scores, which disqualified it from the Krol meta analysis.

50. Donald Ray Taylor, *A Longitudinal Comparison of Intellectual Development by Black and White Students from Segregated to Desegregated Settings* (doctoral diss., University of South Florida, 1974), p. 50. (University Microfilms Order No. 74-10,126.)

51. Ibid., pp. 51–52.

52. Ibid., p. 52.

53. Ibid., pp. 53–54.

54. Annie D. Smith, *The Impact of Desegregation on the Florida Statewide Twelfth Grade Achievement Test Scores of Black and White Students in a Rural and an Urban Florida County* (doctoral diss., University of Florida, 1975), p. 74. (University Microfilms Order No. 76-12,133.)

55. Dora C. Baltzell, *A Longitudinal Analysis of Reading and Arithmetic Achievement and Court-Ordered Desegregation (With "Forced" Busing) in a Large Urban School District in the South* (doctoral diss., University of Florida, 1970), p. 61. (University Microfilms Order No. 78-7848.)

56. Kenneth D. Thomas, *The Effect of Busing on School Success of Minority Students in Urban Elementary Schools* (doctoral diss., North Texas State University, 1977), pp. 66–68. (University Microfilms Order No. 78-7848.)

57. Alton B. Smith, *A Study of the Educational Effectiveness of Desegregation: A Comparison of Pupil Educational Performance Before and After One Year of Desegregation* (doctoral diss., University of Oklahoma, 1978), p. 62. (University Microfilms Order No. 7824614.)

58. Paula C. Calhoun, *A Study of the Effects of the Forced Desegregation Pairing of a Low Socioeconomic Status White Elementary School on Achievement, Social Interaction, and Enrollment* (doctoral diss., Georgia State University, 1978), p. 10. (University Microfilms Order No. 7908485.)

59. Ibid., p. 121.

60. Leonard W. Phillips and William B. Bianchi, "Desegregation, Reading Achievement, and Problem Behavior in Two Elementary Schools," *Urban Education* (January 1975), p. 330.

61. See James S. Coleman and others, *Equality of Educational Opportunity* (Washington, D.C.: U.S. Government Printing Office, 1966).

62. Elmer A. Lemke, "The Effects of Busing on the Achievement of White and Black Students," *Educational Studies*, 9 (Winter 1979), p. 405.

63. See Gretchen E. Schafft, "White Children in a Majority Black School: Together Yet Separate," *Integrateducation*, 14 (July–August 1976), p. 7.

64. James Schellenberg and John Halteman, "Busing and Academic Achievement. A Two-Year Follow Up," *Urban Education*, 10 (January 1976), p. 363.

65. Daniel S. Sheehan and Mary Marcus, "Busing Status and Student Ethnicity, Effects on Achievement Test Scores," *Urban Education*, 13 (April 1978).

66. Maurice J. Eash and Sue Pinzur Rasher, "Mandated Desegregation and Improved Achievement: A Longitudinal Study," *Phi Delta Kappan* (January 1977), p. 395.

67. Ibid.

68. Ibid.

69. Ibid., p. 397.

70. *Brown v. Board of Education*, 347 U.S. 483 (1954).

71. *Brown* v. *Board of Education*, 349 U.S. 294 (1955).

72. Gary Orfield, *Must We Bus?* (Washington, D.C.: Brookings, 1978), p. 114.

73. Ibid.

74. Gary Orfield, "Examining the Desegregation Process," *Integrateducation*, 13 (May–June 1975), p. 129.

75. Bradley and Bradley, p. 401.

8

Moving from Desegregation to Integration

Desegregation means the removal of systematic barriers to the attendance of children of all racial-ethnic groups in the same schools. It may be achieved by legal directives of courts or administrative agencies, by voluntary means, or by a combination of both. A desegregated school may be a wholesome place to learn. Or, it may simply be a new way to practice racism and unequal education. Curiously, it can be some of each at the same time.

Ideally, desegregation develops into integration, which is a social situation marked by mutual respect and equal dignity in an atmosphere of acceptance and encouragement of distinctive cultural patterns. An integrated school educates all children effectively, without regard to race or class. Neither racism nor unequal education can thrive in an integrated school. There are many fewer integrated than desegregated schools.

In the preceding chapter, we have seen how some desegregated school experiences have been, on balance, very constructive for black youth. (Only a few studies deal with other minority youth.) All in all, academic achievement for blacks rises in desegregated schools. The rate of college-going rises. Interracial interaction among students develops. Minority children make broader career choices. Communities come to accept desegregated schools as ordinary events. But the list of negatives is long. We read earlier of teacher and administrator prejudice against minority students, of discriminatory suspensions and expulsions of black students,[1] of racially discriminatory placements in classrooms for the mentally retarded, and of discriminatory ability grouping and tracking systems.[2]

It is important not to idealize conditions in segregated schools of the past because there is little evidence that many were effective educators of the great mass of poor black youth; nor were they designed to be. But desegregated schools must be judged by a higher standard. After all, one cannot leap from segregation directly to integration. Desegregation is the bridge between them and that process is crucial for the future of integration.

It is best, therefore, if we conceive of desegregation as coexisting with phases of integration, and not as a completely distinct stage. A desegregated school may be improving education for all, but lagging in the rejection of some racist practices. It is, on the whole, moving toward integration but at a slow and irregular pace. It may, in fact, never reach that goal. Whether it does depends upon how effectively community and school forces combine to produce success. The upper reaches of such success seem to depend upon factors external to the school. Few, if any, schools appear to be anywhere near success.

What light does research shed on the process of moving from desegregation to integration? We will examine this question from two viewpoints: the development of racial self-concept in young children, mainly of preschool age; and the character of interracial interaction in desegregated schools. Both perspectives bear on the issue of integration since, for the black child especially, racism may fundamentally block the achievement of self-knowledge and self-concept. As Curtis and Bennett put it, "the process of self-discovery is continuous as long as the child is discovering new potentialities."[3] Through constructive interaction with others, those potentialities may take shape.

Charles Wheeler studied eighty-two preschool children attending four day care centers in Washington, D.C.[4] Two were all-black and the other two interracial. He found no differences in self-concept among black children attending the four schools. Mona Thornton explored the racial attitudes of thirty-two white preschoolers attending a preschool at the University of Connecticut.[5] One test revealed an increasing tendency for them to evaluate white positively and black negatively as they grew older. (The children ranged from thirty-seven to seventy months old.) The research could not discern a specific age at which racial stereotypes could be said to take definite shape. When a story was read by both a black and a white storyteller, the white children "sat closer to the white storyteller, touched the white one significantly more, made more verbalizations to the white storyteller and looked at the book while listening to the story with the white storyteller more than they looked at the storyteller or the environment."[6] The younger children seemed less aware of the race of the black storyteller.

Clifford Moore examined sixty poor black children, with a mean age of five years.[7] They were shown photos of black and white adults and were asked which one they preferred as a teacher. Most chose the black person but they also perceived that person more negatively than they did the white person. Moore then divided responses by IQ score. His findings were as follows:

Black males with higher I.Q.s tended to perceive the black model negatively and prefer the white model . . . while black females with higher I.Q.s preferred the black models over the white models. . . . The children with higher I.Q.s tended to perceive the black models more positively than the white models.[8]

Moore does not report the racial composition of the school but it may have been all black.

Judith Langlois and Cookie Stephan investigated the comparative importance of physical attractiveness and race or ethnicity on young children's
preferences and characterizations of others.[9] They analyzed responses of
120 kindergartners and fourth graders in two desegregated schools near
Austin, Texas. Each child viewed thirty-six photos which included, for each
racial-ethnic group, a clearly attractive person and an unattractive person.

The researchers found that a child's "level of attractiveness has wide-
ranging implications for friendship choices, peer interaction, and ethnic relations."[10] The older children tended to select members of their own racial-
ethnic group or from the attractive group; the younger children did less of
this. Black fourth graders were the only ones who failed to select from their
own group or from the most attractive group. For all children, attractive
persons were liked more than persons deemed unattractive; they were rated
smarter, and regarded as more likely to be friendly and nice. Correspondingly, unattractive persons tended to be rated as meaner. Physical attractiveness seemed more important to females than to males, possibly because
people constantly talk to young females of being pretty!

Langlois and Stephan observed that "stereotypes associated with physical
attractiveness are learned by children of different ethnic groups early in
life."[11] Clearly, these preconceptions carry with them a set of loaded evaluations which are consequential for the development of the ability of many
disvalued children to learn and to grow. The researchers also note the possible implication of the fact that the black children in their study might have
"accepted a negative societal stereotype of blacks," especially with reference to smartness and attractiveness.[12]

Physical attractiveness, like skin color, is a highly visible basis for making
invidious distinctions among people. It is even more, however, a subjective
product of social experience, and thus would seem to be rather readily dealt
with by the school. At the same time, physical attractiveness is less invidious
than skin color since—depending on what criteria are used—physically attractive children can be found among all ethnic groups. This is especially
true of younger children.

Ronald Lacoste sought to discover whether three- and four-year-olds of
both races would express racial conceptions.[13] Given a series of photographs of black and white children, the subjects were consistently unable to
"classify by race." A novel feature of this study was the portrayal in some
of the photographs of separate facial features (nose, lips) rather than entire
faces. Black girls did tend to prefer persons resembling themselves but they
did not succeed in identifying whites as racially distinct. Lacoste raised the
question of whether the absence of racial conceptions arose from the lack of
exposure to others that is inherent in segregated schooling. He concluded in
the negative, and cited literature to support his view. (The schools were in
Austin, Texas.)

The issue of segregation-integration and racial attitudes among young
children was also investigated by Carole Goldstein and associates.[14] They

analyzed the responses of fifty-six black and fifty-six white students ranging in age from five to six years in three northeastern schools. All students came from roughly comparable neighborhoods in terms of socioeconomic composition; some attended segregated classes and some integrated classes. The researchers found that attendance in the integrated classes was significant for both black and white children.

For one thing, white children in interracial classes "exhibit higher other-race [black] preference than segregated white children. . . ."[15] On the other hand, black children in interracial classes "displayed significantly less white and more black preference than did segregated blacks."[16] In fact, "to varying degrees . . . all children in interracial classes exhibited more preference for and acceptance of blacks . . . and less preference for whites than did the children in segregated classrooms."[17]

In both black and white segregated classrooms, preference for whites was found to be "strikingly high."[18] Segregated black children preferred whites at a higher rate than segregated white children preferred blacks. Black and white children in interracial classrooms, however, did not differ in the rate by which they preferred other-race children.

How did the researchers interpret some of these findings? Take the finding that blacks in interracial classrooms tended to prefer more blacks and fewer whites. Some researchers have interpreted this sort of finding negatively. They contend, for example, that the finding demonstrates the futility of school desegregation by illustrating how desegregation intensifies racial separation by minority children.[19] Goldstein and associates disagree. They tentatively offer two alternative interpretations, both of which could be true:

> One may speculate that, in this study, the choice of more blacks and fewer whites by interracial blacks may reflect increased racial self-esteem and decreased own-race rejection, rather than negative attitudes toward whites. . . .
> It seems possible that, for members of the racial majority group, segregated classrooms contributed to a "cocoon effect" that permitted and may have encouraged an attitude of psychological nonrecognition toward minority members.[20]

Little racial stereotyping was found among black or white children. Yet, both groups preferred whites over blacks on five measures. On two of these, black preference increased and white preference decreased over a period of time. The researchers' general conclusion is that while white preference prevailed in both racial groups, "in comparison with earlier findings, acceptance of blacks has increased somewhat, particularly by blacks, and negative stereotyping of blacks by both black and white children has decreased considerably."[21]

Some researchers suggest that black children need reinforcement for their self-identity before entering a desegregated school. They view the segregated school as a nurturing environment.[22] Goldstein and associates, however, observe that "for minority members the segregated classroom seemed to permit white preference to flourish, while apparently contributing little to enhancing the black child's own-race attitudes."[23] Few other researchers have studied racial attitudes in segregated school contexts and compared these with attitudes in desegregated schools.

William Estes made a somewhat related study recently.[24] He investigated racial self-identification among 190 black and white students, aged five to eight years old, in southwestern Michigan. Apparently, they attended a desegregated school. All in all, the children were easily able to identify the race of white or black dolls. Very few blacks identified with the white doll. Estes concluded that "experiences in an integrated school and an integrated community can have impact which reverses the findings of an earlier study in a segregated situation which reduces or eliminates self-derogation by black children and racial attitudes leading to informal segregation by white children."[25]

Glen Toney studied racial attitudes of ninety-two first graders in three San Francisco Bay area schools; one, all-white, another, all-black, and a third, desegregated. While a distinct antiblack bias was evident among white children in the all-white and desegregated schools, blacks in the all-black and desegregated schools rated non-biased in their attitudes.[26]

Deborah Best and associates attempted to modify racial bias among fifty-six black and white kindergartners in Winston-Salem, North Carolina.[27] Their mean age was 5.4 years. Two research techniques were utilized: responses were elicited on a teaching machine and students were rewarded for correct responses with pieces of candy. The second technique was the use of a black studies curriculum. The former technique was successful but not the latter.

The researchers' comparison of the two techniques was of considerable practical interest.

The operant procedure, i.e., teaching machines, was directed at changing the children's evaluative responses to both Euro and Afro persons, while the curriculum procedure relied solely on the development of more positive responses to Afro persons. In other words, the curriculum may have promoted a somewhat more positive view of Afro persons which was still not sufficient to compete with the much stronger tendency toward the positive evaluation of Euro persons in the test materials. . . . The successful elimination of racial bias may require procedures aimed at the extinction of pro-Euro attitudes, as well as the reinforcement of pro-Afro attitudes. An extension of this would be a curriculum in which an attempt would be made to teach the children that race is irrelevant to the evaluation of persons.[28]

This analysis bears closer examination.

It would probably be fair to say that most black studies curricular materials aim to develop positive assessments of the role of black persons in American life and history. While evaluations of their efficiency are not numerous, there is reason to believe that a number of such curricular interventions have been successful. But Best and associates point to an aspect of the matter that is almost unnoticed in the literature: none of the black studies material addresses the assumption of white superiority. Unless this is countered, only marginal advances can be expected in the area of student racial attitudes.

Donna Boswell and John Williams—the latter a well-known researcher in the field—explored the comparative importance of racial and nonracial factors in racial attitudes of fifty white five-year-olds in Winston-Salem, North Carolina.[29] They found a substantial correlation between racial attitudes of children and their mothers toward blacks. Boswell and Williams reported also, however, that "those children who had the greatest degree of pro-white/anti-black bias had the greatest degree of aversion to the darkness of night and thunderstorms. . . ."[30] They conclude that part, at least, of what is called racial attitudes originates not in a racial context but in a context of color. As the researchers write: "The young human is a diurnal animal who is able to cope and satisfy his needs in the light, and experiences disorientation and deprivation in the dark. This 'natural' . . . bias creates a receptivity to cultural usages involving light (white) to symbolize goodness and dark (black) to symbolize badness. . . ."[31]

Janet Schofield sought to determine whether 324 black and white first and second graders would express their racial self-identity in a free-hand crayon drawing of a person.[32] Children were directed to "draw a person," but no racial information was given them. Her findings included the following:

> Blacks tend to draw blacker figures than whites. . . . White children were more likely to draw figures which were clearly white than black children to draw figures which were black. . . . Black children were more likely to draw whites than whites were to draw blacks. . . . Blacks were much less likely than whites to color in the faces of the figures they draw. . . . Not a single white child drew a picture of a black.[33]

The exercise, which was exploratory only, encouraged Schofield to develop it further. One advantage of the technique is that young children are not asked to respond verbally. Unlike the use of dolls and photographs, the drawing technique requires no speech or writing by the children.

In 1974, Elaine Brand and others did an overall analysis of the psychological literature on ethnic identification and preference.[34] The review was not limited to studies of young children. "The most consistent finding in this ethnic research," they wrote, "is preference by both white and black children for white experimental stimuli."[35] They question the significance of this finding, however. "Under present empirical and theoretical gaps," they explain, "it is moot whether studies reflect minority preferences for white stimuli or mirror subject responses within biased designs."[36] In other words, the observed outcome might be due to faulty research procedures rather than to an empirical reality.

Two years later, in 1976, a study by Curtis Banks went even further.[37] He concluded that "white preference in blacks has not . . . been convincingly demonstrated by that body of research thus far accumulated."[38] Examining twenty-one studies of racial preferences of blacks, he found white preference in two, black preference in four, and either no preference or ambiguous findings in fifteen. Of twelve self-identification studies of blacks, none showed misidentification with whites, four showed correct identification with whites, four showed correct identification with blacks, and eight showed nonpreferential self-identity. Stated another way, Banks writes that "69 percent of the reviewed studies showed nonpreference, 25 were found to have demonstrated black preference, and only six percent demonstrated a pattern of white preference in black subjects."[39]

We have seen that racial self-identity appears rudimentary in three-year-olds,[40] but within two years or so, it tends to take shape. Racial bias, especially on the part of white children, can be detected at that age and, at times, even earlier. More or less formed in the home, the racial issue is imported into the school. In segregated schools white preference by blacks may develop since it is not the physical presence of whites that gives rise to white dominance but rather its prevalence in the community and the media. In three studies reviewed here, black children in desegregated schools seemed to benefit in terms of greater self-acceptance.

Two studies cautioned against hasty conclusions. One pointed out the greater role of attractiveness over race in young children's attitudes. The other contended that nonracial color factors played a role in what appeared to be wholly racial attitudes. Neither factor has yet been widely explored in the research literature. It is unlikely that either or both are of such weight to make the racial factor insignificant.

The preschool years are a critical time for the generation of racial attitudes. The potential influence of the school will never be greater than during these early years and desegregated classrooms have the greatest promise of developing into integrated classrooms. If they do so, their contribution to later schooling can be great. With the expansion of day care and preschool facilities, that contribution can increase sharply. But much more attention must be paid to deliberate teacher preparation for integration during early education. (Virtually none of the early education studies just reviewed pays any attention to the role of the teacher and little research exists on the preschool teacher in the integration process.)

At present, students enter elementary and secondary schools with a large backlog of racial bias by virtue of inattention to racial integration in preschool. By junior and senior high grades, racial attitudes may have become encrusted with age and teachers and principals concerned with integration at those levels face a formidable task. The research literature relating to interracial interaction in the years after preschool reflects the problems schools face in breaking through the incrustation of racism.

Nancy Tuma and Maureen Hallinan, studying eighteen predominantly black fourth-, fifth-, and sixth-grade classrooms in California, probed into friendship relations between minority white and majority black students.[41] Whiteness was not clearly a highly valued characteristic in these schools. "Nonblacks (mainly white Anglos)," report Tuma and Hallinan, "both received and made more nonfriend choices and fewer friendly choices than did blacks."[42] With reference to children designating others as "friend," "best friend," or "nonfriend," the researchers found that there were more same-race pairs designated as friend and best friend than would have occurred by chance. There were also fewer same-race pairs in the nonfriend sample than expected by chance. The results point up the minority status of whites in these situations and the simultaneous tendency of majority black students to select one another as friends.

In Riverside County, California, Beverley Jackson studied social acceptance and adjustment among 482 black and white fifth- to eighth-graders in elementary and junior high schools attending nine majority white schools.[43] Her overall findings were as follows:

> Black children seem to be more socially acceptable to other black children than to white children. Black children seem to prefer black children to white children. Integration has apparently not markedly increased social acceptance between blacks and whites. Differences in social status seem to be a factor in white nonacceptance of blacks, even in settings in which blacks have attained middle-class status while some whites have not.[44]

Both black and white students accepted very bright black and white classmates at comparable rates. On the other hand, black middle-class children were more readily accepted by middle-class whites than by lower-class whites. Junior high school black boys accepted black girls more readily than they accepted white girls. White elementary school children accepted black children and other white children with no distinction.

"In the settings chosen for this study," concludes Jackson, "integration is not fostering better social relationships between black and white and therefore is not ensuring those social benefits the desirability of which has generally been cited in justification of school desegregation and busing."[45] Unfortunately, she does not specify any aspect of "the settings" that might have influenced the outcomes. Also, she acknowledges that "the differences in terms of social acceptance between the two groups may have been due to a number of variables other than integration—age, grade level, and exposure to social issues being the most obvious."[46]

Early investigations of classroom desegregation gave considerable emphasis to the possible harm academically underprepared black children suffer while competing with better prepared white children.[47] There have been few empirical classroom studies of this aspect of desegregation. Charles McCormick and Robert Karbinus studied black self-esteem in relation to anxiety over school success.[48] They found:

In general, high performance was associated with low anxiety, and there were more significant differences found in test anxiety than in general anxiety. However, the significant differences in both types of anxiety and in . . . self-esteem inventory scores were unevenly distributed across ethnic groups and grade levels. . . .[49]

Those who had higher self-esteem tended to be the high scorers in reading and arithmetic. This was truer for Spanish-speaking and white students than for blacks, but it was true for blacks in two of three grades when it came to arithmetic alone. (The study was made in the Chicago metropolitan area and included fourth-, fifth-, and sixth-grade students. The white students were of a higher socioeconomic status than were the black and Spanish-surnamed students.) The McCormick-Karbinus study suggests black students are more resilient and autonomous in a desegregated setting than some have been led to believe.

Patricia Milazzo, in a somewhat related study, examined the effect of desegregation on the cultural orientations of children from different socioeconomic backgrounds.[50] Four orientations were studied: time, authority, self-image, and peers. The subjects were an equal number of black and white children in Pasadena, California. The children were allocated to socially homogeneous and heterogeneous classrooms. By "time" was meant orientation to present or future; by "authority," orientation to individualism or collectivism; by "self-image," was meant self-esteem; and by "peers," submission to peer leadership.

Whites and blacks, Milazzo found, shared common cultural orientations. Both poor and affluent blacks in racially desegregated but socially segregated classrooms had a rather high self-image. But lower-income black students in a racially desegregated and socially heterogeneous classroom might have suffered a drop in self-esteem. She concludes that racial desegregation should be limited to students of like socioeconomic backgrounds.[51]

Claude Dulan investigated self-identification and attitudes of 1,000 black elementary students in eight desegregated school districts in California and Washington.[52] He summarized his findings by sketching what he called a "composite" black child in the typical desegregated school studied:

Black children in desegregated elementary schools are more likely to have black friends, to perceive schools in a positive way regardless of their achievement level, and to perceive their own ethnic group as having positive characteristics. In addition, they are more likely to identify more strongly with members of other ethnic groups than with members of their own group. Furthermore, they are more likely to receive average to below average grades, but to perceive themselves as well-liked by others in the school. High achievers are more likely to have low identification with their own group and to have few friends. Finally, children with positive self-concepts and/or positive achievement are more likely to have lower anxiety in school.[53]

While large majorities of black children said pictures of Anglos were not "like" themselves, a sex difference emerged. Nearly twice as many black boys as black girls gave this response (37.2 and 19.0 percent). In response to a question whether they would like to be a white child, more than twice as many black girls as boys responded affirmatively. These two latter responses are contrary to the usually strong black self-affirmation of black girls as compared to black boys.

There was also an age factor at work. In the upper grades, black children tended to see themselves as more like blacks but they also increasingly wanted to be less like blacks. Dulan did not probe further, unfortunately. (One might ask whether this latter view expressed, for example, a denigration of their own race or an acknowledgment of the privileged status of whites in a racist society.) In choosing friends, blacks tended to favor their own race. The best readers among black children were least likely to select Anglo classmates for friends or for work-mates. "A clear rejection of outgroup friendships by blacks," writes Dulan, "may indicate either, that blacks purposefully attempt to maintain cross-racial barriers, or that they do not feel accepted by Anglos and Mexican-Americans in the context of the school."[54] This rejection is not a consequence of self-rejection by blacks for, as Dulan reports, "blacks generally perceive themselves in a very positive light."[55] Black children in the study were found to have a "very positive" attitude toward school and felt they were perceived positively by other students and by teachers.[56]

Steven Asher and Louise Singleton studied cross-race acceptance among twenty-two third graders in desegregated schools, perhaps in Urbana, Illinois.[57] Three years after initial desegregation in 1973, the researchers studied the same children, who were now sixth graders. At the same time, in 1976, they drew another sample of third graders. Instead of ascertaining children's choice of *best* friend or with whom they would *most* like to work in class, Asher and Singleton simply determined *how much* each would like to play with others and work with them. The measure, in other words, aimed at discovering degrees of acceptance rather than the most intense involvement with others.

Very little racial discrimination (or selectivity) emerged, and quite a bit less than is customary in "best friend" studies. (Indeed, sex discrimination was far more salient than racial discrimination.) Children interacted very positively in about 95 percent of the cases observed by the researchers, who stated that "the data are particularly encouraging since many of the black children were bused to school and had minimal opportunities for before- or after-school contact."[58] Three years later, sex bias had not receded and racial selectivity in attitudes was still slight. Asher and Singleton did note, however, a "modest trend" toward black children choosing more black children.

The new third-grade sample drawn in 1976 closely resembled their peers of 1973 but with one difference: black evaluation of white children as workmates rose over the level of 1973. Thus, simultaneously, black children were identifying more with other black children while becoming more accepting of white children. This two-direction development is evident in other studies.[59]

Donald Carter and associates examined interracial peer acceptance in a K-8 school in Buffalo.[60] The school, located in a white neighborhood, enrolled about one-third blacks, all of whom were bused in from three other schools. They studied a total of 322 seventh- and eighth-grade students and found that a child's grade point average was predominant "as a determinant of social and academic acceptance which overshadows racial differences in all groups except black social acceptance."[61] High achievers of both races were rated equally high in academic and social acceptability while low achievers of both races received low acceptance scores. Without reference to academic achievement, blacks tended to select other whites to work with but not to play with. For their part, whites tended to select other whites both for academic and social interaction. On the other hand, white rated blacks as a whole more acceptable for social than for intellectual reasons. Sex preferences were powerful and seemed more important than race in a number of contexts. Carter and associates did not report on the role of teachers, nor did they dwell on the interracial climate of the school.

Francis Terrell made a novel study of black-white communication in terms of black dialect.[62] (He calls the latter "Aflish," a contraction of African-English—following W. L. Taylor.) What factors determine one's ability to communicate in Aflish? Terrell's subjects were 123 black and white male fifth- and sixth-graders in a school in the Pittsburgh area divided into five groups:

—	Lower-class blacks	43
BH	Middle-class blacks who associated with lower-class blacks	20
WH	Middle-class whites who associated with lower-class blacks	20
BL	Middle-class blacks who don't associate with lower-class blacks	20
WH	Middle-class whites who don't associate with lower-class blacks	20
Total		123

All were given dialogue in Aflish to read which was written by three lower-class blacks who regularly associated with others like themselves.

Terrell's findings were as follows. Association rather than race was fundamental to understanding Aflish. Yet, "black subjects outperformed white subjects of a comparable association level." (Social class was not a factor since all four test groups were middle-class.) Terrell points out that "only the BH group significantly outperformed the white subjects," thus implying that the BL group scored lower than WH on recognition of Aflish.[63] Blackness as such did not play a role. One implication of Terrell's study is that the interracial communication that is basic to the transition from desegregation to integregation is quite feasible.

Findings of studies of junior and senior high schools are not very different from those done in preschools and elementary schools.

"New Powerton High School" is a desegregated facility in an undesignated state. Robert Young studied 385 white and black students in the school; 246 were white and 139 were black.[64] They were divided as follows by socioeconomic status: low, 10 percent; middle, 65 percent; and high, 25 percent. Young found it an essentially segregated school:

> Invariably, less successful and disadvantaged black students were channeled into low-achieving and low-status courses, whereas white students "selected" or were given the high achieving courses. This kind of system reinforces and perpetuates stereotypes, as well as negative self-images, among less successful students.[65]

Documentation for the latter statement is all too frequent in Young's work.

While self-esteem of blacks and whites did not differ at New Powerton, black academic self-concept was lower, especially among poor blacks. One out of three white students felt whites were "smarter"; they were joined in this view by one out of ten blacks. In other words, most students, by far, believed the races were equal in intellectual ability. Two out of five whites subscribed to prowhite stereotypes; only one out of ten blacks held to a pro-black stereotype.

Interracial interaction in the school was slight. About three out of four students studied "seldom" or "not at all" with peers of the other race. Low-status blacks tended to have fewer whites as friends but they also seemed to hold fewer antiwhite stereotypes. (Young did not find a relationship.) Members of debate teams, music groups, and drama clubs tended to engage in interracial interaction. On the other hand, Young reports, "athletes on interracial teams tended not to form substantially more interracial friendships than non-athletes. . . ."[66] (The present writer recalls the bitterness with which a black football player in a Maywood, Illinois, high school recounted how, after the season was over, few whites even said hello to him in the school corridors. This contrasted with near-adulation during the season.) Young's further observation indicates a disparity in athletes' perceptions: "For whites, 68 percent said they got along very well with other-race teammates and only 50 percent of the blacks indicated that this was true."[67] But the gap is not very great.

What role did the school play in perpetuating the patterns of separateness and stereotypical knowledge? "In general," Young stated, "students consistently rated their school low in providing for a more positive environment which may have enhanced race relations and provided for minority support within the social system of the school."[68] Even those blacks who shared the higher aspirations of white students, Young insisted, were not truly sharing so much as mimicking the attitudes of the whites. Such a process, he wrote, "does little to promote perceptions of equal status—a 'goal' of integrated schools."[69] Young's distinction between equal respect and mimicry is exceedingly important but also extraordinarily difficult to establish.

Young acknowledged that others have asked whether the structure of desegregated schools discriminates against black students. He believes, however, that such a question is academic. With respect to black students who attend a desegregated school and still define themselves as poor or inferior students, Young contended, "the more profound question is: What kind of implication does this have for changing schools to make them more suitable to the needs of black and white students alike?"[70] He mentioned the need to reexamine teacher qualifications and teacher training, to reformulate the curriculum, and to review human relations practice.

Young's study is a sobering one. It reminds us not only that a desegregated school may fail to develop into an integrated one; it may even regress into segregation.

Cheryl Travis and Sharon Anthony studied the personal adjustment of fifty-nine black and white juniors and seniors during the second year of desegregation in an unnamed high school.[71] Testing occurred in the Fall and in the following Spring, a five-month period. As a whole, the group could be rated upper-lower-class and lower-middle class. In the Fall testing, they found that "all differences suggested better self-actualization in white than in black students," but "there were no significant differences between blacks and whites in terms of spontaneity, self-regard, self-acceptance or capacity for intimate contact."[72] By Spring, all black-white adjustment differences had disappeared, "indicating in most cases a gradual improvement in the self-actualization of the black students."[73] Travis and Anthony underscored the gains of black students "in the area of the acceptance of aggressive feelings and in their own improved self-acceptance in spite of weaknesses or shortcomings."[74] In conclusion, the researchers wrote: "Even if the experience of integration is stressful for black students, it is clearly a transitory type of stress which can be overcome within a period of months."[75]

The research instrument used, the Personal Orientation Inventory, was basic to the Travis-Anthony study. It needs to be evaluated before research results based on its use are fully accepted. The fact that desegregation effects were studied only during the second year of the process and that one is left in the dark about desegregation effects during the first year raises another research issue in the study.

School morale among eleventh graders was studied by Elizabeth McAdams in seven desegregated Nashville schools.[76] Her central finding was that the "school morale scores for both black and white students were significantly higher when the students were members of their schools' majority rather than minority race."[77] This did not, however, reflect simply the students' preference to be in a majority—being in a majority usually meant attending a neighborhood school in which students were more comfortable. Because of housing segregation, it also meant attending a racially homogeneous school. In Nashville, most students who were bused were blacks and were transported away from black neighborhoods. In the two all-black high schools, both principals were black and thus more attractive to black students. McAdams suggests this as one reason why school morale in these two schools was high.

Mutual fear was still an important factor in relationships of blacks and whites in the city. Black students frequently stated that they feared going into white neighborhoods. Obviously, blacks tended to have lower morale in those schools, if only because of the fear. McAdams also reported a special factor at play in the white community:

A practice within some families opposed to busing is to place daughters in private schools while allowing their sons to be bused to their assigned public school. Such a practice, if frequent, might well result in white males in public school more strongly opposed to busing than the females remaining in public school, with their opposition reflected in school morale score differences.[78]

McAdams's study is unusual if only because it does not abstract school morale just from the community context of the school.

Darrel Drury studied black self-esteem in non-segregated schools. This was not a desegregation effects study, which would have required the use of schools once segregated but now desegregated. Drury used a sample of 194 high schools located in 173 school districts. All were part of a federal program, the Emergency School Assistance Program.[79] Three groups of schools were delineated: predominantly black (over 60 percent black); racially balanced (40–60 percent black); and predominantly white (over 60 percent white).

Black self-esteem, Drury found "is *lower* in racially-balanced high schools . . . than in predominantly black schools but *higher* than expected in predominantly white schools."[80] Levels of schoolwide self-esteem depended in part on the magnitude of the achievement discrepancy between black and white students in the school:

In approximately 66 percent of those schools in which mean white achievement exceeds mean black achievement by not more than 50 percent, contact between blacks and whites is "medium high" to "high," as compared with only 47 percent of those schools in which the racial achievement gap exceeds 200 percent. . . .[81]

The difference between the two groups is certainly significant. It is still striking that nearly half the latter groups—with the larger achievement discrepancy—were characterized by fairly frequent contact. It would be instructive to probe into the relationships in such schools to discover the dynamics at work.

Drury also examined the effects of tracking or ability grouping. Black self-esteem was found to be "lowest in schools which assign students to classrooms according to ability and highest in schools which do not. . . ." At the same time, and somewhat unexpectedly, he found that "black and white students in tracked schools tend to interact more freely than those in untracked schools."[82]

In conclusion, Drury wrote that "while cross-racial exposure apparently has a deleterious effect upon the self-concept of blacks, we do not know what other effects—possibly advantageous—desegregation may have."[83] One such advantage, he suggested, might be higher academic achievement. Unfortunately, Drury was unable to examine the community context of the schools in his study to determine what external factors were operating in the area of self-esteem. He did close by declaring that "younger black children (especially those of kindergarten age) are, it seems, least likely to suffer from low esteem in desegregated schools and most likely to demonstrate academic improvement."[84] As we saw earlier in this chapter, kindergarten is also a time when black children are the least subject to white racism and thus least burdened by depressants to their self-esteem. A school which does little or nothing about racism may appear to be accomplishing a great deal in the kindergarten. A similar failure on the high school level, however, is both more obvious and perhaps more consequential for the children involved.

Bernard Dooley investigated the relationship of student unrest and the quality of integration in six desegregated high schools in Florida.[85] He studied a total of 480 students and measured student unrest by the number of student suspensions from class during a sixteen-month period ending in December, 1973. Dooley found that unrest was not related in any systematic way to differences in academic achievement between black and white students. Thus, Dooley found unimportant a factor reported by Drury as important. (It should be noted that the two researchers were studying different effects.)

Dooley did find some relationships between student unrest and other factors. Most of these relationships hinged on a disparity between black and white perceptions of one another. For example, in relation to students' feelings about themselves, their teachers, and their futures, "a large variance between the perceptions of black and white students in these three areas would seem to presage much unrest while a small variance would seem to indicate a relatively stable situation."[86] He also observed that "re-segregation by choice within the school appears to correlate positively with a high degree of unrest."[87] (Many school people have observed racial patterns in lunchroom seating, which they regard as a situation needing to be changed. Dooley would seem to regard it as a symptom of race relations in the school as a whole.) Uneven patterns of participation in extracurricular activities may be related to student unrest, Dooley reported. A difficulty with this finding is that—as we saw earlier—extracurricular activities very frequently exhibit differential patterns of racial participation. Dooley did not explain why these patterns were linked with unrest in this study.

Charles Bullock III investigated the role of maturation in racial attitudes of eighth, tenth, and twelfth graders in Georgia.[88] His central finding was that "as youngsters progress through high school their racial attitudes increasingly approximate the attitudes they see in both their friends and the community."[89] Bullock assumed that differences in attitudes among the three grades studied at one time were equivalent to attitudes over a five-year period of time. In the earlier grades, student and parent attitudes were similar. By the twelfth grade, however, the correlation dropped for white students while it rose for blacks. Bullock addressed the question of what the school can do about racial attitudes:

Since perceptions of friends' racial attitudes become increasingly important with maturation, and since most teenagers' friends attend the respondents' school, school authorities can play a role in promoting tolerance. To some extent, classes and activities can be structured to facilitate biracial interaction among equals in pursuit of common goals.[90]

Bullock, a major writer in the field, is one of the few who gave attention to the practical implications of his studies.

Richard Ayling examined a desegregated school that was far from being integrated.[91] Nearly every day for four months in 1971–1972, Ayling was in the school. He found administrative overreaction to racial conflict as a norm: "Administrative efforts go toward avoiding situations where black and white students will group. . . ."[92] Administrators even "put an abrupt stop to the establishment of a human relations committee by the student council."[93] Teachers, too, were wary of mixing among students: "In integrated classes teachers make every effort to avoid interracial interaction."[94] In one incident cited by Ayling, "when a teacher did make an attempt to discuss race relations hostile feelings surfaced which caused great concern on the part of the teacher."[95]

Students of different races were strangers to each other: "Black and white students avoid each other completely," Ayling wrote.[96] More of the coolness originated from whites: "Black students are not as consciously aware of whites as whites are of blacks."[97] There was the familiar specialization along racial lines in extracurricular activities. Whites were found principally on the yearbook staff and in dramatics, language, Red Cross, debate, career, and ski clubs. Blacks belonged to the campus NAACP and intramural sports. Some seventy-six black athletes played in varsity sports, nearly all in just four activities: football, basketball, wrestling, and track. Three played baseball and one was on the swimming team; the tennis, golf, and cross-country teams were all-white.

Ayling found few productive relationships in the school. He noted that "three of every five students are absent one day a week and . . . six students are suspended each day."[98] (The total enrollment is 1,800, of which one-quarter is black). On the educational side, Ayling declared, "teachers make minimal demands on the students and the students, in turn, give minimal compliance to the teacher."[99]

Court-ordered desegregation was implemented here in a formal sense only. Stormy circumstances that accompanied that implementation seemed to have frozen the administration into a defensive posture. Having defined peace as the absence of war, the administration believed that they must pursue negative goals of separation in order to keep the lid on a desegregated school. Teachers and students readily found appropriate goals within this novel framework. One can hardly speak of integration in such a context.

Charles Bullock studied the effects of interracial contact on student prejudices.[100] He used a sample of 5,770 students in Georgia, 58 percent white and 42 percent black, and found that whites in desegregated schools were more prejudiced than those in segregated schools. Partly in explanation he noted that his study focused "on schools which were quite reluctant to desegregate and where racial prejudice has been common."[101] Blacks in desegregated schools, on the other hand, were less prejudiced than their peers in segregated schools.

Bullock stressed the importance of contact on attitudes:

From among all the variables used, interracial contact and crossracial friendships were found to be the strongest correlates of racial tolerance. Thus, while other characteristics such as age, grades, or father's occupation influence racial tolerance, personal interaction with students of the other race is more important. While racial tolerance seems to be generally increasing among Georgia's students, it is developing more rapidly among those who develop friendships or have school-related contacts across racial lines.[102]

These attitudes were only slightly affected by the precise racial mix of schools the students attended: prejudice did not vary by degree of racial mix of the school. Bullock found seniors in desegregated schools less prejudiced than eighth graders whereas in segregated schools no such difference emerged.

Most striking to Bullock were "the generally positive racial attitudes that exist among all groups."[103] Fewer than one-seventh of the students revealed prejudices in their responses. It was this wider moderation of southern white attitudes that, in Bullock's view, accounted for the racially positive views recorded by whites in segregated schools. In other words, southern white attitudes in general were changing, but those of southern whites attending desegregated schools were changing more.

Bullock and Joseph Stewart reported a puzzling contrary finding in another study which concluded that "interracial contact in and out of school and friendships with members of the other race do not appear from this analysis to have great effect on students' tolerance of members of another race."[104] Most puzzling is the fact that both studies apparently used the same sample.

During the early 1970s, Lorenzo Thomas, a black poet, was employed by the Texas Commission on the Arts and Humanities to visit desegregated schools in East Texas. Some years earlier he had taught school in the area, so he was familiar with conditions there. He wrote an article about his experiences in desegregated schools in a small town of 5,000 people.[105]

In this atmosphere of face-to-face knowledge and intimacy, Thomas found both black and white students "very concerned about racial issues" but simultaneously repressed and subdued in their feelings toward one another. He attributed this pattern "to the experience of a desegregation process that has been seriously mismanaged by their elders." A number of whites resented black teachers while many blacks adopted militant black-power rhetoric. In some classes, he faced an almost complete black-white split.

The black students, once they discovered that I was not there specifically to talk to them, refused to respond vocally and spent their time chatting among themselves about community gossips. . . . I put them on the spot because it was easy for me to prove that I was (when I wanted to be) much [more] militant than they had ever imagined themselves to be.[106]

Thomas sought especially to encourage black students to lead discussions of black culture and literature and he observed: "In some cases this experience led students to assume greater roles in more general discussions."[107]

To Thomas, teaching in a desegregated school was an educational experience: "I was more interested in helping students use the techniques of creative writing to improve personal communication and I was in a form of 'attitude adjustment'." Yet, he could not ignore the racial aspects of the learning situation. "Progress has been made," he conceded, "but it is imperative that more new, 'for real,' and *effective* programs be designed and instituted to ensure that black and minority students are encouraged to assume the responsible participatory roles that the integration thrust anticipated."[108]

The movement from desegregation to integration is a journey from statistical ratios to cooperation by equals in an atmosphere of mutual respect. Many desegregated classrooms are moving toward the goal of integration. The pace, however, is exceedingly mixed, more often gradual than rapid. Only infrequently do the schools seem mobilized around the task. As researchers consult daily practice more carefully, the promise of school integration will become more concrete. Meanwhile, the reality of unformalized school progress is all the more impressive.

Notes

1. For an analysis of suspensions in Jefferson County, Kentucky, see Nancy L. Arnez, "Implementation of Desegregation as a Discriminatory Process," *Journal of Negro Education*, 47 (Winter 1978), pp. 32–37.

2. For the findings of a wide-ranging study on this, among other factors relating to high schools, see John I. Goodlad, "An Agenda for Improving Our Schools," pp. 12–17, address to the 41st Annual Convention of the National School Board's Association, Dallas, Texas, April 12, 1981.

3. Willie M. J. Curtis and Clifford T. Bennett, "The Role of Self-Concept in Teaching the Black Child and Adolescent: A Critical Appraisal," *Negro Educational Review*, 29 (July–October 1978), p. 218.

4. Charles Wheeler, III, *The Relationship of the Black Pre-School Child's Self Concept to the Degree of Integration and Other Racially Relevant Variables* (doctoral diss., Purdue University, 1974), p. vii. (University Microfilms Order No. 74-26,695.)

5. Mona Williams Thornton, *Racial Attitudes in White Preschoolers: An Exploratory Investigation* (doctoral diss., University of Massachusetts, 1978). (University Microfilms Order No. 7903853.)

6. Ibid., p. 66.

7. Clifford L. Moore, "Racial Preference and Intelligence," *Journal of Psychology*, 199 (1978), p. 42. See also, same author, "The Racial Preference and Attitude of Preschool Black Children," *Journal of Genetic Psychology*, 129 (1976).

8. Ibid., pp. 37–44.

9. Judith H. Langlois and Cookie Stephan, "The Effects of Physical Attractiveness and Ethnicity on Children's Behavioral Attributions and Peer Preferences," *Child Development*, 48 (1977).

10. Ibid., p. 1697.

11. Ibid.

12. Ibid.

13. Ronald J. Lacoste, *Preferences of Three and Four Year Old Children for the Facial Features of the Negro and Caucasian Races When Skin Color is Not a Racial Cue* (doctoral diss., University of Texas, 1975), p. 62. (University Microfilms Order No. 76-8057.)

14. Carole G. Goldstein and others, "Racial Attitudes in Young Children as a Function of Interracial Contact in the Public Schools," *American Journal of Orthopsychiatry*, 49 (January 1979).

15. Ibid., p. 93.

16. Ibid.

17. Ibid.

18. Ibid.

19. See, for example, the research of David Armor.

20. Goldstein and others, "Racial Attitudes in Young Children," pp. 95, 96–97.

21. Ibid., p. 98.

22. See, for example, Benjamin J. Hodgkins and R. S. Stakenas, "A Study of Self-Concepts of Negro and White Youth in Segregated Environments," *Journal of Negro Education*, 38 (1969), pp. 370–77; Kennard White and J. H. Knight, "School Desegregation, Socioeconomic Status, Sex and the Aspirations of Southern Negro Adolescents," *Journal of Negro Education*, 42 (1973), pp. 71–78; and Robert L. Williams and H. Byars, "The Effect of Academic Integration on the Self-Esteem of Southern Negro Students," *Journal of Social Psychology*, 80 (1970), pp. 183–88.

23. Goldstein and others, "Racial Attitudes in Young Children," p. 97.

24. William Clark Estes, *Racial Identification Revisited* (doctoral diss., Wayne State University, 1978). (University Microfilms Order No. 7908908.)

25. Ibid., p. 37.

26. Glen O. Toney, *An Estimate of Racial Attitudes of First Grade Students in Segregated and Desegregated School Environments* (doctoral diss., University of Southern California, 1975), p. 70. (University Microfilms Order No. 75-15,586.)

27. Deborah L. Best and others, "The Modification of Racial Bias in Preschool Children," *Journal of Experimental Child Psychology*, 20 (1975).

28. Ibid., pp. 203-4.

29. Donna A. Boswell and John E. Williams, "Correlates of Race and Color Bias Among Preschool Children," *Psychological Reports*, 36 (1975).

30. Ibid., p. 152.

31. Ibid., p. 153.

32. Janet W. Schofield, "An Exploratory Study of the Draw-a-Person as a Measure of Racial Identity," *Perceptual and Motor Skills*, 46 (1978).

33. Ibid., pp. 317-20.

34. Elaine S. Brand and others, "Ethnic Identification and Preference: A Review," *Psychological Bulletin*, 81 (1974).

35. Ibid., p. 883.

36. Ibid.

37. W. Curtis Banks, "White Preference in Blacks: A Paradigm in Search of a Phenomenon," *Psychological Bulletin*, 83 (1976).

38. Ibid., p. 1179.

39. Ibid., p. 1184.

40. For an analysis of earlier literature, see Meyer Weinberg, *Minority Students: A Research Appraisal* (Washington, D.C.: U.S. Government Printing Office, 1977), pp. 160-68.

41. Nancy Brandon Tuma and Maureen T. Hallinan, "The Effects of Sex, Race, and Achievement on Schoolchildren's Friendships," *Social Forces*, 54 (June 1979).

42. Ibid., p. 1274.

43. Beverley Dobson Jackson, *Social Acceptance and Personal and Social Adjustment Among Integrated Black and White Elementary and Junior High School Students* (doctoral diss., California School of Professional Psychology, 1975). (University Microfilms Order No. 76-10,420.)

44. Ibid., p. 73.

45. Ibid., p. 71.

46. Ibid., p. 72.

47. See especially the work of Irwin Katz, "Review of Evidence Relative to Effects of Desegregation on the Intellectual Performance of Negroes," *American Psychologist*, June 1964 and "Research on Public School Desegregation," *Integrated Education*, August-September 1966.

48. Charles H. McCormick and Robert A. Karbinus, "Relationship of Ethnic Groups' Self-Esteem and Anxiety to School Success," *Education and Psychological Measurement*, 36 (1976).

49. Ibid., p. 1098.

50. Patricia Ann Milazzo, *Busing and Socio-Economic Class: Effects of Enforced Contact on Several Cultural Orientations of Children from Distinct Socio-Economic Classes* (doctoral diss., University of California, Irvine, 1975). (University Microfilms Order No. 76-13,877.)

51. Ibid., p. 118.

52. Claude G. Dulan, *Ethnic Identification and Stereotyping by Black Children*

in Desegregated Elementary Schools (doctoral diss., University of California, Riverside, 1975). (University Microfilms Order No. 78-3918.)

53. Ibid., p. 157.

54. Ibid., p. 108.

55. Ibid., p. 109.

56. Ibid., pp. 122, 124.

57. Steven R. Asher and Louise C. Singleton, "Cross-Race Acceptance in Integrated Schools," *Integrateducation*, 16 (September–October 1978) pp. 17–20.

58. Ibid.

59. See Weinberg, *Minority Students: A Research Appraisal*, pp. 148–54.

60. Donald E. Carter and others, "Peer Acceptance and School-Related Variables in an Integrated Junior High School," *Journal of Educational Psychology*, 67 (April 1975) pp. 267–73.

61. Ibid., p. 271.

62. Francis Terrell, "Dialectal Differences Between Middle-Class Black and White Children Who Do and Do Not Associate with Lower-Class Black Children," *Language and Speech*, 18 (January–March 1975), pp. 65–73.

63. Ibid., p. 71.

64. Robert Elliot Young, *Interethnic Behavior in Desegregated Secondary Schools* (doctoral diss., Columbia University, 1975). (University Microfilms Order No. 75-13,917.)

65. Ibid., p. 147.

66. Ibid., p. 110.

67. Ibid., p. 112.

68. Ibid., pp. 118–19.

69. Ibid., pp. 134–35.

70. Ibid., p. 143.

71. Cheryl B. Travis and Sharon E. Anthony, "Some Psychological Consequences of Integration," *Journal of Negro Education*, 47 (Spring 1978).

72. Ibid., p. 154.

73. Ibid., p. 155.

74. Ibid., p. 156.

75. Ibid., p. 157.

76. Elizabeth E. McAdams, *Relationship Between School Integration and School Morale* (doctoral diss., George Peabody College for Teachers, 1974). (University Microfilms Order No. 74-29,178.)

77. Ibid., p. 63.

78. Ibid., p. 68.

79. Darrel W. Drury, "Black Self-Esteem and Desegregated Schools," *Sociology of Education*, 53 (April 1980).

80. Ibid., p. 98.

81. Ibid., p. 99.

82. Ibid.

83. Ibid., p. 100.

84. Ibid., p. 101.

85. Bernard J. Dooley, *The Relationship Between the Quality of Integration and the Level of Student Unrest in Six High Schools of a Desegregated School District* (doctoral diss., University of Miami, 1974). (University Microfilms Order No. 75-4152.)

86. Ibid., p. 118.

87. Ibid.

88. Charles S. Bullock, III, "Maturation and Changes in the Correlates of Racial Attitudes," *Urban Education*, 12 (July 1977).

89. Ibid., p. 234.

90. Ibid., p. 236.

91. Richard H. Ayling, *An Exploratory Study of the Formal and Informal Relationships between Black and White Students in a Large Racially Mixed, Urban High School* (doctoral diss., Michigan State University, 1972). (University Microfilms Order No. 73-5320.)

92. Ibid., p. 147.

93. Ibid., p. 151.

94. Ibid., p. 147.

95. Ibid., p. 137.

96. Ibid., p. 122.

97. Ibid., p. 151.

98. Ibid., p. 78.

99. Ibid., p. 116.

100. Charles S. Bullock, III, "Interracial Contact and Student Prejudice. The Impact of Southern School Desegregation," *Youth and Society*, 7 (March 1976).

101. Ibid., p. 304.

102. Ibid., pp. 306-7.

103. Ibid., p. 304.

104. Charles S. Bullock, III and Joseph Stewart, Jr., "Perceived Parental and Student Racial Attitudes," *Integrateducation*, 15 (November-December 1977), pp. 121-22.

105. Lorenzo Thomas, "Creativity and Stress in Recently Integrated Schools," *Freedomways*, 15 (Third Quarter 1975), p. 222.

106. Ibid., p. 224.

107. Ibid., p. 225.

108. Ibid.

9

Mexican Americans and American Indians

Mexican Americans

Research interest in Mexican-American life and history is rising, especially among Mexican-American researchers. Seven separate research areas are discussed in the following pages: (1) history, (2) social mobility and assimilation, (3) community power, (4) reading problems, (5) Mexican-American literature, (6) higher education, and (7) desegregation. Virtually all the studies are buried in doctoral dissertations, and few of their findings have yet found their way into articles or books.

History

Three works deal exclusively with the development of the Mexican-American community in Los Angeles.

Griswold del Castillo discusses the impact of the American conquest of California (1846–1848) on the life of Spanish-speaking persons in Los Angeles in the years from 1850 to 1880. During this period, the group declined in economic and social position:

Their occupational structure stagnated as upward mobility into new occupations was limited and as older occupations declined. The bulk of the Spanish speaking experienced downward property mobility as their real and personal holdings dwindled in size and number. Due to discrimination and depression, upward socioeconomic mobility was severely limited and by 1880 the Chicanos were an economic minority.[1]

In 1844, nearly three out of four working Chicanos were employed as unskilled laborers. The proportion remained essentially unchanged up to 1880.

Under American rule, the Chicano middle class remained underdeveloped and the tiny upper class declined in size. While the city as a whole developed an expanding economy, few of its fruits were shared by Chicanos.

A Spanish-language public school was permitted until 1853, but after that date all-English schools were organized; they were taught by Anglos. During the years 1850 to 1880, Chicano children made up from 25 percent to 40 percent of all students, comparable with the Anglo enrollment, which ranged around 40 percent. Three times during the 1850s parents petitioned municipal authorities to conduct a bilingual school, but each time the request was turned down. In 1861, a Roman Catholic school was opened and conducted in both languages. In 1870, what Griswold calls "the first bilingual secondary school in the state was organized under Catholic auspices."[2] The public school board had only three Mexican-American members over a period of 120 years.

Chicano literacy was low. In 1880, less than one-fourth of Spanish-speaking adults, as compared with some 85 percent of the state as a whole, were reportedly literate. Griswold stresses the non-comparability of Mexican Americans and European immigrants: "The Europeans came as landless foreigners hoping to adapt themselves to the American culture while the Chicanos were a conquered people who were forced to confront a foreign culture that had invaded their ancestral lands."[3] During the last half of the nineteenth century, Chicanos were all but excluded from public life. Three out of 194 lawyers admitted to the bar between 1887 and 1900 were Chicano. Between 1887 and 1896, only eight of over 2,000 persons on federal juries in Los Angeles had Spanish surnames. Meanwhile, as a reflection of their dissatisfaction, the equivalent of nearly one-fifth the entire Chicano population voluntarily returned to Mexico to stay during the period from 1850 to 1890.

A *barrio*, an area of concentrated Chicano residence, grew rapidly from 1850 to 1880. This was the obverse of another development: growing exclusion of Chicanos from Anglo society. By 1880, more than one-third of all Chicanos would have had to move in order to create a population distribution representative of the ethnic distribution of the city as a whole.[4] Chicano participation in politics was the property of "scions of the older families, who had proved their loyalty to the Anglo-American majority."[5]

The Catholic Church increasingly took on the appearance of a foreign church. Priests and prelates were Spanish, French, or Italian; none was Mexican. Church officials were oriented toward the wealthy and politically powerful. When a second Catholic church was built in 1876, it became exclusively Anglo while the older church became Chicano. Informal religious elements prospered among the people, sometimes in secret. Spiritual healers, *curanderos*, operated widely near the surface of Chicano lower-class society. Fiestas, unsanctioned by the Church, prospered.

Despite internal conflicts of economic class and social consciousness, the Chicanos developed "their own unique social responses which enabled them to survive as a culture."[6]

Ricardo Romo studied Los Angeles during the years 1915 to 1930, with special emphasis on the Mexican-American worker. He noted, at the outset, a difficulty in discovering primary sources: "English-language newspapers such as the *Los Angeles Times* ignored much of the community activities of the Mexican population."[7]

As the central business district of the city grew, houses in adjacent poor neighborhoods were eliminated. Mexican-American workers followed expanding industry into the suburbs where they established new barrios or *colonias*. Numerous third-generation workers who remained in the city were employed in white-collar pursuits. As Romo notes, however, all worked as clerks and "none in the ranks of proprietor, semi-professional, or professional ranks."[8] Indeed, he adds: "Only a small percentage of the first, second and third generation Mexicanos found opportunities in the skilled trades and professions."[9] There was little upward mobility.

Residential dispersion increased somewhat from 1918 to 1925, diminishing to some extent the cultural cohesion of the community. On the other hand, three institutions helped maintain that cohesion. One was the Mexican consulate, which represented to many persons a protector against American injustice. Another was the Spanish-language press. A third was the great number of voluntary associations of a cultural, economic, self-help, and recreational character. The schools' Americanization program was a highly negative factor in developing community interests as it "attempted not only to change the Mexican's standard of living, without improving his income, but also to convince him to shed completely such cultural baggage as language and customs."[10]

Gilbert George Gonzalez studied the decade of the 1920s with a major emphasis on the public schools. He summarizes much of his work in a simple formulation: "For the Mexican child, a hostile, at times liberal, society looking forward found ways to socialize him or her but not necessarily to make the child a social equal."[11]

The twenties were a crucial period for the education of Chicano children. In the three years from 1923 to 1926 alone their proportion in the city's public schools rose from 8.8 percent to 11.5 percent.[12] Fatefully, the twenties also witnessed the blooming of the IQ test. Judging from the test results for 1928 to 1929, Gonzalez writes: "Nearly three fourths of all children who scored below 70 were from either a foreign or semi-foreign neighborhood."[13] "Foreign" meant, of course, Mexican. After analysis of the 1931 test results, Gonzalez concluded: "There was a very high probability that nearly one-half of the Mexican children would find themselves placed in slow-learner rooms and development centers."[14]

How limited was the educational effect of development centers is underscored by Gonzalez's finding: "The development rooms produced unskilled labor for the economy. Of the 325 who graduated from the development centers in 1928–29, 65 were working in agriculture as fruit pickers, 60 sold newspapers, and the remainder scattered over a wide range of unskilled manual occupations."[15] These centers had their analogues in other cities and other minority groups.

Studies of Santa Barbara, California; Texas; and New Mexico have been made in three separate works.

Albert Michael Camarillo examined the development of the Chicano community in Santa Barbara from 1850 to 1930. During the first half or so of this period, Chicanos constituted considerably more than half the city's population. This fact was reflected in the schools.

The sparse public schooling available before 1855 had been conducted in Spanish only; a state ruling of that year required English-only instruction. This meant little in Santa Barbara, where the change produced a single English-only class for Anglo children. When financial stringencies brought about a merger of the two kinds of classes, bilingual instruction was to begin. Anglo parents, however, took their children out of the school, where they represented only one-third of enrollment. In 1858, a parochial bilingual school was organized that permitted Anglo students to receive English instruction.

There was a confluence of strong forces in the Chicano community during the mid-1870s. A national economic depression affected Chicanos severely. The rising Anglo presence and domination in Santa Barbara brought new stresses. As the historic pastoral economy receded and was replaced by new industries and employments, the Chicano community found itself unprepared and unwelcome. Political and social isolation became the new norm. "After 1873," writes Camarillo,

political insignificance, occupational dislocation, residential segregation, social ostracism from Anglo society, and increasing impoverishment characterized the conditions of the evolving Chicano community. By 1890, the depressed socioeconomic and political position of the Spanish-surnamed people in Anglo Santa Barbara determined the status of the Chicano community for future generations.[16]

In 1874, for example, the boundaries of the heavily Chicano Third Ward were redrawn to make it even more Chicano, and citywide elections were changed to ward elections. This minimized the impact of the Chicano vote. It is not surprising, therefore, that an Anglo mayor was elected for the first time in 1874. Soon, Chicanos lost nearly all direct governmental power. "Without political, judicial, and law enforcement representatives," writes Camarillo, "the Chicano people were defenseless against Anglo racism."[17] Anglo physical assaults upon Chicanos went unpunished.

In the 1880s, spreading poverty forced women and children into the labor market to supplement meager paternal incomes. They often replaced low-paid Chinese laborers as almond pickers and shellers. "Chicano children who worked in both [Fall and Winter] harvests were usually absent from school until February," writes Camarillo.[18] Some picked olives. Orchard operators increased child employment, despite state labor laws. In 1911, the California Labor Commission reported that "so many children [were] in the orchards that the schools were all but depopulated."[19] The state began to demand that operators cease their illegal use of child labor. "During the following walnut picking season," according to Camarillo, "the president of the Walnut Growers Association threatened to use Japanese labor if an extension of summer vacation was not granted to the native Chicanitos." The Growers Association obtained a decision from the Superior Court which in 1912 held that "if a family pleaded hardship, children could work."[20] Nine years later, the Growers Association signed an agreement with the county school board permitting children of adult laborers to enroll temporarily in the Goleta schools; such children were allowed to work in the fields outside school hours.[21]

Ethnic separation inside Santa Barbara grew during the latter years of the period under study: "The Bath House or swimming pool located on the beach excluded Chicanos, especially the darker-skinned ones. Some of the theaters required, by rule or by gentle persuasion, that 'visible' Chicanos (the *prietos*) sit together with other people of color in a segregated section."[22] During the 1920s, members of the local Ku Klux Klan paraded brazenly through public streets, not even bothering to wear masks.[23]

Arnoldo De Leon studied Anglo racial attitudes toward Mexicanos in Texas from 1821 to 1900. Throughout this long period, dating from Mexico's revolt for independence from Spain, a firm racist conception of Mexicanos took shape among Anglo-Texans. In De Leon's words:

First, white men convinced themselves that Mexicanos were going nowhere. Then, placing a cultural gulf so vast between themselves and Mexicans, they determined that Mexicanos could never really get anywhere. And by speaking of Mexicans as lazy, indolent, stupid, ignorant, present-minded, and fun-loving, they justified the imposition of social mores that relegated Mexicans to a place outside the American cultural milieu. And then, blaming that subjugation on the Mexican nature itself, and thinking of Mexicanos as unworthy entities in this world of theirs, they took advantage of their "indolence" to insure white supremacy.[24]

During these years, Anglo contempt led to widespread lynching of Mexicanos without any legal penalty. After an initial period of development, the Texas Rangers, according to De Leon, became "a legal corps that enjoyed the legal consent and tacit sanction of the white community to do to Mexicans what others were doing extralegally."[25]

Before the Civil War, *Tejanos* (Mexicans from Texas) in general opposed the institution of slavery and this became another issue of conflict with the Anglos. In some cases they helped fugitive slaves to escape to Mexico. During the Civil War itself, Mexicanos, in cooperation with federal soldiers, harassed Confederate troops. After the war, many Mexicanos regarded themselves as radicals in the reconstruction struggles. "They concurred," according to De Leon, "with Republican advocacy of general suffrage without distinction of race or color, and criticized the conservatives for their attempts to form a white man's party, especially as they were attempting it with the assistance of the privileged Mexican population, which, if successful, would disfranchise both the [poor] Mexican and black element."[26] (Eventually, blacks were disfranchised, but De Leon reports that disfranchisement of poor Mexicanos, although "attempted many times, never came to pass.")[27]

A spectacular event in 1894 placed a sudden strain on the long tradition of Mexican-black cooperation. In that year, a riot broke out in Beeville between the two groups. For several years, blacks had been forced to compete against increasing numbers of unskilled Mexicano laborers willing to work for lower wages than the blacks received. Now, in the midst of a very severe national economic depression, blacks in Beeville protested in a raid upon a Mexicano living area. Whites, De Leon notes, supported the Mexicanos in the conflict.

In the eight decades after 1821, the Mexicano had come to be viewed as an inferior human being, fitted by his inferiority to work for exceedingly low wages. Segregation and substandard public services accompanied this seemingly fixed status.

Robert Johnson Rosenbaum has analyzed the course of Mexicano resistance to Anglo dominance in New Mexico during 1870–1900.

In San Miguel County an armed Mexicano resistance movement arose, known as *Las Gorras Blancas*, or the White Caps. It stood, if vaguely, for a defense of Mexicano cultural rights and against exploitation by Anglo or Mexicano elites. After the American conquest of 1846 to 1848, a small group of the latter had cooperated with Anglo governing forces. The Americans excelled in becoming office holders and organizing new kinds of economic enterprises. "Some powerful native New Mexicans," writes Rosenbaum, "were officers of banks, railroad corporations and mining companies. They probably gained these positions because of their political influence rather than their capital investment or technical expertise."[28]

The White Caps articulated a popular sentiment for ethnic solidarity while rejecting any racist conceptions. In Las Vegas, they posted a sign: "We are down on race issues, and will watch race agitators. We are all human brethren, under the same glorious flag."[29]

Education was another popular issue the White Caps dealt with. Public schools were all but unknown in the years from 1870 to 1900. The few wealthy Mexicanos, or *ricos*, "sent their children to private schools in Santa Fe and perhaps on to St. Louis University or Notre Dame."[30] The two greatest obstacles to public education were not the poverty of New Mexico Territory but the attitudes of the *ricos* and the Catholic Church. *"Educar un muchacho es perder un buen pastor"*—"To educate a boy is to lose a good shepherd"—said one *rico*.[31] Nor did the aristocratic *ricos* wish to help pay for educating the poor.

To the Catholic hierarchy, public education was Protestant—that is to say, non-Catholic—and thus repulsive. Catholic prelates lobbied success-

fully against the creation of a meaningful public school system. Archbishop
J. B. Salpointe charged that nonsectarian schooling was "in reality either
sectarian, non-religious, godless, or agnostic."[32] All were equally bad.
Protestant zealots, for their part, were no less dogmatic. W. S. Burke,
editor of the *Albuquerque Daily Journal*, equated the Catholic Church with
the practice of polygamy in nearby Utah: "They require precisely the same
treatment, and there are but two remedies—the one being the sword and the
other the schoolhouse. I favor the latter as more consonant with our institution, our religion and our civilization."[33]

In time, according to Rosenbaum, the advent of state-financed public
schools had less to do with the White Caps than with three factors unrelated
to the protestors. One was the eagerness of territorial leaders to gain
congressional approval for statehood; low literacy rates were among the
criticisms congressmen brought up in early attempts at statehood. Another
was the rising demand for schools voiced by Anglos as they settled in the
territory. Still another was the attraction of patronage opportunities to be
had in a statewide system of public education.

It is all but impossible to summarize six historical works in a few pages.
The six works, however, share certain characteristics. They deal with principal areas of Mexican-American settlement (California, Texas, and New
Mexico) and thus are representative in a geographical sense. A central emphasis is the subordinate economic and political position of Mexican Americans in every community; each also touches on the presence of a very small
privileged subgroup. Education is portrayed as heavily dependent on the
social structure of the given area. Segregation and planned deprivation in
the schools were part of communitywide patterns. Each study is concerned
fundamentally with understanding how—or whether—the contemporary
Mexican-American culture evolved from the historic Mexicano experience.

Most of the six researchers document to a degree the persistence of Mexicano cultural patterns well after the midcentury American conquest. At
the same time, they stress the effect of racism in stimulating an in-group
feeling. Griswold del Castillo declares: "Had the development of Spanish-
speaking culture depended only on persecution . . . it would have disappeared in a short time."[34] Yet, without exception, the six researchers
devote far more space to persecution than to cultural life. Consequently,
their accounts of culture sometimes strike the reader as ethnology without
ethnography. But, in the main, their accounts add greatly to the reader's
understanding of the evolution of modern Mexican Americans and their
efforts to educate their children.

Social Mobility and Assimilation

Throughout the historical works reviewed above, the topics of social
mobility and assimilation are frequently linked. In New Mexico Territory,
for example, a tiny group of affluent Mexicanos was accepted by Anglo
elites and, in time, came to resemble the new dominant forces in that

nineteenth-century society. At the same time, it is observed that the historic culture persisted among the poorest Mexicanos. In other words, upward social mobility is associated with the discarding of Mexicano ways. In the absence of detailed historical studies of this process we are able only to examine several social science explorations of the contemporary scene. Researchers have studied this subject in California, Arizona, Texas, and New Mexico.

Two studies concern Arizona, one in Tucson the other in Phoenix.

Jacqueline Joann Taylor, in Tucson, addressed two questions: "(1) What happens to ethnicity in an upwardly mobile population of definable ethnics? (2) Is there an ethnic mobility system which differs in some respects from the dominant mobility system?" She interviewed thirty-five upwardly mobile Mexican Americans and a slightly larger group of Mexican-American university students. Mexican Americans in Tucson make up nearly one-sixth of the population; about three-quarters of them live in a fairly concentrated area.

The older sample of thirty-five persons was not typical of the city's Mexican Americans. Two-thirds were college graduates; another six had some college education. A third were educators. Two-thirds of their parents had been skilled or unskilled laborers.

Of the thirty-five, twenty-one grew up in Tucson. Their experience in the public schools was not encouraging, as Taylor points out: "In elementary school, many had experiences—which are vividly remembered to this day—of being punished or humiliated by Anglo teachers for using Spanish in class or on the playground. Many regarded Anglo teachers with some apprehension."[35] The high schools had not been any more pleasant:

Many of the urban residents spoke of school counseling as discouraging. Several . . . had been put on vocational tracks and . . . told . . . they were not college material. . . . The urban high schools . . . did not provide a milieu that encouraged achievement. . . . The incidence of tracking or counseling [for] vocational training was . . . highest among women. . . . Other factors . . . include[d] segregation, which was reinforced by the school counseling program, and limited participation of Mexican Americans in extracurricular activities and student government.[36]

During late adolescence, their prevailing educational goal was to complete high school and thereby gain a "steady job."

The upwardly mobile group was divided equally on the importance of speaking Spanish. Since they live all over the city, "mothers must make an effort to find Spanish-speaking playmates for their children."[37] For a number of mobile persons, a traditional loyalty to family remains so strong that it moderates the mobility: "In order to take full advantage of wider opportunities, Mexican Americans may have to move to other urban areas. Many are unwilling to leave their families, particularly aging parents. In not becoming geographically mobile, they limit occupational chances to some extent."[38] It is these less mobile persons who tend more to maintain Mexican customs and visit Mexico with some frequency.

"Being Mexican" is not necessarily regarded as a limitation on mobility. Those of darker skin seemed at least as mobile as persons of lighter hue. As Taylor points out: "Confident Mexican Americans who perceive themselves as visibly ethnic may be high achievers and may seek public office or other conspicuous positions."[39]

The sample of Mexican-American college students differs significantly from the other group surveyed. Over a third of them, for example, graduated from parochial schools; in the first group only one-fifth did. Eight out of ten had siblings attending college. At the same time, nearly nine out of ten had fathers who were skilled or unskilled laborers, or worked in service or sales occupations. In the city as a whole in 1970, somewhat over one-ninth the Spanish-surnamed population had completed one or more years of college. In the college sample group, however, nearly all had friends who were also college students. At the university, where until the 1960s Mexican-American students were excluded from fraternities or sororities, they are now permitted to join with Anglos. Taylor doubts that this means the end of discrimination on campus: "The climate of the university is different for Mexican Americans than it is for Anglos."[40]

Taylor concludes that Mexican Americans' upward mobility, at least in a moderated form, is not inconsistent with their ethnic identity. Adjustments in career choices, though they bring higher incomes and more interaction with Anglos, also are made in the interest of maintaining ethnic ties. Thus, assimilation is not necessarily the end of the road for those seeking a higher social status. The mobility system of Tucson's upwardly mobile Mexican Americans is distinctive. Its goals are modest and its approach genteel.

Eugene Acosta Marin studied certain aspects of the Mexican-American community in Phoenix. He was interested in its relations with the Anglo community as well as in its internal divisions. The sample was made up of 417 Mexican Americans who were active in ten civic organizations and 375 Anglos who represented the dominant social group in the city's affairs. Over half the former and over three-quarters of the latter were college graduates. Three-fifths of the Mexican-American sample had attended a grade school which was entirely or predominantly Mexican American. Nearly all the Anglo leaders had attended grade schools in which there were few or no Mexican Americans. On the whole, there was a high degree of correspondence between the political attitudes of the two samples. When asked whether it was advisable to allow more Mexicans to enter the country to seek jobs, half the Mexican Americans and three-quarters of the Anglos answered in the negative. To a question about the advisability of greater political cooperation between Mexican Americans, blacks, and American Indians, over four-fifths of the Anglos and about three-fifths of the Mexican Americans replied in the negative.

An internal division revolved around the matter of a label, as between

"Chicano" and "Mexican American." The division was substantial and not a mere matter of words. Acosta Marin reports that self-designated " 'Chicanos' see social unrest as desirable and advantageous to the aggrandizement of Mexican Americans, but 'Mexican Americans' see social unrest as undesirable."[41] Those in the sample identifying themselves as Mexican Americans tended to be older and were more favorably inclined toward Anglos. Acosta Marin regards the internal split as of secondary importance. In all, then, the study shows little if any possible causal interrelationship between upward social mobility and assimilation.

Patterns of social mobility among middle-class Mexican Americans in four Texas cities were analyzed by Raymond Herman Charles Teske, Jr. He studied 151 subjects in Waco, McAllen, Austin, and Lubbock and found that upward social mobility had occurred mainly in the second or third generation. Well over half the respondents were the first in their families to have achieved middle-class status; more than eight out of ten came from lower-class or working-class families. In all four cities, upwardly mobile middle-class persons tended to identify more strongly with and interact more with members of their ethnic group the more they perceived prejudice and discrimination against their group.

Social mobility was found to be related to perception of discrimination. Teske reports that "in communities where there is a limited middle-class Mexican American population and relatively greater perceived prejudice and discrimination by Anglos, the rates of upward mobility are comparatively lower."[42] City-to-city differences were apparent in numerous measures. This led Teske to deny the existence of a general pattern of collective assimilation for middle-class persons; nor could he find any evidence of a distinctive middle-class Mexican American subculture as such. (The finding could hardly be otherwise since no class group other than the middle class was studied. Therefore, no comparative conclusion can be reached.)

Nevertheless, certain principles were evident in Teske's data. The likelihood of a young Mexican American leaning toward assimilation into Anglo society was heightened when that person had understood English upon entering school or lacked a Spanish accent. "Looking Mexican" operated against assimilation. The ethnic character of childhood playmates was of some significance in determining assimilation in later life.

Actually, Teske writes not of assimilation as such but of three separate scales constituting a measure of assimilation. These are interaction with Mexican Americans, interaction with Anglos, and Mexican-American identity. Responses from the 151 interviewees are broken down by four cities on three scales. The whole picture becomes highly complex and fractionated. Characteristics are true of one scale in one of the cities but not of another scale in the same city. No wonder Teske arrives at very few general findings on the issue of status mobility and assimilation.

Diane Adele Trombetta Reynolds, in a study in San Jose, California, considered the "relationship between the economic integration of a

Mexican American individual in U.S. urban society . . . and his accul-
turation and assimilation to U.S. society and culture as a whole.''[43] She
studied twenty-four persons of Mexican-American background, aged eighteen to twenty-five years, who were enrolled in a single job rehabilitation
program; and ten staff members in the same program. Each informant was
interviewed for four hours.

Trombetta Reynolds found that there was no consistent relationship
between economic adaptation and cultural assimilation. Staff members had
"made it" economically, and in many respects such as language, dress, and
recreation, they were assimilated. Yet, "in the areas of social interaction,
intermarriage, models for behavior, personal friendships and articulated
values, ties to Mexican ethnicity are strong and apparent.''[44] She concluded
that upwardly mobile individuals "will assimilate behaviorally and ideo-
logically in areas they perceive necessary to such success.''[45]

The students, whose average age was almost twenty, were apparently
downwardly mobile. Fifteen of the twenty-four had blue-collar fathers and
one or more parents had supported the families regularly. But the students
were chronically unemployed. While the program formally aimed at job
rehabilitation, students viewed it as "easy money." They had only to attend
and collect their stipend. One could hardly speak of the students seeking
any "place in society other than as a way of survival." This fact had no
connection with their ethnic character except for the probable discrimination experienced by them in their earlier job searches.

The resarcher reached an unusual conclusion about the staff. She noted
that they "emphasized . . . their desire to be accepted and treated by everyone as individual persons rather than primarily as Mexican Americans.''[46]
This led her "to believe that with elimination of social and economic barriers to participation with Anglo Americans, these staff members and others
like them would be likely to lose many of the ethnic ties they now maintain.''[47] Already, she holds, the informants are highly acculturated. The
future may well complete the process. (Too much faith, however, should
not be lodged in the future. David Emmett Hayes-Bautista has studied a
process of "disassimilation" whereby young medical professionals in
training, who had little consciousness of being Chicano, go on to develop
just such a new self-conception.)[48]

Thomas R. Lopez, Jr. presents the most pessimistic, but probably a real-
istic, perspective on prospects for the Spanish-American culture in New
Mexico. He stresses the need to confront the great poverty of Spanish
Americans rather than what he calls a "sentimental commitment to preserv-
ing a culture apart from solving . . . dire economic problems. . . .''[49] The
Roman Catholic Church, one of the historic bases of traditional culture in
New Mexico, is, according to Lopez, shunting the poor aside:

Spanish Americans are among the least able to pay tuition costs or financially support the parishes and [parochial] schools; the schools particularly are rapidly becom-

ing the domain of middle-class, Catholic Anglos. . . . It would appear that the Spanish American population on the basis of financial considerations . . . [is] being "written off" . . . by parochial schools.[50]

The Spanish-American poor, Lopez writes, are hardly interested in the problems of retaining a particular "culture" but are consumed by their economic problems. He holds that the principal sustaining force of traditional culture in the state is the social and geographical isolation of the people. "The pervasive and continuing isolation of Spanish Americans," declares Lopez, "may be attributable to two interrelated factors: economic deprivation and racism, i.e., the complex of attitudes and practices which make ethnic and racial consideration important in society."[51] As the geographical isolation gives way before urbanization, it is replaced by ethnic segregation in the schools and other urban institutions. Willy-nilly, therefore, the future of traditional culture will be secure, predicts Lopez, because of "(1) the absence of a national commitment to eliminate poverty and (2) the failure to foster human diversity and cultural pluralism seriously and deliberately."[52] Yet, even within this bleak context, he believes "schools can positively contribute to American pluralism by being models of pluralism through a professional commitment to educating children for competence across cultures."[53]

Community Power

About seventy-five miles south of San Antonio, Texas, and about 125 miles north of the Mexican border lie the towns of Pearsall and Cotulla. Pearsall, with a 1970 population of 11,159, and Cotulla, with 15,014 people, are some twenty-five miles apart. The population of the county in which Pearsall is located is over two-thirds Mexican American, and that of the county in which Cotulla is located is over three-fourths Mexican American. Between November, 1972, and January, 1974, Donald Post studied the efforts of Anglos and Mexican Americans to retain or gain control over the public schools in the towns. He interviewed 146 persons.

The schools in both towns have done little for Mexican Americans, whose academic achievement lags two or three years behind that of Anglos. "The school system," Post writes, "primarily operates on behalf of an Anglo minority. This further enhances the Anglos' dominance of the economic sphere and retards the Spanish-surnames' involvement socially and economically. . . ."[54] Anglo dominance was traditional inside the schools, as well. In Cotulla, for example, until the late 1960s when Mexican Americans became the majority, they were all but excluded from certain key student extracurricular activities. In Pearsall's high school, "Anglos continued to control the organizational sector of school life," even into the early 1970s, although Mexican Americans had for more than two decades been the majority.[55] A school board rule forbidding the use of Spanish on the campus was not rescinded until June, 1972.

Historically, the Anglos were dominant in economic life, comprising almost all the landowners. Mexican Americans were primarily low-paid laborers on farms. Economic and political subordination was nearly complete. Extreme poverty was widespread; nearly four out of ten families in Cotulla were on welfare. The city council was traditionally Anglo until the 1970s. The few Mexican-American businessmen who were invited to join the Pearsall Rotary Club and the Chamber of Commerce, Post observed, "exhibited subordinate behavior when in the presence of Anglos, that is, . . . downcast eyes, excessive amount of smiling, agreeability, humbleness, and so forth."[56]

Mexican-American elementary schools were traditionally segregated; one, in Pearsall, remained segregated until 1970. Post reports:

Some informants described the manner in which, historically, Anglos allocated the "used" school resources to the Mexican American and black schools. In the board minutes for September 1953, the board sent used desks to the black school. Mexicanos point out that in the past if they "accidentally" got a good teacher from out-of-town, that teacher was inevitably transferred to the Anglo school.[57]

None of the respondents could recall a time when the elementary schools were not segregated.

Anglo control of the Pearsall schools is still effective and pervasive, although, as discussed below, it is being challenged. Mexican Americans usually regard the public schools as "their schools," that is, as belonging to the Anglos. Drawing on his interviews, Post describes several examples:

The Mexican American school leaders are aware that local Anglos make the least desirable teachers for Mexican children because they tend to broker local Anglo culture regarding Anglo cultural superiority, yet these teachers are given preference in hiring. . . . Mexican Americans tell numerous stories concerning the covert, and overt, manners in which Mexican American students have been told they are dumb. . . . When the Mexican Americans acquired a plurality of the [high school] student body [the Anglo response] was to create a parallel system of awards. . . . To parallel the elite status of Mr. and Mrs. Pearsall High School the Anglos set up a Senor and Senorita position. In 1968 the Mexican American students refused to participate in this process and it was dropped.[58]

During the 1960s, Anglo control of the schools began to weaken under the combined impact of two sets of powerful forces. The first was the new federal school legislation with accompanying mandatory guidelines. This legislation included compensatory education as well as desegregation. State regulation became more stringent as the Texas Education Agency was compelled, for financial reasons, to exercise closer supervision. Moreover, in a sweeping statewide decision of a desegregation case in which it was a plaintiff, the Texas Education Agency was designated as agent of the federal court to monitor the implementation of the court's order. A new statewide teachers' organization made itself felt on new state legislation. A second set of forces can be summed up as the rise of Mexican-American leadership. The latter was still being exercised haltingly in Pearsall late into 1973.

Cotulla's schools have not differed appreciably from those of Pearsall. Before World War II, there seemed little point in young Mexican Americans attending high school and less so college, but today the situation has changed a great deal. Post states: "It would be safe to describe the contemporary Mexican American parental population as viewing schooling as the most viable means to upward social and economic mobility."[59] Most Mexican-American teachers in Cotulla are reported to see their role as one of accommodating assimilation of their students into the Anglo system rather than as fostering the development of an autonomous cultural group.

Changes in the traditional order were brokered by two groups in Cotulla: veterans from World War II and migrant laborers. The former were less willing to resume their historical roles, having experienced more egalitarian treatment in the armed forces. Migrant laborers were economically dependent on the Anglos but they were not permanent parts of the local social order. Thus, they felt freer to strike out in independent political directions. Also, an important external impetus to collective action came from Crystal City, a nearby town where Chicanos had formed Le Raza Unida Party (RUP) and had brought about a complete change in control of the city government and school board. As early as 1969, RUP members began visiting Cotulla regularly. They "conducted rallies and staged dramas depicting local Anglos as oppressors."[60]

In 1970, the Cotulla RUP's mayoral candidate won along with several city council candidates. Two RUP school board members were also elected; two years later, another two joined the board. So tense was the atmosphere during the 1972 elections that the high school employed police to patrol the halls in order to prevent physical violence between Chicanos and Anglo students. Elections the following year swept all RUP candidates out of city office.

Prior to 1973, writes Post, "most Anglos in Pearsall believed that 'their Mexicans' were not like those of Crystal City."[61] That year, however, for the first time in the town's history, Mexican Americans ran candidates for a range of offices, won two school board positions, and almost gained the mayoralty. As in Cotulla, the tenseness of the political confrontation was reflected in student behavior inside the schools.

"School leaders," observes Post, "are the subordinates within a local power domain."[62] As the ethnic conflict sharpened in both towns, school officials toed the line and had less latitude to express their own views and enforce their own policies. But Post also comments that the Chicano students in Cotulla may well complete the task begun by their elders. When he had finished his study, it appeared to Post that the students were well on their way to mobilizing Mexican-American voters to capture the school board.

Reading Problems

Edward Joseph Casavantes, who was a social science analyst for the U.S. Commission on Civil Rights' Mexican American Education Study, explored various aspects of reading achievement and nonpromotion policies for Mexican-American and black students. (Unfortunately, the reading scores used by Casavantes are only principals' estimates but he believed there was a high probability of accuracy.)

"It can *conservatively be said*," contends Casavantes, "that two years of effective achievement can be subtracted from the 'year of education' figures of the census to arrive at a more accurate picture of the true educational level of Chicanos today."[63] In Texas, even among those Chicano students who remained in high school after 47 percent of their Chicano classmates dropped out, nearly two out of three read below grade level.

Casavantes doubts that anything of educational value was gained by holding back low-scoring minority students. In Texas, for example, the nonpromotion rate for Chicano children in grade four is half again as large as the rate in California. Yet, the California children do not read any more poorly than Texas youngsters. In both states, Mexican-American children are nonpromoted at a higher rate than Anglo children. Casavantes notes that in the literature of nonpromotion he failed to find a single study of the subject that deals with minority children.

Researchers have studied the frequently observed drop in academic achievement over the school summer vacation. A common finding is that children from poor homes often suffer the greatest loss. Andrea Frieder-Vierra investigated the issue in Albuquerque, New Mexico. She was interested in minority and nonminority children, but in addition divided the former into those who lived in the barrio and those who did not. Finally, all the children were analyzed in terms of income group. A total of 746 Chicano and Anglo fourth, fifth, and sixth graders made up the sample. The study was conducted during the 1972–1973 school year. There were too few low-income Anglo children to compare with the more plentiful low-income Chicano children.

Specifically, Frieder-Vierra wanted to know whether "the difference in reading achievement between certain groups of children increases more rapidly over the summer than during the school year."[64] Assuming, in other words, the lag between Anglo and Chicano: did it grow worse over the summer? She predicted that "poverty and ghettoization [that is, living in the barrio] would produce more difference than ethnicity itself."

As it turned out, the ethnic factor was quite secondary in importance; level of income was hardly more important; but residence in the barrio seemed highly significant. Taking low-income Chicanos, Frieder-Vierra found "their scores at any single point in time as considerably higher if they reside outside the *barrios*." The advantage is considerable: "The reading performance of low-income non-*barrio* Chicano children benefits more than that of any group from exposure to school and does not suffer any loss relative to other children during the summer vacation period. Their *barrio* counterparts, however, do much less well while in school but more than make up for that relative loss during the summer."[65] It is not clear just why the barrio Chicanos experience a relative summer gain.

Middle-class non-barrio Chicanos score lower than Anglos but resemble closely their pattern of learning during the entire year. Both hold their own. Middle-class barrio Chicanos also gain over the summer. Frieder-Vierra stresses that "the group that gains the most on an annual basis . . . is the low-income non-*barrio* Chicanos and, contrary to the picture for their *barrio* counterparts, almost all of this improvement in relative standing is made during the school years."[66]

Frieder-Vierra draws a rather sweeping and suggestive conclusion from the findings:

Some dimensions of minority status seem more amenable to the schools' intervention than others. In Albuquerque, school is only successful in increasing the reading achievement of Chicano children relative to Anglo children when they are not socially isolated. Poverty itself does not seem to be a barrier; school closes the gap for poor Chicano children, as long as they do not reside in the *barrio*.[67]

It should be recalled that we are not speaking here of the year-round gap between Anglo and Chicano children, which is sizable, but of the gap in achievement between the end of the Spring semester and the opening of the Fall semester. In other words, while the achievement of non-barrio poor Chicanos and middle-income Chicanos who live in the barrio is relatively high during the school year, low-income Chicano barrio residents do poorly during the school year but, for some reason, do not suffer from being out of school, or suffer less than the others. Frieder-Vierra states that having poor barrio children attend summer school will not necessarily narrow any achievement gap. The research is thin on this question.

Mexican-American Literature

Albert Dwight Trevino studied the place of Mexican-American literature in high school English programs in Texas. He found no mention of Mexican-American literature in state-adopted literature textbooks. A guideline issued by the Texas Education Agency does provide that "the State Textbook Committee shall choose a minimum of two textbooks at each level which shall be a departure from the regular anthology and shall be designed especially for students who have difficulty in the regular literature program."[68] It is stipulated further that such literature "should be of a type with which cultural minorities can identify strongly, shall be representative of the cultural patterns of minority groups, and should contain numerous selections written from the point of view of the minority groups." Trevino objects to conceiving of minority literature as appropriate only to students not performing up to standard in the literature program. Apparently, students performing satisfactorily are "above" minority literature. Upon examining two textbooks prepared in accordance with the above-listed guidelines, Trevino found them seriously wanting. Only one of the books contained a single Mexican-American selection, and that was an autobiographical sketch by Pancho Gonzalez, the tennis star. Thus, there were not "numerous selections" nor could the Gonzalez entry be properly regarded as "representative of the cultural patterns" of Mexican Americans.

Trevino outlines a curriculum, consisting of short stories, poetry, and novels, for Mexican-American literature in integrated high school classes.

Dorothy Clauser Moyer studied children's fiction and nonfiction books about Mexico and Mexican Americans published in this country between 1925 and 1971. "None of the early books about Mexicans in the United States," she writes, "depicted them as members of a recognized minority group. . . . Even in books since 1961 there have been only a few stories about Mexican Americans as a minority group and only a few informational books which include descriptions of the minority group."[69] More recently, Moyer found a considerable improvement both in fiction and nonfiction; yet she concluded that "numerous . . . books portray Mexico and Mexican Americans in a stereotyped, patronizing manner." Moyer includes in her report a 167-page bibliography of the works she reviewed. It is a valuable starting point for research in the area.

Desegregation

Patrick E. McBurnette and James W. Kunetka conducted a very preliminary and restricted study of Mexican-American students in desegregated schools in five Texas cities: Houston, San Antonio, Lockhart, McAllen, and Waxachachie. Only ninety-nine Anglo and Chicano students were surveyed. About the only warranted conclusion one could arrive at from the study is that there seems to be much verbal harassment between Chicano and Anglo students. Just how conflicts arise, their significance, and how they are distributed—nothing of this is clarified.[70] A number of studies on Mexican-American students in desegregated schools are under way.

Observations

Social science research is notoriously ahistorical. In this tradition, however, the study of minority education is a puzzle without attention to historical roots. These roots, like all others, are extremely tangled. They reach into other growths, making it impossible to treat a single subject in isolation. Minorities in American life bear a distinctive relationship to the political and economic institutions of the country. Therefore, a study of minority education leads inevitably to the broader social picture. Structures of segregation and deprivation were a long time building. While one can tell something about a dwelling without examining the foundation, it is advisable to find out all you can about it before moving in.

The six historical works reviewed above succeed well in establishing the historical nature of some important educational problems.

One dominant theme is the economic decline of Mexican Americans while the larger economy expanded during the nineteenth century. This was seen to be the case in both Los Angeles and Santa Barbara. In a real sense, few Mexican Americans gained directly from the larger economic expansion. As a consequence, Mexican-American history cannot be approached from a European immigrant perspective of "from rags to riches." In each instance studied, Mexican Americans occupied the lowest rung of southwestern rural and urban society. Courses and teaching units on the history of Mexican Americans need to come to grips with this historic reality.

Another theme concerns the language problem in school. Griswold del Castillo's account is clearest on the persistent efforts of Mexican-American parents to gain bilingual instruction for their children, as early as the 1850s. The reception they met with hardly differed from that of a century later. Bilingualism has a more ancient lineage than is generally recognized, as has the anti-bilingual sentiment. The latter won out decisively; as Post points out, in one Texas high school speaking Spanish was forbidden until 1972.

Still another point of interest is the educational role of the Catholic Church. In sketches of the historic culture of Mexican Americans much attention is usually paid to the subject of Catholicism. But the discussion is often restricted to Catholicism as a religious value; the institutional history of the Church is slighted. As is clear from the historical materials, the Church never aimed at nor achieved mass education in the Southwest. It was somewhat more open to bilingual education but for a rather selective enrollment. In more recent years, with the financial crisis of Church schools, the patronage of these schools has narrowed even more, in a social and ethnic sense. The opposition of the Church to public school expansion in areas of large Catholic population was not, however, peculiar to the Southwest. Around the turn of the century, this view was still widespread in Catholic circles.

The problem of the educational quality of Mexican-American schooling is a long-standing one. There were no "good old days" of high-quality mass education of Mexican Americans. Attendance of Mexican-American children in the schools of Los Angeles before the Civil War was relatively high, but as noted earlier, literacy among Mexican Americans was lagging even a century ago. There is abundant historical evidence relating to the institutionalizing of low achievement by Mexican Americans. This would include Gonzales's material about Los Angeles, as well as Post's on two Texas towns, and other studies cited elsewhere in this chapter.

The studies of social mobility and assimilation deal with a topic that is very familiar in the literature. They are concerned largely with income levels, occupational choice, and ethnic self-concept. All in all, the upward strivers seem to entertain modest life goals; they are not aiming at the sky. Perhaps this is more an adjustment to the limited opportunities available to them than an expression of any cultural restraint indigenous to Mexican Americans.

Ethnic identity means something different to each researcher: language used by self and one's family; geographical nearness to the nuclear family; interaction with others of one's own group; celebration of traditional holidays; physical appearance; and location of dwelling. One gains from the studies a conception of culture that is somewhat amorphous, even fragmented at times. In any case, it is difficult to grasp precisely the subject of ethnic character.

An older, rather romantic conception of assimilation suggested that the poor are more culturally authentic and don't "need" to assimilate. What's more, they were believed to lack any economic motive to assimilate. Since none of the studies deals with the poor, it is not possible to judge whether any of the findings are peculiar to the middle-income upward strivers or whether upward-striving itself is unique to middle-income persons.

Unfortunately, the exigencies of writing a doctoral dissertation usually dictate that when there is a choice between a need to complete the work and a need to encompass many factors, the former will win out. But much of the published material in this research field also reflects the same problem.

Few researchers have come to grips with a further issue which hovers over the investigations. This is the matter of the form of Mexican-American culture in the long run. Lopez comes close to saying that if racism and poverty were to disappear, Mexican-American ethnic consciousness would be severely weakened. Most of the other researchers adopt a very different view, taking for granted the maintenance of Mexican-American culture without regard to its eventual configuration.

Both the historical and social mobility studies afford a glimpse into the operation of community power on a local scale. Post's case study of two towns enables us to study the process in contemporary detail and in historical perspective at the same time. (It is a valuable work, matched in the literature only by Parsons's 1965 study of Castroville, California.)[71] Especially important is the fact that Post clarifies the political nature of the school. In a time when charges are heard about this or that group using the schools "for political purposes" it is well to be reminded that this is quite unexceptionable.

Indeed, political action by Mexican Americans is on its way to becoming a community norm, at least in South Texas, where they are concentrated. The schools are bound to reflect this situation and so we may well look forward to significant changes in the schools. But in another respect, change is bound to be slow. Post stresses throughout his work that Anglo control derives from ownership of the economic power centers of the community, with Chicanos playing a subordinate economic role. From Post's account, it is not clear that RUP and other Chicano political movements have yet disturbed the traditional basis of Anglo control.

The practical import of Post's work lies not in the realm of classroom instruction so much as in the area of reorienting school personnel.

The Casavantes and Frieder-Vierra studies deal with the narrower question of academic achievement of Mexican-American children. Casavantes's work rests on a possibly unsteady base since he utilizes reading outcomes from several states without the benefit of standardized scores. Instead, he uses principals' estimates. Nevertheless, his main point is at least plausible and very possibly quite correct: nonpromotion of minority students yields no discernible educational benefit. Frieder-Vierra's findings, like so many others in educational research, cry out for interpretation in order to convert them into usable guideposts to school policy.

The remaining works represent single studies of restricted aspects of a broad subject and are thus difficult to discuss in a meaningful way.

Indian Americans

Few researchers have been interested in the education of Indian Americans. One can easily page through standard research compendia and textbooks without once running across the subject. Ignorance runs rife. The absence of Indian researchers is a principal reason for this lack of interest. Another is the failure of the research community to acknowledge the existence of deliberate, intentional educational disadvantage. The attempt to destroy Indian culture and society is deeply rooted in the United States.

Only recently have some researchers begun to study and document efforts by Indian parents to ensure their children an adequate education. Historical perspective is a very important part of the research. Social science studies of specific reservations and Indian schools are of great potential value. Questioning of established governmental policy in the field of Indian education is crucial. Studies representative of each type of research are discussed below.

History

Two historical studies deal with the Colville Indians (Washington) and the Fort Berthold Indians (North Dakota).

The first, by Susanna A. Hayes, stresses the century-long campaign by federal educators to inculcate in Colville children a feeling of shame for the native culture. At present, she writes, "Indian children interpret the differences between their way of life and that of the white population as indications of their ignorance and cultural inferiority."[72] Since English is the present language of school instruction, few parents teach their children the native language.

In 1873, when the reservation's first school opened, many more children applied than could be accommodated. Two years later the Indian agent reported that five children applied for each vacancy. Near the end of the decade, however, there was a grand total of eight-five students actually enrolled in two schools. Federal authorities constantly promised to build more facilities but decades of inadequate ones were the rule. At times the degree of administrative bungling was ludicrous. A day school was built but no teacher was provided. As a result, for three years the school building was used as a warehouse. During many years of failure to provide the promised schools, Hayes points out, "the major obstacle to more extensive and improved educational services was attributed to limited financial provisions for buildings, staff, and supplies, rather than the children's inability to learn or parental indifference to education."[73] During a century, fewer than one-tenth of Colville children were afforded an opportunity to attend school.

Since federally built facilities were chronically inadequate, Colville parents sent their children to public schools whenever possible. Often, such schools were located on the reservation but were designed principally for children of whites who worked on the reservation; whites paid the expenses of the public schools. By 1931, the public schools on or near the Colville reservation enrolled a majority of Indian students from the reservation. After 1934, federal funds were channeled to such public schools to cover the cost of Indian students.

Still, Hayes reports, the Indian children are viewed by the public schools as a liability. Teachers are critical of their reluctance to speak up in class. Hayes notes, however, that "it is possible for Indian children as young as six and seven years old to spend hours talking together about their experiences in the open country with great animation and enjoyment."[74] High school athletics is the single public arena where Indian skill is acceptable to the white community. In all other respects, Indian children "know the cold stares from whites on the streets and in the stores of towns are signs of disapproval and rejection" and frequently they, themselves, "adopt the name-calling practices of white men and refer to themselves as 'dumb Indians'."

In 1971, some 85 percent of the Colville children attended public schools on or near the reservation. But these are "white men's schools." Faculty, administration, school boards, and fellow students are mainly white. Despite the fact that, according to Hayes, all Colville children speak English when they enter school, they find the environment foreign and inhospitable.

The second historical study, by Wallace Henry Stockman, concerns the Fort Berthold Indians in North Dakota. Three tribes live there: the Mandans, Arikaras, and Hidatsa (Gros Ventres).

Formal relations between the Indians and the federal government began with the Treaty of Fort Laramie, in 1851. During the following fifteen years, Indian parents requested federal authorities to provide schools for their children, but the requests went unanswered. In 1866, a new treaty was signed under which the United States agreed to spend up to $3,000 a year on various Indian matters, including education. Four years later the first school was opened in December. During the following Spring, few children returned and the teacher offered a free meal as an inducement to attend. In May, the school was closed down altogether since reservation authorities decided the structure was needed for other purposes. Because, however, the three tribes had not joined the Sioux in their wars during the 1850s and 1860s, they received extra concessions, including some jobs.

In 1875, a government school was opened. Instruction was in the native language. But within five years, this had changed. Jacob Kaufman, Indian agent, reported in 1880 that "the English language is taught exclusively in the school, which I believe is the proper language to be taught in an Indian school."[75] Occasionally, Christian missionaries seemed to have a somewhat greater respect for Indian culture. In 1876, the American Board of Commissioners for Foreign Missions sent Rev. C. L. Hall and his wife to the reservation. They used the Dakotan language in church services.

Whatever the reason—Stockman does not evince any interest in searching for one—Indian parents became deeply antagonistic to the federal schools. George E. Gerowe, the school superintendent, complained that the Indian parents would gather near the boarding school grounds and he had to drive them away "since they exerted an undue influence over the Indian children."[76] Whenever possible parents withheld their children from such schools. To counteract this action, in 1888 federal Indian authorities in Washington, D.C., ordered the local Indian agent to withhold rations from Indian families until they sent their children to the schools. Five years later Congress passed a law providing that "the Secretary of the Interior may, at his discretion, withhold rations, clothing, and other annuities from Indian parents or guardians who refuse or neglect to send and keep their children in some school a reasonable portion of the year." Two important factors, among others, helped alienate the three tribes from the educational facilities they had demanded in vain for so long. First was the language of instruction; English was a foreign language and all but useless in the life on the reservation. Second was the profound unpopularity of boarding schools, where Indian children were not only sent far away from home, but where their culture was also subjected to a systematic process of suppression and denigration.

During the early years of the present century, academic goals of Indian education were almost nonexistent. In 1911, for example "the boys were given instruction in gardening and the girls in sewing, cooking, and housework. In the schoolroom of the day [that is, non-boarding] schools, the classwork was limited to the primary level and few pupils remained in school long enough to complete the fifth grade."[77] By the 1930s the major government drive was to shift Indian children into public schools. The facilities were modest at best. In his report for 1932, Carl M. Moore, supervisor of Indian education, reported three "new" public schools on the Fort Berthold reservation: "One of these is to be conducted in a worked-over Indian dance hall. Another will be housed in a Catholic chapel and the third in a Mormon church."[78]

While Stockman does not supply enough evidence to establish his conclusions firmly, they are consistent with the evidence he did examine: "The majority culture has achieved its initial goal—the destruction of the original social forms of the Fort Berthold people."[79] The schools played an important role in that process of destruction.

Teachers

To what extent are teachers in schools educating both Indian and Anglo pupils aware of sociocultural differences between the two groups of children? Joseph J. Centrone set out to answer this question by studying third graders and 222 teachers in fourteen elementary schools.

By and large, the teachers—apparently all Anglo—were assimilative and optimistic about social interaction between Indian and Anglo children. They felt, for example, that the children were adjusting well to each other. But Centrone found that "as the Indian pupil progresses in school, he interacts less with pupils of other ethnic groups."[80] Teachers were confident that Indian pupils were coming to resemble their Anglo classmates in basic beliefs and values. Centrone found the contrary to be the case, at least with respect to several subjects under scrutiny. Thus, instead of Indian parents preferring integrated schools they expressed a desire for an all-Indian school. Teachers thought the two groups of children shared a common conception of citizenship. "Indian children," Centrone discovered, "are taught that they are members of a separate nation."[81] Indeed, writes Centrone, "Indian people, especially those of the Longhouse religion, wish their children to learn the Indian tongue, to fully participate in tribal customs, folkways, mores, and religion, but are not interested in their children's learning and acceptance of the Anglo culture."[82]

Teachers' expressed values seemed to have little effect on their students' academic achievement. The teachers most sensitive to differences between the two cultures had no "substantial bearing" on the reading or arithmetic achievement of their students. This finding can be contrasted to the frequent finding in other studies—especially of white teachers and minority students other than Indians—that students whose teachers are less prejudiced and more "understanding" tend to be more successful academically.

Two questions, among others, are raised by Centrone's research. First, how capable are teachers when it comes to gauging cultural differences of students when they themselves are part of the dominant community group? Centrone's research is hardly encouraging on this score. Second, what are the practical consequences of cultural understanding? If Centrone's report on parent preferences is accurate, the Indian community under study does not wish to be "understood" so much as to be left alone to develop its own cultural ways.

Considerations such as these create a framework of doubt as to the educational significance of more traditional research findings. Donald E. Hjelmseth, for example, studied ninety-five teachers from four public elementary schools near Indian reservations in Montana. He found "very encouraging" the fact that "nearly half . . . of all elementary teachers sampled have had academic course work in Indian studies in the past five years. . . ."[83] This trend is national in scope. Does such training merely enable Anglo and other non-Indian teachers to implement more effectively an Anglo-oriented program of instruction—without consulting the educational interests of the Indian community? Or, does the training form a new path to Indian culture, enabling teachers to create effective instructional strategies that fully take into account the goals of the community?

The School and Indian Culture

An anthropologist studying Navajo mothers born between 1940 and 1949 wrote: "One woman reported having been beaten with a rubber hose for speaking Navajo."[84] She had attended a mission school. (One can easily tell what cultural mission the school conceived for itself.) The rubber hose has receded as an instrument of cultural suppression. By no means, however, are Indians of one mind on converting the public school into a place where their own cultural ways are taught.

Among the Hopis, for example, there does indeed seem to be near unanimity on the undesirability of teaching Hopi ways in school. In a three-year study—from May, 1970, to July, 1973—Murray L. Wax and Robert G. Brennig found that most Hopis regarded the schools "as places where they send their children to learn 'white man's ways'."[85] A fourth-grade teacher told interviewers: "The PTA president said that Hopi culture could not be taught in the schools, that this was something to be done in the village and not at the school. The school was set up to teach white ways and they wanted it kept that way."[86] Since Hopis do not distinguish between their religion and their culture, most consider public discussion of cultural—others might say religious—matters highly inappropriate. On the basis of interviews of 178 parents, Wax and Brennig report: "Although some parents did mention that they would like to see some aspect of Hopi language or culture taught in the school, a majority of mothers volunteered opinions opposed to such activities."[87]

Parents seemed to have drawn a very sharp line between the merits of their traditional culture and the advantages of knowing the white man's ways. Parents, the researchers inform us, believe that "when today's children are adults, virtually no one will be engaged in traditional subsistence activities."[88] Thus, to prepare their children to engage in nontraditional—in effect, in the *white* man's—economy it appears sensible to utilize the white man's schools for the requisite training. As a result, report Wax and Brennig, "in all our visits to PTA meetings on the reservation, we heard nothing of how Hopi children were unique, or that they had particular or peculiar capabilities and potentials that could be utilized in the overall education process [or] personality development of Hopi children."[89] Instead, energetic efforts were under way to "bring everyone up to the 'national average'."[90]

Contrary to expectations of superficial observers, then, an ethnic group with a rising presence in the schools chose not to convert the school into an ethnic "thing." Instead, it insisted that the school perfect its present goals and make them work for Indian children. This approach was freely chosen by Indian parents, although it did not satisfy educators' preconceptions as to how persons of certain ethnic groups should behave.

On the other hand, Dominic J. Cibrario studied four groups of Pueblo Indians and found differing practices with respect to bilingual and bicultural practices.

At Taos Pueblo (New Mexico), a teacher had once tried to initiate such a program but parents protested that they wanted English to be the language of instruction. At the time of Cibrario's study, several years later, a kindergarten teacher observed that the children tended to speak Tiwa less and English more during playtime than they had done four years earlier. This was attributed to greater parental use of English at home and the consequences of a Head Start program. When, however, an English teacher had students write about the San Geronimo Festival, a sacred event, and posted the essays on a bulletin board, the Tribal Council ordered the teacher to remove the essays.

The people of San Juan Pueblo, however, had bilingual instruction in Tewa and English as well as a bicultural program which included Pueblo history. In fact, Spanish is also rather widely used in the community. Cibrario reports that "of the nineteen pueblos in New Mexico, San Juan has thus far been the only pueblo to introduce bilingual and bicultural studies into the elementary school."[91] No explanation is offered as to the uniqueness of San Juan Pueblo.

A different situation exists at Zia Pueblo. "Although the community did not approve of bicultural studies," observes Cibrario, "they wanted to have the Keresan language taught at the school by a Keresan Indian aide; however, they did not want an Anglo teacher present in the room while the language instruction was being conducted."[92] So determined were the Zia to maintain the privacy of their culture that they rejected requests of linguists to record the Keresan language. According to Cibrario, "the general attitude seemed to be that the Indians in this attitude would rather see their tribal language perish than allow the ancient language to be recorded by linguists."[93]

At the Zuni Pueblo, no bilingual instruction was given in schools. Young people who dropped out of school in large numbers were deeply involved in the Zuni culture by the ease with which they got jobs making jewelry. Since an immediate market existed, a Zuni labor supply was needed.

Chemawa School

Carol J. P. Colfer conducted an ethnographic study of the Chemawa boarding school for Indians in Oregon. During six months in 1971, she was employed as a matron at Chemawa.

The school, begun in 1880, enrolls students between the ages of thirteen and twenty-two, and is surrounded by high fences. Until 1968, military nomenclature was used in many school records. An assignment to do a housekeeping task was described as a "detail," students who were absent without adequate explanation were recorded as "AWOL," and when a student returned from a visit home, a notation might read: "Mary Whitefoot Leave to Duty." Over the years, students tended to come from specific areas or tribes; undoubtedly, this resulted from official policy. Following is an indication of the predominant tribal attendance pattern since 1880.[94]

1880–1948	Northwest coast and Montana
1948–1961	Navajo
1961–1971	Alaska
1971 to present	Northwest coast

Recently, enrollment ranged between 700 and 1000.

However advanced her academic training, Colfer occupied a very ordinary position at the school. As matron in a dormitory, she was able to glimpse intimate aspects of life which eluded other investigators. It is not intimate events so much as intimate aspects of everyday routines that emerge in Colfer's work.

Alaskan and Northwest students differed in important aspects. As Colfer writes:

Students from the Northwest have had long experience with the white man, and have frequently come to hate him. They expect whites to demand subservience, to consider themselves superior, to cheat and lie to Indians. This attitude is quickly transmitted to the less "acculturated" Alaskans who have sometimes known no whites.[95]

Students from Alaska tend to be nonaggressive and quiet while Northwest students are outgoing and uninhibited; nearly all of them came to Chemawa "because their local school ha[d] expelled them or [was] about to do so."[96]

The dormitory staff, many of them Indians, have more or less adopted the value judgments of students put forward by the faculty. The latter view students as unprepared, unmotivated, and bored. Such denigration is often expressed outside the classroom. Colfer comments: "Several Alaskan students were pointed out to me as being "stupid" or "not all there." On closer inspection, it developed that the girls in question simply could not understand what they were being told to do. In Barrow Dorm one hears Eskimo and Aleut as much as English."[97] Tribal divisions are by no means insurmountable although they play a predominant role in the making of personal friendships.

Alaskan students adapt well to the school while Northwest students resist it. Colfer points out that for neither group, however, is the education they receive there of any significance for the future. "Schooling," she writes, "is a hardship that Alaskans as conquered people must undergo, but at the end of the ordeal a return to the familiar, secure (emotionally, if not economically), loving homelife is envisioned."[98] Attendance at Chemawa is for many students a commitment to change their traditional way of life. Academically, however, the experience is seriously inadequate and is the end of the road for virtually all the students.

School as an avenue of upward social mobility is an uncongenial idea to many Chemawa students. Indeed, the very idea of a class society finds little precedent in Indian lives. Colfer explains:

Most students . . . are from societies where there has not been a great institution-alized discrepancy in status and wealth among individuals, either in the past or the present. . . . The student, who is not accustomed to ranking human beings in hier-archies where one human being has a wide latitude of control over another human being *for no apparent reason*, is confused by this strange set of behaviors. He repeatedly sees staff members who are incompetent, in the eyes of both students and other staff members, in positions of authority over adequate or even superb human beings; and these inferior beings remain in positions of authority. Hierarchy in the home community was a familiar fact but there it rested on palpable factors such as age, expert knowledge, or a degree of community consent.[99]

Indians were well aware of their own low position in the national class structure. Colfer stresses, however, that the Indian's status "is not a particu-larly significant part of his own self-concept (though it is of extreme signifi-cance in his life)."[100] At Chemawa, the student is constantly reminded by his daily experience of the very low status he occupies: "The student is seen by staff members as being the lowest in the hierarchy and is treated accord-ingly."[101] (The process whereby the student comes to accept the lowest social position for himself is not documented in Colfer's study nor, perhaps, any-where else.)

The comparative few who succeed at Chemawa are not the special objects of appreciation or respect by the rest. For most students at Chemawa, the school year is more a nine months' captivity than anything else.[102]

Since ethnographic studies such as Colfer's are not plentiful, few schools, Indian and non-Indian, have been the object of careful probing into the homely details of school life. Yet, some comparisons come to mind. The norm of little academic achievement is found in many large-city schools attended by poor and minority children, some of them Indians. In a perceptive study of New York City schools, Miriam Wasserman wrote that in those schools the parent was considered "the least adult" and students were "the least persons."[103] The lesson of learning one's "place" in an inhospitable class structure was mastered all too well in such schools. And, as at Chemawa, there was little or no evidence of a positive connection between schooling and later upward social mobility.

Urban Indians

Two studies of Indians in Detroit, completed three years apart, are available.

Thomas E. Glass, author of the earlier study, used data collected by a previous public opinion survey. In the Cass Corridor, a part of the city that attracts very poor people, unemployment among heads of Indian families stood at 46 percent. Most of the parents had attended federal Indian schools or public schools on or near a reservation. When asked what they thought of the Detroit public schools, many failed to answer. Glass explains: "For every ten months of school the Indian child usually only makes five months of academic progress. . . . Children have traded non-achievement in rural schools for non-achievement in urban schools."[104] This conclusion is based on examination of test data. Apparently, Glass did not visit any schools to observe the classroom aspects of this non-achievement.

The second Detroit study was done by Beatrice A. Bigony; field work was conducted between Fall, 1971, and Spring, 1973. She worked through the Associated Indians of Detroit, primarily in the Cass Corridor. Unlike Glass, Bigony spoke with many Cass people.

"Many Indian people in the Cass Corridor," Bigony found, "eat only one meal a day. Adults appear to survive principally on cups of coffee, doctored with sugar and powdered cream, and cigarettes."[105] Most do not have telephones. Their children's high rate of absence from school is another reflection of their poverty: "Their children are teased at school because they are Indians and because they wear faded or old clothing. To save the children from this embarrassment some of the parents deliberately keep their children out of school part time."[106] Few of these parents see much point in their children finishing high school; there is little opportunity awaiting them afterwards.

Many of the Indian people in Cass Corridor share a prevailing attitude described by Bigony as follows: "This is a general feeling of despair, of somehow being cheated out of the best years of life without knowing why. This feeling of despair is coupled with frustration because the people do not know how to make life change for the better."[107] Yet, Bigony observes that "it is the people from this neighborhood who have spearheaded fights for change among the Indian populace of Detroit."[108] (No explanation is offered of the emergence of a force for change out of a general context of despair.)

While nearly all Indian parents in the Cass Corridor had grown up on reservations, few consciously transmitted their cultural heritage. Bigony reports that "most people of the Ottawa, Chippewa, and Potawatomi tribes do not know their specific traditional beliefs, they do not know their folklore, and they do not know their language. . . ."[109] Solidarity among Indians who are economically self-sustaining is weakening. Many, Bigony writes, are "refusing to acknowledge obligations to their kin, who act as drains on their financial resources."[110]

Bigony explored varying Indian attitudes toward education and the city schools. In general, high dropout rates were associated with low levels of parental education and unstable employment. Those parents who worked at low-paying jobs tended to find more to criticize in the schools. (One exception was criticism from parents who were employed as professionals.) The two major school problems reported by a broad range of parents were discrimination by teachers and prejudiced behavior by non-Indian classmates. Skilled workers tended to be less critical of schools than were unskilled workers. Since Bigony did not investigate actual discrimination in the schools, it is impossible to know how realistic the parental attitudes are.

Eskimos make up 2.1 percent of the population of greater Anchorage, Alaska. It is this group of people that Patrick J. Dubbs studied. Actually, his sample included nearly three-quarters of all Anchorage Eskimos twenty years of age and older.

At the time of the study, the unemployment rate for Eskimo workers was 38.1 percent, some four times greater than the rate for Anchorage as a whole. While a high school diploma is nearly always expected of an applicant for a job, 56.5 percent of the Eskimos haven't finished high school. "Although there are many able Anchorage Eskimos with a vast amount of experiential knowledge," Dubbs writes, "these individuals are often denied employment because they lack a certain credential."[111]

Since all Eskimos in Anchorage are bilingual, one might expect that they would interact a good deal with persons of other ethnic backgrounds. Whether because of employment or for other reasons, the greatest amount of interaction occurs between Eskimos and whites, considerably less with Indians, and almost none with blacks. There is a considerable amount of Eskimo-white intermarriage but it almost always involves an Eskimo woman and a white man.

Living in Anchorage takes its toll of traditional kinship relations. "Many Eskimos, although not the majority," reports Dubbs, "take great pains not to have their addresses or phone numbers made public so as to avoid having to fulfill kinship obligations and suffer the attendant personal and economic consequences."[112]

Anchorage Eskimos are what Dubbs calls "reliable employees." Only about one-fourteenth live on nonwage income such as welfare or child support funds. While they suffer much employment discrimination, they are often hesitant about making a formal complaint to a government bureau: "This reluctance stems from a fear of being rejected and a feeling that the black or Caucasian administrative agent will not be interested in a Native claim."[113]

Dubbs sees the Anchorage Eskimos as outsiders. "Many, if not most, Anchorage Eskimos are balanced," he writes, "on the edge of a precipice—they are isolated, they have a low level of adaptation, they are not receiving support from agencies and they are developing serious drinking problems."[114] The source of the problems, Dubbs emphasizes, lies not in the Eskimo but in the larger social system of Anchorage and beyond.

Federal Policy

In 1864, a formal treaty was signed between the Klamath Indian tribe and the federal government. The economic resources owned by the tribe—timber, range land, pulpwood—were held in trust and managed by the Bureau of Indian Affairs (BIA). Outside users of these resources paid fees and royalties to the BIA which then distributed part of the proceeds to each member of the tribe.

The per capita payments were interpreted by many outsiders as government largesse, but such an interpretation was quite mistaken. As William T. Trulove, the author of the study under review, explains:

Since 1918, the Klamath were never a "burden" on taxpayers. From tribal income they paid for most BIA administration, forest and range management, extension services, health, welfare, law and order, and various credit schemes either directly from timber revenues or, in the case of loans, from obligated future revenues.[115]

In 1923, it was estimated that four out of five able-bodied Klamath were self-supporting, that is, they earned an income over and above the per capita payments.

Paternalism was (and remains) the operating principle of federal Indian policy. As trustee for Klamath property, the BIA performed as the all-knowing father. It alone made final decisions on important economic issues. For example, it concentrated on preserving the value of Klamath resources but "few serious attempts were made to encourage or develop Indian owned and operated manufacturing facilities."[116] Trulove points out the bureaucratic reasons for this policy:

First, developmental and industrial activities were risky. Indians might fail and under BIA direction that would be equivalent to BIA failure. Careers would be jeopardized and claims might be lodged against the government which would lower the BIA's status with Congress.[117]

Individual Klamath were all but excluded from management responsibilities in BIA enterprises.

The exclusion of Klamath from self-directed economic activity could not help but underscore the importance of per capita payments. By the early 1950s, it was estimated that "only 35 percent of all Klamath families were able to make a living without per capitas."[118] As its salience grew, the per capita system came to influence many aspects of Klamath society, both on and off the reservation. An example of the latter was the growing practice of Klamath obtaining credit from nearby merchants by mortgaging their future per capita payments. Trulove comments that "area businessmen, while criticizing social effects of the system, consistently pressed for its continuation."[119]

In his study, Trulove frequently characterizes per capita payments as "unearned income" and then traces the harmful effect of such payments on their recipients. He refers often to these effects as depriving Klamath adults and young persons of personal incentives to work and study. From another perspective, however, it could be stressed that the per capita payments were not designed as rewards for individual enterprise. Children, for instance, were entitled to full payments because of their tribal membership and not because of productive work. As indicated above, a half-century ago the Klamath were predominantly self-supporting despite the per capita system. One *earned* per capita by *being* Klamath. But one *made a living* by participating in the *white* economy. As the latter became more difficult, the inadequacy of per capita payments became more obvious.

Given the framework of federal paternalism and narrowing employment opportunities, the per capita system proved destructive to the Klamath.

It became a common practice for parents to borrow from children's per capita accounts in order to cover various expenses. "As parents sank more deeply in debt to their children," writes Trulove, "and with little hope of repayment, they found their parental influence severely restricted."[120] Klamath youth found themselves poorly prepared to compete for jobs in the outside economy because their schooling was inadequate. According to Trulove, "the Klamath were generally unconvinced as to the importance of education and local schools provided little room for enthusiasm."[121] This had not been the case a half-century earlier when, Trulove writes, the rate of school attendance for Klamath children was higher than the national average. During 1938–1947, non-Klamath taxpayers in the county paid about three-fifths of the cost of the education of Klamath children; the rest was supplied by the federal government. "Klamath county schools had no incentive to provide special services to meet Indian needs, and, in fact, had to resist strong incentives to discourage Klamath attendance," Trulove reports.[122]

In 1954, Congress, responding to non-Indian pressures, enacted a law permitting the federal government to "terminate" Indian reservations and convert all tribally owned assets into individual property. Termination, as Trulove explains clearly, "was specifically aimed at ending federally controlled Indian reservations and thereby eliminating all special rights and privileges granted when the reservation was originally created."[123] Seven years later, the Klamath reservation was "terminated."

Under congressional pressure, the BIA negotiated sale of the Klamath forest for a final price one-quarter less than originally offered. Formally, the sales revenue was to yield a per capita payment of $43,000; only a third (34 percent) of the tribe actually received this amount "free and clear." In April, 1961, the cash distribution was made. For the most part, Klamath used their shares for "domestic needs such as living and medical expenses, automobiles, home improvements, household furnishing, and housing."[124] For the first time in their lives, Indians needed to employ lawyers to aid them in unfamiliar transactions. The Klamath County Bar Association took advantage of the situation by promulgating a fee schedule which charged

Indians twice the fees that non-Indians paid.[125] (Trulove is contradictory on the speed with which the Klamath spent their funds. In one place he writes that "about half used their funds fairly rapidly" and in another that "most proceeds were probably disposed of fairly rapidly."[126])

Writing about a dozen years after termination, Trulove noted that the position of the Indians in local society was virtually unchanged. Klamath were not "flooding" the welfare rolls as many whites had expected. Patterns of residence and employment had not changed. Thus, "the pro rata shares were usually exhausted as the Klamath adjusted their style of life, but not the incomes, upward."[127]

Governmental paternalism until termination proved a disabling rather than an enabling policy for the Klamath. Termination itself was the ultimate in paternalistic decision making. It did not convert the supporting Klamath into the self-regarding entrepreneur so dear to American myth. Instead, it integrated him into a class society in which he could take his place—a very lowly one—and function as dependent poor.

In 1963, the BIA pledged to close the educational gap between Indian and non-Indian students in seven years. In 1972 the U.S. General Accounting Office (GAO) reviewed the pledge and found that not only was the goal far from being achieved, but that the BIA had made no real preparation to achieve it.[128] In 1976 the GAO undertook another probe that found:

As was the case at the time of our 1972 report, we did not find evidence that BIA had established realistic goals and objectives or implemented comprehensive programs to meet the needs of Indian students. As a result, the major national goal established by the Congress to provide the quantity and quality of educational services and opportunities which will permit Indian children to compete in the careers of their choice is no nearer to being achieved than it was four years ago.[129]

The GAO also noted that from 1966 to 1976, fifteen different persons served as director or assistant director in the BIA's Office of Indian Education Programs. The average term was seven months.

If a new day in Indian education is dawning, the researchers have yet to glimpse it. The historical works document the persistence of deeply rooted patterns of subordination as well as inadequate and misdirected education. While certain quantitative progress is evident—more children in school— the inadequacy of the education received has eased little.

Contemporary school reform hinges much on teacher training and retraining. This emphasis is especially prominent in discussions of the teaching of ethnic minority children. The Centrone research must give pause to these efforts. In searching for evidence of educational benefits to children of increasingly enlightened teachers, Centrone met with considerable disappointment. It is not that cultural understanding is unimportant. Rather, the cultural sphere lies beyond the realm of mere book knowledge and must encompass knowledge of specific children living in concrete situations different from those familiar to most teachers.

Researchers who explore the school and Indian culture lead the reader to this conclusion: Indian parents, *to the degree that they trust the school*, favor school responsibility for teaching about Indian culture. If efforts by Indian parents to achieve greater control over schools meet with success, the schools will be assigned greater cultural responsibilities.

The study of Chemawa must be measured against less extensive and less formal studies. In general, Chemawa does not seem exceptional in any major sense. In autobiographical accounts written by Indians who attended boarding schools, one finds many of the same phenomena. Reading Colfer's study is a very welcome relief from many recent studies of Indian education that depend heavily upon questionnaires and demographic data.

Whether in Detroit or Anchorage, Indians occupy the lowest level of urban society. Unfortunately, in neither of the studies examined here was any attention paid to the conditions of Indian schooling in the schools actually attended. These conditions are very distant from the treatment of other poor or minority children. Not only is there educational deprivation but cultural oppression and discrimination of unique gravity.

Trulove's study of the Klamath is especially strong in analyzing the strategy and content of the termination policy. (Unfortunately, he does not note the deleterious effects of termination on education.)[130] He is also helpful in enabling the reader to understand the federal bureaucratic framework which surrounds Indian life. This, in turn, clarifies why the contemporary American Indian movement for self-determination necessarily concentrates on the character of future federal regulation.

Notes

1. Richard Allan Griswold del Castillo, *La Raza Hispana Americana: The Emergence of an Urban Culture Among the Spanish Speaking of Los Angeles, 1850-1880* (doctoral diss., University of California, Los Angeles, 1974), pp. 63-64. (University Microfilms Order No. 74-18,772.)

2. Ibid., p. 156.

3. Ibid., p. 189.

4. Ibid., p. 249.

5. Ibid., p. 270.

6. Ibid., p. 302.

7. Richardo Romo, *Mexican Workers in the City: Los Angeles 1915-1930* (doctoral diss., University of California, Los Angeles, 1975), p. 19. (University Microfilms Order No. 761157.)

8. Ibid., p. 145.

9. Ibid., pp. 145-46.

10. Ibid., p. 171.

11. Gilbert George Gonzalez, *The System of Public Education and Its Function Within the Chicano Communities, 1920-1930* (doctoral diss., University of Cali-

fornia, Los Angeles, 1974), p. 121. (University Microfilms Order No. 75-9392.)

12. Ibid., p. 130.

13. Ibid., p. 149.

14. Ibid., p. 150.

15. Ibid., p. 167.

16. Albert Michael Camarillo, "The Making of a Chicano Community: A History of the Chicanos in Santa Barbara, California, 1850-1930" (doctoral diss., University of California, Los Angeles, 1975), pp. 104-5. A revised edition was published more recently: *Chicanos in a Changing Society: From Pueblos to American Barrios in Santa Barbara and Southern California, 1848-1930* (Cambridge, Mass.: Harvard University Press, 1979). All citations following are from the unpublished dissertation.

17. Ibid., p. 134.

18. Ibid., p. 172.

19. Ibid., p. 246.

20. Ibid.

21. Ibid., pp. 246-47.

22. Ibid., pp. 301-2.

23. Ibid., p. 303.

24. Arnoldo De Leon, *White Racial Attitudes Toward Mexicanos in Texas, 1821-1900* (doctoral diss., Texas Christian University, 1974), pp. 91-92. (University Microfilms Order No. 75-3458.) A revised version was published more recently: *The Tejano Community, 1836-1900* (Albuquerque: University of New Mexico Press, 1981). All citations following are from the unpublished dissertation.

25. Ibid., p. 219.

26. Ibid., pp. 161-62.

27. Ibid., p. 278.

28. Robert Johnson Rosenbaum, *Mexicano versus Americano: A Study of Hispanic-American Resistance to Anglo-American Control in New Mexico Territory, 1870-1900* (doctoral diss., University of Texas, 1972), p. 34. (University Microfilms Order No. 73-18,492.) A revised version was published more recently: *Mexicano Resistance in the Southwest: "The Sacred Right to Self Preservation"* (Austin: University of Texas Press, 1981). All citations following are from the unpublished dissertation.

29. Ibid., p. 163.

30. Ibid., p. 187.

31. Ibid., p. 253.

32. Ibid., p. 252.

33. W. S. Burke to Sen. George T. Edmunds, December 21, 1883, in ibid., footnote 34, p. 254.

34. Griswold del Castillo, *La Raza Hispana Americana*, p. 302.

35. Jacqueline Joann Taylor, *Ethnic Identity and Upward Mobility of Mexican Americans in Tucson* (doctoral diss., University of Arizona, 1973), p. 162. (University Microfilms Order No. 74-11,464.)

36. Ibid., p. 160-61.

37. Ibid., p. 136.

38. Ibid., p. 123.

39. Ibid., p. 185.

40. Ibid., p. 205.

41. Eugene Acosta Marin, *The Mexican American Community and the*

Leadership of the Dominant Society in Arizona: A Study of the Mutual Attitudes and Perceptions (doctoral diss., United States International University, 1973), p. 179. (University Microfilms Order No. 73-16,759.)

42. Raymond Herman Charles Teske, Jr., *An Analysis of Status Mobility Patterns Among Middle-Class Mexicans in Texas* (doctoral diss., Texas A & M University, 1973), p. 185. (University Microfilms Order No. 74-13,110.)

43. Diane Adele Trombetta Reynolds, *Economic Integration and Cultural Assimilation: Mexican Americans in San Jose* (doctoral diss., Stanford University, 1974), p. 21. (University Microfilms Order No. 74-27,093.)

44. Ibid., p. 54.

45. Ibid., p. 80.

46. Ibid., p. 140.

47. Ibid.

48. David Emmett Hayes-Bautista, *Becoming Chicano: A "Dis-Assimilation" Theory of Transformation of Ethnic Identity* (doctoral diss., University of New Mexico, 1971), p. 240. (University Microfilms Order No. 72-30,759.)

49. Thomas R. Lopez, Jr., *Prospects for the Spanish American Culture of New Mexico: An Educational View* (doctoral diss., University of New Mexico, 1971), p. 240. (University Microfilms Order No. 72-30,759.)

50. Ibid., p. 245.

51. Ibid., p. 274.

52. Ibid., p. 275.

53. Ibid., p. 294.

54. Donald Eugene Post, *Ethnic Competition for Control of Schools in Two South Texas Towns* (doctoral diss., University of Texas, 1974), p. 119. (University Microfilms Order No. 76-7984.) A related work is Douglas E. Foley, Clarice Mota, Donald E. Post, and Ignacio Lozano, *From Peones to Politics: Ethnic Relations in a South Texas Town, 1900 to 1977* (Austin: University of Texas Press, 1977).

55. Post, *Ethnic Competition for Control of Schools,* p. 120.

56. Ibid., pp. 150-51.

57. Ibid., p. 168.

58. Ibid., pp. 182-83.

59. Ibid., p. 230.

60. Ibid., p. 264.

61. Ibid., p. 293.

62. Ibid., p. 422.

63. Edward Joseph Casavantes, *Reading Achievement and In-Grade Retention Rate of Differentials for Mexican-American and Black Students in Selected States of the Southwest* (doctoral diss., University of Southern California, 1973) (emphasis in original). (University Microfilms Order No. 74-28,425.)

64. Andrea Frieder-Vierra, *School-Year and Summer Reading Growth of Minority and Non-Minority Children in Albuquerque, New Mexico* (doctoral diss., University of New Mexico, 1975), p. 45. (University Microfilms Order No. 75-7957.)

65. Ibid., p. 57.

66. Ibid., p. 58.

67. Ibid., p. 99.

68. Albert Dwight Trevino, *Mexican-American Literature in the High School English Program: A Theoretical and Practical Approach* (doctoral diss., University of Texas, 1974), p. 8. (University Microfilms Order No. 75-4468.)

69. Dorothy Clauser Moyer, *The Growth and Development of Children's Books About Mexico and Mexican Americans* (doctoral diss., Lehigh University, 1974), p. 181. (University Microfilms Order No. 74-21,432.)

70. Patrick E. McBurnette and James W. Kunetka, *Mexican American Perceptions of Isolation in Desegregated School Settings* (April 1976). (ERIC ED 121 555)

71. See Theodore W. Parsons, Jr., *Ethnic Cleavage in a California School* (doctoral diss., Stanford University, 1965). (University Microfilms Order No. 66-2602.)

72. Susanna Adella Hayes, *The Resistance to Education for Assimilation by the Colville Indians, 1872 to 1972* (doctoral diss., University of Michigan, 1973), pp. 8-9. (University Microfilms Order No. 74-3641.)

73. Ibid., p. 164.

74. Ibid., p. 238.

75. Quoted in Wallace Henry Stockman, *Historical Perspectives of Federal Educational Promises and Performance Among the Fort Berthold Indians* (doctoral diss., University of Colorado, 1972), p. 155. (University Microfilms Order No. 72-25,221.)

76. Ibid., p. 161.

77. Ibid., p. 205.

78. Ibid., p. 220.

79. Ibid., p. 294.

80. Joseph John Centrone, Jr., *Teacher Sociocultural Awareness in Selected Schools in New York State Accountable for American Indian Education* (doctoral diss., Syracuse University, 1972), p. 72. (University Microfilms Order No. 73-9585.)

81. Ibid., p. 88.

82. Ibid., p. 114.

83. Donald E. Hjelmseth, *A Study of Attitudes of Selected Elementary School Teachers Toward American Indian Students in the State of Montana* (doctoral diss., University of Montana, 1972), p. 74. (University Microfilms Order No. 72-25,075.)

84. Ann Hillyer Rosenthal Metcalf, *The Effects of Boarding School on Navajo Self-Image and Maternal Behavior* (doctoral diss., Stanford University, 1975), p. 110. (University Microfilms Order No. 75-13,558.)

85. Murray L. Wax and Robert G. Brennig, *Study of the Community Impact of the Hopi Follow Through Program* (October 1973), p. 12. (ERIC ED 096 037)

86. Ibid., p. 27.

87. Ibid., p. 14.

88. Ibid., p. 22.

89. Ibid., p. 14.

90. Ibid., p. 13.

91. Dominic J. Cibrario, *The Pueblo Indians of New Mexico: An Analysis of the Educational System* (1974), p. 28. (ERIC ED 096 030)

92. Ibid., pp. 33-34.

93. Ibid., p. 35.

94. Carol Jean Pierce Colfer, *An Ethnography of Leaderlong Indian School* (doctoral diss., University of Washington, 1974), p. 100. (University Microfilms Order No. 74-15,509); see also Dean Baker, "Americanization of the Native American," *Eugene Register-Guard*, February 8, 1976; Lehman L. Brightman, "Chemawa Indian School: A Case Study of Educational Failure," *Journal of Non-white Concerns* (July 1973), pp. 207-13; and Burton C. Lemmon, *The Historical Development of the Chemawa Indian School* (master's thesis, Oregon State University, 1941).

95. Colfer, *An Ethnography of Leaderlong Indian School*, p. 57.

96. Ibid., p. 101.

97. Ibid., p. 41.

98. Ibid., p. 124.

99. Ibid., pp. 132, 135 (emphasis in original).

100. Ibid., pp. 132–33.

101. Ibid., pp. 135–36.

102. Ibid., p. 44.

103. Miriam Wasserman, *The School Fix, NYC, USA* (New York: Outerbridge and Dienstfrey, 1970), p. 57.

104. Thomas Eugene Glass, *A Descriptive and Comparative Study of American Indian Children in the Detroit Public Schools* (doctoral diss., Wayne State University, 1972), pp. 238, 241. (University Microfilms Order No. 72-28,436.)

105. Beatrice Anne Bigony, *Migrants to the Cities: A Study of the Socioeconomic Status of Native Americans in Detroit and Michigan* (doctoral diss., University of Michigan, 1974), p. 147, footnote 8. (University Microfilms Order No. 76-5548.)

106. Ibid., p. 133.

107. Ibid., p. 149.

108. Ibid., p. 150.

109. Ibid., p. 224.

110. Ibid., p. 154.

111. Patrick James Dubbs, *The Urban Adaptation Patterns of Alaska Eskimos in Anchorage, Alaska* (doctoral diss., Michigan State University, 1975), p. 106. (University Microfilms Order No. 76-5548.)

112. Ibid., p. 88.

113. Ibid., p. 223.

114. Ibid., p. 220.

115. William Thomas Trulove, "Economics of Paternalism: Federal Policy and the Klamath Indians" (doctoral diss., University of Oregon, 1973), p. 172.

116. Ibid., p. 101.

117. Ibid., p. 102.

118. Ibid., p. 121.

119. Ibid., p. 122.

120. Ibid., p. 123.

121. Ibid., p. 126.

122. Ibid., pp. 134–35.

123. Ibid., p. 156.

124. Ibid., p. 236.

125. Ibid., p. 243.

126. Ibid., pp. 236, 242.

127. Ibid., p. 250.

128. See Meyer Weinberg, *A Chance to Learn* (New York: Cambridge University Press, 1977), pp. 228–29.

129. General Accounting Office, *Concerted Efforts Needed to Improve Indian Education* (Washington, D.C.: Comptroller General of the United States, January 17, 1977), p. 19.

130. See Weinberg, *A Chance to Learn*, p. 224.

10

The Minority Community
and its Schools

Ignoring and ignorance can be closely related. By failing to acknowledge a social reality—"ignoring it"—"ignorance" of that reality is created. There is much of this going on in racial-ethnic matters in the literature of the subject as well as in the world of action. The great bulk of writing on minority parents, slim as it is, seldom views them as active initiators. They are regarded as passive objects of white policy. In this chapter, we will examine materials that place minority parents in a more realistic frame. First, we will review the evidence of public opinion polls, both national and local, bearing on attitudes toward busing, then, studies of school-community relations focusing on minority parents, taking special note of Hispanic segregation. Finally, we will analyze some studies of the role of parents working in classrooms.

National Public Opinion Polls

Public opinion studies dealing with desegregation almost wholly concern white opinion.[1] Researchers have been uniformly uninterested in the opinion of black persons on this subject, perhaps because, as in so many other areas, blacks tend to be taken for granted by whites. In 1956 and 1957, Gallup polled blacks on their opinions on desegregation, but did not conduct another poll until 1969. Meanwhile, whites were polled numerous times.

During 1972–1978, two separate polling organizations—the National Opinion Research Center (NORC) and the Survey Research Center (SRC) of the University of Michigan—tapped national black opinion nine times. Respondents were asked their opinion of busing, and the findings were expressed in percentages, as follows:[2]

	Favor	Oppose	Don't Know/ No Answer
NORC, 1972–1978			
1972	52.9	42.9	4.2
1974	59.5	35.3	5.2
1975	45.4	50.3	4.3
1976	50.4	47.3	2.3
1977	45.5	50.0	4.6
1978	48.7	45.6	5.7
SRC, 1972–1976			
1972	53.9	36.3	9.7
1974	49.9	31.0	19.0
1976	57.2	26.8	16.0

In seven out of nine cases, blacks favored busing. The NORC figures show that black support for busing never fell below 45 percent, while opposition to busing fell as low as 35 percent at one point. According to SRC, black support of busing was more decisive, and opposition fell below 30 percent in one year. In these same polls, whites opposed busing at extremely high levels. In the NORC series, white opposition fell below 80 percent only once while in the SRC series it ranged around 66 percent.

In 1970 Gallup introduced a series of questions to blacks and whites on busing. Respondents were asked: "In general, do you favor or oppose the busing of Negro and white school children from one school district to another?" The replies of a national sample of whites and blacks were as follows, in percentages:[3]

Favor   11
Oppose   86
No opinion   3

Instead of presenting a racial breakdown, the poll reported: "When Negro parents are asked the same series of questions, the weight of sentiment is also found to be against busing."

Twice during 1971, Gallup reported responses to the question asked the year before and gave a racial breakdown. In September, responses were reported in percentages:[4]

	Favor	Oppose/No Opinion
Whites	15	85
Blacks	45	55

In November, the report read this way:[5]

	Favor	Oppose	No Opinion
Whites	15	79	6
Blacks	45	47	8

In August, 1972, at the opening of a presidential campaign, Gallup listed a number of stands on disputed issues and asked respondents "whether you would be more likely or less likely to vote for a candidate who took that position." On the issue of "busing school children to achieve racial balance," the responses were in percentages:[6]

	More	Less	No Opinion
Whites	19	70	11
Non-Whites	52	32	16

This marked the first time blacks registered a clear majority in favor of busing on a Gallup poll.

Two years later, in October, 1974, potential voters in the upcoming congressional elections were asked how they would vote on issues as well as on candidates on election day. On the issue of favoring busing, the results were, in percentages:[7]

Whites	28
Non-Whites	75

Once more, an increase in probusing sentiment among blacks was apparent.

Two Harris polls on busing were taken in this period, one in 1972 and another in 1976. The earlier one found 74 percent majority against (20 percent in favor of) busing but Harris provided no breakdown of results by race.[8] In the later poll, there were two questions about busing. Respondents were asked to agree or disagree with the statement that "the courts have made a decision, therefore busing is the law and should be followed." Responses were in percentages:[9]

	Agree	Disagree
Whites	48	45
Blacks	73	17

However, Harris added, "when asked directly an overwhelming 85-9 percent of whites and a 51-38 percent majority of blacks oppose busing."[10]

A national poll conducted in 1979 by the Darden Research Corporation asked, "Do you favor busing to achieve racial integration?" Affirmative replies were received from 57 percent of blacks and 16 percent of whites.[11] A Harris poll the same year reported somewhat comparable findings. It reported opposition to busing by 85 percent of whites and 43 percent of blacks.[12]

In 1981 there were more polls on busing than during any previous year.

In February, Gallup reported responses to the question: "Do you favor or oppose busing children to achieve a better racial balance in the schools?" Responses were in percentages:[13]

	Favor	Oppose	No Opinion
Whites	17	78	5
Blacks	60	30	10

A month later, Harris reported replies to a question whether respondents "would like to see their children bused to another part of town to go to school with children of all races." While the sample as a whole was negative, 74 percent to 21 percent, a breakdown by race found that "by 79 percent-16 percent, whites feel busing is too hard, while blacks favor it by 61 percent-31 percent."[14] These two sets of findings constitute the closest the findings of Gallup and Harris had been since polling on the question began.

Curiously, however, only a few days before this latest Harris poll was published, the *New York Times* reported the finding of its own poll that, with respect to busing, "among blacks the figure was 45 percent opposed to 37 in favor."[15] The *Times* gave no specific date for the poll, stating only that it had been taken "recently."

Meanwhile, *Newsweek* magazine had commissioned Gallup to poll blacks on busing, among other issues. It asked a new kind of question—"Has school busing for integration been helpful to black children on balance—or has it caused more difficulties than it is worth?" Forty percent thought it had been helpful and 50 percent that it had caused more difficulties than it was worth.[16] The *New York Times* headlined this finding in a story: "Half of Blacks in a Poll Question Busing's Value."[17] When the present writer asked an editor of the paper why the *Times* had not reported the Gallup poll finding of a month before that blacks favored busing by 60 percent to 30 percent, he replied that he had not known about that poll. A year later, the *Times* still had not mentioned it.

Gallup had thus found in February, 1981, that blacks supported busing two-to-one, but less than a month later it reported to *Newsweek* that by a margin of five to four blacks regarded busing as more troublesome than it was worth. Were blacks this fickle or did the explanation lie with the two very different questions asked by Gallup within weeks of each other? The second is a far more probable explanation.

Reviewing all the national polling data, two conclusions can be made. First, more times than not, blacks favored busing rather than opposed it, and second, there is no basis in national data for asserting that blacks have opposed busing in numbers approaching those of whites.

Statewide Polls

During 1974–1975, two statewide polls were conducted in Ohio. In the first, persons were asked whether they favored or opposed integration with or without busing. The following were the responses in percentages:[18]

	Without Busing:			With Busing:		
	Yes	No	Undecided	Yes	No	Undecided
Blacks	78	14	8	62	36	2
Whites	74	17	9	18	74	8

The second Ohio poll asked: "Would you favor or oppose a federal constitutional amendment to prohibit forced busing of school children to achieve racial integration in the public schools?" Responses follow in percentages:[19]

	Favor	Oppose	No Opinion
Blacks	47	42	11
Whites	68	23	9

In 1975, the Texas Poll queried: "Do you favor or oppose the busing of children to bring about racial integration in the schools?" Respondents answered, in percentages:[20]

	Favor	Oppose	Don't Know
Anglo-Americans	8	87	5
Mexican Americans	31	55	14
Blacks	51	37	12

This is one of the few statewide polls that reports opinions of Mexican Americans. In Delaware, during 1974, blacks split 53 percent–47 percent against busing.[21]

In the main, statewide data indicate fairly definite black support for busing.

Local Polls

During the late 1960s and early 1970s, a few local polls on busing were taken. Four cities in Connecticut were polled in 1966:[22]

Negro and white opinion on proposal to bus Negro children to schools in white neighborhoods, four Connecticut cities, 1966 by percent

	Bridgeport		Hartford		New Haven		Waterbury	
	White	*Negro*	*White*	*Negro*	*White*	*Negro*	*White*	*Negro*
Total	100.0	100.0	100.0	100.0	100.0	100.0	100.0	100.0
Agree	19.0	30.7	24.3	59.3	19.1	45.5	17.5	29.6
Disagree	69.2	24.0	62.4	24.4	67.1	36.4	70.4	56.3
Mix, both agree and disagree	5.0	40.0	5.9	9.8	6.4	14.0	5.5	5.9
Don't know	6.8	5.3	7.5	6.5	7.5	4.0	6.5	8.1
N =	516	75	510	123	425	99	382	135

Negro and white opinion on proposal to bus white children to schools in Negro neighborhoods, four Connecticut cities, 1966 by percent

	White	Negro	White	Negro	White	Negro	White	Negro
Total	100.0	100.0	100.0	100.0	100.0	100.0	100.0	100.0
Agree	14.7	33.3	14.7	55.3	13.9	43.4	22.8	45.2
Disagree	76.4	25.3	74.5	27.6	76.5	40.4	62.8	44.4
Mix, both agree and disagree	3.1	38.7	4.3	9.8	5.2	12.1	6.3	6.7
Don't know	5.8	2.7	6.5	7.3	4.5	4.0	8.1	3.7
N =	516	75	510	123	425	99	382	135

The following year, a poll in Washington, D.C., found opinions on busing were as follows, in percentages:[23]

	Favor	Oppose	Not Sure
Black	45	41	14
White	21	69	10

Three polls were taken in Los Angeles. In 1970, respondents were asked whether they favored busing to achieve desegregated schools. They responded in percentages:[24]

	Favorable	Opposed	Undecided
Blacks	56.4	34.9	8.7
Mexican Americans	38.5	47.7	13.8
Whites	16.2	80.8	3.0

Findings in a poll in Los Angeles County the next year were virtually identical. Fifteen percent of whites favored the use of busing, as did 37 percent of Mexican Americans, and 57 percent of blacks.[25] Five years later, in response to a similar question, replies, in percentages, were:[26]

	Favor	Oppose	Not sure
Blacks	68	31	1
Mexican Americans	43	54	4
Whites	12	86	2

During 1970–1976, then, black and Mexican-American support for busing rose while white opposition increased.

In Louisville, during 1976, nearly a year into court-ordered desegregation, 35 percent of blacks and 91 percent of whites expressed opposition to busing.[27] The same year, in Philadelphia, opinions were expressed on the use of busing to achieve racial balance. Responses were, in percentages:[28]

	Approve	Disapprove	Don't Know
Blacks	39	45	16
Whites	8	86	6

In Detroit, also in 1976, blacks and whites opposed busing in differing proportions: 40 percent of the blacks and 76 percent of whites.[29] In Milwaukee, 55 percent of blacks and 24 percent of whites favored busing.[30] Busing for integration in Buffalo was the subject of a poll released in 1976. The responses in percentages were:[31]

	Blacks	Whites
Favor	68.3	15.5
Oppose	24.5	70.0
No opinion	7.2	14.5

In Hamilton County (Cincinnati) blacks favored desegregation without busing (80 percent) or with busing (54 percent). Figures for whites were 82 percent and 13 percent.[32] Long Islanders in Suffolk and Nassau counties were split over busing black children into white schools as follows, in percentages:[33]

	Blacks	Whites
Favor	48	22
Oppose	32	71
Undecided	20	7

Late in 1976, less than a year after an earlier poll, Philadelphians' opposition to busing rose somewhat among blacks and fell slightly among whites.[34] A San Diego poll asked in 1978 whether respondents would favor their child being transported to another school if it meant she or he would get a better education. The responses, in percentages, were:[35]

	Alaskan/Indian	Black	Hispanic	Asian	White
Yes	17	63	46	32	30
No	66	32	42	59	61

In Cleveland, during 1978, whites opposed busing by a margin of 86 to 9, while blacks rejected it by a margin of 54 percent to 33 percent.[36] In the San Bernardino Valley, California, area a Harris poll found minorities favored busing for desegregation by 52 percent, with 38 percent opposed to it. Whites opposed it by a 53 percent margin. (Several years earlier, the figure for whites had been 79 percent.)[37] In Milwaukee, early in 1979, 74 percent of whites but only 39 percent of blacks opposed busing their children to other neighborhoods.[38]

During the same year, 1979, Chicagoans were polled twice on busing. In the first, results were, in percentages:[39]

	Blacks	Whites
Favor	48	14
Oppose	46	80
Don't know	6	7

Following are the responses on the second poll, in percentages:[40]

	Blacks	Latinos	Whites
Acceptable	56	38	9
Not acceptable	29	57	82

It is difficult to compare the two sets of responses since the questions differed.

In 1980, respondents in Pinellas County (St. Petersburg), Florida, were asked whether or not the busing of their children had worked out satisfactorily. In percentages, findings were as follows:[41]

	Blacks	Whites
Satisfactory	69	38
Not satisfactory	29	57
Don't know	2	5

Late in 1980, after a year of a desegregation plan involving busing, respondents in Seattle were asked whether the plan should be continued or discontinued. They replied as follows, in percentages:[42]

	White/Asian	Other
Continue	27	63
Discontinue	68	31
Don't know/No answer	5	5

In New Castle County, Delaware (Wilmington), after one year of extensive busing as part of a metropolitan desegregation plan, black parents' attitudes toward desegregation grew more positive.[43] This finding is striking because far more black children than white children are bused in the plan.

Blacks in local polls favored busing in a large majority of cases. While it is not possible to "add" results from local, statewide, and national polls, clearly the main tendency of black opinion in each category is to favor busing. Nor does there seem to be a decline in black approval during the past five or more years. One reason is the fairly uniform positive findings of inquiries into how black parents of bused children evaluate the experience. With the spread of desegregation through busing blacks have had experiences with busing that they tend to view positively.

How accurately are those poll findings perceived by the learned public and the mass media? Stated succinctly: not very.

Some ten days after Gallup reported in February, 1981, that blacks favored busing by a 60–30 margin, Thomas Sowell wrote: "Central to the civil rights crusade is school busing—which has never had majority support among blacks."[44] CBS News twice within a week informed its viewers inaccurately. Fred Graham said "polls show that seventy-seven percent of all Americans including the majority of blacks, oppose it [busing]."[45] Richard Threlkeld stated that "most Americans, black and white, think that busing is the wrong vehicle."[46]

One reason for this widespread ignoring of available evidence is the failure of polling organizations to relate the most recent of their surveys to older ones. The March, 1981, Gallup poll which found—and reported to *Newsweek*—a majority of blacks regarding busing as more troublesome than it was worth contained no hint that less than a month earlier Gallup had found that most blacks favored busing. Editors hastily incorporated selective findings into headlines. The principal finding of Gallup's *Newsweek* poll had been headlined both in the magazine and in the *New York Times*. Yet, when *that* finding was contradicted three weeks later by a new Harris poll, neither *Newsweek* nor the *Times* took note of it. Late in March, 1981, Harris reported that of black families who had experienced busing, 74 percent found it satisfactory and another 21 percent partly satisfactory. (Figures for whites whose children had been bused were 48 percent and 37 percent.)[47]

Social scientists who have continued to ignore black opinion on busing thereby add to the general misimpression of the findings.

The black press has not perpetrated inaccuracies about busing as much as the white press has. But black civil rights organizations, principal proponents of school desegregation, seem to have been somewhat intimidated by repeated erroneous assertions that blacks oppose busing. It is difficult to find statements by civil rights leaders rectifying the errors. Nor can one easily find counterassertions that blacks favor busing. Almost entirely overlooked, in the black press and elsewhere, are the strongly probusing sentiments of black students attending black colleges, a group often assumed to be less "integrationist" than others. Yet, in Fall, 1980, 75.1 percent of freshman students in black public colleges favored busing for "racial balance." Their peers in black private colleges favored it by a 71.4

percent margin.[48] In either case, their probusing levels exceeded those even of the general black population.

The black community has frequently criticized busing because the burden of busing is distributed unequally. In some communities, they have mounted demonstrations on the issue. Charlotte, for example, responded with a revision of busing that tended to equalize assignments between black and white children. When the small black population of Portland, Oregon, was asked to boycott the schools on the issue, many did so. In Milwaukee, however, a much larger black community refused to heed such calls although the inequality in busing burdens was manifest in that city.

Since the desegregation movement in this country has been largely a black movement, it is no wonder that blacks rally to busing. The distortions of the mass media, or claims to the contrary of individuals who assert that they represent black opinion, should not obscure this basic quality of black opinion.

Hispanics and Residential Segregation

In public opinion surveys on desegregation, Hispanics usually place themselves midway between black and white positions. They favor busing less than blacks and oppose it less than whites. Yet, only a handful of national polls have included Hispanics, so generalizations should be made carefully. A more basic question is: What has been the Hispanic experience with segregation? In the Southwest, school boards enforced school segregation for many years.[49] Mexican Americans felt the full force of exclusion, isolation, and planned deprivation. To a lesser degree, Puerto Ricans had a parallel experience on the Island as well as in New York City. Residential segregation is the principal mechanism for perpetuating school segregation, now that *Brown* forbids direct exclusion; but until recently, the subject, as it affected Hispanics, was virtually unexplored.

Ghetto-like *colonias* where recent immigrants from Mexico were concentrated resulted from extralegal exclusory actions by real estate interests in the Southwest. During the first half of this century, such segregated settlements could be found in numerous locations. In large cities in the North a more formal process was used. During the 1930s, for example, realtors in Chicago policed restrictive covenants that prohibited the transfer of real property to certain classes of persons including blacks, Mexican Americans, Jews, Catholics, and others.[50] These private covenants were enforced in state courts. The process was repeated in city after city. In 1948, the U.S. Supreme Court, in *Shelley* v. *Kraemer*, prohibited further enforcement by state courts, but did not invalidate restrictive covenants as such. Federal housing agencies, which had formally endorsed the idea of ethnically homogeneous housing, continued to refuse mortgage guarantees for purchases that would make an "undesirable" change in the neighborhood. Although blacks were the main target of such regulations, Hispanics were also affected.

In 1977–1978, the first comprehensive analyses of residential segregation among Hispanics were made. There were three separate studies: Manuel Lopez and Rosario Torres-Rainer examined Mexican Americans in the Southwest while Douglas Massey investigated Hispanics in twenty-nine urbanized areas of the country.[51]

Massey used the 1970 Census as the base of his work, as did the other two researchers, but his had the broadest compass. He focused on two points of interest: the segregation of Hispanics from whites and blacks, and socioeconomic influences on Hispanic segregation. (Massey writes of "Spanish Americans" rather than Hispanics but we will use the latter term except in direct quotations.)

Hispanics are far less segregated from whites than they are from blacks, although this varies among metropolitan areas. In Seattle, Washington, D.C., and New Orleans, the degree of Hispanic-white segregation is only half that in New York and Chicago. Whether in suburbs or central cities, blacks are highly segregated from whites, while Hispanics in suburbs are much less segregated from whites than are Hispanics in central cities. In the suburbs, too, Hispanics live far away from blacks. They are much less concentrated in central cities than are blacks, and Massey declares: "The larger inner-city 'ghetto' is simply not as pervasive a feature of the urban experience of Spanish Americans as it is for blacks."[52] Segregation from blacks does not differ among American-born or immigrant Hispanics. Within the Hispanic population itself, blacks and whites are highly segregated. Indeed, writes Massey, "the pattern of concentration for white and black Spanish Americans parallels those for whites and blacks in general."[53]

Puerto Ricans, Massey found, are less segregated from blacks than are other Hispanics, and are more concentrated in central cities. They are also more segregated from whites than are Cubans and Mexican Americans. Except for black Hispanics, contends Massey, "Puerto Ricans behave the most like a segregated urban minority in the classical sense."[54]

Massey inquired whether Hispanic segregation was more ethnic than socioeconomic. In the latter term he included education, family income, and occupation. These socioeconomic factors proved to be at the heart of Hispanic-white segregation. With increased education, Hispanics tend to be less segregated from whites. This does not hold, however, for Puerto Ricans. With reference to economic factors, Massey found that "Spanish-white segregation declines with increasing income while Spanish-black and black-white desegregation do not."[55] Once more, however, Puerto Rican segregation from whites does not fall with increasing income of Puerto Ricans. This leads Massey to conclude that "Puerto Ricans are more like black Americans than they are . . . [like] other Spanish Americans."[56] When considering occupation, Massey found:

The difference between the most highly segregated occupational group and the least segregated group is 29.4 points for Spanish-white segregation. In contrast black-white and Spanish-black segregation scores are generally invariant across occupational groups. Segregation [for these groups] is maintained at a high level no matter what the occupation.[57]

The higher the occupational group of Hispanics the less they were segregated from whites. Once again, this did not hold for Puerto Ricans. Blacks and Puerto Ricans, regardless of socioeconomic level, continued to be segregated from whites and Hispanics at undiminished levels.

Hispanics who lived in largely white suburbs were barely segregated, if at all. As Massey pointed out, they were also likely to share the socioeconomic position of their white neighbors. When, however, Hispanics lived in concentrated fashion within inner city areas, their socioeconomic position was usually quite low. Why? Massey suggested, "Inferior school systems and poorer job opportunities in central cities certainly must act as a restrictive force in determining the potential for socioeconomic advancement of Spanish Americans who live there."[58]

Massey stated that to prescribe a common remedy for the housing segregation of blacks and Hispanics is a mistake. In the light of his research, he stressed that blacks still suffer chiefly from racial discrimination. Any remedy for black housing segregation, therefore, must be based on strong legal action to prevent discrimination in the purchase of property and in credit markets. Hispanics, on the other hand, suffer principally from socioeconomic disadvantages in gaining housing equality. Improved education and more equitable income, Massey contended, would greatly improve the housing position of Hispanics. He doubted that it would lessen discrimination against blacks.

In the course of his analysis, Massey several times addressed possible reasons behind the considerable and persistent Hispanic housing segregation from blacks. He considered it in part, at least, as a preference by Hispanics. He wrote: "Spanish Americans apparently tend to follow the lead of the white majority in their residential behavior towards blacks."[59] This conclusion is not based on public opinion or other data on attitudes, but is an interpretation of demographic data. Its possible significance for understanding Hispanic attitudes on school desegregation and busing is considerable.

Lopez studied the housing segregation of Mexican Americans in fifty-six southwestern cities during the decade of the 1960s. Using essentially the same sources of information as did Massey, the Census of 1960 and the Census of 1970, he found the greatest decline in Mexican-American Anglo segregation and the least decline in Mexican-American black segregation. Like Massey, Lopez found that Mexican-American Anglo segregation followed income level, and that those with higher incomes were less segregated. This does not mean that no segregation at all exists for Mexican

Americans if their incomes are high. Indeed, in the cities studied, racial or ethnic segregation for all three groups exceeded segregation based on occupational distribution.

"Affordability," Lopez wrote, "is not a major factor in assessing majority-minority residential segregation."[60] Along with Massey, Lopez indicated "a distinct possibility that the case of the Mexican American's segregation from the Anglo majority is different from that of the black minority."[61] Just as white housing was segregated by socioeconomic factors, so was Mexican-American Anglo housing, but somewhat less so. This was far different from the case with black-white housing or Mexican-American black segregation. Thus, observed Lopez, "Whereas blackness continues to be a serious handicap, the implication is that prejudice against Mexican Americans, especially those of the 'high type,' has diminished to the point where their segregation from the majority parallels the overall class segregation for the city."[62]

Lopez reported that "Mexican Americans view themselves, and are more frequently viewed by Anglos as 'white'."[63] He noted, too, that Mexican-American black relations in the Southwest have long been strained as "Mexican Americans perceived, and continue to perceive, themselves as 'white' and 'superior' to blacks, a sentiment not much discouraged by the Anglo majority."[64] Blacks repaid this prejudicial reaction in like ways. "Mexican Americans from Texas appeared to have internalized the dominant white population's negative attitudes toward blacks."[65] Lopez's statements on racial attitudes seemed to be based on personal familiarity rather than on any data reproduced in his work. Their possible relation to attitudes on school busing and desegregation is clear.

In discussing remedies for housing problems of Mexican Americans (and other ethnic groups), Lopez proposed that equal housing rather than integrated housing is the real problem. He acknowledged the harm of segregation while he welcomed the improvement of ghetto housing. At the same time, he wondered whether segregation will ever become a voluntary affair. If it did and people were given a choice to live among their "own," an attack on segregation "could only come from an assimilationist system and its cultural premises."[66]

Torres-Raines studied housing segregation of Mexican Americans in twenty cities in Texas and California. Most of the households studied in these cities were found to be in barrio areas, heavily concentrated, and patterned by socioeconomic positions. Yet, the obvious segregation of Mexican Americans could not be explained solely by socioeconomic factors —ethnic discrimination also played a part. Torres-Raines found that nearly two-thirds of the segregation she studied in twenty cities was explained by housing expenditures rather than by ethnic factors. This was truer of Texas cities than of California cities. Nevertheless, Torres-Raines found that "as similarities in socioeconomic status have increased over time, such changes have not been accompanied by significant reductions in the magnitude of residential segregation of Mexican Americans in the Southwest."[67] This was an unexpected finding, given the large component of housing segregation due to socioeconomic factors and the rise in average incomes of Mexican Americans during the 1960s. This finding also contradicted those of both Massey and Lopez, which were that segregation decreased during the same period.

Lopez and Massey dealt with two dimensions of housing segregation—the racial/ethnic factor and socioeconomic factors. Torres-Raines added a third—an ecological factor. By this she meant distinctive factors in individual cities. She found, for example, that exclusion of Mexican-American families in Galveston and Lubbock, Texas, and in San Francisco, California, was far greater than in Brownsville and McAllen, Texas, and in Fresno, California. Part of the explanation for such differences is demographic, according to Torres-Raines. In the cities near the Mexican border of both Texas and California, there is less housing segregation. Perhaps the large size of the Mexican-American population in these cities dictates that the smaller Anglo population has less space in which to relocate.

Unlike Massey and Lopez, Torres-Raines did not deal with Mexican-American/black segregation. She did, however, speak to the comparative neglect by researchers of the subject of housing segregation of whites:

In the final analysis . . . it is Anglo-American residential segregation that continues to be the greatest and their residential dispersion that continues to be the least evident. Further investigation must recognize and focus on this fact, and researchers should deal with it equally as scientifically as they are doing in studying minority housing problems.[68]

The point is important since in a racist society "problems" tend to be defined as "minority" in nature even when the dynamic of their development lies with the "majority."

The three works just reviewed permit several generalizations. First, they agreed on the existence of housing segregation of Hispanics. Second, the segregation varied among Hispanic subgroups—it was highest for Puerto Ricans and black Hispanics, and lowest for Cubans. Third, socioeconomic rather than ethnic factors explained most of the segregation. Fourth, Hispanic-black segregation was high and does not seem to be dropping. All these generalizations are based on the experiences of the 1960s.

The Census of 1980 has not yet been analyzed to permit precise updating of these generalizations. Several observations, however, may be in order. As Hispanics move increasingly to suburbs, their places—and more—are taken in the barrios by poor immigrants from Mexico, and a greater class division seems to be in the offing. The relative growth of Hispanic school segregation during 1968–1976 also implies increased residential segregation.[69] Thus, America's Hispanic population seems to be in for heightened experience with segregated housing and schools, but how this experience will impact upon desegregation-related issues remains to be seen.

Effects of Parents on Schooling

Generalizations abound in this area of interest while solid studies are rare. Just as school administrators and teachers generally view parents as factors external to the task of education, researchers have seen little point in studying the effects of parents on schooling. In very recent years, however, it has become increasingly difficult to ignore the role of parents as dissatisfaction with the educational performance of schools has risen. One sees them more frequently on the school premises, and not only for "open houses" or other special occasions.

Organized parents are learning to wield political power in order to exert greater parental influence in school affairs. This is especially true in the areas of compensatory education, bilingual education, desegregation, and Indian education. Federal and state statutes and administrative guidelines often require parental participation in programs. Litigation around this right has grown rapidly in courts on all levels, but little of this activity has yet influenced research.

Indeed, the subject of organized parental action is virtually absent from standard guides to educational research. For the most part, research on parents focuses on their individual relationship to their own children in the home. Or it is designed simply to discover some inert characteristics of parents—income, occupation, education—in the conviction that such data are important for determining academic achievement. Seldom, however, are parents studied from the viewpoint of their role in the school or in changing the school.

But educational research does yield, however reluctantly, to new currents of interest.

Contemporary educational research assumes a certain fatalism with respect to the home, which it views only as an inactive expression of socioeconomic position. Parents who are poor are expected, by virtue of poverty, to provide a less favorable learning climate for the child. Thus, the school's failure to educate poor children is frequently ascribed to parental poverty. Two recent studies are of interest in this respect.

Since 1968, the Educational Testing Service (ETS) has been conducting a project entitled "Disadvantaged Children and their First School Experiences." Recently, study director Virginia Shipman and associates dealt with, among other things, parents in families of varying degrees of poverty and their roles in the academic success of their children.[70] In one report, relating to a study of 103 black third graders of low socioeconomic status, the researchers found a constant pattern: "The most common picture that emerged for those children who showed the most gain in academic achievement was the . . . continuing warm and stimulating classroom environment combined with a home environment that provided the child emotional support in general and support for school activities in particular."[71] The researchers also found that positive home influences were strengthened by participating mothers who received information and emotional support from the schools. "In response to greater acceptance [by the school]," Shipman wrote, the mother "participated more; and from such participation there appeared to develop an increased sense of efficacy and optimism with greater awareness and use of community resources to meet family needs."[72]

The ETS researchers learned that a family's help to its children depended on more than beneficent interactions between parent and child. As Shipman put it, "cognitive gains are likely to be largest and to be substantial when there is [also] support in the total ecology of the child . . . in adequate health care, nutrition, housing, and general family support."[73] Thus, Shipman cautioned, "Parent-to-child or teacher-to-child models appear too simplistic for characterization of minority children's achievement behaviors."[74]

In a related report on the ETS project, Shipman and associates interviewed 1,375 mothers during Year 6 of the project; 71 percent of the mothers were black.[75] They emphasized the pitfalls of viewing the role of the family solely through its social status: "Even though family status remains relatively constant over a number of years, the way in which the family operates within the environment may change considerably."[76] Residential mobility of the family and absence of the father, two factors dearly beloved by many educational researchers and educators as explanations of low achievement by poor students, were found to be almost unrelated to the academic achievement of children in the project.

The economic conditions of inner-city families in the study had deteriorated over six years; yet, the achievement of their children had not declined. At the same time, economic support to impoverished families seemed to help set the stage for the educational improvement of their children. Precisely how this influence worked out is not known. It is surely worth further investigation. Shipman observed the need among the children of impoverished families in the project for extensive community services: "Despite the low representation in the study sample of those in the most impoverished circumstances, a considerable minority of the mothers reported that: (1) their child had not been to a doctor since entering grade school [the children were now third graders]; (2) they had no friends; and (3) their child had a problem which was of serious concern."[77]

In another study, David Armor and associates investigated, among other things, the role of parents in aiding schools to implement successful reading programs.[78] Between 1972 and 1975, poor black and Mexican-American sixth-grade students in twenty elementary schools in Los Angeles showed significant increases in reading scores.[79] To what degree could any of the success be attributed to parental action?

"In black neighborhoods," reported Armor, "the more vigorous were the schools' efforts to involve parents and community in school decision making, the better did sixth grade students in those schools fare in reading attainment."[80] It is noteworthy that Armor placed the emphasis in this respect on school initiative, but he also found that mere parental presence in the school played a constructive role:

We examined whether the individual students whose parents met with the teacher had improved reading scores; they did not. Parents visiting in classrooms apparently affect students as a group; this finding contributes to our belief that parent visits reflect the atmosphere of a classroom.[81]

The specific mechanisms whereby the atmosphere is communicated to the children are still to be explored.

The degree of community involvement, Armor found, was very low in the areas in which the twenty schools were located. This extended to participation in reading programs as well. The level of income and residential stability gave no clue to the degree of community involvement. One finding was perplexing: "For black schools, levels of parent involvement appear to relate rather closely to student reading gains. . . . No such relationship appears in the Mexican-American subsample."[82] One possible explanation which Armor did not mention is that the schools in Los Angeles were especially resistant to Mexican-American parental influence. Another is that Mexican-American parents may not be focusing their interest on the improvement of reading as much as on bilingual instruction.

Several studies have examined the role of parents in desegregated schools. While this was not Willis Hawley's major interest, he touched on it in his study of 2,142 fifth-grade students in seventy-nine classrooms in North Carolina.[83] He found that "parental support for school . . . accounts for just under 10 percent of the variance in students' reported interest in achievement."[84] This is a modest factor but not to be ignored. Of considerable interest was Hawley's finding that "for the students in this study, the relationship between parental education and parental support for achievement in school is very weak."[85] This finding contradicts a very widely held conviction by educators and researchers. And it bears further exploration.

During 1975–1977, the System Development Corporation evaluated the operations of the Emergency School Aid Act (ESAA). John Coulson wrote annual reports on a national scale while Jean Wellisch reported on a sample of twenty-four elementary schools.[86] In the 1976 report, Coulson wrote: "Parent involvement can apparently be beneficial to student achievement, when those parents are present in the classrooms as paid instructional aides, volunteers, or visitors."[87] One of the conditions he found to be important in the more successful programs was that "parents were more heavily involved in the classroom. . . ."[88] The evaluation of the third year of the ESAA project did not mention the role of parents.

In the first of her two in-depth studies, Wellisch found the parent role important. "In the ESAA in-depth schools, the key elements of success in both reading and math achievement included: (1) parent participation in the classroom; (2) the use of objectives; and (3) relatively high per-pupil costs of remedial specialists."[89] Analyzing the relative contribution of various factors in predicting reading and mathematics achievement, Wellisch ranked "parent involvement in the classroom" as second (for reading) or third (for mathematics) among five of seven factors. Indeed, with respect to prediction of reading achievement, parent involvement was more important than "per pupil costs for remedial reading specialists."[90] Wellisch stressed that by parent involvement she did not mean just any school-related activity:

Two features of the relation of parent involvement to achievement should be underlined: first, that involvement in the classroom, rather than in the school in general, is related to academic success; second, that parent involvement specifically, and not the use of instructional aides in general, is associated with school success in the in-depth study.[91]

Further, she specified that it is "the use of paid parent aides in the classroom" that matters rather than the use of paid outsiders.[92]

Wellisch detected still other parental effects. In schools where principals reported that parent visitors were racially representative of the school as a whole, two conditions were noticeable: multiethnic materials were used more frequently and students reported improved student-teacher interaction.[93] Wellisch offered no explanation. One could argue plausibly that the presence of minority parents in force, so to speak, influenced teachers and other school staff positively in the direction of racial fairness.

In her second-year report, Wellisch did not detect any parental effects.

Forehand, Ragosta, and Rock barely touched on the subject of parental effects in their study of desegregated schools, and then only cryptically.[94] An experienced official, formerly with a federal agency deeply involved in desegregation implementation, wrote: "One basic problem that occurs in practically every community that must desegregate its schools is the failure of the school administration to thoroughly inform parents of what is to take place."[95] In the years since this statement was made, the problem has probably eased because of the rise of organized citizen participation in desegregation planning. A detailed account of a black parent's futile efforts to probe into low black student achievement in the Madison, Wisconsin, schools suggests the persistence of administrative resistance to parental inquiry.[96]

Jesse Kinard studied the effect of parental involvement on the achievement of first and second siblings in two compensatory education programs, Head Start and Follow Through.[97] At the time of the research, conducted in Hillsborough County, Florida, children from the former program were at least in second grade, and from the latter program in second through fifth grades. Kinard found: "The children who attended Head Start and Follow Through programs tend to achieve higher scores than those attending only Head Start; children with directly involved parents tend to achieve higher scores than siblings with indirectly involved parents; parental involvement tends to have a greater effect on achievement of second siblings than of first siblings; [and] parental involvement and duration of program had a significant effect on both siblings."[98] Unfortunately, Kinard did not provide an explanation of those outcomes, nor did he propose a theory that would predict the outcomes. Consequently, the practical value of his findings was minimized, and we are left with a desirable outcome but with no idea of how it might be duplicated with other children.

Wilda Winters surveyed the role of black mothers in urban schools, possibly located in New Haven, Connecticut.[99] She chose two heavily black schools, one experimental, the other a control. Specifically, she sought to discover whether mothers would be less alienated in a school which encouraged participation and involvement. One hundred sixty mothers, equally divided among the two schools, were matched by age, number of children, education, marital and employment status, socioeconomic status, and other factors. As Winters expected, mothers whose children attended the experimental school were less alienated. In what ways was this true? They were more actively involved in school activities; they tended less toward normlessness, that is, to approval of illegal and illegitimate means of goal attainment; they demonstrated a greater understanding of events that helped determine their lives; and they saw the school as facilitating skill acquisition by their children.

At the same time, the actions of the mothers in both schools converged, in part or wholly, with respect to two factors. Winters found that while mothers in the experimental school were considerably more involved, around half the mothers in the control school were also quite active in visiting classes, raising funds, attending workshops, and parent-teacher meetings. This finding, Winters declares, "belies the continued posture of many urban school administrators and educators concerning the so-called apathy and pervasive disinterest of their parent constituents."[100] In another respect—a feeling of powerlessness—the two groups of black mothers felt alike. This sentiment attached, of course, more to structures and processes outside the school. Even the less alienated mothers did not feel that their heightened activity within the school could change appreciably the kind of world their children would inherit.

Reginald Clark made an unusual study of black families as educators.[101]

He visited and observed thirteen poor black families in Chicago in an effort to discover patterns of family living which encouraged academic success of high-achieving black students. More formally stated, Clark's hypothesis was that "the family's culture is important to successful educational performance."[102] (It was a relief to meet some real persons rather than statistical representations of them.)

Clark observed twenty-two practices characteristic of families of academically successful black high school students, and nine that characterized the homes of less successful students. The first group was as follows:

1. The parents view the role of the family in the educational process as an important one.

2. The parents have consistently stressed the importance of schooling and education to the student.

3. Students believe in the importance of post-secondary education.

4. Schooling (per se) is seldom pursued solely for the attainment of knowledge.

5. Students view school attendance as a normal part of their responsibility.

6. Parents guide and direct the student into social activities requiring intellectual functioning.

7. When assisting the students with schoolwork, the mother uses a complex of progressive and traditional instructional techniques.

8. Homework is a regularly performed, almost ritualistic, activity.

9. Ritualistic discussions on school concerns (e.g., teachers, new school policies, etc.) occur between family members.

10. Parents make attempts to visit the school and communicate with the students' teachers.

11. The parents have established clearly delineated parent-child roles.

12. The parents wield the ultimate power and control in the home.

13. We find clearly outlined parentally imposed rules and regulations governing the child's behavior.

14. The student expresses pride in his/her parents.

15. While insisting upon obedience and respect from the student, the parents temper their demands with warmth and love.

16. In these families, the students' time and space are parentally governed inside and out of the house.

17. The student has been highly involved with household responsibilities and tasks.

18. There is a high level of interaction and involvement between siblings.

19. Parents provide the young child with a strong moral foundation.

20. The child usually had early home experiences in mastery learning.[103]

21. Each student appears to be characteristically autonomous and independent, somewhat assertive, and highly structured.

22. The student tends to be possessed of a sense of urgent purpose in the pursuit of goals.

The folowing are the nine characteristics of homes of less successful students:

1. There is little or no overt support (from family members) for this student in his/her quest for educational achievement.[104]

2. There are no consistent, regularly performed learning rituals in the home.

3. The parents and older siblings almost never visit the school.

4. Parents exhibit little awareness of the student's day-to-day school activities and school performances.

5. Parents do not expect students to be responsible for home chores.

6. Parents make few demands on the students.

7. Parents exhibit a sense of helplessness over children's behavior.

8. Early parental life experiences have often been agonizing.

9. Parents are not aware of the extent of their child's school problems.

The first group of characteristics stressed parental initiative and control in the home, with ample consultation and discussion among family members. Students in these homes were functioning family members with specific duties to perform. They also operated as independent, though structured, individuals whose life goals were definite. "Insurrection and rebelliousness," Clark noted, "were never seen with these students."[105] The second group were, for the most part, negatives of practices in the first group. Points seven and eight merited comment, however. Before characterizing the second group, Clark had observed: "Although all these parents were interested in their child's education, they were imbued with a stronger sense of powerlessness over their lives. 'I can't do nothin' about it' was a typical response among this group."[106] (Winters had observed a similar sense of powerlessness among black mothers of varying degrees of alienation.) Perhaps this sense of powerlessness was connected with the "agonizing" early parental life experiences Clark reported. In any event, one may guess that both lists of characteristics could easily be applicable to white children and homes.

The advent in 1971 of limited administrative decentralization in Los Angeles brought citizens advisory councils (CACs) into the school system. Jenkins studied their operation from July, 1972, to October, 1974.[107] Principals, she found, saw the councils as potential competitors for authority in the school. More generally she discovered:

Administrative professionalism, expertise, and experience are considered the overriding criteria for access to decision making, regardless of the qualifications or the socioeconomic status of persons in the school's community. Of thirty-seven principals interviewed, only three mentioned that they would allow increased community involvement in decision making if the parents were intelligent and knowledgeable.[108]

Thus, intelligence without professional credentials was considered insufficient preparation for access to decision making although in other areas of our society, such as voting, one without the other is quite acceptable.

During 1976, the Citizens' Management Review Committee (CMRC) evaluated administrative decentralization in the Los Angeles schools.[109] The group conducted an undetermined number of interviews at area offices during the last two months of 1975, and 223 at individual schools during the Spring of 1976. A CMRC subcommittee reported: "Parents generally want significantly greater involvement in personnel, budget, and program decisions than they currently have or than teachers or principals want them to have."[110]

It was very clear to all concerned just who made decisions regarding single schools. The following table summarizes how four types of respondents perceived the principal decision-maker.[111]

Perceptions about Who Makes Most of the Decisions, by Percent Respondent

Decision-Makers	Principal	Teacher	CAC Chairman	Parent	Average
Principal	25	36	32	40	33
Teachers	27	20	9	20	19
Parents	4	5	5	4	5
District and area offices	0	0	4	0	1
Students	2	2	0	0	1
No response	0	0	11	2	3
Combination of decision-makers	43	38	39	35	39

Principals and teachers were the most frequently cited individual decision-making groups. All respondents had virtually identical perceptions of the weakness of parents in decision-making roles.

The parties concerned differed sharply on the desired extent of CAC involvement in four areas of decision making: goals, program, budget, and personnel. Here is a listing of views by four groups: principals, teachers, CAC presidents, and parents:[112]

Desired Extent of CAC Involvement, by Percent

Respondent	Goals	Program	Budget	Personnel
Principals				
More	73	57	46	18
Less	2	14	27	52
Teachers				
More	46	50	48	21
Less	21	18	21	54
CAC Presidents				
More	79	77	79	54
Less	4	7	5	32
Parents				
More	78	73	67	47
Less	7	11	13	32

(Some pairs equal less than 100 because of lack of responses in some cases.)

Clearly, principals and teachers resisted an increased citizen voice most in areas of "business," that is, budget and personnel and, less so, in program. Parents, on the other hand, favored a strong parental voice in all four areas of interest but were less united on personnel than on the other three areas.

The CMRC subcommittee found school board members and central staff administrators reluctant to delegate any significant degree of authority to lower administrative levels. It also singled out "the apparent ambiguity of authority relationships between different levels of the system" as its most consistent finding.[113] On the lowest administrative level, the principal, whose authority over budgets appeared decisive to local people, turned out to have only marginal control.

While the CMRC study was underway, investigator Irving Croshier was studying advisory councils in west central Los Angeles.[114] These schools enrolled some 46,000 students. Croshier interviewed 136 council members and 44 principals. Principals tended to evaluate the councils' decision-making power as greater than did the members themselves. Considerable apathy characterized the work of the councils. "A major cause of apathy or upheaval . . . ," Croshier wrote, "was the feeling of manipulation or being a 'rubber stamp' of the school administration, be it local or at the district level."[115] Being a member of a council brought little prestige, either in the school or the community. Yet, parents of all racial-ethnic and socio-economic groups wanted more to say about their schools.

Two studies have been made of school-community advisory councils in Detroit.[116] It is difficult to believe that the two researchers were writing about the same city. In 1971, the state legislature, in a momentary enthusiasm for citizen participation and as an alternative to desegregation in Detroit, decentralized the public schools of that city. Eight regional boards were organized and every school in each region was to have an advisory council. The citywide board of education continued in operation.

In the first of the two studies, Robinson Hammonds examined one school and interviewed twenty-three persons, including ten former students. He reported that "two issues surfaced frequently in the majority of interviews: the general lack of citizen involvement, now and in the past, and the general lack of awareness of community people about what goes on at the school."[117] (Hammonds was writing three years after passage of the decentralization law.) On the question of the activity of advisory committees, Hammonds also reported that "the concern expressed was that physical presence of more community people would be of little value without much greater understanding of how the school might best address the educational needs of students."[118] Many of the respondents expressed concern over the poor educational record of the school and were confident that heightened community participation was a prerequisite to educational improvement. This had not yet worked out in practice.

Eleanor Barnwell, an administrator in the decentralization program, analyzed its operations in one of the eight regions. She observed:

Since decentralization, every school program, every major decision and every administrative change under region board authority, required local-school-community council approval. It was virtually impossible to separate the council influence from any of the accomplishments or failures in the schools.[119]

She added that "the region board removed the veil of secrecy from the educational system which had frustrated parents."[120] In general, Barnwell noted, very few community groups participated in the region board's affairs after the fashion of the 1960s. A single organization, the Black Christian Nationalist Church (BCNC), has fairly well dominated the region board since in recent years its representatives have been chairpersons of the board and a majority of the board members. The BCNC pressed schools to install a black studies program and to employ more blacks as school leaders.

Barnwell did not analyze the educational consequences of region board and advisory council activity. She did relate, however, that "parents met, wrote and secured approval of a goal statement from all councils. This statement has been sent home by students annually, and parents have been asked to sign their names indicating their intent to cooperate."[121]

Hammonds's study found decentralization and advisory council activity problematical whereas Barnwell viewed both as accomplished facts with a positive effect on parents' determination of policy. The two studies are directly contradictory on whether or not "the veil of secrecy from the educational system" has been raised. Barnwell said yes, but Hammonds said no. A much more detailed study of the Detroit case is necessary.

Three separate studies have been made of the role of parents in advisory councils mandated under Title I of the Elementary and Secondary Education Act, a compensatory education program for "educationally disadvantaged" children of poor families.[122] The basic law was passed in 1965, but provision for parent participation was not required until six years later. (In 1981, Congress dropped the mandatory feature.)

In the first of these studies, conducted in 1976, Roy Dawson analyzed parent committees in six school districts located throughout Camden County, New Jersey, including the city of Camden. Council members, according to Dawson, "play a limited role in non-decision activities such as attending conferences, observing the Title I instructional program, volunteering their time in the Title I classrooms and in limited cases, act as paid workers in the Title I program."[123] They participated even less in decision-making roles; when they did, it was most likely to be in the preparation of Title I proposals and in evaluation activities around ongoing programs. Parents of higher socioeconomic status tended to occupy key positions on the councils, although all families in Title I were low-income. Many mothers could not attend because of the lack of council funds for babysitting and transportation even though Title I regulations required such funds to be made available. Overall, parents wanted more of a say in decision making but did not want outright control of Title I programs.

Andres Vallado studied Title I Parent Advisory Committees (PACs) in fifty Texas school districts. He found a rather dismal situation. Most PAC members did not know whether their recommendations were ever implemented, few had received any training, and many did not know much about Title I programs in their district. Planning, implementation, and evaluation, in descending order, were the areas in which PAC members participated. Administrators seemed well aware of the limited nature of PAC work:

A number of administrators feel defensive when inquiries are directed at the PACs. There seems to be a feeling of "don't rock the boat," and that if the PACs know their rights and understand what is expected of them, they could cause problems for the district. Therefore, a feeling seems to exist that it is best to keep PACs uninformed whenever practical.[124]

This was consistent with the feeling of a number of PAC members that the committees were "paper committees."[125]

Norman Gross made the third Title I study, which involved Rochester,

New York, and a suburb, Geneva, New York. For part of the period of the study, which extended from 1969 to 1973, Gross was Title I Administrator in Rochester.

The first Parent Advisory Committee on Title I (PACT—as the parent group was called in Rochester) was exceedingly active and skilled. Despite its supposed poverty basis, 48 percent of the first PACT's members were college graduates! (It will be recalled that national guidelines for PACTs were not formulated until 1971.) One effect of PACT's activity was felt in the area of Title I budget composition:

In amount of money budgeted, basic skills represented some 64 percent of the total to some 36 percent for cultural enrichment prior to PACT's input. After PACT's input, 89 percent of the money was budgeted for basic skills and only 11 percent for cultural enrichment.[126]

So effective was PACT in the first year that school officials, including Gross himself, made efforts to co-opt its members.

Late in 1971, the central administration reorganized PACT and produced a dilution of "the sophistication of the committee in its ability to deal with the school administrators."[127] PACT leaders were given jobs in the school system. People from the poor community were also employed in increasing numbers. This trend fitted the viewpoint of the PACTs expressed so well by a member in 1972-1973: "Get some gravy for the folks!"[128] While some skirmishes continued to be fought, the school district tended to have its way.

PACT did, in fact, accomplish some educational changes. Certain programs it deemed marginal or even harmful educationally were eliminated against initial school district opposition. Other programs were initiated at PACT's insistence.

A fundamental reason for PACT's early success lay in its close connection with sophisticated community organizations. As a result of the 1971 reorganization, however, organizational types of members gave way to grass roots representatives who had little or no experience dealing with top administrators and few, if any, connections with citywide sources of political influence.

The PACT in Geneva was far less successful, although it did count a few victories. From the outset, unlike the one in Rochester, the Geneva PACT was a grass roots affair and developed something of a siege mentality. In 1972, it filed a lawsuit in federal court against the school board, charging two violations of Title I regulations. First, PACT asserted that it was not being properly involved in planning and other aspects of Geneva's Title I programs, and, second, that federal funds were being improperly used by the district. This referred to a part of the Title I law which required that Title I funds be compensatory, that is, be in addition to funds spent out of local taxes and state contributions. It was illegal for a school board to finance some programs out of local funds in nonpoverty schools and to fund the same type of programs in poverty schools with federal funds. When this happens, it is called "supplanting," that is, federal funds supplant local funds in poverty schools. Title I funds must be spent over and above what the local school district spends in all schools equally. Otherwise, Title I funds are not truly "extra" or compensatory.[129] Three years after the lawsuit began, it was still in the courts.

While PACTs in both Rochester and Geneva accomplished some changes in Title I programs, they were circumscribed by school authorities. As Gross puts it: "In both cities the school administrations were able to reorganize the PACTs when it appeared that they were becoming too powerful. . . . The school administrators were able to influence and redirect the activities and efforts of the PACTs."[130] Gross's work is notable for its openness and for the comparative lack of personal distortion that could easily have occurred in a study made by a central administrator. As such, it is almost unique. Its substantive findings were very much in line with other research reviewed above.

Two other studies concerned advisory councils outside the context of poverty. John Mason Hill studied the Citizens Advisory Committee program in San Diego, California, which had been created in 1971.[131] After that, Hill found, it became very difficult to evaluate the precise effects of CACs since there had also been a proliferation of other parent participation programs. In some high schools he found as many as twelve different parent advisory groups, each with a special focus of interest (attendance, gifted, discipline, and others). Hill's study found that "many of these groups . . . duplicated efforts, functioned at cross purposes, and seldom communicated."[132]

Although some 1,500 citizens sat on one or another of these advisory groups, most of them, according to Hill, were dominated by principals:

Although the principal is an ex-officio, nonvoting member of the advisory committee, most principals were found to be heavily involved in the planning of CAC meeting agendas, and a majority were also found to dominate the operation of the meetings. . . . All principals involved in the study, as reported by themselves and advisory chairpersons, made use of, to varying degrees, manipulative strategies in order to influence the impressions of advisory committee members as to the principal as the legitimate decision-maker and/or the degree and nature of committee involvement in decision-making.[133]

Within this context, it was not surprising to learn from Hill that "the perceived philosophy seemed to be that 'the schools are doing OK'."[134]

Given such a structure, local community expression was muted. Hill concluded flatly that "citizen involvement in decision-making is only as effective as those in power want it to be."[135] Seldom was staff domination of decision making seriously challenged. "Community involvement in decision-making is generally viewed by educators with a mixture of resentment and apprehension despite educational rhetoric to the contrary," Hill wrote.[136] In the face of an intense public relations effort by educators to convince citizens that the schools were "OK," Hill commented sharply: "It is time to stop selling the schools to the citizens who already own them."[137]

Barbara Hatton, in 1972, studied the operation of School-Community Councils (SCCs) which were part of a funded project, the Urban/Rural School Development Program, in black communities of Dayton, St. Louis, and Bacon County, Georgia.[138] She found little enthusiasm by school authorities to integrate the program into their day-to-day operations. "Take the money and run" seemed to Hatton an accurate description of school district behavior. "None of the districts," she reported, "instituted specialized procedures in administration or accounting to accommodate the U/R program."[139] Hatton pointed out how central an institution the local school was in the three black communities. In the St. Louis neighborhood dominated by the empty shell of the notorious Pruitt-Igoe housing project, "the schools remained as the *only* community institution."[140] Yet, local community opinion failed to find an organizational form for expression.

Practically all the advisory council studies reviewed above dealt with poor and minority children. Robert Francy, however, studied a heavily white, middle- and upper-class Orange County, California, district, located between Los Angeles and San Diego.[141] He interviewed 156 members of parent-advisory committees and twenty-five principals in the Newport-Mesa Unified School District where over 90 percent of the families were white. During 1976, when Francy did his research, 88 percent of committee members had attended college; some had done graduate study. Nearly half had volunteered. Strikingly, slightly over half the parent members were past or present employees of the school district. All in all, even within this affluent community, the composition of the advisory committees was unrepresentative. The upper crust was overrepresented. As in poorer communities, Francy found in Newport-Mesa that "most advisory councils were under the guidance of the school principal."[142] His conclusion parallels that of Hill: the literature suggests that parent advisory councils are a "sham." The present study tends to confirm the findings from the literature.[143] Thus, social class alone did not explain the weakness of parent-advisory councils.

Leaving the topic of advisory councils, let us review a study of Chicano influence on school boards in nineteen districts within Los Angeles County. Mary Montes, a researcher and an activist in Chicano circles, sought to discover whether "the way Chicanos organized on school-related issues in fact produced variation in school policy outputs."[144] Chicano organizations played an important role in political mobilization; such rallying of support was critical for the attainment of demands for bilingual programs and Chicano studies. Those Chicano groups who interacted with governmental sources and outside supportive groups gained more of their school-related

objectives. In school districts with sizable Chicano enrollments administrators tended to be more responsive to Chicano demands. Chicano high
school students received important aid from Chicano college students in
negotiating with school administrators or helping to implement new
Chicano-related programs. College students were also significant in stimulating communitywide activities.

When Montes made her study during 1972–1973, Chicanos were beginning
to occupy a few administrative posts but they tended to be staff rather than
line personnel. Montes characterized the gains as "incremental" rather than
"substantial."

After completing her formal analysis, Montes reproduced in an appendix
a fascinating collection of firsthand comments by Chicanos in each of the
nineteen districts. They are, of course, anecdotal and quite "unscientific,"
but their historical value is considerable. They address the kinds of issues
frequently ignored by educational researchers and thus are suggestive of
research leads for further investigation.

In Montebello, one informant stated that "we . . . have been through
two racist superintendents who have publicly stated that Mexicans are lazy
and stupid, should be in vocational education classes because they're good
with their hands and that their parents aren't interested in the education of
their children."[145] In Baldwin Park, another related:

We have a Chicano working for the school administration as a liaison. She goes out
and scolds the parents for what their kids aren't learning, all the while defending the
superintendent of schools. She and the superintendent eat out of the same plate;
she's their stool pigeon.[146]

Another informant, in ABC district, told Montes: "The superintendent that
helped us was later fired. . . . He went back to teaching in Paramount. We
believe that this occurred because he was so supportive of our efforts—too
supportive of minority people."[147] In Culver City: "Some first and second
generation [Chicano] students are lost sheep; lost in a mass of Anglos."[148]

In Pasadena, an informant dealt with a central issue, thus far largely
ignored by researchers:

When you get a conservative board, their mind-set is the black problem. They don't
see the Chicano as a problem. They see us as buffers between them and the blacks
and thus offer us some token jobs. Before they would put up ten Negroes and say,
"Here's what we're doing for minorities. . . . I suspect . . . [the school board] will
try to use the *Mexicanos*—not so much against the Negroes but in helping keep the
Negroes away from them.[149]

This short lesson in ethnic politics is a valuable one.

The same informant also addressed another important, but neglected,
issue:

Despite the fact that we had made gains such as Chicano studies programs, Chicano skills courses, Chicano surnamed teachers [and] Chicano students are now attending college, our kids are still failing academically. They were failing in the social sciences [and] in English. . . .[150]

She or he was calling upon the Chicano community to pay heed to the entirety of the educational scene. Attaining only some objectives such as ethnic representation in the curriculum and staff did not automatically spell academic success for the children.

Two more informants highlighted another issue. One, from either Downey or Temple City, told Montes: "Some of the [Chicano] kids don't know what a barrio is; their parents have pretty good jobs and maybe that's why they don't have the desire to do something."[151] And in Temple City: "The Chicanos who live here are very much assimilated into the community."[152] Together, these comments suggest a need to analyze class differentiation in the Chicano community more carefully.

Eileen Byrne studied community participation in one decentralized school district in New York City between 1970 and 1977.[153] In 1969, the state legislature divided the city's schools into thirty-one districts and gave each a grant of power that was minimal but included appointment of a superintendent and principals. The local school boards were to be elected by voters of each community. Byrne chose District 22, in southeast Brooklyn, a predominantly Spanish district with substantial numbers of Irish and Italian residents. During the period studied, the number of blacks and Puerto Ricans increased. In 1970, most minority children in the district's schools were not residents but were bused in; by 1976, a majority were residents. By the latter date, the three heavily minority schools were the district's largest and registered the lowest achievement scores. In the district as a whole, 64 percent of students read above grade level.

Turnover in local board elections was modest although somewhat higher than in the city as a whole. The elected boards, however, were unrepresentative of the district population. As Byrne put it:

School District 22 houses a school population that is over 20 percent black, and over 7 percent Spanish. Only 26 percent of the community population are professionals or hold managerial positions. Yet, the board elected in 1975 and reelected in 1977 was 100 percent white, all college graduates, all professionals.[154]

(She herself was one of those elected.) Supporters of the state decentralization law assumed that elections would be nonpartisan, especially with reference to the major political parties and organized interest groups. This did not turn out to be the case in District 22 or elsewhere. Byrne wrote: "Most groups which had power under the highly centralized education system tended to maintain power under decentralization."[155] These included the teachers' union, the administrators' organization, the Democratic party, and Jewish and Catholic groups.

Racial desegregation was the issue that most upset whites in District 22. In 1973 a federal court permitted the city school board to transfer twenty-five minority children from a housing project located outside the district into a school inside the district. Whites resisted; in one case they broke into the school and occupied it. Court action finally settled the case. By 1976, the disparity in overcrowding between predominantly white and minority schools in the district led the local board to propose a rezoning that would transfer minority children to the predominantly white schools. "Home-owners in the southern [that is, white] end of the district," wrote Byrne, "pressed to have their neighborhood schools 'protected' from both an increased number of [minority] students . . . and to be protected from the threat of being closed."[156] The demands were contradictory but powerful nonetheless.

Rezoning of attendance areas to equalize educational opportunities became the single most controversial issue in District 22. Since minority groups were among the least powerful groups in the district, the local school board responded least to their views. As Byrne explains: "The local decision-making process tended to favor those community residents who had financial vested interests in the district and had the freedom to attend the rather time-consuming meetings which drafted the zoning proposals presented to the community school board."[157] The most important decisions were reached at these committee meetings rather than at the public meetings.

Examining the content of speeches made by citizens before the local school board during the years 1970–1977, Byrne found that fully 70 percent dealt with subjects outside the local board's jurisdiction. The remaining 30 percent tended to be negative comments which were ignored: "Except in the area of zoning, negative views expressed by community members at these meetings had little or no effect on the board's passage of the resolution."[158]

Under the 1969 state decentralization law, the central school board retained jurisdiction over school desegregation policies.[159] Decentralization, however, tended to work against desegregation. In District 22, for example, there were nineteen separate neighborhoods. In the white areas, residents resisted linking their neighborhood schools with those of minority parents in other parts of the same district. Under the blinking eye of the U.S. Office for Civil Rights (which, during 1970–1977, was little disposed to enforce desegregation through the Civil Rights Act of 1964) and the halting supervision of the citywide board of education, the local school board compiled reluctantly.

A final comment on the decentralization law. When it was implemented in 1969, Byrne noted, none of District 22's schools had a Catholic principal. By 1977, however, there were three such principals and a Catholic superintendent had been selected by the local board. (Byrne herself is a

Catholic religious.) Since the law gave the vote to all qualified residents, rather than just to parents, a large bloc of Catholic voters helped elect local school boards although many of their children attended parochial schools. They pressed District 22 to keep the schools open after 3:00 P.M. to accommodate the parochial school students in recreation facilities. And they were able to increase Catholic employment in the district schools. Although more sedately handled, this was reminiscent of Rochester's "get some gravy for the folks!" (See above, p. 257.)

In District 22, decentralization probably brought increased parent participation but over 80 percent of those eligible to vote in local school board elections always failed to vote. Compared with the total adult population of the district, only a small number of activists formulated policy, and they paid little heed to the equity of the minority position.

Studies of parental participation tended to emphasize the unrealized educational potential of schools and thus did not share the prevailing research view of the school as an inert, passive educational factor. Clearly, if parents did not feel dissatisfied with the schools, they would have little reason to seek to change them. Yet, the schools, by and large, did not appear eager to change. To call upon parents to become more involved in their children's education while denying them meaningful avenues of institutional participation is to preclude any real change from occurring.

Shipman reported on the basis of her six-year study:

The majority of parents in the present sample say that most teachers in their child's school do not understand community needs. Also, although a number of parents visited their child's school and assisted with extracurricular activities, very few had been involved in discussions of the curriculum their child studied. A substantial number of families would appear to require concerted outreach efforts from the schools; 19 percent of the mothers did not know the name of their child's teachers.[160]

Educationally adequate schools seemed to require a readiness to acknowledge their own shortcomings and a consequent need to change.

In the absence of sufficient research, numerous attractive-sounding proposals have been made to improve education of poor and minority children by manipulating parents. Frequently, such approaches were based on the overly simplistic idea that the quality of education offered by entire school systems can be improved by inducing individual parents to pledge firmly that they will enforce better study habits by their children. This assumes that parents are presently not sufficiently concerned and also that any shortcomings of the schools themselves are incidental obstacles or even irrelevant to educational improvement.

Recently, civil rights leader Rev. Jesse Jackson formulated a program of educational improvement known as "Excel" which shares the basic outlook sketched in the preceding paragraph.[161] "Contracts" are signed between student, parent, and school whereby parents agree to enforce strict study standards at home. The school's signature does not commit it to any program of internal change, thus furthering the idea that widespread educational failure is an individual responsibility. The Los Angeles school board agreed to budget $400,000 to finance the first year's "Excel" program, and the federal government has contributed more than two million dollars. Private foundations have also made grants to the effort.

"Excel's" approach, so popular among educators since the early 1960s, is that failing students who are poor or of minority origin lack certain personal qualities necessary to academic success. In this case, a lack of parental concern is the quality highlighted. Parental cooperation with the school is, of course, desirable, but the research reviewed above suggests that schools generally do not welcome such cooperation except in narrowly defined terms. Parental cooperation is resisted in areas such as teachers, budget, and program. It will be of interest to see whether "Excel" can succeed in the face of such institutional resistance to change. The record thus far is not encouraging. Two interim evaluations suggest the organizational inability of "Excel" to translate its viewpoint into functioning school programs.[162] Financial stringencies have eliminated local school district funding of "Excel," and, thus, a full-scale test of the "Excel" idea seems unlikely.

Notes

1. Two such recent studies are A. Wade Smith, "Tolerance of School Desegregation, 1954–77," *Social Forces*, 59 (June 1981), pp. 1256–74; and D. Garth Taylor and others, "Attitudes Toward Racial Integration," *Scientific American*, 238 (June 1978), pp. 42–49.

2. Data kindly supplied by the Social and Demographic Research Institute, University of Massachusetts, Amherst. The writer is grateful to Dee Weber Burdin for her cooperation.

3. *The Gallup Poll, Public Opinion 1935–1971*, Vol. 3 (New York: Random House, 1972), p. 2244.

4. Ibid., 1971, p. 2323.

5. Ibid., p. 2329.

6. Ibid., 1972, pp. 51–52.

7. Ibid., 1974, p. 370.

8. *Current Opinion*, 3 (November 1975), p. 107.

9. Ibid., 4 (September 1976), p. 91.

10. Ibid., p. 92.

11. *Integrateducation*, 17 (May–August 1979), p. 67.

12. Ibid., 17 (September–December 1979), p. 60.

13. *Chicago Sun-Times*, February 5, 1981.

14. *Cleveland Plain Dealer*, March 26, 1981.

15. *New York Times*, March 22, 1981.

16. *Newsweek*, March 9, 1981.

17. *New York Times*, March 2, 1981.

18. *Integrateducation*, 12 (November–December 1974), p. 15.

19. *Current Opinion*, 3 (April 1975), p. 38.

20. Ibid., 3 (November 1975), p. 106.

21. *Integrateducation*, 13 (January–February 1975), p. 9.

22. Data from tables 1.8.13 and 1.8.14 in Irving L. Allen and J. David Colfax, *Urban Problems and Public Opinion in Four Connecticut Cities* (Storrs, Conn.: Institute of Urban Research, University of Connecticut, December 1968), pp. 155–56.

23. A. Harry Passow, *Toward Creating a Model Urban School System: A Study of the Washington, D.C. Public Schools* (New York: Teachers College, Columbia University, 1967), p. 71.

24. David O'Shea and others, "Desegregation in Los Angeles School District: Report of a Public Opinion Survey," *Educational Research Quarterly*, 1 (Spring 1976), p. 6.

25. *Integrated Education*, (March–April 1971), p. 53.

26. *Integrateducation*, 15 (September–October 1977), p. 27.

27. Ibid., 14 (November–December 1976), p. 29.

28. Ibid., 14 (March–April 1976), p. 48.

29. Ibid., 14 (May–June 1976), p. 52.

30. Ibid., 14 (July–August 1976), p. 35.

31. Ibid., 14 (September–October 1976), p. 38.

32. Ibid., 14 (November–December 1976), p. 32.

33. Ibid., 15 (January–February 1977), p. 33.

34. Ibid., 15 (July–August 1977), p. 32.

35. Ibid., 16 (September–October 1978), p. 40.

36. Ibid., 16 (November–December 1978), p. 28.

37. Ibid., 17 (January–April 1979), p. 66.

38. Ibid., p. 86.

39. Ibid., p. 69.

40. *Chicago Tribune*, April 20, 1980. Strictly speaking, the question did not use the word busing: "Suppose a plan is put into effect, and your children are required to go to a school outside your neighborhood. Is that acceptable?" The education editor of the newspaper, Casey Banas, in reporting the entire poll's results, referred to this one as related to busing.

41. *St. Petersburg Times*, October 19, 1980.

42. *The Seattle Public Schools: A Study of Attitudes, Expectations, and Perceptions* (Seattle, Wash.: McClure Zig, Inc., March 1981), p. 71.

43. Margaret A. Parsons, "Attitudinal Changes of Students and Parents Following Court-Ordered School Desegregation," p. 12. (Paper prepared for presentation at the annual meeting of the American Educational Research Association, Los Angeles, California, April 1981).

44. Thomas Sowell, "Blacker Than Thou," *Washington Post*, February 13, 1981.

45. CBS News, "Monday Morning," April 20, 1981.

46. CBS News, "Sunday Morning," April 26, 1981.

47. Harris Survey, "Busing Receives Passing Marks," *Cleveland Plain Dealer*, March 26, 1981.

48. *Chronicle of Higher Education*, February 9, 1981, p. 8.

49. Jorge C. Rangel and Carlos M. Alcala, "De Jure Segregation of Chicanos in Texas Schools," *Harvard Civil Rights-Civil Liberties Law Review*, 7 (March 1972).

50. See Homer Hoyt, *One Hundred Years of Land Values in Chicago* (Chicago: University of Chicago Press, 1933).

51. Douglas S. Massey, *Residential Segregation of Spanish Americans in United States Urbanized Areas* (doctoral diss., Princeton University, 1978) (University Microfilms Order No. 7905634); Manuel Mariano Lopez, *Patterns of Residential Segregation: The Mexican American Population in the Urban Southwest* (doctoral diss., Michigan State University, 1977) (University Microfilms Order No. 78-10,086); Rosario Torres-Raines, *Casas Ricas y Pobres: The Effects of Housing Market Expenditures on Residential Segregation of Mexican Americans in Texas and California* (doctoral diss., Texas Woman's University, 1978) (University Microfilms Order No. 78-15,602).

52. Massey, *Residential Segregation of Spanish Americans*, p. 82.

53. Ibid., p. 94.

54. Ibid., p. 100.

55. Ibid., p. 169.

56. Ibid., p. 172.

57. Ibid., p. 173.

58. Ibid., p. 238.

59. Ibid., p. 243.

60. Lopez, *Patterns of Residential Segregation*, p. 121.

61. Ibid., p. 128.

62. Ibid., pp. 156–57.

63. Ibid., p. 163.

64. Ibid., p. 164.

65. Ibid., p. 169.

66. Ibid., p. 170.

67. Torres-Raines, *Casas Ricas y Probes*, p. 329.

68. Ibid., p. 361.

69. For an enlightening analysis of the school side of the equation, see Abdin Noboa, *Segregation of Hispanic Students* (Aspira, forthcoming).

70. See *Research Review of Equal Education*, 1 (Winter 1977), pp. 9–11.

71. Virginia S. Shipman and others, *Notable Early Characteristics of High and Low Achieving Black Low-SES Children* (Princeton, N.J.: Educational Testing Service, December 1976).

72. Ibid., p. 38.

73. Ibid., p. 52.

74. Ibid., p. 53.

75. Virginia C. Shipman, "Stability and Change in Family Status, Situational, and Process Variables and their Relationship to Children's Cognitive Performance" (based on a paper of March, 1977, to the Society for Research in Child Development).

76. Ibid., p. 14.

77. Ibid., p. 24.

78. David Armor and others, *Analysis of the School Preferred Reading Program in Selected Los Angeles Minority Schools* (Santa Monica, Calif.: Rand, August 1976).

79. *Research Review of Equal Education*, 1 (Winter 1977), pp. 8–9.

80. Armor and others, *Analysis of the School Preferred Reading Program*, p. vi.

81. Ibid., p. 25.

82. Ibid., p. 47.

83. Willis D. Hawley, *Teachers, Classrooms, and the Effects of School Desegregation on Effort in School: A "Second Generation" Study* (Durham, N.C.: Center for Policy Analysis, Institute of Policy Sciences and Public Affairs, Duke University, April 1976).

84. Ibid., p. 17.

85. Ibid., p. 16.

86. John E. Coulson, *National Evaluation of the Emergency School Aid Act (ESAA): Summary of the Second-Year Studies* (Santa Monica, Calif.: System Development Corporation, July 1976); Jean B. Wellisch and others, *An In-Depth Study of Emergency School Aid Act (ESAA) Schools: 1974-1975* (Santa Monica, Calif.: System Development Corporation, July 1976).

87. Coulson, *National Evaluation of the Emergency School Aid Act*, p. 20.

88. Ibid., p. 22.

89. Wellisch and others, *An In-Depth Study of Emergency School Aid Act*, pp. viii-11.

90. Ibid., p. viii-8.

91. Ibid., p. ix-9.

92. Ibid., p. vi-15.

93. Ibid., p. vii-15.

94. See Garlie A. Forehand, Marjorie Ragosta, and Donald A. Rock, *Conditions and Processes of Effective School Desegregation* (Princeton, N.J.: Educational Testing Service, July 1976), pp. 100, 114, and 169.

95. Ben Holman, "Desegregation and the Community Relations Service," *Integrateducation*, 13 (January-February 1975), p. 27.

96. See Dorothy H. Holden, "Academic Achievement of Black Students: A Black Parent's View," *Integrateducation*, 14 (July-August 1976), pp. 39-43.

97. Jesse E. Kinard, *The Effect of Parental Involvement on Achievement of First and Second Siblings Who Have Attended Head Start and Follow Through Programs* (doctoral diss., Florida State University, 1974), pp. 50-51. (University Microfilms Order No. 75-6285.) See also Dorothy J. Zupperer, *Parent Knowledge and Attitudes toward ESEA, Title I Programs and Their Ability to Assess Child Achievement* (doctoral diss., Florida State University, 1978). (University Microfilms Order No. 7822217.)

98. Kinard, *The Effect of Parental Involvement*, pp. 50-51.

99. Wilda Glasgow Winters, *Black Mothers in Urban Schools: A Study of Participation and Alienation* (doctoral diss., Yale University, 1975). (University Microfilms Order No. 76-14,574.)

100. Ibid., p. 60.

101. Reginald M. Clark, *Black Families as Educators* (doctoral diss., University of Wisconsin, Madison, 1977). (University Microfilms Order No. 77-19,752.)

102. Ibid., p. 44.

103. Ibid., pp. 328-34.

104. In the literature of black achievement, one of the rare personal examples of lack of family encouragement of further schooling appears in Thomas Sowell, *Black Education: Myths and Tragedies* (Philadelphia: McKay, 1972), pp. 26-32.

105. Clark, *Black Families as Educators*, p. 334.

106. Ibid., p. 335.

107. Jeanne Kohl Jenkins, "Advisory Councils and Principals in Los Angeles," *Integrateducation*, 14 (January-February 1976).

108. Ibid., p. 28.

109. Citizens' Management Review Committee, Decentralization Subcommittee, *Decentralization in the Los Angeles Unified School District: An Appraisal* (Los Angeles: CMRC, June 1977).

110. Ibid., p. 17.

111. Ibid., p. 50.

112. Ibid., p. 49.

113. Ibid., p. 25.

114. Irving C. Croshier, *The Participatory Role of the School Community Advisory Council in the Local School: The Study of Differing Perceptions* (doctoral diss., United States International University, 1977). (University Microfilms Order No. 7909534.)

115. Ibid., p. 113.

116. Robinson R. Hammonds, *A Case Study of the Views of Key Participants in Local School Affairs Relative to Community Participation Under Decentralization* (doctoral diss., University of Michigan, 1974) (University Microfilms Order No. 75-707); Eleanor S. Barnwell, *An Analysis of the Development of School-Community Councils in Region One, Detroit Public Schools* (doctoral diss., Wayne State University, 1978) (University Microfilms Order No. 7908891).

117. Hammonds, *A Case Study*, p. 175.

118. Ibid.

119. Barnwell, *An Analysis*, p. 154.

120. Ibid., p. 211.

121. Ibid., pp. 243–44.

122. Roy J. Dawson, Jr., *A Study of Title I Parent Council Member Participation in Selected Title I Programs* (doctoral diss., Rutgers University, 1977) (University Microfilms Order No. 78-4590); Andres Nicolas Vallado, *Parent Involvement in Compensatory Education through Title I ESEA Parent Advisory Committees in Selected School Districts in Texas* (doctoral diss., University of Houston, 1975) (University Microfilms Order No. 75-23,950); Norman N. Gross, *Participation of the Poor in Educational Decision Making: A Comparative Case Study* (doctoral diss., University of Rochester, 1975) (University Microfilms Order No. 75-22,795).

123. Dawson, *A Study of Title I Parent Participation*, p. 134.

124. Vallado, *Parent Involvement*, p. 117.

125. Ibid., p. 116.

126. Gross, *Participation of the Poor*, p. 134.

127. Ibid., p. 204.

128. Ibid., p. 215.

129. See above, Chapter 6.

130. Gross, *Participation of the Poor*, p. 322.

131. John Mason Hill, *Citizen Advisory Committees and their Relationship to Decision-Making in the Schools* (doctoral diss., United States International University, 1977). (University Microfilms Order No. 7909565.)

132. Ibid., p. 53.

133. Ibid., pp. 56–57 and 62.

134. Ibid., p. 59.

135. Ibid., p. 73.

136. Ibid.

137. Ibid., p. 78.

138. Barbara R. Hatton, *Schools and Black Communities: A Problem Formulation* (doctoral diss., Stanford University, 1976). (University Microfilms Order No. 76-26,011.)

139. Ibid., p. 122.

140. Ibid., p. 113.

141. Robert C. Francy, *Processes and Practices of Parent Advisory Councils: A Study of Twenty-Five Elementary Schools* (doctoral diss., University of Utah, 1978). (University Microfilms Order No. 7821672.)

142. Ibid., p. 73.

143. Ibid., p. 109.

144. Mary Montes, *School Community Relations: A View from the Barrio* (doctoral diss., Claremont Graduate School, 1974), p. 46. (University Microfilms Order No. 75-12,749.)

145. Ibid., p. 123.

146. Ibid., p. 144.

147. Ibid., p. 164.

148. Ibid., p. 208.

149. Ibid., pp. 215–16.

150. Ibid., p. 218.

151. Ibid., p. 221.

152. Ibid., p. 225.

153. Eileen E. Byrne, *Community Participation After Decentralization in One New York City School District, 1970–1977* (doctoral diss., Fordham University, 1979).

154. Ibid., p. 167.

155. Ibid., p. 222.

156. Ibid., p. 211.

157. Ibid., p. 212.

158. Ibid., p. 223.

159. For contrasting views on the success of desegregation under these auspices, see Irving Anker, "Integration in New York City Schools," *Integrateducation*, 13 (May–June 1975), pp. 137–42; and Kenneth B. Clark, "New York's Biracial Public Schools," pp. 153–55, in the same issue.

160. Shipman, "Stability and Change," p. 25.

161. See *PUSH for Excellence* (Chicago: Operation PUSH, 1977); Jesse L. Jackson, "A Plan to Nourish Roots," *Los Angeles Times*, May 23, 1977; Jesse Jackson, "PUSH for Excellence," *Chicago Sun-Times*, September 25, 1976; Jesse L. Jackson, "Encouraging Learning," *Chicago Tribune*, November 7, 1976 (letter); Jesse L. Jackson, " 'Give the People a Vision,' " *New York Times Magazine*, April 18, 1976; and Eugene E. Eubanks and Daniel U. Levine, "The PUSH Program for Excellence in Big-City Schools," *Phi Delta Kappan*, January 1977, pp. 383–88.

162. See Saundra R. Murray and Charles A. Murray, *National Evaluation of the PUSH for Excellence Project: Phase I*, 2 parts, July 1979 (ERIC ED 177 744-5); Saundra R. Murray and others, *The National Evaluations of the PUSH for Excellence Project: 1. The Evolution of a Program*, March 1980 (ERIC ED 185 693); Saundra R. Murray and others, *The National Evaluation of the PUSH for Excellence Project, Technical Report 2: Implementation*, November 1980 (ERIC ED 199 322); and Edward B. Fiske, "For Jackson, Failures and Some Success," *New York Times*, January 27, 1981.

11

Minorities in Higher Education – I

Discrimination against racial and ethnic groups in higher education is deeply rooted. Before the Civil War, fewer than fifty blacks graduated from American colleges. After the Civil War, southern private and public colleges and universities simply excluded blacks. For a number of years, southern states refused to build colleges for black citizens even though the latter paid taxes which were used to support institutions attended by white students. In the North, exclusion was only slightly less sweeping. Stringent quotas were enforced. Where a few blacks were admitted, frequently they were not permitted to live or eat in residential halls and dining rooms. Enforced segregation was the rule in extracurricular activities also. Subordination was exacted as the price of attendance and racism thrived on these campuses.[1]

Black higher education on a meaningful scale was restricted to the black colleges which were built soon after the Civil War almost wholly in the South, principally under sponsorship of black and white church denominations. After 1890, southern states built black land grant colleges in order to qualify for federal monies to build white counterparts. Deliberately starved for operational funds and restricted as to the breadth of educational offerings, the black colleges nevertheless endured. In the face of political obstacles of a monumental order, they educated a teaching force for the equally penurious black common schools of the South. They trained a cadre of black professionals—including physicians and lawyers. Miracles, however, were beyond the power of the black colleges. While their capacity to "make do" was astonishing, the confines of the racist society dictated ultimately that they would remain unable to produce a first-rate collegiate education for every capable black youth.

Mexican-American youth had even fewer opportunities for a higher education before the 1960s. Concentrated in Texas, they were segregated in elementary schools and not infrequently excluded from high schools there. At the end of World War II Mexican-Americans represented only a small fraction of higher education enrollment even in Texas. Puerto Rican youth, if they belonged to the small middle class on the Island, had a slight chance at higher education. On the mainland, even this order of opportunity was lacking until the 1960s and 1970s. There was a longer history of opportunities for American Indian youth but this record was of no greater consequence in terms of actual outcomes. Indians were frequently used in order to qualify for institutional grants and awards, but few of these benefits accrued directly to the Indian student. Asian Americans, a complex grouping, showed up relatively well in overall statistics. These, however, obscured a number of specific groups such as very poor and ghettoized Chinese Americans. Yet, when Asians successfully completed a higher education, they met with considerable discrimination in employment, regardless of their educational attainment.

The higher education establishment more or less perpetuated these constrictive tendencies. State education officials sternly enforced segregation and exclusion laws and administered state appropriations in discriminatory fashion. They also discouraged black higher institutions from raising their academic level since to do so would require increased state expenditure. Until 1961 regional accrediting associations refused to permit black institutions to join as full-fledged members. Graduate schools of education accepted the situation as normal and rarely, if ever, voiced criticism of racism. Learned societies also coordinated their policies along the same lines. In a number, blacks were excluded outright; in others, they were accepted but treated as second-class members. Federal educational authorities also enforced the racial order of things. Before 1945 or so, federal concern was limited to an occasional survey of black higher education but there were few practical consequences.

The rise of the civil rights movement during the 1950s and 1960s marked the beginning of a change in higher education. During the 1930s and 1940s, a series of Supreme Court rulings expanded the rights of individual blacks to attend white state universities, but they stopped short of declaring the system of segregation illegal. While the *Brown* decision of 1954 arose out of the common schools, the high court tentatively applied it to post-secondary education, at least in the case of public community colleges.[2] Only in 1968 did a lower federal court in Tennessee apply *Brown* to public higher education and require the state to produce a desegregation plan. Not until 1979, eleven years later, was the final order in that case implemented.) In 1964, Congress passed the Civil Rights Act which forbade the use of federal funds for racially discriminatory purposes. Enforcement was lodged with the U.S. Department of Health, Education, and Welfare (HEW). When, in 1970, it appeared to civil rights groups that enforcement was lagging, they filed a lawsuit, *Adams* v. *Richardson*, asking that the court order HEW to enforce the law against illegally segregated state systems of higher education. Three years later, a lower court found against HEW, and was upheld on appeal. Finally, by 1977 HEW released formal criteria for the dismantling of racially dual systems of public higher education in ten states.

The exclusory nature of white higher education in the South began to give way not so much because of the pressure of litigation as because of the growing black political strength in that region. Expanding black representation in state legislatures and on governing bodies pried open higher education doors and black students determined to take advantage of these openings. In 1952, 63,000 black college students in the South attended only predominantly black institutions (PBIs). Twenty-six years later, that number had expanded seven-fold. In 1978, 176,000 (triple the number in 1952) were attending PBIs and, unprecedentedly, 266,000 attended predominantly white institutions (PWIs) in the South.[3]

Black students continued to attend black colleges, but there were relatively few such institutions in the South. Thus, black students chose also to go where there were openings, that is, the PWIs. As a consequence, the percentage of all blacks attending PBIs fell from 100 in 1952 to 40 in 1978. It should be noted that black enrollment in higher education during these years was not a "zero-sum game." That is, the enrollment of blacks in PWIs did not mean the loss of the same number in PBIs. Attendance grew at both types of institutions, although at different rates.

This was true in a number of states. As Stephen Wright points out, South Carolina State College at Orangeburg, the one-time state college for blacks, enrolled in 1976 only one-half the number of black students attending PWIs in the same state. Similarly, in Texas, "there [were] 43,000 black students enrolled in the white public colleges and universities . . . and only 12,500 black students in the two public black colleges in this state."[4] Clearly, without the opportunity to attend the PWIs, far fewer blacks in the South could have attended any college. Also, as Wright stresses, growing black specialization in engineering, dentistry, medicine, law, business, and physical science was one result of the broadened choice of higher institutions increasingly available to black students. The black colleges also extended somewhat the range of career choices of black students.

While statistics alone give the impression of continued progress, further analysis reveals a number of shortcomings. For one thing, a large number of black students attend community colleges whose record of preparing students for the baccalaureate degree is relatively poor. J. LeVonne Chambers pointed out that "in 1976, 78 percent of black students in predominantly white institutions in North Carolina were in two-year colleges."[5] In a study of community colleges in Maryland, James Tschechtelin found that "six times as many blacks as whites left community colleges because of inadequate financial aid."[6] In very large cities, community colleges are frequently segregated institutions. Those with predominantly black enrollments often exhibit features of segregated education such as truncated curricula and inadequate guidance and counseling services. Another sobering feature of the growth of black higher education is the disproportionately large group of part-time black students. This is largely a result of their relative poverty and underscores the special financial needs of this group.

Perhaps the most unsettling aspect of black higher education is the climate of race relations black students encounter on predominantly white campuses, whether North or South.

"Only a fool," wrote Bernard Watson, "would deny that there has been progress."[7] Only research, however, can tell us whether and to what degree that progress has resolved long-standing problems in minority higher education.

Chicanos in Higher Education

Catherine Putnam has written the most rounded and systematic treatment of recent works on Chicanos in higher education; it deals with Chicanos in California.[8] She established four standards of equal educational opportunity and examined data bearing on each: (1) equality of access; (2) equality of educational attainment; (3) equal subsidies for public education; and (4) equal effects on life outcomes.

In elementary schools, Chicanos and others attend at comparable rates with whites; in secondary schools Chicanos are somewhat underrepresented but Chicano underenrollment in higher education is severe. Chicanos constitute about one-fifth of California's population, but Putnam found that their "undergraduate enrollments in California's systems of higher education range from around eight percent at the community colleges to about five percent at the University of California. Graduate student enrollments are also around five percent." Chicanos are far behind Anglos in educational attainment. As Putnam reported, "47 percent of the Anglos who entered public school in first grade enter higher education, while 28 percent of the Chicano children who started in the system at age six will do so."[9] Chicanos also drop out of college more frequently than Anglos. In 1975-1976, further, some 21 to 25 percent of Anglo undergraduates at the University of California and the state colleges received a bachelor's degree; only 15 percent of Chicano undergraduates did so. Putnam stresses the significance of shortchanging during early school years: "Not only do Chicano students receive fewer years of instruction overall, but there is evidence that educational programs, facilities, resources, and personnel available to Chicano children are inferior to those available to educate Anglo children."[10]

Tax funds used to support local schools are regarded as subsidies by Putnam. She reported that there was no difference in per-student expenditures on Anglo and Chicano children in the public schools. If, however, one considers not merely the children actually attending but all who are eligible to attend, an inequality favoring Anglos emerges. "Statewide," Putnam wrote, "California saves about $59,700,000 a year by spending less on Chicanos than Anglos when total eligible populations are taken into account."[11] There was a similar finding for higher education. Putnam declared of spending for the public higher education of all college-aged Anglos and Chicanos in the state: "The higher education investment in the average Anglo is more than double the investment in Chicanos of the same age range, regardless of whether scholarship aid is included in the calculations."[12]

Assessment of life chances means "how the education . . . translates into differences in employment and earnings."[13] Education, including higher education, pays off more for Anglos than for Chicanos; Chicanos as a whole experience 40 percent more unemployment. Yet, for certain Chicano age groups education seems more productive of earnings and employment than for others. "What if Chicanos were as educated as Anglos?" Putnam asks. Inequality would shrink but not disappear.

Certainly, then, education is not equal for Chicano and Anglo in California. What are the limits of educational reforms aiming at equalization? Putnam states her case cogently:

> Educational reform will not alter the social disparities which exist in the community and the workplace as well as within the schools. And education policies will not be able to effect economic and social reform to end discrimination. Equalizing educational opportunities is a worthwhile goal in and of itself and it does not require justification through equal economic outcomes for everyone. But for equal life outcomes to be realized for all Californians, any policy of educational reform must be accompanied by improvements in other social services and by government sanctions against discrimination.[14]

Putnam thus is willing to settle for the schools becoming more equal whether or not the rest of society's inequalities also moderate. At the same time, it is equally clear that, to her, the elimination of broader social inequalities is a further guarantee of equality in education. It is notable that Putnam's analysis pays little significant attention to cultural factors in equality.

Amarante Fresquez investigated another aspect of the subject, the educational success of Chicano scientists.[15] He reported that according to a survey by the recently founded Society for Advancement of Chicano and Native Americans in Sciences, there were only about 100 native-born Chicanos with Ph.D.'s in science in the entire country. During 1972–1973, the National Academy of Sciences found that Chicano doctorates were more or less in the same fields as those of the Anglos. Two exceptions were education, which attracted nearly one-third of the Chicanos but less than one-quarter of the Anglos; and engineering, which attracted one-fourteenth of Anglos but about one-hundredth of Chicano doctorates. (Seven years later the situation was changing for the better: in 1980, the number of Hispanic bachelor's degrees in engineering had risen to 2,327, up from 1,419 in 1975. During the 1980–1981 academic year, a total of 9,043 Hispanics were enrolled in undergraduate engineering programs.[16]

Fresquez compared a group of thirty-three Chicano scientists with one of twenty-seven Anglo scientists. About half the former reported that they had been discriminated against in their career because of ethnicity.[17] Chicano scientists came from poorer homes and their parents were less educated. They tended to begin their higher education careers at smaller, lesser-known colleges and completed their graduate work at elite universities. Anglo scientists, on the other hand, tended to begin and finish at elite institutions. After graduation, Chicanos tended to teach in colleges while Anglos were more concentrated in industry. Among Chicano scientists, Fresquez observed, there tended to be fewer full and associate professors and more assistant professors. Only Chicanos with doctorates in biology, chemistry, physics, and mathematics were covered in this study.

Kaufert and associates analyzed various characteristics of 114 Chicano medical students, drawn from all over the country.[18] He compared them with Anglo medical students and found that "Chicano medical students tend to be drawn from families whose economic and educational background [is] well above the mean levels for the total national Chicano population." Nearly one out of five fathers of Chicano medical students was a laborer; the percentage was slightly greater for fathers of Anglo students. The numbers of fathers in both groups who were professionals were fairly comparable. The Chicano students had high academic records in high school; 55 percent ranked in the top tenth of their graduating class and another 29 percent had been in the top third.

Probing the career plans of the Mexican-American medical students, Kaufert found that family practice and community medicine ranked high among first-year medical students but low among seniors. For example, 56 percent of the former chose family practice but only 5 percent of the latter did so. Clearly, as Kaufert and associates note, the nearer actual practice appeared, the more attractive a speciality seemed. Thirty-seven percent of freshmen said they expected to practice internal medicine, surgery, pediatrics, obstetrics, and gynecology. Among seniors the percentage rose to 90. This suggests that poorer Chicano communities and families, who can afford a general practitioner at best, will not be treated by many of these students after graduation.

Access problems of Mexican-American students will persist, even in areas of fairly heavy Mexican-American settlement. B. E. Aguirre and Patrick Bernal, for example, studied underenrollment of Chicanos in Texas A & M University: of a total enrollment of 31,000 only 2 percent are Chicanos.[19] One reason they cite is poor recruitment. "Apparently," Aguirre and Bernal write, "the few that attend . . . now do so in part because other persons significant to them also attend the university. In other words, they attended because their friends did. Chicanos at Texas A & M were high-ranking students. Nearly two-thirds were in the top quarter of their high school graduating classes and one out of eight was earning a B+ average now. While one out of six had felt discriminated against, two out of three did not identify with the Chicano movement.

The Kaufert and Aguirre-Bernal studies presented groups of Mexican-

Americans who were relatively privileged. This is less true in Fresquez, although the group analyzed—scientists—had an elite occupation. Isaac Cardenas studied lower-income students enrolled in three post-secondary compensatory education programs in San Antonio during the early 1970s, but his account is too episodic to analyze.[20]

Carlos Arce has begun to outline what he sees as the operation of "academic colonialism" in higher education. This he defines as "the selective imposition of intellectual premises, concepts, methods, institutions and related organizations on a subordinate group and/or the unselective and uncritical adoption and initiation of those premises by selected members of a subordinate group, with the selection processes not being in the control of the subordinate group."[21] In this view, American higher education is an arena in which Anglo dominance is expressed by ideologies and groupings designed to instruct the colonized in acquiescence, or to become junior partners to Anglos. The future will very likely bring a more detailed and comprehensive documentation of this view.

Indian Higher Education

Indian higher education has attracted few researchers although scholars are increasingly at work in the field. Ward Churchill and Norbert Hill surveyed some aspects.[22] They criticized severely the setting up of ethnic studies departments or programs: "As a mechanism to confuse social issues and priorities these programs have been amazingly effective. As educational developments, however, they are largely a transparent devotion to posture and gloss at the expense of scholarly content." The greatest concern for Churchill and Hill, however, is the implicit assumption behind an ethnic studies department: "The school as a whole becomes an institution of 'white studies': nonwhite studies are separate entities attached to the campus."[23] Nonwhites, they point out, "have a perfectly valid, if ignored, status *within* all curriculum content areas." In history, literature, and other substantive content areas, the perspectives and roles of nonwhites should be considered seriously. To help develop and monitor the inclusion of such materials in what are frequently called the "regular" courses is, according to Churchill and Hill, "the logical function of a Minority Studies Department (or any of its components).

Louis Jacquot has written one of the very few connected analyses óf Indian higher education, in this case of Alaskan Natives. He established his viewpoint concretely when he observed that "when reflecting on the achievements of the Alaska Native peoples over the past half century, and particularly during the last two decades . . . it is striking that the bulk of their leaders had a minimum of education for success in the United States.[24] Following acquisition of Alaska in 1867, the federal government supplied Alaskan Natives with an inadequate education in legally segregated schools.[25] Between 1895 and 1950, twenty-four Natives received college degrees, nearly all in institutions connected with a religious organization. During the next seventeen years, another 101 received degrees. Only in 1935 did the first Native receive a degree from the University of Alaska. In general, school authorities, at least until the 1930s, did not encourage Natives to attend colleges.

The meaning of formal education among the Native people was highly traditional until very recently. Native organizations concerned with education, however, adopted a broader view:

A theme that is repeated consistently . . . is that such training must be of a dual nature: It must prepare the young to live in a village environment (the "traditional ways") and in an urban setting (the "new ways"). The young person will make a choice, when he matures, as to where he will live, and he may in fact migrate back and forth between the two societies several times in his life. In either case, he must be prepared for the life he will encounter, and that is a major concern of the adults.[26]

It is difficult to tell how well this goal has been achieved. Jacquot does not make a straightforward statement on the matter.

An unresolved problem is the ethnic content of Native schooling. Jacquot writes that the Natives' basic question is: "Who will teach it?"

For there is a fear that a false culture will develop if misinformation is passed on to the young, it is thought to be doubly dangerous when clothed by institutional authority. . . . The mistrust described is basically the result of a fear that the "real history" or the "real story" will not be told. . . .[27]

Perhaps the Native people have experienced hasty attempts by schools to establish intercultural understanding by superficial means. Also, as Jacquot emphasizes, they do not accept the assumption that intercultural instruction is a one-way enterprise in which Native children are instructed by school personnel: "There is a keen yearning among the Native peoples: They not only want to know more about themselves, but they also want to pass such information on to others."[28]

In 1971, Congress passed the Alaska Native Claims Settlement Act, which awarded one billion dollars to be paid over ten years to some 80,000 Native beneficiaries. Regional and village corporations were organized to own and manage over 40 million acres of land. Passage of the law was the culmination of a long campaign by Native people to assert their right to ownership of Alaskan land. The land claim movement, Jacquot noted, brought "together, in mutual concert, all of the Native peoples for the first time in their histories."[29] A feeling of collective pride arose out of this successful effort at self-determination.

Just two years after passage of the Settlement Act, Jacquot completed his research on a high note of expectation by the Native people. By 1981, there was widespread questioning of the act's benefits. Willie Hensley, a foremost

Native leader, feared the ill effects of formal education: "Unfortunately, the school has been a tool for the disintegration of viable cultures which had evolved to allow us to live in this most hostile of climates."[30] This contrasted with the double-paths that had been expected of the school. Another leader in Anchorage reported that in the city's high schools some two-thirds of Native students dropped out. Hensley declared: "What we have accomplished in the last 15 years is quite useless if our identity and our spirit does not survive. We can be destroyed by the pressures of government, politics, and the economy. Or by the internal decay of the spirit. Some might call it Americanization." It is essential to note that Hensley and others are not bemoaning political and economic change so much as calling for two-sided development that will find an equal place for traditional culture.

By the opening of the 1980s, over one million black students attended some kind of post-secondary institution. Only about one out of five was in a traditionally black school. How did black students fare in these institutions? And what of their white classmates?

Black Colleges

DeWitt Williams found during the years 1969–1974 that the boards of trustees of private black colleges had increasing numbers of black members. The occupational composition of the boards did not seem to have changed much and was not greatly different from that of white colleges.[31] Only in one respect, the larger representation of clergymen, were the black college boards different. Williams did not extend his inquiry into the area of actual policies.

Changes in the black land grant colleges between 1965–1966 and 1970–1971 were traced by Freddie Nicholas. He studied fifteen institutions and visited three. It was during these years that four predominantly black colleges began to enroll considerable numbers of white students, as follows, in percent white:[32]

Institution	1965–1966	1970–1971
Kentucky State College	21	42
Lincoln University (Mo.)	29	54
University of Maryland, Eastern Shore	8	23
Delaware State College	4	35

Numerically, black enrollment in these institutions during this period declined from 3,822 to 3,733 while that of whites rose from 946 to 2,798. It is worth noting that the change in racial composition did not result from any determined federal policy of collegiate desegregation. As will be seen below, such a policy emerged only after 1973. On the other hand, in Maryland the state university had absorbed a formerly predominantly black college and made it into a branch of the university.

Taking all fifteen colleges as a group, Nicholas found that during his period of study the percentage of faculty holding doctorates rose from 23 to 29; the percentage of black faculty fell from 91 to 76; the percentage of blacks sitting on boards of trustees rose from 16 to 21; and the percentage of administrators who were black declined from 99 to 96. At the University of Maryland-Eastern Shore, 42 percent of administrators were white. Nicholas also discovered a handful of tentative programs involving cooperation between neighboring black and white institutions. The picture gained from Nicholas's work is one of the fifteen black colleges holding their own—overall, enrollment increased by 23 percent—but also one of significant changes in racial composition occurring on a few of the campuses.

Monroe Little studied black colleges from 1880 to 1964 from the viewpoint of the students. Much of the work is an argument with sociologist E. Franklin Frazier, who had theorized that students at black colleges before World War I were children of light-skinned and newly freed blacks while, after the war, they were principally, in Little's words, "urban lower-middle and second generation middle class black youths."[33] At some points in the work, Little seemed to accept the contention; at other points there appeared to be some self-contradiction. In his introduction, Little wrote that "a higher percentage of the students at black colleges did come from middle class backgrounds, but there were some who did not."[34] Some pages on, however, he noted that "a very large proportion of black undergraduates, in 1940 as well as in 1930, came from upper socioeconomic families."[35] Yet, just a page earlier he had written that "well over 50 percent of the undergraduate population at black colleges in 1930 and 1940 was from lower-middle class family backgrounds."[36] Too much seemed to hinge on undefined distinctions between lower middle, middle, and upper socioeconomic strata.

Before 1920, Little writes, "few, if any, black oriented courses were offered at black colleges. . . ."[37] Indeed, he specifies, the curriculum of the colleges "attempted to acculturate students to white middle-class values and institutions."[38] Nevertheless, Little contended, "despite the failure of teachers and the course of instruction to show a full appreciation for black life and culture, it appears that black students still managed to develop a strong identification with their ethnic roots."[39] Little was able to arrive at such an unexpected conclusion because he used a most unusual conception of "ethnic roots":

Yet racial awareness among most students did not extend to lower-class Afro-American culture, but was limited primarily to the contributions of blacks to Western civilization. . . . Most often it was due to students' attitudes about lower-class culture: (1) it was something they already knew about and thus did not deserve their careful attention, (2) represented the legacy of slavery, and as such, had no place in black efforts at racial pride and assertiveness, and (3) was not fully appreciated by whites (especially faculty and visitors), but looked upon by them simply . . . [as] a means of entertainment and amusement.[40]

This curiously elitist conception of ethnic roots is at odds with just about every principal black theorist of black culture. During the 1930s, Carter G. Woodson, the eminent black historian, attacked black colleges for their subordination of black culture.[41] Unfortunately, Little did not mention Woodson's critique.

In part because of the availability of materials, Little depended mainly on observations at Howard, Fisk, Spelman, and Tougaloo. These were among the highest-ranking black colleges. Whether a detailed investigation of more typical institutions would have led Little to different conclusions is problematical. In his eagerness to argue down Frazier, he may have become too defensive of black college practices attacked by Frazier.

Preston George examined the financial health of thirty-three black colleges, twenty-five public and eight private.[42] He collected the data in 1977–1978 but they concerned 1972 and 1974. Presidents of the institutions submitted the data; over two-thirds queried cooperated. George constructed a scale ranging from A (Healthy) to E (Unhealthy). The institutions were ranked as follows, in percentages:

A	6.3
B	6.3
C	43.7
D	31.2
E	12.5

Asked whether the situation had improved since 1974, two-thirds replied in the affirmative. Only one president cited increased state aid as a reason, however. Since George completed his work, financial pressures on black colleges have multiplied.[43]

James M. Richards recently analyzed the psychosocial environments of black colleges by comparing these with a representative sample of white institutions. His primary interest was in determining the capacity of institutions to prepare students for various types of occupations. (Richards used Holland's occupational types: realistic, investigative, artistic, social, enterprising, and conventional.) In part, he found that the distribution of students between the two types of institutions resembled the occupational distribution of blacks and whites in the general population. In other words, the colleges tended to reproduce the existing racial pattern of occupations. Thus, Richards found that "instruction which would prepare students for technical and executive careers is relatively less available at black institutions and instruction which would prepare them for social service fields is relatively more available."[44]

Clearly, Richards observed, "a black high school student planning to become a mechanical engineer, business executive, or lawyer *currently* is more likely to find an appropriate environment at an integrated college and might be so counseled."[45] At the same time, it should be noted that Richards underscores the word *currently*. As he explains, *"in the absence of some intervention* the environmental presses of black colleges and universities may perpetuate the current occupational distribution of black college graduates."[46] As was noted on page 272 above, Wright reported that greater black enrollment in hitherto white institutions was accompanied by broader black representation in the professions. This finding squares with that of Richards.

In 1975–1976, Thomas and associates report, black colleges granted more than one-third of all degrees awarded to blacks in the country as a whole.[47] Since these colleges make up a very small part of all American colleges, it is clear that they are important beyond their numbers for black attainment. Little is known, however, about the relative success black and white institutions have had with regard to graduation of black students.

Recently, the State Council of Higher Education for Virginia studied retention and completion rates of black and white students attending the fifteen predominantly white and black state-supported institutions in Virginia.[48] Completion was treated as enrolling as a freshman in Fall, 1975, and receiving a bachelor's degree by Summer, 1979. (Since blacks often take more than four years, the State Council's figures underestimate black graduation rates. However, black-white institutional comparisons are little affected by this factor.) Two institutions—Norfolk State and Virginia State—are predominantly black while the remaining thirteen institutions are predominantly white.

About one-sixth (16.9 percent) of black students in all fifteen state institutions received a baccalaureate within four years, as contrasted with over two-fifths (41.6 percent) of white students who had been freshmen in 1975. The two black colleges had very different graduation rates, however: Norfolk State, 8.6 percent, and Virginia State, 24.6 percent.

Fall, 1975, entrants who did not graduate by Summer, 1979, fell into one of two groups: (1) some were still enrolled and working for a degree and (2) some were no longer enrolled in any of the fifteen state institutions. Statewide, about a third (33.6 percent) of black 1975 entrants were in the first group; only about a sixth (16.9 percent) of white 1975 entrants were still enrolled. At Norfolk State and Virginia State, as previously, the persistence rates differed considerably; they were 43.6 percent and 26.9 percent, respectively. Nearly half (49.5 percent) the state's black 1975 entrants had dropped out without a degree by Summer, 1979, as had 42 percent of their white peers of 1975. Attrition rates for the two predominantly black institutions were almost identical (47.8 percent and 48.5 percent).

Did Virginia's black students "do better" in white or black colleges? As measured by the educational attainment of a baccalaureate degree, their record was better at predominantly white colleges. While no white school's graduation record for blacks was as low as that for Norfolk State, eight of the ten predominantly white colleges exceeded the black graduation rate of Virginia State.

Two comments seem in order. For one thing, black graduation rates would undoubtedly rise if a six-year period were studied, since twice as many blacks as whites were still persisting beyond the four-year limit. The magnitude of such a rise cannot be determined at this point. For another, it may be a considerable error to equate black students enrolled in the fifteen institutions. Selectivity varies among at least some institutions and this should be considered before calculating graduation and other rates. It would be especially important to learn which institutions have the most success with comparable students. Nevertheless, the Virginia data give reason to temper the frequent assertion that black colleges are more successful with black students in terms of educational attainment. Similar studies should be made in other states.

Historically, public black colleges were designed to be and remain inferior institutions. State legislatures and departments of education withheld financial aid and placed numerous other obstacles in the way of improving these colleges. One of the most telling obstacles was the failure of private and governmental funding agencies to encourage scientific research at black colleges. As a result, Lawrence Marcus and Franklin Smith state, at the black colleges "black faculty have found themselves in positions with heavy teaching demands, poor research facilities, little, if any, time for research, and no real opportunity for sabbaticals."[49] Over the years, black faculty developed their own techniques to encourage scientific research on black campuses. Marcus and Smith called these mechanisms "survival systems."

In 1923, at black Lincoln University in Pennsylvania, young Horace Mann Bond and some classmates formed the Beta Kappa Chi Scientific Honor Society for undergraduates. (BKX, as the group came to be known, operated as a black equivalent to Sigma Xi, a purportedly national honor society for science students but in fact a white-only organization.) By 1946 BKX had twenty-eight chapters and had held its first national conference. At the following year's conference, scientific papers were read for the first time. A journal was published and it carried the texts of scientific papers. During the earlier years of BKX, black scholars were virtually excluded from the pages of the leading American scientific journals. As Marcus and Smith report:

For the most part, the European journals served as the primary publication outlet (until the last decade or so). One of those we interviewed has published 77 articles; nearly two-thirds appeared in European journals. The referees across the Atlantic apparently did not know which colleges were black and which were white![50]

Other researchers have made similar reports.[51]

In 1945, professors from black colleges formed the National Institute of

Science (NIS). This gave some, at least, recognition withheld from them by exclusion from white scientific organizations. From 1954 on, NIS and BKX met together each year. During the 1960s, when white groups opened their doors under pressure of the civil rights movement, some members of NIS dropped out to join white associations. A number returned to NIS in the 1970s but retained membership in the white groups. By the late 1970s, NIS enrolled some 500 members.

Marcus and Smith observed that "since there is such a small community of black scientists and since most have been involved in BKX either as faculty-sponsors or students, one had the impression of a kinship system whose genealogy is readily traceable."[52] One may perhaps add that substantial progress in the future will make black scientists less of a family.

Black Students in Predominantly White Institutions

There have been few studies of black students in predominantly black colleges, but the situation is different with respect to black students in predominantly white colleges. A growing number of such studies have emerged in recent years. In many cases, the name of the college was not cloaked, thus giving the reader an increased sense of assurance about the validity of the research.

Mary Merritt and associates studied interracial interaction among black and white students at the University of Maryland and found:

> Regardless of race, students tended to feel most comfortable in an integrated situation, less comfortable when they were in the majority and least comfortable when they were in the minority. . . . Both blacks and whites preferred to be in a majority at parties and on blind dates [and this] underscores the importance of considering social situations separately. . . . The only situations where blacks were more comfortable than whites involved living in an integrated dorm or neighborhood. . . . Whites are usually more comfortable than blacks in interracial situations.[53]

These rather disjointed findings are difficult to integrate into a coherent statement. Perhaps they indicate the need of blacks to be with other blacks in an integrated situation in order to feel most comfortable. In other words, simply being with whites—as a tiny minority, for example—does not make for comfort.

Marvin Peterson and some colleagues at the University of Michigan studied the impact of increased black enrollments at thirteen predominantly white colleges and universities during 1974–1975. The institutions were Lewis University, Bradley University, the University of Missouri-Kansas City, California State University (Pa.), Bowling Green University, Carleton College, Macalester College, Northwestern University, Clarion State College (Pa.), State University of New York-Brockport, and three whose names were disguised. The researchers were primarily concerned with institutional changes occasioned by black enrollment. Their probe of individual student response to the changes was a secondary issue.

Zelda Gamson and Carlos Arce, two members of the Peterson group, noted that "in reading reports of the period, one is struck by the level of confusion and fear which pervaded faculties and by the suddenness with which normally deliberate and slow-moving faculties were confronted with the necessity of making major curricular changes."[54]

The assassination of Martin Luther King in 1968 moved many colleges to institute programs to recruit black students. Gamson reviewed those programs which operated during 1968-1974. These support programs included remedial instruction, financial aid, counseling, and other goals. "Generally speaking," observed Gamson, "these support programs were initiated and carried out by administrative staff and not by regular faculty."[55] Recruitment of black students verged on the indiscriminate with some participants using the term "by the busload."[56] This changed over the years, Gamson wrote:

Early in the period the more selective institutions had been able to attract a number of black students who met their traditional admissions standards. But by 1974 . . . even these institutions were beginning to talk about the need to recruit large numbers of students who were better prepared.[57]

On some of the less selective campuses studied, students and some faculty "began to raise the question of 'reverse discrimination' in financial aid allocations and other areas."[58] Indeed, writing about the institutions as a whole, Gamson reported that "supportive service programs in general were viewed with suspicion by the faculties."[59] Minority programs ranked very low in the academic hierarchy on the typical campus.

Marvin Peterson and Roselle Davenport examined student life at the thirteen institutions. White students did little or nothing to force the colleges to recruit blacks. On each campus, white and black students remained largely separate. The institutions, however, seemed uninterested in this fact: "The paradox is that, despite this reported concern, not one of the institutions attempted to ascertain in a systematic way what made it more or less attractive to black students or how black students' perceptions of the institution differed from those of white students."[60]

How, if at all, did the advent of black students change the staffing and structuring of the thirteen institutions? More blacks were employed, but as administrators rather than as faculty, and even then, most presided over minority-related programs. Peterson writes that "the presence of top-level minority administrators with other than minority responsibilities was seen by both blacks and whites as evidence of serious commitment to minorities."[61] Wherever they worked, black administrators tended to become advocates for institutional change on behalf of black students. The regular machinery of the institutions contained no standing or permanent committees to study minority programs and issues. Black faculty, almost always recently appointed, were under great pressure from "both" directions. Black students wanted their leadership and support while the goal of tenure dictated involvement in research and writing, two pursuits that took time from involvement with students.

Other problems affecting black faculty related to administrative domination of financial resources for expansion of black programs. Allocations to these programs were made without departmental and faculty review, even, adds Peterson, "at the more prestigious institutions with strong traditions of departmental and faculty autonomy."[62] The black programs thus developed in the shadows of academe. Peterson comments that "this was more acceptable in a period of expansion, but it becomes more problematic in periods of retrenchment."[63] He is referring apparently to programs that did not become full-fledged departments. Peterson seems to be saying that the white faculty was not disturbed as long as there was money enough for all. When, however, funds grew scarcer, competition between departments and black programs developed and previously unexamined procedures and standards of employment came under scrutiny.

The departments of the institutions did relatively little and changed even less as a result of the influx of black students. Some responded with black courses, tutorial programs, or remedial courses. James Mingle calls the departmental response "inconsequential."[64] Among the faculty and the departments, he observed "a pervasive ambivalence" to the presence of black students.[65]

In a closing chapter of the Peterson group's study, Robert Blackburn reported that "blacks are no longer among the top concerns of hard-pressed administrators, even in the relatively responsive institutions examined in this study."[66] By 1974-1975, he reported further, "several campuses had settled down to a pattern of mutual indifference between the races."[67] The administration and faculty dozed on.

The Peterson group tried hard to avoid cynicism in appraising the experiences of the thirteen colleges and universities. Yet, the weight of the facts reported in the volume is overwhelmingly clear. The institutions bent slightly and reluctantly under the moral-political pressure generated by the civil rights movement. After adopting certain tangential changes, by the mid-1970s they had snapped back to their accustomed stance. Apparently, they had learned little other than how to avert serious institutional change. While the Peterson group does not insist that the thirteen institutions were representative the literature on the subject suggests that they reflect the general situation in American higher education. This heightens the importance of the Peterson work.

For six weeks during 1979, Donald Smith of the City University of New York visited seven unnamed, predominantly white universities to study the problems of black students. He interviewed 131 black students, faculty, and administrators and 38 white faculty and administrators. For some reason he did not interview white students.

Smith dwelt at some length on the changing socioeconomic composition of black students at the seven institutions:

A growing lack of interest in underachieving black students from inner-city high schools was evident among most of the universities investigated, even though they have taken some steps to provide assistance. For example, 75 percent of the current black population at East Private University is middle class and upper class and the product of predominantly white communities and predominantly white schools. By contrast, in 1969, 40 percent of the black population came from the lower class.[68]

This finding accords in general with that of the Peterson study. Undoubtedly, heightened recruitment of financially better-off black students will reduce attrition rates. But Smith notes the potentially disastrous effect of such a policy on black students who need special academic and financial aid in order to complete college.

Black students were unhappy on the campuses: "By and large, they feel depressed, lonely, and alienated. They perceive their universities as hostile places in which their relationships with white professors and white students are often demoralizing."[69] (Veteran black educator Stephen J. Wright had this to say on the same subject: "Very many black students on predominantly white campuses encounter attitudes that range from tolerance to cold indifference and even to hostility, and which have been reciprocated.")[70] Black students complained to Smith of police harassment. On campus, they tended to associate with other black students more as a defensive measure than as an expression of "black cohesiveness." They felt denigrated by prevailing attitudes among white students that blacks were not genuine students but were on campus only because of the requirements of a special admissions program.

Black students were ambivalent toward black faculty and administrators. Many black students, according to Smith, "believe that the placement of some blacks in high-level administrative posts is intended to keep students from protesting what they view as legitimate grievances."[71] The Peterson study contradicted this finding. It will be recalled that black administrators in the thirteen universities were frequently advocates of black student interests. Smith did find that black faculty and staff understood and sympathized with the problems black students were encountering. Few, however, did much about it. This failure was interpreted by black students as indifference and lack of concern.

The picture derived from Smith's study is unrelievedly bleak for black students. While it differs from the Peterson study in some respects, the two are basically consistent.

In reviewing studies of black students on white campuses, a significant methodological problem should be taken into account. If black students are found to feel powerless and isolated, is this because they are *black* in heavily white contexts or does it reflect the fact that they are *students*? In other words, feelings of powerlessness and isolation can be found among many white students. Universities may be alienating institutions for both black and white. The proliferation of mental health services on American college campuses suggests as much. It would, however, be all too easy to attempt to write off the racism on American campuses by attributing its effects to racially neutral alienation. White students do not suffer alienation because of their race; black students do.

Indeed, Richard Shingles has studied an issue that is very close to the one just indicated. He wanted to discover the dynamics of life on a predominantly white campus which engendered black alienation. Shingles interviewed 105 black students at an institution that may have been Virginia Polytechnic. He found two types of alienation: black alienation from white society, and black alienation from black society or self-debasement. Shingles stated that a liberal arts education reduced self-debasement "largely by freeing the students from the cultural stereotypes of the dominant society."[72] Self-debasement appeared to be linked with dissatisfaction with the institution. Why should this be so?

Shingles speculated that self-debasement is related to a clash of views within the black community:

Some of the more frustrated and militant of black students harbor embarrassment and disdain for those among the black masses whose behavior serves to reinforce negative stereotypes. This type of ambivalent, love-hate relationship between potential leaders and followers is not uncommon among minority and third world peoples. Typically, a lingering sense of inferiority exists alongside new-found pride; the desire to emulate contrasts with the simultaneous demand for autonomy and distinct identity.[73]

In this sense, self-debasement is seen to originate in a conviction by would-be leaders that their projected leadership will be withheld until the supposed followers act more deservingly. Whether or not Shingles's elaborate speculation is valid, it did not account entirely for the alienation. As he concedes in conclusion, "a large proportion of the alienation experienced by black students may be credited to the same frustrations, complaints, and realizations experienced by other college students."[74]

Smith, in his study of black students at seven predominantly white institutions, observed that "poor academic preparation in secondary schools appears to be the main barrier to access to higher education at the seven universities investigated."[75] Maureen Sie's study of minorities in science careers, conducted among 474 juniors and seniors at Wayne State University in Detroit, casts some light on this problem. She characterized the institution as enrolling "the highest percentage of black students . . . of any non-black university in the country. . . ."[76] (A fifth of Wayne's students are black.)

Four-fifths of the whites and over half of the blacks in the study had enrolled in college preparatory courses in high school. "Over 70 percent of the
white science majors felt their high school training was adequate while less
than 50 percent of the black science majors did."[77] Sie and her colleagues
found that a number of black students had taken advantage of special opportunities in secondary school: "Of the twenty-four black science majors,
thirteen went to Cass Technical High School where science is emphasized."[78]

Sie also examined the perception of discrimination. She found black and
female students perceived the most discrimination by faculty and administrators. Black science majors also perceived a high degree of discrimination
by fellow students and secretaries. In addition, "within the sciences, the
black students were the least content with their interpersonal relationships
with the faculty."[79] In her report of the research, Sie stressed what she characterized as a lack of cooperation by the science faculty and implied that the
cause lay in her concern about discrimination against black students.

Steven Rosenthal, a sociologist, studied racism at Old Dominion University.[80] Very possibly as a result his contract as a teacher was not renewed.
Black students make up 6 percent of enrollment; Rosenthal queried 363
white students and 136 black students. Blacks perceived far more racism
than did whites. Following is a tabular summary of responses to two questions expressed in percentages:[81]

	Agree		**Disagree**		**No Opinion**	
	Blacks	*Whites*	*Blacks*	*Whites*	*Blacks*	*Whites*
"There are too few blacks at O.D.U."	82	28	10	34	8	38
"Many faculty at O.D.U. are prejudiced."	33	7	25	48	42	45

Except for the strong affirmative black response to the first question, there
was not a monolithic response in any respect. The large "no opinion" response from both groups in answer to the second question is notable.

Students were asked whether they had encountered racism in the following areas during the preceding six months. Their affirmative responses,
again in percentages, were:[82]

	Black	**White**
"In the remarks or behavior of faculty members in the classroom"	65	26
"In grades given by an instructor"	48	7

"In treatment by administrators or staff"	40	11
"In behavior of campus police"	38	13

Blacks reported many more acts of racism than whites. Rosenthal also noted that "among both black and white respondents, those who perceived more racism within the University were more likely to favor further desegregation [that is, the enrollment of more black students] than respondents who perceived less racism."[83]

The results of Rosenthal's study were widely disseminated throughout the state of Virginia. According to his account:

Shortly thereafter, two deans in the University administration attacked this research as politically motivated and harmful to the University. Three months later, in December 1978, the author, who had previously been praised for his teaching, research, and community service, was notified that he would not be reappointed for the 1979–1980 academic year. . . . The University chose to act against the researcher rather than act upon the research findings.[84]

Any program to eliminate racism in higher education rests on a prior affirmation of its existence, and if the facts were as Rosenthal stated them, the freedom to inquire into racism in academe is precarious, indeed. It would be of interest to discover whether sociological and other professional organizations were involved in any investigation of this episode.

Discrimination in intercollegiate sports has a long history in American higher education, but the subject as a whole has hardly been studied nor do standard histories of higher education usually mention it.[85] Donald Spivey and Thomas Jones recently completed a detailed study of the history of racial discrimination in athletics at the University of Illinois. It is one of very few such studies and covers the years 1931–1967.

Spivey and Jones pointed out that until 1931 blacks were excluded from intercollegiate sports at the U. of I.; during the next five years a single black athlete competed, on the track team. In 1937, football was desegregated when Alphonse Anderson became the first black to be awarded an athletic scholarship at Illinois but he remained an isolated instance. In 1946, a study quoted by Spivey and Jones reported that "Negroes are not allowed on baseball, basketball, tennis, and swimming teams."[86] This pattern continued for eleven more years until, in 1957, two black star players joined the basketball team. (Black students also faced discrimination on other fronts. Until 1955, blacks were not permitted to live in university housing.) Black football players, even if they were outstanding members of the first team, were seldom allowed in starting lineups. Bill Burrell, such a player during 1956–1960, said: "I actually made All-American from the second team."[87]

The university did not consider the academic interests of black athletes very seriously. Nearly two-thirds of black athletic scholarship recipients failed to receive baccalaureate degrees. Nine out of ten had attended all-black high schools in Chicago. Nearly all of them scored below the minimum score on an aptitude test that predicted probable academic success. Two-thirds majored in physical education; only a third of white athletic scholarship holders did the same. In addition the black athletes were subjected to the indignity of having their social activities policed, especially in any instance of interracial dating, which was severely discouraged by university authorities.[88]

Notes

1. For the historical background, see Allen B. Ballard, *The Education of Black Folk: The Afro-American Struggle for Knowledge in White America* (New York: Harper & Row, 1973); and Meyer Weinberg, *A Chance to Learn* (New York: Cambridge University Press, 1977), Chapter 7.

2. See *Frazier v. Tennessee Board of Higher Education*, 240 F. 2d 689; Jessie P. Guzman, *Twenty Years of Court Decisions Affecting Higher Education in the South* (Tuskegee, Ala.: Tuskegee Inst., 1969), p. 22; and Jack Greenberg, *Race Relations and American Law* (New York: Columbia University Press, 1959), pp. 260–67.

3. James R. Mingle, "The Opening of White Colleges and Universities to Black Students," in Gail E. Thomas (ed.), *Black Students in Higher Education: Conditions and Experiences in the 1970s*, (Westport, Conn. : Greenwood Press, 1981), p. 20.

4. Stephen J. Wright, "The Impact of Current Desegregation Policy on Students and American Society," in Jeff E. Smith (ed.), *The Impact of Desegregation on Higher Education*, (Durham, N.C.: Institute on Desegregation, North Carolina Central University, 1981), p. 35.

5. J. LeVonne Chambers, "The Impact of Supreme Court Decisions on the Desegregation of Statewide Systems of Higher Education," in Smith, *The Impact of Desegregation*, p. 186.

6. James D. Tschechtelin, "Black and White Students in Maryland Community Colleges," in Thomas, *Black Students in Higher Education,* p. 163.

7. Bernard C. Watson, "Through the Academic Gateway," *Change* (October 1979), p. 25.

8. Catherine E. Putnam, *Examination of Equality of Educational Opportunity for Chicanos in California Public Higher Education* (doctoral diss., Stanford University, 1978) p. 57. (University Microfilms Order No. 7822561.)

9. Ibid., p. 66.

10. Ibid., p. 73.

11. Ibid., p. 107.

12. Ibid., p. 122.

13. Ibid., p. 124.

14. Ibid., pp. 221–22.

15. Amarante A. Fresquez, *Socio-Economic, Education, and Employment Status*

Factors Relating to Educational Success for Chicano and Anglo Scientists (doctoral diss., University of Arizona, 1979) p. 7. (University Microfilms Order No. 7916871.)

16. Gene I. Maeroff, "Minority Engineers Cultivated," *New York Times*, June 16, 1981.

17. Fresquez, p. 58.

18. Joseph Kaufert and others, "A Preliminary Study of Mexican-American Medical Students," *Journal of Medical Economics*, 50 (September 1975), p. 859.

19. B. E. Aguirre and Patrick Bernal, "Mexican American Students at Texas A & M," *Integrateducation*, 17 (September–December 1979), p. 39.

20. Isaac Cardenas, *Equality of Educational Opportunity: A Descriptive Study on Mexican American Access to Higher Education* (doctoral diss., University of Massachusetts, 1974). (University Microfilms Order No. 74-25,28.)

21. Carlos H. Arce, "Chicanos in Higher Education," *Integrateducation*, 14 (May–June 1976), p. 14.

22. Ward Churchill and Norbert S. Hill, Jr., "An Historical Survey of Tendencies in Indian Education: Higher Education," *Indian Historian*, 12 (Winter 1979), p. 39.

23. Ibid., p. 40.

24. Louis Fred Jacquot, *Alaska Natives and Alaska Higher Education, 1960–1972: A Descriptive Study* (doctoral diss., University of Oregon, 1973), p. 144. (University Microfilms Order No. 74-6838.)

25. See Meyer Weinberg, *Race and Place: A Legal History of the Neighborhood School* (Washington, D.C.: U.S. Government Printing Office, 1968), pp. 19–22.

26. Jacquot, pp. 158–59.

27. Ibid., p. 183.

28. Ibid.

29. Ibid., p. 201.

30. Quoted in Wallace Turner, "Alaskan People See a Fading of 'Spirit,' " *New York Times*, June 18, 1981.

31. DeWitt S. Williams, *Policy Boards of Private Predominantly Black Colleges and Universities* (doctoral diss., Indiana University, 1975), p. 60. (University Microfilms Order No. 76-6360.)

32. Freddie W. Nicholas, *The Black Land Grant Colleges: An Assessment of the Major Changes Between 1965-66 and 1970-71* (doctoral diss., University of Virginia, 1973). (University Microfilms Order No. 73-31, 149.)

33. Monroe Henry Little, Jr., *The Black Student at the Black College, 1880-1964* (doctoral diss., Princeton University, 1977), pp. 40–41. (University Microfilms Order No. 78-186.)

34. Ibid., p. ix.

35. Ibid., p. 48.

36. Ibid., p. 47.

37. Ibid., p. 88.

38. Ibid.

39. Ibid., p. 95.

40. Ibid., p. 96.

41. See Carter G. Woodson, *The Mis-Education of the Negro* (Washington, D.C.: Associated Publishers, 1933).

42. Preston A. George, *An Analysis of the Financial Health of Predominantly Black Graduate Institutions of Higher Education* (doctoral diss., Kansas State

University, 1978), p. 60. (University Microfilms Order No. 7821913.)

43. See Judith Randal, "Money and Management: Meharry's Double Trouble," *Change* (October 1979), pp. 60–61; Reginald Stuart, " 'Black' Medical College Battles Deficit," *New York Times*, March 4, 1981 (Meharry); Dan Balz, "A Black Dream Goes Awry," *Washington Post*, June 30, 1980 (Bishop College, Dallas); Paul Anthony, "He Conquered Lost Causes: An Epitaph for Lucius Pitts," *Southern Voices*, 1 (May–June 1974), pp. 71–73 (Miles College, Birmingham); and Thomas A. Johnson, "Fisk Commencement Hears Alumni Report on Endowment Drain," *New York Times*, May 11, 1976.

44. James M. Richards, Jr., *Psychosocial Environments of Black Colleges: A Theory-Based Assessment* (Baltimore, Md.: Center for Social Organization of Schools, Johns Hopkins University, September 1980), p. 7.

45. Ibid., p. 8.

46. Ibid., p. 7.

47. Gail E. Thomas and others, "Recent Trends in Racial Enrollment, Segregation, and Degree Attainment in Higher Education," in Thomas, *Black Students in Higher Education*, p. 123.

48. *A Comparison of the Retention and Completion Rates of Black and White Freshmen Who Enrolled at Virginia's State Supported Institutions of Higher Education in Fall, 1975* (Richmond: State Council of Higher Education for Virginia, December 1980), p. 9.

49. Lawrence R. Marcus and Franklin O. Smith, "Black Faculty and Survival Systems," *Integrateducation*, 17 (May–August 1979), p. 31.

50. Ibid., p. 34.

51. See Michael Winston, "Through the Back Door: Academic Racism and the Negro Scholar in Historical Perspective," *Daedalus*, 100 (Summer 1971).

52. Marcus and Smith, "Black Faculty and Survival Systems," p. 35.

53. Mary S. Merritt and others, "Quality of Interracial Interaction among University Students," *Integrateducation*, 15 (May–June 1977), p. 38.

54. Zelda F. Gamson and Carlos H. Arce, "Implications of the Social Context for Higher Education," in Marvin W. Peterson et al. (eds.), *Black Students on White Campuses: The Impacts of Increased Black Enrollments*, (Ann Arbor: Institute for Social Research, University of Michigan, 1978), p. 35.

55. Zelda F. Gamson, "Programs for Black Students 1968–1974," in Peterson and others, *Black Students on White Campuses.* p. 164.

56. Ibid., p. 168.

57. Ibid., pp. 169–70.

58. Ibid., pp. 173–74.

59. Ibid., p. 191.

60. Marvin W. Peterson and Roselle W. Davenport, "Student Organizations and Student Life," in Peterson and others, *Black Students on White Campuses*, p. 206.

61. Marvin W. Peterson, "Impacts on Administrative, Faculty, and Organizational Structures and Processes," in Peterson and others, *Black Students on White Campuses*, p. 216.

62. Ibid., p. 230.

63. Ibid.

64. James R. Mingle, "Faculty and Departmental Response Patterns: Individual and Contextual Predictors," in Peterson and others, *Black Students on White Campuses*, p. 267.

65. Ibid., p. 276.

66. Robert T. Blackburn and others, "The Meaning of Response: Current and Future Questions," in Peterson and others, *Black Students on White Campuses*, p. 317.

67. Ibid., p. 319.

68. Donald H. Smith, *Admission and Retention Problems of Black Students at Seven Predominantly White Universities* (Washington, D.C.: National Advisory Committee on Black Higher Education and Black Colleges and Universities, December 1980), p. 5.

69. Ibid., p. 6.

70. Stephen J. Wright, in Smith (ed.), *The Impact of Desegregation on Higher Education*, pp. 37–38.

71. Smith, *Admission and Retention Problems of Black Students*, p. 11.

72. Richard D. Shingles, "College A Source of Black Alienation," *Journal of Black Studies*, 9 (March 1979), p. 283.

73. Ibid.

74. Ibid., pp. 284–85.

75. Smith, *Admission and Retention Problems of Black Students*, p. 19.

76. Maureen A. Sie and others, "Minority Groups and Science Careers," *Integrateducation*, 16 (May-June 1978), p. 44.

77. Ibid., p. 45.

78. Ibid.

79. Ibid., p. 46.

80. Steven J. Rosenthal, "Racism and Desegregation at Old Dominion University," *Integrateducation*, 17 (January–April 1979), p. 41. See also "Symbolic Racism and Desegregation: Divergent Attitudes and Perceptions of Black and White University Students," *Phylon*, 41 (Fall 1980), pp. 257–66.

81. Rosenthal, "Racism and Desegregation," pp. 257–66.

82. Ibid.

83. Ibid., p. 42.

84. Ibid.

85. See Meyer Weinberg, *A Chance to Learn*, pp. 305–8.

86. Jean Knapp, quoted in Donald Spivey and Thomas A. Jones, "Intercollegiate Athletic Servitude: A Case Study of the Black Illinois Student-Athletes, 1931-1967," *Social Science Quarterly*, 55 (March 1975), p. 944.

87. Ibid., p. 945.

88. Ibid., p. 946.

12

Minorities In Higher Education—II

North Carolina Studies

A small number of studies of black students in colleges in North Carolina have been made and are reported below.

Recently, Augustus Burns traced the history of efforts by state officials in North Carolina to exclude blacks from public graduate and professional education in the years 1930–1951.[1] "Many of the state's leaders," he wrote, "were strong believers in racial segregation, and they waged the legal fight against desegregation as a matter of conscience."[2] The officials also sought to protect the state university's flagship campus at Chapel Hill from voluntary desegregation. When legal segregation appeared to be doomed, state officials continued to fight in the courts in order to place the onus for desegregation on federal officials.

Cleon Thompson made a comparison of black and white public higher education institutions in the state. Wherever possible he used data within the period of 1964–1974; in those years, white enrollment almost tripled while that of the black colleges rose by only about two-thirds.[3] In 1964, both types of institutions enrolled fewer than 1 percent of opposite-race students. By 1974, whites made up 7.4 percent of enrollment at predominantly black institutions while blacks constituted only 3.1 percent of enrollment at predominantly white institutions. The percentage of freshmen graduating with a baccalaureate four years later (in 1966) was 47.2 in black institutions and 43.5 in white institutions. Eight years later the black percentage was 74.9 but the white percentage was 86.7. During this latter span of years, blacks advanced but lost in relative standing.

Thompson used another measurement, "Advanced to next level," a measure of whether students were progressing normally. Blacks in black schools progressed at somewhat higher rates than did blacks in white schools. In 1974–1975, black students in black schools persisted at a higher rate than did white students in white schools (68.8 percent v. 60.8 percent). The following year, however, the rates were virtually identical (59.6 percent v. 59.1). During the same two years, retention rates—that is, the number of returning students in relation to enrollment—were distinctly higher for blacks in black colleges than for whites in white colleges (83.7 percent v. 76.0 percent and 81.7 percent v. 74.7 percent). While these measures are not identical with those used by the State Council of Higher Education for Virginia, it appears that black colleges in North Carolina were more productive educationally than those in Virginia. On the other hand, little is known about the academic comparability of the two groups of colleges.

Between the late 1960s and mid-1970s, some changes occurred in the faculty of black and white colleges of North Carolina. In 1966, there were no black faculty employed in white colleges; seven years later the figure rose to 1.9 percent. In the black institutions, the figures for white faculty, for the same period, were 22.7 percent and 29.5 percent. Thus, from the viewpoint of student enrollment and faculty employment, the black colleges were far more desegregated. Faculty members holding doctorates rose from 24.3 percent to 33.8 percent in black colleges but the gap between the two groups of colleges expanded as doctorates in white colleges grew from 35.7 percent to 56.2 percent.[4] Faculty-student ratios were slightly more favorable at the black institutions.

On a number of other measures, Thompson found some more favorable at the black colleges, others at the white colleges. Per-student expenditures for libraries, for example, favored white institutions in 1966–1967 but very slightly favored black institutions by 1973–1974. Thompson found the two groups of institutions comparable on twelve of twenty-three tests. Even where recent state expenditures had made some headway toward equalization, Thompson emphasized how recent the effort was.

Are the black institutions inferior to the white ones? Thompson, who had set out to settle this question, concluded that "this study has neither proved nor disproved this particular assumption. . . ."[5]

David and Anna Kleinbaum studied the black student experience at the University of North Carolina, Chapel Hill, during 1972. "Black students . . . ," they found, "are generally disenchanted with their total experience on campus."[6] They were troubled about the lack of social life and they missed having black faculty and advisors.

In response to a questionnaire distributed by the Kleinbaums, black and white students expressed opinions on six items, in percentages, as follows:[7]

	Blacks	Whites
Would not come to UNC if could choose again	30 + 5	10 + 5
UNC not trying at all to improve status of minorities	23 + 5	2 + 2
Came to UNC because of social life	18 + 4	53 + 9
Dissatisfied with social opportunities	68 + 5	39 + 9
"Strongly" concerned about not enough minority faculty	90 + 3	24 + 8

	Blacks
Experienced some discrimination from instructors	
Men	58 + 8
Women	52 + 8
Undergraduate Student	59 + 6
Graduate Student	41 + 11

Acknowledging the generally negative cast of black student opinion, the Kleinbaums observed that during Fall, 1973, the university had made significant changes in administration and student facilities. "The experience of black students at UNC during the next few years," wrote the Kleinbaums, "should help determine whether or not improvements in university structure will affect the social and academic atmosphere on campus in such a way as to cause positive change in student attitudes."[8]

In 1977, four years after the Kleinbaum study, Walter Allen investigated 135 black undergraduates at Chapel Hill.[9] He found that they fell into two groupings. The first included those who "positively perceived campus race relations and the university's supportive services for black students."[10] This group was more satisfied with the campus, was better adjusted, and performed better academically. The second group was marked by "strong feelings of alienation and academic anxiety," and members of this group did not do as well academically. While Allen made no precise apportionment of the 135 students among the two groupings, he treated the alienation of the second group as a serious problem.

He wrote:

Black students enter white universities as the victims of sustained personal and institutional discrimination. After their entrance, such incidents of discrimination evidently do not cease and black students subsequently experience adjustment and academic performance difficulties.[11]

While Allen did not document in detail the nature of the discrimination, the continued existence of such perceptions by black students suggests that the Kleinbaums' expectations may have proved to be premature.

During these same years—to be precise, 1973–1976—Chapel Hill was engaged in an affirmative action program pressed on it by the Office for Civil Rights. Barbara Kramer studied the effort from the "inside" as a member of the Affirmative Action Program Committee appointed by the Chapel Hill chancellor.[12] The committee met twenty-two times and drew up and adopted a program which changed many employment procedures. Kramer noted that "there has been a considerable increase in the amount of record keeping and secretarial time. . . ."[13] But little else changed. Between 1973 and 1976, the percentage of faculty that was black rose from 0.9 to 2.1, while that of whites on the faculty dropped from 96.4 to 95.9.

In interviews with sixty-six deans or department chairpersons at Chapel Hill, Kramer found that two-thirds said the approved plan had not affected the number of minorities offered employment as faculty. She reported also that "not a single chairman gave any indication that departmental standards had been lowered in any way in order to obtain female and minority faculty members."[14] According to Kramer, during that period of the study every department hired at least one faculty member and a total of 356 were newly employed as assistant, associate, or full professors.

Kramer did not dwell on the issue of institutional responsibility for the minimal outcome of the plan. Instead, she declared that "the affirmative action regulations have not addressed the subject of student 'pools' and there appears to be overwhelming evidence that changing this 'pool' is really the critical issue."[15] (A pool in this sense is the totality of persons eligible for some specific task or function.) Thus, Kramer contended that, apparently, the minimal representation of blacks on the Chapel Hill faculty was an expression of some absolute shortage of blacks who have completed the appropriate graduate training that would otherwise qualify them for university teaching positions. This is, of course, a possibility. Kramer, however, did not present evidence that would permit making an independent judgment on the issue.

In Spring, 1977, Donald Richard studied black and white students at a predominantly black (North Carolina Central University) and a predominantly white (University of North Carolina—Greensboro) institution.[16] He found, more or less, that both groups of students viewed the educational benefits of attendance in similar ways. Black and white students seemed equally satisfied with their education. It should be noted that the black contingent of graduating seniors at UNC-G was quite small (18) as compared with white seniors (488). Fewer than two out of five of the black seniors had responded to Richard's questionnaires, so there is some question of whether his sample is representative.

The City University of New York (CUNY)

During the 1930s, CUNY enrolled a tiny number of black students. No blacks were on the faculty and during the middle years of the decade no blacks worked on the clerical staff of City College even though 500,000 blacks lived in New York City.[17] In 1942, the lack of black academic appointments became a political issue in the black community. As a result, token numbers of black professors were added to CUNY's lily-white faculty.[18] A few more were added in the first years after World War II. By 1950, only 5 percent of the total student enrollment was made up of nonwhites. Ten years later the figure was unchanged.[19]

In 1955, a system of community colleges was created which became part of CUNY. The new institutions were expected to provide for minority groups especially. Searching the records of CUNY for the years 1961–1969, Sheila Gordon found that undergraduate enrollment increased by some 40,000 students but half of them attended community colleges. Gordon reported, "Senior college full-time enrollment was up during this period by less than 40 percent, compared with 850 percent among the community colleges."[20] Entry of minorities into the senior colleges remained low during the 1960s.

As the decade drew to a close, however, the black and Puerto Rican communities demanded a fundamental change. They insisted on the right of their children to gain a higher education in every facility of CUNY. As a result of protracted struggles, CUNY agreed in 1969 to an open admissions program.[21] The new system began to operate in Fall, 1970. All high school graduates were guaranteed entry to CUNY; specific placement in a senior or community college depended on high school scores, placement in high school graduating class, and availability of space.

The first entering class under Open Admissions was three-quarters larger than its predecessor a year before. In 1969, 2,815 black students had entered CUNY; by 1974, the number enrolled was over 12,000. (The number of Puerto Rican students rose from 1,215 to 5,624.)[22] The latter year CUNY Chancellor Robert Kibbee testified that CUNY "may very well be the largest black university, as well as the largest Puerto Rican university, in the country."[23] Black faculty rose from 1,050 in 1970 to 1,670 two years later.[24]

In 1960, a minimum high school average of 85 percent was required for entrance into any of the senior colleges and a minimum average of 77 percent to enter a community college. During 1970–1973, Leslie Berger and Jeanette Leaf wrote, "the percentage of students with high school averages below 70 ranged from 31–36 percent at the community colleges, in comparison to 4.5–12 percent at the senior colleges."[25] Clearly, CUNY had to shoulder a large remedial burden. CUNY had initiated a compensatory education program in 1966–1967 which included student stipends, with a total expenditure of $1.5 million for 1,200 students. The program known as SEEK spent over $28 million for the benefit of 12,427 students in 1974–1975.[26] This sum by no means comprised the entire cost of compensatory education in CUNY.

Was broadened access translated into heightened educational attainment, especially in terms of graduation at the baccalaureate level? The question was answered by then City College president Robert Marshak as follows: "It is clear . . . that open admissions does not mean open graduation or a guaranteed degree at the end of four years of college unless the faculty itself relaxes standards."[27] David Lavin and his colleagues provide data which enable us to examine the graduation record of blacks and Hispanics who attend the senior colleges of CUNY. After five years of attendance, here was the experience of the two groups, in percentages:[28]

	Regular Admission Students			Open Admission Students		
	Graduated	Retained	Dropout	Graduated	Retained	Dropout
Entered 1970						
Blacks	48	14	38	23	21	56
Hispanics	34	18	48	19	22	59
Entered 1971						
Blacks	30	40	30	18	43	39
Hispanics	19	38	43	7	26	67
Comparative National Rates (for all students)	49	9	42	21	14	65

Overall, blacks achieved in CUNY more or less in line with national averages while Hispanics did more poorly.

While open admission was designed primarily for blacks and Puerto Ricans, and they benefitted greatly from it, others gained even more. Several writers cite data indicating that whites—including Jewish, Irish, and Italian youths—benefitted. As Gordon wrote: "The children of working-class whites whose high school averages would have been too low for CUNY admission under the old system—and whose families could not afford private college fees—now found CUNY open to them."[29] Lavin and associates said flatly: "Open-admissions Jewish and Catholic students generally outnumbered open-admissions blacks and Hispanics throughout the CUNY system."[30]

In any event, the experiment seemed to be the rare kind that benefitted every group—black, Hispanic, and whites. Yet, by the mid-1970s the promise of open admissions began to crumble, but not for want of support by potential and present students. The financial stringencies of New York City struck hard at open admissions. Lavin and associates wrote:

The impact of faculty retrenchment has hit hardest at those staff providing the remedial and counseling services so important to the open-admissions effort. Free tuition has been abolished, with consequences made more dire by the information gap resulting from the reduction in the numbers of high school guidance counselors.[31]

The additional weight of inflated economic stagnation cut many minority students out of CUNY. A decade that had begun with one of the most daring adventures in higher educational history ended under a surfeit of imposed disadvantages.

Other Colleges

Austin Frank studied graduation rates of students admitted to various universities on an affirmative action basis. In each case, rates were calculated five years after students entered as freshmen, except at the University of Michigan, where the rates covered four years:[32]

University	Year of Entry	Graduation Rate, in Percentages			
		Black	Hispanic	White	Asian
University of California	1972	41	43	52	67
California State University and Colleges	1973	14	16	34	33
University of Delaware	1973	25	N.A.	64	N.A.
University of Maryland	1974	25	N.A.	48	N.A.
University of Michigan	1975	30	30	51	52

Graduation rates among the five institutions seem to correlate directly with the degree of selectivity of admissions, especially for blacks. This was not necessarily the case for whites and Asians. In examining graduation rates among predominantly black institutions, the same distinctions must be kept in mind.

At Michigan State University in 1979 an official committee evaluated and pronounced successful the Developmental Program for Admissions (DPA) which had been set up to aid students from disadvantaged backgrounds.[33] Data showed "a general pattern of increased retention or persistence of DPA students, particularly since 1971 when the Office of Special Programs and Supportive Services was established."[34] The committee also reported: "The percentages of minority and DPA students with majors in the Colleges of Natural Science and Social Science are higher than for Caucasian students. The growth in enrollments of DPA students in Natural Science is a recent phenomenon. . . ."[35] In Fall, 1978, around three-quarters of DPA freshmen were enrolled in eight remedial programs. The persistence of racism, however, was stressed by the committee's observation that "there is concern . . . that there is increasing intolerance of behaviors deriving from racial/ethnic and cultural differences."[36]

Maurice Taylor explored some problems of black students on white campuses.[37] A central issue he discussed was the "institutional advocate" for these students. In the eyes of the "college gatekeepers," the advocates are customarily near the bottom of the university's status ranking. Thus, Taylor advised black students to seek to convert the gatekeepers into advocates: "Professors, chairpersons, and administrators are the advocates who are unquestionably accepted as being 'in'. They have the time and know-how to avoid or cut across maintenance measures and virtually assure, if not success, at least an opportunity for success."[38] Taylor cautioned against black students confusing advocacy with lack of academic standards. "It is not inherently racist to require or even demand, quality academic performance. Indeed, it would be racist not to demand it."[39] Gerald Dillingham, a black person who attended a state university during the late 1960s, expressed a similar view:

> As black students, we were often patronized when we arrived on the campus. The attitude was "You are underprivileged." "You are behind and need help," and "You are not as good as we." Black students reacted by drawing together, not on ideological grounds, but in search of psychological security.[40]

In this context, institutional advocates may be an urgent academic necessity.

One result of the advent of black students throughout American higher education has been the organization of black studies programs. There are numerous statistical surveys of the field, but few practitioners in black studies have written as understandingly about the field as Julius Lester of the University of Massachusetts. He contended that the importance of black studies in the curriculum did not depend on the presence of black students. Even if there were no black students in a university "black studies would have a place, just as English literature had legitimacy for me as an undergraduate at an institution where there were no white students."[41] He described the mission of black studies in universal terms: "To invite and guide students into human experience as it has affected the lives of blacks and to examine the variety of ways in which blacks have responded."[42] Yet, Lester observed, "few white academicians perceive black studies as legitimate." Indeed, white students on his own campus have told Lester that "faculty advisors have counseled them against courses in [his] department" on the ground that black studies offered nothing of value to whites.[43]

Jomills Braddock and James McPartland traced the effect of having attended desegregated elementary and high schools on the later academic success of black students in predominantly white colleges.[44] Their overall finding is that "black students in desegregated colleges fare better (that is, they have higher educational attainment levels) if they also had attended elementary and secondary classes which were desegregated."[45] They also found that black students who had early desegregated schooling were twice as likely as blacks who attended segregated schools to enroll in a traditionally white college in the South. With the growth of desegregation in the South over the past two decades, it is thus to be expected that many more black students would enroll in hitherto white institutions; as, indeed, they have.

Graduate and Professional Schooling

"The analysis of data on black student enrollment in professional schools," declared James Blackwell, ". . . depicts a process of exclusion, retardation, and decline."[46] J. Christopher Lehner characterizes the movement for increased black participation in graduate and professional studies as "a losing battle."[47] Lehner reported that only twenty-nine historically black colleges (HBCs) conferred master's degrees in 1976–1977. During 1979, only six HBCs granted doctorates. (The latter were Atlanta, Howard, Morgan State, Texas Southern, Meharry, and Interdenominational Theological Center.)[48] Black graduate and professional schooling cannot grow significantly if it remains within its present constricted bounds. Yet, as Blackwell and Lehner pointed out, black representation in predominantly white graduate and professional schools has been declining for several years.

Before examining the racial factor, let us pause to review Leonard Baird's suggestive finding about the role of social class in influencing the rate of entry into graduate and professional schools.[49] Using the 1971 findings of the College Senior Survey as well as a one-year follow-up which covered 7,734 seniors in ninety-four colleges, Baird found that "among the B+ students, those from the wealthiest families were nearly twice as likely to attend graduate or professional school than those from the poorest homes."[50] This advantage was greatest in professional schools for medicine, law, and business. Black students, whose economic status is very low, thus bear the brunt of disadvantage in this respect.

Lehner pointed out that black graduate students are concentrated in education and the social sciences, "academic disciplines that will offer severely reduced career opportunities in the near future."[51] Much federal financial assistance has helped to produce this concentration. With the decrease in federal aid and in the demand for graduate teachers and social scientists, the number of black graduate students has declined. Here, for example, is a listing of the number and percentage of black doctorates received during 1974–1979:[52]

Year	Number	Percentage of Total
1974	846	2.6
1975	989	3.0
1976	1,085	3.3
1977	1,109	3.5
1978	1,029	3.3
1979	1,050	3.4

Black enrollment in graduate schools rose during the first half of the 1970s, but according to Lehner, it "has regressed to the situation as it existed in 1970."[53]

Even in graduate fields such as education, in which blacks are comparatively numerous, certain subfields are almost wholly white. Take the specialty of educational policy research. Wright queried forty knowledgeable black educators and social scientists as to the reason for the absence of blacks in this area. A number referred to "the tendency of many professors in major graduate schools to discourage black students from selecting black oriented problems for investigation."[54] Another factor was the small number of black institutions offering doctoral work. The entire arena of public policy on black education has been off-limits to blacks. As Wright pointed out:

> Blacks have been systematically excluded, over the years, from educational policy-making—specifically from educational governing boards of various types and from the staffs of such boards, and until relatively recently, from many state legislatures and the boards of major voluntary educational associations, including accrediting associations.[55]

This entire pattern of denials, combined with the exclusory practices of university graduate schools, determined that black scholars would not participate in the making of, or advising on, public policy.

Three research studies analyzed the functioning of black graduate students in predominantly white universities. Donald Cunningen, a student in the Harvard Graduate School of Education, found most of his black classmates were from middle or upper-middle class families and that they had gone to white undergraduate colleges. Cunningen, who had graduated from a black college, reported that "as a black college graduate I was an invisible student among blacks in a white graduate school."[56] He sensed a tendency to devalue the black college, and responded: "In my opinion, the black college has a two-fold responsibility to its constituency: (1) to give the black college students the necessary tools to compete with all students in American society, and (2) to make the black college students aware of all the opportunities available to them."[57]

Freeman Hrabowski studied black graduate students at the University of Illinois. These were master's and doctoral students who had begun graduate work between 1968 and 1973.[58] Two hundred ten of the students had graduated from a total of fifty-five black colleges; 140 were graduates of forty-eight white colleges. The former were called Group A, the latter Group B. Students in each group were matched on graduation rate and retention level. Of the 350 black graduate students, 103 were seeking a doctoral degree, and 247 were seeking a master's degree. The fields of specialization for the two groups were as follows, in percentages:[59]

	Group A	Group B
Education	26	29
Social sciences and public service	30	46
Humanities	11	11
Pure and applied sciences	33	14

Hrabowski found that the groups were very similar in graduate grade point averages, in graduation rates for master's candidates, and in retention rates for doctoral students. "Despite the inferior resources of most black colleges," Hrabowski concluded, "many of the graduates of these institutions are capable of successfully completing graduate programs at a major university."[60] Financial assistance was especially critical for black graduate students, having much to do with staying power. "Master's level students . . . who did not receive financial aid were more likely to drop out than those who did; the retention rate for the group of students who received financial assistance was significantly higher than the retention rate for the group without financial support."[61]

Beverly Bruce studied minority graduate achievement in the humanities and social sciences, except for sociology, at the University of California, San Diego.[62] She found that minority students, even when they began at a disadvantage on entrance examinations and in grade point averages, nevertheless commonly performed at a satisfactory level (that is, were in academic good standing). Surprisingly, perhaps, "almost one-fourth of the blacks and a little less than one-half of the Chicanos had attended a junior college."[63]

Together, the Hrabowski and Bruce studies suggest—at least for those few minority students who enter graduate study—that prior attendance at many black colleges and community colleges, despite their meager resources, is not incompatible with the highest academic attainment. Academic folklore would reject that possibility.

Until 1970, the medical school of the University of California at Los Angeles had not graduated a single black student.[64] This was quite typical of standard medical schools. The great majority of black medical graduates had attended either the medical school of Howard University or Meharry Medical College. In 1969–1970, for example, 47.6 percent of all black medical students attended Howard or Meharry. Five years later, however, the figure had dropped to 20.7 percent.[65] While in the half-decade the number of black medical students rose from 1,042 to 3,555, the growth seemed large only in relation to the minuscule number at the outset.[66] Ada Fisher wrote that "in 1978, only 1 percent of 200,000 eligible black college students applied to medical school."[67] While a number ultimately graduated as physicians, special efforts were required. As Fisher reported: "In all medical schools combined, 12.9 percent of the black students had to repeat the first academic year and 6.3 percent had to repeat other years; only 1.6 percent of the whites had to repeat the first year and 0.7 percent had to repeat other years. . . ."[68]

At the same time one should not lose sight of the fact that the overwhelming majority of black medical students made normal progress. This was true of other minorities as well, as demonstrated by figures supplied by John Rolph and associates.[69] They reported retention rates of minorities in medical school as follows—in percentages.[70] (All references to year designate the year of admittance, not that of graduation.)

Year	Black	American Indian	Mexican American	Puerto Rican	All Students
1971–1972	86	100	94	91	96
1972–1973	87	90	96	95	98
1973–1974	87	84	94	98	97
1974–1975	95	98	97	98	99

Ralph Smith has written an enlightening analysis of black law students. He presented a listing of gross attrition rates in American Bar Association approved law schools, 1969–1977, in percentages.[71]

Year	Blacks	Mexican Americans	Puerto Ricans	Asians
1969–1970	31.7	30.6	37.9	N.A.
1971–1972	29.7	32.8	49.0	20.5
1972–1973	30.3	19.4	23.3	3.4
1973–1974	25.3	29.3	0.0	12.2
1974–1975	22.1	20.2	14.5	11.9
1975–1976	26.3	19.8	11.5	3.0
1976–1977	26.1	17.9	6.7	17.8

Again, it was clear that the majority, although a less resounding one than in the case of medical students, did not drop out of law school and presumably completed their tour successfully.

The law school experience is frequently a crushing one for blacks. "It is not uncommon for these students," Smith wrote, "to leave law school with loan obligations in excess of $20,000 to be repaid with interest during the initial stages of their professional career."[72] Smith also reported numerous complaints by black law students about wretched human relations in the schools: "Given the certainty of being outperformed by whites, perceived alienation from the law school environment, and a lack of adequate support and assistance from law schools, it should not be surprising that many of the black students who do get past the admission process are emotionally crippled by the law school experience."[73] A national organization has been formed to help cope with some of these pressures: the Black American Law Students Association.

The creativity of the civil rights movement is nowhere clearer than in the changes wrought in the admission practices of the Harvard law and medical schools. Between 1955 and 1968, the medical school admitted a grand total of nine Afro-Americans. But during the next decade, according to Lee Daniels, "Harvard trained over 500 black lawyers and doctors. This figure is several times greater than the number of blacks enrolled in the two schools during the entire previous century."[74] In the early 1970s, blacks at the law school failed and dropped out at a higher rate than did their white classmates. By the end of the decade, there was no longer any important difference in black and white failure rates. Even by the mid-1970s, blacks' scores on the Law Students Aptitude Test "more closely resembled those of their white peers."[75]

Desegregation of Higher Education

Policy Problems

The single greatest factor favoring college desegregation has been the large number of individual decisions by black students to attend formerly all-white institutions. After legal means were used to open those doors, black students began acquiring skills and knowledge that led them into careers which had been a white monopoly, especially in the South. Scientific, technical, and business fields attracted growing numbers of black students, and it was the availability of training in these fields that drew blacks rather than the opportunity to study with whites. Such training was not typically available in the black colleges.

But individual decisions alone did little to dismantle the illegal dual structure of higher education in the South and elsewhere. Further legal action was required. After the 1972 *Adams* v. *Richardson* ruling was upheld in 1973, the U.S. Department of Health, Education, and Welfare formulated criteria for desegregating colleges in 1977. During the Nixon and Ford administrations, enforcement of *Adams*-related measures was minimal, if not inconsequential. HEW tended to accept desegregation proposals from the states that could only have produced a token measure of actual desegregation. The civil rights plaintiffs returned to the courts, complained about the failure of HEW to carry out the *Adams* mandate, and usually saw the court demand further action. In the Carter administration, 1977–1981, HEW began to crack down, although tardily. Just days before Carter left office, a series of directives to states were issued. When President Reagan took office, many of the Carter initiatives were diluted and reversed. Exceedingly little desegregation had occurred on the campuses.

Let us examine some of the central issues in this arena. Whenever public higher education systems had been segregated there was, under *Adams*, an obligation to desegregate. In several respects, however, it is far more complicated to desegregate higher education than the common schools. For one thing, attendance in higher education is not compulsory and thus individual students cannot be mandated to attend a certain college or, indeed, any college. For another, colleges are far less interchangeable than elementary or high schools. Students may select one college because it is different in some manner deemed educationally advantageous. Further, the number of higher institutions is far less than the number of common schools and thus the possibilities for linking institutions in a plan are relatively few. Also, attendance in a specific college—whatever its racial composition—is frequently regarded as an acceptable accompaniment of wealth or social status; this feature has few equivalents in the common schools.

Nevertheless, federal courts have accepted the proposition that a legally segregated public higher education system offends the Fourteenth Amendment and must be dismantled. The features noted in the preceding paragraph relate, at most, to the practicability of a remedy rather than to the propriety of a finding of illegal segregation.

In one critical respect, desegregation of higher education and of the common schools is quite alike. That is, the white institutions were deliberately favored at the expense of the black ones. The burden of inequality grew over the years as official policy sought successfully to maintain black schools and colleges as inferior institutions. The purpose of desegregation, in either case, was to eliminate the privileged status of formerly white institutions and to institute a system whereby race was no longer a barrier to educational achievement and attainment by any group of students.

In no case have formerly dual systems of higher education hastened to eliminate white privilege. The prime device used to postpone this crucial step was the effort to diminish the degree of material inequality between black and white institutions. In a number of cases, a bargain was struck between state officials and persons representing black institutions in search of desperately needed funds. In exchange for these funds, the black institutions would not press for the transfer of popular curricula or programs from the white to the black institutions. (At times, they were located within a few miles of each other.) Black attendance at white institutions was scheduled to rise somewhat while efforts were pledged to increase white enrollment at traditionally black colleges.

Some advocates of black colleges viewed desegregation as a threat. They feared that these institutions would be eliminated since American race lore usually reserved the description "desegregated" for predominantly white institutions. Other advocates of black colleges viewed desegregation as an opportunity to secure the future of black colleges as they came to absorb white colleges under a principle of black leadership.

Elias Blake, Jr., president of Atlanta's black Clark College, is a proponent of the first view. He contended that merely changing the racial composition of colleges will not do.[76] Instead, he wrote, the emphasis should be "on the need for white institutions to emulate black institutions in producing more black professionals."[77] His concern was practical: that college is most desirable that produces the greatest number of black professionals. He asked: "Will desegregation address itself specifically to the creation of a genuinely new world, or will it simply be an attempt to convert the world to a new, multicolored version of the old?"[78] The "new world" he spoke of is one in which black and white alike would occupy the heights of academic and professional life.

Leonard Haynes, a frequent writer on the subject, held the *Adams* ruling in high regard:

> The *Adams* mandate provides, for the first time in history, a blueprint for eliminating the dual system and providing more—and better—educational opportunities for blacks and other minorities. The mandate, explicated in HEW's new criteria [of 1977], represents the most comprehensive effort to date toward achieving the goals of equal educational opportunity and increasing the participation and completion rates of blacks in higher education systems.[79]

Referring to the stipulation in the 1977 HEW desegregation criteria that the interests of black colleges must be protected, Haynes stated that "no other federal regulation or laws have ever acknowledged that these institutions should receive special treatment to improve and expand their capacity to educate blacks and other minorities."[80]

In an earlier study, completed in 1975, Haynes explored the effects of desegregation on public black colleges.[81] He interviewed the chief executives (president and vice-president) of twenty-six colleges. He found one effect of desegregation was the increasing difficulty of black colleges to hold on to black faculty. White institutions, under federal pressure to desegregate their heavily white faculties, were raiding black colleges for likely candidates. Similarly, many bright black students were receiving scholarships and other irresistible aid offers from white colleges to change the racial composition of their student bodies. According to the interviewees, Haynes reported, "black faculty . . . have been especially alarmed over the desire of authorities (federal and state) to use affirmative action as a tool of desegregation, because it encourages whites to compete with blacks for the same positions."[82] For many black academics, the black colleges have been the sole source of employment as teachers and for administrative positions. To set those opportunities aside in the name of a desegregated staff could only constitute, to many, another form of white privilege.

Yet, Haynes found support for desegregation everywhere: "In no instance did the respondents suggest or imply that their institutions would profit by supporting a policy of segregation."[83] At the same time, a heightened sense of prudence was leading black colleges to consult with one another on possible consequences of desegregation. Haynes also found his interviewees deeply concerned that adequate financial resources be committed by the states to support expanded roles for black colleges. All acknowledged some increase in state funding since 1972 (the date of the district court decision of *Adams*). Black college officials advised Haynes that the problem of desegregating black colleges was not so much one of discovering how to attract white students as it was recognizing that "whites are going to find it difficult to adjust to the missions and goals of a traditional black institution."[84]

At the time of his study, Haynes was informed that black communities in general did not give much support to the black colleges. Since then, however, black political support has increased significantly.

J. LeVonne Chambers, a prominent black civil rights lawyer in North Carolina, examined the desegregation problem in that state.[85] Recently, he served a term on the state university governing board. Chambers argued that state authorities are attempting to disturb only minimally the preferred status of whites in higher education. In the state's premier institution, the state university at Chapel Hill, for example, nearly one-quarter of the white college students of the state are enrolled but only one-fourteenth of the state's black college students. The state's desegregation proposal did not promise to change that situation materially. Chambers declared that over the years the state had "simply built in and perpetuated a superior funding for white institutions while at the same time locating additional programs and faculties at those institutions."[86]

Chambers examined the word *enhancement*, a term used to indicate the upgrading of the academic offering of black colleges. "Enhancement," he wrote, "does not mean separate but equal."[87] It meant much more, in fact: "Genuine enhancement of the black colleges requires money, priority placement of new programs at black colleges, postponement of new developments at white institutions and elimination of unnecessarily duplicative programs by taking away programs from or curtailing programs at traditionally white institutions."[88] Enhancement has been the principal point at issue between the state and federal authorities. When an agreement was negotiated between the two parties in mid-1981, however, little more than token enhancement was provided. No programs were to be denied white units nor were they to lose any of their ongoing programs.

Chambers charged that the state does not treat the black colleges, including staff, faculty, and students, as equals, nor is it committed to do so. He also criticized "some black leaders in the state" for lacking the same commitment to the equality of black colleges. He predicted that unless equality became a reality, the better faculty and students would continue to leave the black colleges until a takeover by white colleges would become a real option.

Before proceeding to examine some actual cases of college desegregation, let us review the status of court- and administrative-ordered desegregation as of mid-1981. The following listing refers principally to two types of legal proceedings: (1) *Adams*, decided in 1972–1973 by federal courts and implemented on a systematic basis by HEW in 1977; and (2) actions prompted by a series of investigations during 1978–1979 by the Office for Civil Rights.[89] Tennessee desegregation was the consequence of an independent lawsuit in the federal courts.

State	Impetus for action	Outcome
Alabama	OCR	In negotiation
Arkansas	Adams	Acceptable plan, 1978
Delaware	OCR	In negotiation
Florida	Adams	Acceptable plan, 1978
Georgia	Adams	Acceptable plan, 1979
Kentucky	OCR	In negotiation
Louisiana	Adams	Settled
Maryland	Adams	Ongoing lawsuit
Mississippi	Adams	Ongoing lawsuit
Missouri	OCR	In negotiation
North Carolina	Adams	Settled
Ohio	OCR	In negotiation
Oklahoma	Adams	Acceptable plan, 1978
Pennsylvania	Adams	In negotiation
South Carolina	OCR	Settled
Tennessee	Court suit	Merger, 1979
Texas	OCR	In negotiation
Virginia	Adams	Acceptable plan, 1979
West Virginia	OCR	Acceptable plan, 1981

Since the states with plans deemed acceptable acted only during 1978–1981, there has not been sufficient time to study the consequences. Yet, a few independent studies of other instances of college desegregation have been made.

Examples of Desegregation

In 1972, the University of Arkansas absorbed the state's only public black college—Arkansas Mechanical and Normal, in Pine Bluff—and converted it into a branch. As a black institution it had been severely starved over the years.[90] When the legislature voted the merger, it did not first consult with black educators at A M & N.

Edna Neal studied some of the changes wrought by the merger by comparing the institution in 1970–1972 and 1974–1976.[91] Enrollment figures were as follows:[92]

1970–1971	2,661
1971–1972	2,083
(Merger)	
1974–1975	2,016
1975–1976	2,588

The American College Testing (ACT) scores and average high school grades of the entering freshman class were:[93]

Year	Mean Composite ACT Score	Mean Average High School Grades
1970–1971	11.3	2.6
1971–1972	11.4	2.6
1973–1974	11.8	2.4
1974–1975	10.9	2.5
1975–1976	10.3	2.5

Neal observed that the changes since merger were negligible; the same was true of holding power. The percentage of nonblacks enrolled rose from 6 during 1973–1974 to 14 in 1975–1976.

The faculty underwent certain changes. The percentage of teachers holding doctorates rose from 17.5 in 1970–1971 to 25 in 1975–1976. Whites on the faculty increased over the same period from 12.3 percent to 23.5 percent. As Neal summarized: "The number of white faculty more than doubled between 1971-2 and 1975-6 while the total number of faculty declined."[94]

Enrollment in various curricula underwent rather important changes. Examining the fields of concentration of graduates during the years 1970–1971 to 1975–1976, Neal reported:

Heavy declines were reported in sociology, biology, English-speech-drama, and history-political science. Education also suffered a marked decline. Business/economics and agriculture/technology emerged as the leaders in 1976, whereas sociology, first by far in 1971, 1972, and 1974, dropped to a weak fourth place in 1976.[95]

(Using Neal's own data, however, it is clear that the percentage of graduates in education rose from 12.2 to 15.4.)[96]

While Neal did not present figures for the total number of graduates, it is possible to calculate such figures from the data in the work. Apparently, the number of graduates has declined, although it held up during the first year after merger. Perhaps a special factor was at work of which Neal did not take note. The number of graduates was as follows:[97]

Year	Graduates	Enrollment	% Graduates
1970–1971	598	2,661	22.5
1971–1972	592	2,083	28.4
Merger			
1973–1974	561	N.A.	—
1974–1975	356	2,016	17.7
1975–1976	377	2,588	14.6

These figures are only rough indicators but it seems clear that a significant drop has occurred. Neal did not comment on this, however.

Expenditure per full-time-equivalent student from state funds rose during these years:[98]

1970–1971	$ 786
1971–1972	966
Merger	
1973–1974	1,544
1974–1975	1,701
1975–1976	1,582

Merger brought nine new degree programs, with three more under development by 1976. During 1973–1976, $7 million was spent on physical facilities; two new buildings were constructed and five more were renovated.

Neal's bare-boned report does not permit a judgment as to the overall educational consequences of the merger. Nor was there an indication as to the human content of the changes. How were students affected? What of faculty response? Did the black community respond differently to the institution in its new form?

In 1895, the all-black Bluefield State College was opened in West Virginia. Not until 1955, a year after *Brown*, did the first white student enter. Yet, by 1966 blacks had become a minority in the school (38 percent) and Bluefield was a predominantly white institution. Curiously, only twenty miles away from Bluefield was Concord State College, an all-white institution. It remained white, except for a handful of blacks. Enrollment did not rise appreciably while Bluefield was undergoing change.

R. Thomas Garrett studied the process of change and raised important questions about it.[99] He noted that Bluefield's first white president came in 1966. Suspicion was widespread among blacks that his predecessor, a black, had been forced to resign because of his close identification with the civil rights movement. The new president tightened up the conduct of college affairs and made many enemies. In 1970, an old gym burned, apparently the result of arson. Ten student leaders were suspended. Upon appeal, the governor appointed the state Human Rights Commission to investigate. According to Garrett, the Commission's report was straightforward:

This report maintained that Bluefield was a victim of racial discrimination and was administered with ineptness, poor judgment, and insensitivity. Faculty salaries were inequitable and financing was inadequate for the physical plant, faculty, and student programs. The report also stated that black students were given unfair treatment in terms of disciplinary measures.[100]

By this time, apparently, few administrators were black.

In 1972, the state proposed to merge Bluefield and Concord as two campuses of a single institution. Garrett saw the merger as logical but asked: "Would the Board of Regents . . . have been so anxious to merge the two schools if Bluefield had not become a predominantly white college?"[101] Indeed, several times he raised another pointed question: Why did so few blacks enter Concord and why did not many of the whites choose to attend Concord? Garrett even implied that there might have been a conscious design to convert Bluefield into a white institution, but he did not explore the question further.

Garrett uses his study of Bluefield as the occasion for canvassing a number of aspects of black colleges. "Black students are in white institutions," he wrote, "because they feel they will be provided with better preparation for jobs and feel they can better compete with white job seekers if they have the prestige of a white institution behind them."[102] Black students who were in remedial classes in white institutions often developed strong feelings of isolation. If they were to attend black colleges, they would interact with role models, good students who were black, and their feelings of isolation would moderate. But Garrett stressed that "black institutions cannot survive only for the educationally disadvantaged and the high school dropout."[103] A whole range of students must be present and the black colleges must be superior educational institutions.

Garrett also raised a question which, although frequently asked, may still be a phantom: "Why have the black institutions lost such favor with black students?" In fact, they have not "lost favor" if enrollment data are to be believed. More black students than ever are attending black colleges. But of course, there are even more in predominantly white colleges.

Arthur White studied the desegregation of Florida's community colleges during the years 1954–1977.[104] After 1957, the state had two systems of such colleges: twenty-eight for whites and twelve for blacks. The latter were located in high school buildings. Over a period of time all the black colleges were closed down. By 1966 the process was complete. In St. Petersburg, the closing of the state's largest black community college, Gibbs Junior College, led to no unemployment of black teachers. A number returned to high school teaching. In Volusia County, however, black college teachers continued to be employed, but "at reduced responsibilities." Between 1964, when all blacks attended black community colleges, and 1968, when the majority were enrolled in predominantly white institutions, black enrollment fell sharply from over 2,000 to less than 500. As White comments: "These declines were typical of colleges that lacked recruiting drives and programs geared toward the minority student.''[105] Within a period of just two years, for example, Miami-Dade Junior College experienced a rise in black enrollment from 760 to nearly 1,300. This resulted from a determined recruitment campaign and initiation of special service programs.[106] The short-term fall in the absolute number of black students was not quickly forgotten. When the issue of possible desegregation of the state's four-year institutions arose, at least one writer recalled: "A pervasive fear of Florida blacks is that desegregation of FAMU [Florida A and M University] may have a depressive impact on black university enrollments similar to the effect that the closing of black community colleges had on the enrollment of blacks in the desegregated two year colleges.''[107]

Whites in Black Colleges

Four studies of white students in historically black colleges were made during 1972–1976.

Bowie State College in Maryland had an all-black enrollment from its inception until 1963 when the first white students entered. By 1971, when Ada Elam conducted her research there, nonblacks made up 28 percent of the undergraduates but 48 percent of all students, including graduate students.[108] Her study sample numbered 238, of whom 89 were white. Enrollment by curriculum did not vary greatly by race. About 33 percent of the blacks but only 1 percent of the whites objected to having members of the other race in fraternities and sororities. More than two out of five blacks (42.3 percent) objected to having whites room with them. A possibly unexpected finding was the fact that "college contact was more important than pre-college contact in influencing the positive social attitudes of students.''[109] On the other hand, it was still true that "those students who had a limited degree of pre- and college contact with the other race had the lowest social attitude mean score." In response to a statement that "the average white is more intelligent than the average black," 17.5 percent of blacks and 26.9 percent of whites agreed.[110]

Charles Brown and Phyllis Stein studied white students attending five predominantly black campuses in North Carolina.[111] These were Elizabeth City State, North Carolina Central, Fayetteville State, North Carolina A & T State, and Winston-Salem State universities. Three out of five of the whites were women in their late twenties; most were married, and nearly half were parents. Nearly nine out of ten lived off campus although almost three out of five were full-time undergraduates. Almost none entered directly from high school and most were doing quite well academically. White males, reported Brown and Stein, "were highly favorable and indicated satisfaction with the quality of both their education and their instructors as well as a high degree of social acceptance.''[112] White females were almost as positive. They reported, however, that upon learning of their intention to attend a black college their families and friends expressed many reservations. These doubts receded somewhat over time.

The white students as a whole had not socialized extensively with blacks prior to attending college. About half characterized such contacts as "nonexistent or limited." Three out of four now participated in some extracurricular activity. Nearly half said they did not find participation in the classroom a problem but an equal number indicated "some degree of discomfort." About one out of four felt that "black students used idiomatic or slang expressions difficult to understand."[113] In general, white students indicated that race would not be a consideration if they sought help in an academic or social problem.

James Lyons studied whites in twenty traditionally black colleges from 1969–1972.[114] Academic deans of the institutions supplied much of the information. In addition, however, Lyons visited the five largest campuses and interviewed an average of eleven persons per campus. Lyons noted that black colleges tend to be viewed monolithically, but he declared, "It is just as meaningless to cite a typical black college as it is to cite a typical white college."[115]

On the black campuses there were eight all-black fraternities and sororities. Lyons estimated that not more than 1 percent of the members of all sororities and fraternities were white. White students were little concerned with the future of black colleges. Lyons commented: "Most of them were far more concerned about the more immediate question of being a minority student for the first time in their lives. For many, it had been almost impossible to adjust." They seemed equally divided between those seeking an education and those seeking to know more about blacks. In only one of the twenty colleges was there a definite plan to recruit whites. Some cooperated with nonblack guidance counselors at nearby high schools in order to apprise them of specific programs of interest to whites.

In discussions with administrators of the black colleges, Lyons found "an almost unbelievable paranoia exists concerning the possible merger of these institutions with traditionally white institutions."[116] They shared with Lyons a strong conviction that unless young black personnel were employed in various positions, the present (black) occupants of those positions would be succeeded by whites. At the same time, Lyons reported that during the years 1969–1972 the percentage of white faculty had not risen. Lyons did not fear possible merger, but rather a merger on unequal terms. "If a merger is to take place," he wrote, "the non-black institution must also be required to give up similar kinds of autonomy."[117]

Ida Stevens analyzed the role of white undergraduate students in housing and extracurricular activities at six predominantly black colleges.[118] The institutions and the percentage of whites at each were: Bethune-Cookman, 11.8; Bowie State, 31.5; Central State, 10.7; Delaware State, 36.7; colleges, and Howard University, 28.1; and the University of Maryland, Eastern Shore, 21.0. The average of whites at the six campuses was 22.7 percent.

Stevens summarized her central findings about the white students this way: "While they will enroll in the predominantly Negro college for academic advantages, they are not willing, in most cases, to live in the dormitories on Negro campuses; nor are they active in student activities."[119] Slightly over 80 percent lived at home and 91 percent were full-time students. Convenient location and low cost were the main reasons students gave for attending the respective colleges. More than 90 percent expected to graduate from the black colleges.

One hundred twelve white students from the six colleges responded to a questionnaire Stevens constructed. The items related to judgments about institutional characteristics. All figures on the following table are percentages.

	Strongly Agree	Agree	Disagree	Disagree	No Response
Goals identifiable	23	59	9	7	2
Educational programs	4	44	40	8	4
Learning climate	17	61	19	2	1
Registration easily executed	9	24	22	44	1
Advisement adequate	8	62	22	7	1
Adequate financial assistance	10	55	19	10	6
Adequate personal counseling	14	66	16	3	1
Well-prepared subject matters	16	60	20	4	0
Instruction meets student needs	9	77	9	4	1
Intellectual climate	9	61	22	7	1

In eight of ten items, the assessment was strongly positive. Dissatisfaction with registration procedures was pronounced. Opinion was divided on educational programs, a central concern of these students.

The ten resident white students evaluated their experience positively but since they were apparently not from a single college, it is difficult to know the significance of such scattered data. Faculty encouraged white students in varying degrees to participate in extracurricular activities. Between 20 percent and 25 percent encouraged participation in student government and social clubs but only 14 percent in athletics, and as few as 6 percent in Greek societies. Three of five white students reported friendly relations with black peers and another one said they had satisfying relations with them. Students who were not in extracurricular activities most frequently gave lack of time and lack of interest as the reasons. About a quarter reported that they feared ridicule or were not accepted. Many more white students, on the other hand, ended up participating than had expected to when enrolling. Twenty percent participated regularly and nearly 40 percent seldom.

Friends, rather than parents or relatives, were the main sources of reser-

vations about white students attending a black college. Most of these reservations were social rather than academic. Seven out of ten would recommend to
other whites that they attend the same college. Although the factual basis
for it is not clear, Stevens wrote that if whites "are to be attracted to the
residence halls on traditionally Negro campuses, the residence halls must be
better constructed; better equipped; and staffed with trained personnel."[120]
This observation, while not contradicting Stevens's other findings, seemed
somewhat unrelated to the main line of her inquiry.

Merritt Norvell probed into desegregation problems in four state institutions of higher education: the University of Maryland-Eastern Shore; the
University of Maryland-College Park (the main campus); and Morgan State
and Towson State universities; and declared:

> The most common problems associated with increasing black enrollment at pre-
> dominantly white schools in Maryland are: the racist image of the schools; deadline
> violations by black students; the tendency of high school counselors to refer blacks
> to black colleges; increased competition for black students from all schools; self-
> imposed social isolation by black students; black student attrition; white faculty
> resistance to remedial courses-work; black student stereotyping by white faculty and
> staff; and low matriculation of black students from the community colleges.[121]

The main problems involved in increasing white enrollment in black colleges
were the reluctance of white parents and counselors to recommend such
action; black faculty and student opposition to desegregation; the black
schools' image of low academic quality; and the comparatively low "market-
ability" of degrees from such schools.

Norvell observed that "at both black and white schools there was a preoccupation with institutional preservation, self-preservation, and regional
control."[122] This accorded with Lyons's findings.

The final study to be discussed deals not with the consequences of an instance of desegregation but with the problems of final planning for court-
ordered desegregation in Nashville.

Tennessee State University Merger

John Matlock and Frederick Humphries traced the process whereby representatives of the predominantly black Tennessee State University and the
predominantly white University of Tennessee-Nashville prepared for a
merger of the two institutions, under the leadership of TSU.[123] This desegregation plan was unique because it awarded the leadership role to a black institution. The state fought this case for eleven years and in Spring, 1979,
was still asking for delays. In April, 1979, a federal appeals court turned
down the request and ordered the plan implemented by July, a long-deter-
mined date. The following month a plan was submitted and approved by
the court.

Meanwhile, thirteen subcommittees, staffed by persons from the two universities, had been meeting to prepare detailed procedures. Matlock and Humphries characterized the atmosphere of the meetings this way: "Oftentimes, hostilities, especially on the part of UTN personnel, made meetings counterproductive."[124] Although only six weeks remained before the merger, "UTN [had] been somewhat uncooperative in developing a combined course schedule."[125] At this late date, double sets of officials still held office although one had to be selected for each office for the merger. While the meetings continued during UTN's appeal for court delay, UTN officials were hopeful of winning and they were "reluctant to cooperate with TSU personnel by providing data, budget information, student information, and other materials."[126]

The court had directed that any plan not diminish the role of black administrators. Yet, if most students in the merged institution turned out to be white, "the majority of the administrators, staff, and faculty, as well as the leadership of the institution, will not be black."[127] Or, if the merger were arranged hastily and incompletely total enrollment might fall short of expectations and staff and faculty retrenchment would follow. Blacks stood to lose disproportionately in that event.

The U.S. Court of Appeals for the Sixth Circuit, when it turned down a request for further delay, declared: "The remedy of merger effectively restores the victims of discrimination to their rightful places."[128] The account by Matlock and Humphries suggested that effective restoration of rights was still far removed from the victims of discrimination.

Conclusions

A research examination of minorities in higher education permits only a few generalizations. Recent years have seen the fruits of the civil rights movement in the extension, in part, of equal education to blacks and to a lesser extent to other minorities. Studies in California and elsewhere suggest strongly the unequal conditions of higher (and lower) schooling for Mexican Americans. Only fragmentary coverage of American Indian higher education is possible at this time. The black colleges, which were for long the historic anchor of higher education for blacks in America, now account for about one-fifth of all black college students but still grant one-third of all academic degrees of blacks. Their weaknesses derive largely from the subordinate role assigned them by public authorities who are reluctant to deal with the colleges as equals of white institutions. While by far most black collegians attend predominantly white schools, these institutions have yet to accept them without rancor or racism. This situation is national, not regional.

Significant advances have occurred in such settings as CUNY, whose contributions in the early seventies were of national importance both symbolically and substantively. For a historic moment during that same time, there were minority advances in graduate and professional schooling; but for half a decade or longer, blacks have been losing their gains.

Desegregation of higher education is resisted with the same lavishness of resources and intensity of purpose that marked rejection of desegregation in the common schools. State authorities, encouraged by laxity at the federal level, have opposed significant dismantling of dual college systems. Doubtful of any change in official policy or practice, a number of black educators have preferred a present advantage over a more distant reward, and have lent themselves to a moderation of demands for desegregation in exchange for a modest increase in appropriations. As ever, the black community is not monolithic on the issue.

Researchers have investigated some aspects of this confusion but all in all have yet to realize the richness of the subject. Most surprising—and disappointing—is the failure of researchers to document in detail the life that is lived in black colleges. Most of what appears in the literature deals with policy rather than practice and is frequently filtered through the eyes of administrators who are understandably solicitous of their own institutions. But black colleges are not primarily the victims of vested interest as much as the product of a society that has yet to accord all its citizens an equal chance to learn.

Notes

1. Augustus M. Burns, III, "Graduate Education for Blacks in North Carolina, 1930–1951," *Journal of Southern History*, 46 (May 1980).

2. Ibid., p. 218.

3. Cleon F. Thompson, Jr., *A Comparison of Black and White Public Institutions of Higher Education in North Carolina* (doctoral diss., Duke University, 1977), pp. 113–15. (University Microfilms Order No. 77-31,699.)

4. Ibid., p. 132.

5. Ibid., p. 212.

6. David G. and Anna Kleinbaum, "The Minority Experience at a Predominantly White University—A Report of a 1972 Survey at the University of North Carolina at Chapel Hill," *Journal of Negro Education*, 45 (Summer 1976), p. 324.

7. Ibid., pp. 316–21.

8. Ibid., p. 327.

9. Walter R. Allen, "Correlates of Black Student Adjustment, Achievement, and Aspirations at a Predominantly White Southern University," in Gail E. Thomas (ed.), *Black Students in Higher Education: Conditions and Experiences in the 1970s*. (Westport, Conn.: Greenwood Press, 1981).

10. Ibid., p. 136.

11. Ibid., p. 137.

12. Barbara B. Kramer, *Perceived Effects of Affirmative Action Regulations by Administrators at the University of North Carolina at Chapel Hill: A Case Study*

(doctoral diss., University of North Carolina at Chapel Hill, 1978). (University Microfilms Order No. 7900473.)

13. Ibid., p. 144.

14. Ibid., p. 116.

15. Ibid., p. 147.

16. Donald J. Reichard and others, "Environment of a Predominantly White Campus as Seen by Black and White Students," p. 96, in Smith (ed.), *The Impact of Desegregation on Higher Education*.

17. See Weinberg, *A Chance to Learn* (N.Y.: Cambridge University Press, 1977), p. 305.

18. Dominic J. Capeci, "From Different Liberal Perspectives: Fiorello H. LaGuardia, Adam Clayton Powell, Jr., and Civil Rights in New York City, 1941-1943," *Journal of Negro History*, 62 (April 1977), p. 164.

19. Sheila C. Gordon, *The Transformation of the City University of New York, 1945-1970* (doctoral diss., Columbia University, 1975), p. 162. (University Microfilms Order No. 77-27,856.)

20. Ibid., p. 97.

21. See Allen B. Ballard, *The Education of Black Folk: The Afro-American Struggle for Knowledge in White America* (New York: Harper & Row, 1973), Chapter 7.

22. Leslie Berger and Jeanette B. Leaf, "The Promise of Open Admissions: An Evaluation After Four Years at CUNY," *Educational Record*, 57 (1977), p. 156.

23. Robert Kibbee, "Open Admissions at CUNY," *Integrateducation*, 13 (May-June 1975), p. 176.

24. Ibid., p. 177.

25. Berger and Leaf, "The Promise of Open Admissions," p. 158.

26. Judith J. Piesco and Lawrence Podell, "Graduation of Disadvantaged Students: The Senior Colleges of CUNY," *Evaluation Quarterly*, 2 (November 1978), p. 601.

27. Robert E. Marshak, "Problems and Prospects of an Urban University," *Daedalus*, 104 (Winter 1975), p. 194.

28. David E. Lavin and others, "Open Admissions and Equal Access: A Study of Ethnic Groups in the City University of New York," *Harvard Educational Review*, 49 (February 1979), p. 81.

29. Gordon, *The Transformation of the City University of New York*, p. 243.

30. Lavin and others, "Open Admissions and Equal Access," p. 67.

31. Ibid., p. 88.

32. Austin C. Frank, "Affirmative Action Students: Cognitive and Affective Histories," material used in a symposium at the annual meeting of the American Educational Research Association, Los Angeles, April 13-17, 1981.

33. Committee on Supportive Services for Minority Students from Disadvantaged Backgrounds, *Report to the Provost of Michigan State University* (East Lansing: Michigan State University, July 1979).

34. Ibid., p. 36.

35. Ibid., p. 37.

36. Ibid., p. 19.

37. Maurice C. Taylor, "Academic Performance of Blacks on White Campuses," *Integrateducation*, 16 (September-October 1978).

38. Ibid., p. 30.

39. Ibid.

40. Gerald L. Dillingham, "Blacks and the College Experience— Revisited," *Integrateducation*, 14 (May-June 1976), p. 37.

41. Julius Lester, "Growing Down," *Change* (October 1979), p. 35.

42. Ibid., p. 37.

43. Ibid., p. 35.

44. Jomills Henry Braddock III and James M. McPartland, *The Effects of Elementary-Secondary School Desegregation on Black Student Attendance and Persistence at Traditionally White Four-Year Colleges* (Baltimore, Md.: Center for Social Organization of Schools, Johns Hopkins University), p. 8.

45. Ibid.

46. James E. Blackwell, "The Access of Black Students to Medical and Law Schools: Trends and Bakke Implications," p. 190, in Thomas, *Black Students in Higher Education*.

47. J. Christopher Lehner, Jr., *A Losing Battle: The Decline in Black Participation in Graduate and Professional Education* (Washington, D.C.: National Advisory Committee on Black Higher Education and Black Colleges and Universities, October 1980).

48. Stephen J. Wright, *The Black Educational Policy Researcher: An Untapped National Resource* (Washington, D.C.: National Advisory Committee on Black Higher Education and Black Colleges and Universities, December 1979), p. 8.

49. Leonard L. Baird, "Social Class and Entrance to Graduate and Professional School," *Integrateducation*, 15 (July-August 1977).

50. Ibid., p. 39.

51. Lehner, *A Losing Battle*, p. 7.

52. Ibid., p. 33.

53. Ibid., p. 14.

54. Wright, *The Black Educational Policy Researcher*, pp. 6–7.

55. Ibid., p. 11.

56. Donald Cunningen, "Graduates of Black Colleges in a White Graduate School," *Integrateducation*, 16 (May-June 1978), p. 30.

57. Ibid.

58. Freeman A. Hrabowski, *A Comparison of the Graduate Academic Performance of Black Students Who Graduated from Predominantly Black Colleges and from Predominantly White Colleges* (doctoral diss., University of Illinois, 1975). (University Microfilms Order No. 75-24,322.)

59. Ibid., p. 39.

60. Ibid., p. 91.

61. Ibid., pp. 92–93.

62. Beverly E. Bruce, "A Comparative Analysis of Graduate Achievement at the University of California, San Diego," *Integrateducation*, 15 (July-August 1977).

63. Ibid., p. 23.

64. James E. Blackwell, *Access of Black Students to Graduate and Professional Schools* (Atlanta, Ga.: Southern Education Foundation, n.d.), p. 5.

65. Blackwell, "The Access of Black Students to Medical and Law Schools," p. 193.

66. Ibid.

67. Ada M. Fisher, "Black Medical Students: Too Few for So Large a Task," p. 205, in Thomas, *Black Students in Higher Education*.

68. Ibid., p. 207.

69. John E. Rolph and others, *Predicting Minority and Majority Medical Student Performance on the National Board Exams* (Santa Monica, Calif.: Rand, November 1978).

70. Ibid., p. 4.

71. Ralph R. Smith, "Black Law Students and the Law School Experience: Issues of Access and Survival," pp. 218–19, in Thomas, *Black Students in Higher Education*. All figures have been rounded to the nearest decimal.

72. Ibid., p. 221.

73. Ibid., p. 223.

74. Lee Daniels, "The New Professionals," *Change* (October 1979), p. 40.

75. Ibid.

76. Elias Blake, Jr., "The Impact of Desegregation on Higher Education," in Jeff E. Smith (ed.), *The Impact of Desegregation on Higher Education*, Durham, N.C.: Institute on Desegregation, North Carolina Central University, 1981.

77. Ibid., p. 26.

78. Ibid., p. 29.

79. Leonard L. Haynes, III, "The *Adams* Mandate: Is It a Blueprint for Realizing Equal Educational Opportunity and Attainment?" p. 206, in Smith, *The Impact of Desegregation*.

80. Leonard L. Haynes, III, "The *Adams* Mandate: A Format for Achieving Equal Education Opportunity and Attainment," p. 331, in Thomas, *Black Students in Higher Education*.

81. Leonard L. Haynes, III, *An Analysis of the Effects of Desegregation Upon Public Black Colleges* (doctoral diss., Ohio State University, 1975). (University Microfilms Order No. 75-27,591.)

82. Ibid., p. 120.

83. Ibid., p. 165.

84. Ibid., p. 169.

85. J. LeVonne Chambers, "The Impact of Supreme Court Decisions on the Desegregation of Statewide Systems of Higher Education," in Smith, *The Impact of Desegregation*.

86. Ibid., p. 188.

87. Ibid., p. 185.

88. Ibid., p. 191.

89. See "The Status of College Desegregation in 19 States," *Chronicle of Higher Education*, July 6, 1981. These figures have been updated.

90. For background, see Weinberg, *A Chance to Learn*, pp. 270, 283, and 293.

91. Edna L. D. Neal, *Changes at the University of Arkansas at Pine Bluff Following Merger into the University of Arkansas System* (doctoral diss., Indiana University, 1978). (University Microfilms Order No. 7906021.) All figures have been rounded to the nearest decimal.

92. Ibid., p. 36.

93. Ibid., p. 37.

94. Ibid., p. 51.

95. Ibid., p. 59.

96. See table 15 in ibid.

97. Ibid.

98. Ibid., p. 65.
99. R. Thomas Garrett, *A Study of the Transition of Bluefield State College from a Black Teacher Preparation College to a Predominantly White Liberal Arts College* (doctoral diss., Rutgers University, 1979). (University Microfilms Order No. 8000853.)
100. Ibid., p. 49.
101. Ibid., p. 55.
102. Ibid., p. 83.
103. Ibid., p. 87.
104. Arthur O. White, "The Desegregation of Florida's Public Junior Colleges, 1954–1977," *Integrateducation*, 16 (May–June 1978).
105. Ibid., p. 35.
106. Ibid.
107. Charles J. Stanley and others, "College Desegregation in Florida," *Integrateducation*, 13 (September–October 1975), p. 17.
108. Ada Maria Elam, *Social Attitudes Held and Methods for Change Desired by Black and White Students in a "Reverse Integration" College Setting* (doctoral diss., Pennsylvania University, 1972), p. 77. (University Microfilms Order No. 73-7431.)
109. Ibid., p. 77.
110. Ibid., p. 58.
111. Charles I. Brown and Phyllis R. Stein, "The White Student in Five Predominantly Black Universities," *Negro Educational Review*, 23 (October 1972).
112. Ibid., p. 154.
113. Ibid., p. 155–56.
114. James Earl Lyons, *The Admission of Non-Black Students as an Indicator of a Potential Shift in the Traditional Role of the Black Publicly Supported Colleges and Universities* (doctoral diss., University of Connecticut, 1973). (University Microfilms Order No. 74-14.)
115. Ibid., p. 19.
116. Ibid., p. 60.
117. Ibid., p. 76.
118. Ida Richardson Stevens, *Beliefs of Caucasian Students Enrolled in Selected Negro Higher Education Institutions Concerning Housing and Student Activities* (doctoral diss., Southern Illinois University, 1976). (University Microfilms Order No. 77-6263.)
119. Ibid., p. 8.
120. Ibid., p. 65.
121. Merritt J. Norvell, Jr., *Desegregating Higher Education: An Analysis of the Maryland Plan* (Atlanta, Ga.: Southern Education Foundation, n.d.), p. 46.
122. Ibid., p. 58.
123. John Matlock and Frederick Humphries, "A Blueprint for Merging Higher Education: A Case Study of the Planning of the Merger of Tennessee State University and the University of Tennessee at Nashville," in Smith, *The Impact of Desegregation*.
124. Ibid., p. 165.
125. Ibid., p. 167.
126. Ibid.
127. Ibid., p. 171.
128. *Geier* v. *University of Tennessee*, 597 F. 2d 1068 (1979).

13

Conclusions

Research on minority students has undergone significant changes during the past decade or so.

More studies are being made from the viewpoint of minority parents or students rather than from that of administrators or teachers. In this changed perspective, the school loses much of its beneficent penumbra and its educational contribution becomes much more problematical. The advent of minority researchers has had much to do with this change, although neither the race nor the ethnicity of the researcher wholly accounts for it.

In the foregoing chapters we have seen evidences of this change in research perspectives in the spheres of legal affairs, discriminatory classroom procedures, and higher education, as well as in others. We are in the early stages of the change. Consequently, few general treatises and textbooks used to train future teachers, administrators, and researchers pay much attention to the viewpoint of parents. Indeed, there is a certain defensiveness in the reluctance of schools of education to depart from the customary bureaucratic framework for viewing problems of schooling.

Another change, closely allied with the first, concerns explanatory schemes or theories. Many of these still echo the writings of the 1960s when children of a minority race or low economic status were held responsible for failures of schooling. They were regarded as "different," "culturally deprived," or precluded from learning because of home or family conditions. This left the more privileged children as the most successful, a condition deemed natural by most writers on the subject.

Recently, however, some researchers have begun to view the schools as responsible for the basic educational task. Although they regard the schools as actively choosing to adapt themselves to the class and racial structure of society, these researchers still insist on the possibility of change. They see society's tendency to press the schools into a constrictive role for poor and minority children as being subject to change under organized community pressure by parents. Merely to exhort administrators to effect this change is not considered a very productive course. The studies of parent influence on schools—or the lack of it—reviewed earlier, indicate the magnitude of the challenge. The continuing difficulty of supporters of desegregation to effect change represents another aspect of the problem.

We are accustomed to conservative ideologies that resist trends toward more equalitarian schooling, deny the existence of racial barriers to advancement, and preach patience. Certain radical perspectives have come into prominence which have more or less the same effect. Their supporters contend that problems of racism are fundamentally an aspect of an iniquitous capitalism, and that it is fruitless to struggle for nonracist education while capitalism exists. This radical-sounding approach restates essentially the conservative view: racial change must wait for long-term changes in the society and, when these occur, the problem of racism will fade away. In the writings of these radical researchers, one almost never reads about real human beings or groups in their particularity. Least of all can we learn from their writings about the struggles minority parents and their allies have conducted on behalf of the educational rights of their children. Nevertheless, these same radical authors make a positive contribution in reminding us of the need to study the schools in their overall political-economic framework.

Recently, too, some researchers have begun to seriously consider the role of history. Educational historians of black education have made important contributions in recent years and a few have begun to examine the Hispanic experience more closely. These changes, however, have altered little the general run of educational research. It is more or less standard to begin an account of research with what is generously called "historical background." Most often this bears the same relation to the rest of the research as a stage curtain does to a play. Seldom does the researcher study the implications of recent historical research in his or her subject. As a result, educational research is almost uniformly "presentist," a stance that implies the problem under study was born, at the most, yesterday. While not every problem with a past is a prisoner of history, neither is any problem with a social foundation so free-floating that it lacks roots.

Fifteen years ago, there were no journals dealing exclusively with school law. Today there are two, as well as several shorter bulletins, and research into legal aspects of schooling has become a major enterprise. This change is due to the efforts of relatively politically powerless people to gain a hold on bureaucratic structures in order to educate their children more adequately. School boards and administrators whose former monopoly of power in the schools must be shared, however slightly, with successful plaintiffs perceive the growing salience of law very differently. To the managers, the multiplicity of legal remedies available to citizens is itself a problem. The literature of educational administration is filled with this type of complaint. As we saw above, after a finding of school board guilt has been made, there is much room for the board and administrators to help shape the remedy, and in some cases, the remedy thus formulated may vary little from the condition originally found offensive to the Constitution.

Significant research on Hispanics, especially on Mexican Americans and less so on Puerto Ricans, has begun to appear in the last half-dozen years along a broad front. (Such increased activity has paralleled judicial determinations that Mexican Americans are an autonomous ethnic group under protection of the Fourteenth Amendment. They are not simply a "nonblack minority.") As research proceeds, however, the resulting studies report rather regularly on the heterogeneity of the group called Hispanics. Economic and cultural distinctions among members of the group are found to play an important role in the life of Mexican Americans, Puerto Ricans, Cubans, and others. Some are more segregated residentially than others, with probable differential consequences for school segregation. School and residential segregation of Hispanics seems to be growing and researchers have begun to study the implications of this development for the emergence of a Hispanic minority self-concept.

Desegregation continues to attract much research, but the work is unequally distributed among the various aspects of the subject. Sixty percent of all desegregation studies deal with desegregation and academic achievement, for example. This means that relatively few investigations have been made of teacher-student relations, student interracial interactions, the role of the principal and higher administrators, effects on self-concept and career aspirations, community factors in desegregation, and the movement from desegregation to integration. A firm evaluation of existing studies of these aspects of desegregation is almost as necessary. As of now, both learned and popular discussion of these studies is partial and distorted. The situation is nearly as bad as that sketched in Chapter 10 regarding treatment of black opinion on busing.

Little desegregation research is useful for practical applications in the schools. This is true even of the most numerous achievement studies. All attempted to gauge how achievement was affected by desegregation over a time period, but virtually none tried to discover the classroom dynamics of a particular result—an increase, a decrease, or no change. Thus, practitioners seeking to duplicate the success recorded in a study are unable to do so since nothing beyond scores at two points in time was studied. Sometimes, researchers did analyze the operation of other variables than time and this could be of practical use. For example, a finding that students learned most when teachers accepted them more as individuals could be very suggestive for improving academic achievement. In other cases, the dynamics are more or less clear without further study. Consider the finding that the younger the child in a desegregation program, the higher his achievement.

Some investigators have questioned whether desegregation as such can be said to have "educational effects," positive or negative. Since desegregation merely refers to a way of assigning children, including the way they get to school every day, in a strict sense the effect of desegregation stops at the classroom door. From then on, the problem is one of instruction, broadly conceived. Whether the desegregated children learn more or less is the responsibility of the school. Researchers who speak of the "educational effects of busing" are making the same error. Obviously, the only effect of busing is to transport children from one place to another. Whether enhanced learning occurs in the new setting has little or nothing to do with busing. It has a lot to do with the character of schooling.

During the past few years social science researchers have continued to make a central distinction between race and class. The principal effect of such a distinction is to downgrade the effect of race in the schools and society at large. This results from the artificial and self-confounding way that class is defined. The usual research study designates "race" by one racial-ethnic classification or another while defining "class" by income, occupation, housing, or education. Each of these elements, however, is greatly influenced by race. Blacks or other minorities are regularly discriminated against in salaries or wages, choice of occupation, the purchase or rental of housing, and on various levels of schooling. By using such measures of "class," we deny their "racial" component. Indeed, declarations that class has superseded race have become more familiar, giving rise to the unwarranted conclusion that racial discrimination is disappearing. What is happening, at least in part, is that racial discrimination is merely being defined out of existence.

An obvious resolution of this conceptual difficulty is to define race and class in a mutually exclusive way. In a racist society, however, this is impossible. The pervasiveness of race in America arises, to a large degree, from its incorporation into the institutional orders of American society. In one institution after another, race is handled to the advantage of dominant groups. Whether in housing, employment, or education, racial discrimination profits some and deprives others systematically. To call this phenomenon "economic" or "social" is a matter of words, and it does not eliminate the reality of racial discrimination. In a sense, separating class from race in a racist society is as fruitless an endeavor as trying to separate the red from the white in pink.

The social class structure of American society, to be sure, encompasses both black and white. But "race" is simply another way of apportioning the goods and opportunities in that same structure. While certain types of racial discrimination formally violate the Fourteenth Amendment, economic discrimination and inequality are regarded as unfortunate but unexceptionable. Many regard the latter as inevitable and thus without moral fault. If, by some act of magic, we suddenly cease to speak of racial discrimination, the lives of its victims and beneficiaries would continue unchanged. Denying the existence of "race" by mislabeling it "socioeconomic" merely cloaks this reality.

Still another recent research trend is a growing movement to consider schooling a commodity. By commodity, we mean a good or service which is distributed by means of the market, itself the product of competition between sellers and buyers. Public schooling is described as a localized monopoly industry. Researchers and advocates of various kinds contend that many of the ills of contemporary schools can be eliminated or alleviated by ending the monopoly of the public school through a system of cash vouchers negotiable in any school of choice. Competition among schools to attract voucher-holders would be expected to force "producers" (schools) to offer consumers (students) a standard product (education) at a lower than prevailing price or to offer an improved product at not more than the prevailing price.

There is now a heated debate over whether or not such a system of schooling is workable. The few limited experiments are indecisive. But a broader question than workability is involved: the political implications of viewing schooling as a commodity. First of all, the issue is to a degree nonideological. The voucher approach has devotees of both a capitalist and a socialist persuasion. Second, if schooling is not a commodity it must be regarded as a social necessity offered in a democratic political system. As such, its provision is an obligation of government to be enforced by political means. Much of the content of this book attests to the great difficulty poor and minority parents have had in enforcing the right of their children to an education. A voucher system would relieve government of any responsibility to provide that education. Applied more broadly, the same approach would help weaken governmental obligation in other fields of human services, as well. Thus, a seemingly nonpolitical matter such as vouchers could very well lead to a major decline in governmental response to human needs.

The simplicity of a market approach is attractive. Compared with the anguish and incessant activism required by the present system, it is clearly preferable on mechanical grounds alone. Educational researchers may well choose, as they often do, to ignore the political consequences of a market approach, but the cost of such an approach can be immense.

What might the 1980s hold for educational researchers studying minority students in schools and colleges?

1. *A severe shortage of research funds.* Both federal governmental and foundation expenditures in this area have been declining since the late 1970s. Sharp budget cuts from 1981 on threaten to dismantle a large part of the research structure of the federal government itself as well as that of nonprofit research organizations in universities and elsewhere. Minority organizations continue to be too poor to sponsor relevant research. Undoubtedly, individual scholarship by doctoral students will continue, but the recent decline in financial aid has already led to a fall in the number of minority students in graduate schools. This source of doctoral research has been especially valuable.

2. *The role of housing will be taken into account increasingly.* Legal doctrines of the interrelation of housing segregation and school segregation continue to point out a growing area of research. Comparison of segregation in the two areas will continue to employ statistical techniques readily available to demographers. It seems likely, however, that greater stress will

be laid upon historical and case-study approaches in specific cities and communities. Housing will also be taken into account more in drawing up remedies in desegregation cases. The desegregation of housing as an aid to desegregating schools will come under closer scrutiny. In a real sense, metropolitan school desegregation plans are a means of facilitating housing desegregation, although the effect is not automatic. Another area of inquiry will involve school studies of residentially non-segregated communities. The persistence of segregated schools in some of these communities poses an intriguing research problem.

3. *Intradistrict inequalities in school funding will become a major direction in research.* During the latter part of the 1970s, several researchers, working largely independently, began to explore systematically the occurrence of sizable per-pupil funding differences between schools within the same district. This basic problem of equity will be explored more intensively. With the computerization of school financial operations, theoretical access to detailed expenditure data will grow. But means will have to be discovered whereby school districts release enough data to enable meaningful studies to be made. Minority groups will pay more attention to this area. Studies of inequitable state school funding systems will analyze the impact of changes in interdistrict funding upon intradistrict equity. School board and administrator groups can be expected to resist this area of study since it will tend to diminish the monopoly of knowledge on the part of school bureaucracies.

4. *Racism will be more fully and systematically studied.* Considering the ubiquity and persistence of racism, it is astonishing how little educational researchers deal with it. The number of books on the subject of racism in education can be counted, literally, on the fingers of one hand, while articles on the subject in educational journals are only slightly more plentiful. At best, the concept is equated with individual racial prejudice and researchers take little account of its relation to social structure, to community power, and to prevailing ideologies of social control.

This situation is likely to change for several reasons. For one, the growing numbers of minority scholars who are far more ready to deal with the concept of racism than are Anglo researchers will make a difference. Their writings already show as much. In addition, educational researchers of all backgrounds will find it less possible to avoid coming to terms with a phenomenon that sociologists, economists, and other social scientists are beginning to subject to systematic analysis. Also, minority parents increasingly lodge charges of racism against school boards and central administrations. In one case, in Dallas, the superintendent agreed his school system was guilty of institutional racism. The future may see more examples.

5. *Educational practice and research will move away from an emphasis on desegregation and closer to nonsegregation.* Obviously, in order to desegregate a school it must first have been segregated in some legal sense. In a country in which 81 percent of the population is white, only about

3,000 of the nation's some 15,000 school districts contain a substantial number of blacks and Hispanics. By attending exclusively to the 19 percent and the 3,000 districts, we ignore the 81 percent and the children in the 12,000 districts. In Massachusetts, for example, an all-black school may be regarded as segregated—because it is majority nonwhite—while an all-white school in an all-white district is not segregated—because its racial composition reflects that of the entire district. The situation is similar in Illinois.

According to prevailing theory, the black children in the all-black school must be desegregated. But also, many other changes are prescribed for the curriculum, teaching strategies, in-service training, extracurricular activities, textual materials, and much else. But none of these changes is prescribed for the white children in all-white districts, except by osmosis. How can this be justified educationally? If it is beneficial for new curricula to be considered for blacks in newly desegregated schools, why would whites in all-white schools not benefit similarly? If blacks and whites who attend a desegregated school come to have the benefit of a more soundly researched American history and learn more about the role of blacks and other minorities in that history, what educational justification is there for withholding this information from whites in geographically isolated white communities? The present assumption seems to be that blacks need to know about themselves and their historic role—at least, in theory—but that such knowledge is not the concern of whites. Surely this is mistaken.

In other words, all school districts in the United States can have desegregated curricula, teaching and administrative staffs, training programs, and instructional materials. Indeed, for educational reasons, they should. In addition, they can also have a desegregated enrollment where there are sufficient children of varying racial-ethnic groups. Ultimately, a non-segregated education should be the goal of every school in the country, whether or not minority children are enrolled in the same school or district.

6. *Equity within higher education will become a regular concern of researchers and practitioners.* The large majority of blacks and other minority students attend predominantly white colleges, but a number of blacks who do so attend colleges in southern states which until very recently had legally segregated public higher education. Efforts to desegregate these one-time legally dual systems have been underway for about ten years, but resistance to this kind of desegregation has been politically adroit and thus far highly effective. While the separate-but-equal rule has been rejected by the courts for the common schools, it is presently regarded by other courts as a rather lofty goal for public colleges and universities. Government authorities seem eager to settle for separate-but-equal or even its appearance.

As long as minority participation in higher education was minimal and segregated, pressure for desegregation was considered irrelevant. Now, however, over a million and a half minority students attend colleges and universities, mostly in public institutions. As the pressure of these numbers grows, and it will in the future, and black electoral power expands, the desegregation movement will gain new strength. There is no reason, however, to expect the resistance of white power structures to lessen. They will continue to defend vested interests in higher education as unyieldingly as was the case earlier in elementary and secondary education. Minority students in nonsouthern institutions have a more difficult task before them as the racism they confront is more diffuse and informal.

Barely a generation has passed since blacks were first permitted to teach in predominantly white colleges and universities, North and South. Only during the past decade has any public authority been placed behind an effort to expand the numbers of black professors on the faculties of predominantly white institutions. The record of accomplishment is very slim and the immediate future promises little more.

7. *Greater attention will be paid to equity problems in the educational systems of other countries.* Oppression and exploitation in colonial structures have created racial-ethnic situations that resemble, in some respects, those of the United States. In addition, minority problems are growing in countries such as Britain, France, and Germany. Poverty is everywhere a serious barrier to educational attainment. How do these countries deal with these problems, many of which resemble ours? Can anything be learned from their experience? These questions will be asked more frequently in the future.

The variations in remedies that are used here, as well as elsewhere, are of great interest. Consider, for example, affirmative action. In India, *harijans* (formerly, "untouchables") are granted by law fixed numbers of places in universities which cannot be made available to nonharijans, a reservation that was rejected by the U.S. Supreme Court in *Regents of the University of California* v. *Bakke*. Recently, a series of riots by upper-caste students aimed at eliminating these affirmative action measures. A certain number of seats in India's parliament are also reserved for *harijans*. Several years ago, a Polish university tried open admissions, a sharp departure from the traditional examination-oriented system of admissions. The results of such experiments should be compared and studied. Community colleges, which in the United States are attended disproportionately by minority students, are spreading into other countries. Do they serve the same purpose elsewhere as here? While financial aid to students is critical for American minorities, in some countries, such as Sweden, working-class students— perhaps for cultural reasons—seldom take advantage of such opportunities. Comparing this example with what happens in this country could be profitable.

Public schooling has always been especially important for poor and minority children. Now, however, it is under heavy attack. Financial support is being withheld and the principle of private use of public funds is a further threat. More and better research alone will not make public education whole. It can, however, provide guidance to coalitions of citizens across a broad spectrum of social circumstances. But it is minority people who have played a leading role in recent years in the struggle for public education and their stake in it is the greatest of all. Researchers can help most by elucidating that fact, by illuminating the role of minority students and parents in our national life, and by helping to clarify avenues to a more democratic educational system.

Bibliographical Essay

The literature of our subject is scattered among many separate disciplines, most of whose practitioners are either oblivious or immune to research of workers in the other disciplines. In some lines of inquiry, the number of studies is quite large, while in others work has barely begun. Complementary problems are sometimes investigated simultaneously in different disciplines but interrelationships are not noted. Age-old problems with deep and tangled roots are frequently treated as though they were born yesterday and can be investigated adequately without reference to historical factors. To complicate matters further, pronouncements abound as to the nature of "proper" methodologies, by which are frequently meant favored investigative techniques.

Research in this area is profoundly racist, although exceptions are numerous. Minorities are discussed *in absentia*, as though they had never studied their own plight. Even the most celebrated journals fail completely to cite other journals that regularly carry the work of minority researchers. The world of minority communities is largely unexplored and thus foreign to most studies of minority children. Most often, inferiority of academic preparation and performance of minority children is treated as an unfortunate fact of life, attributable to their family structure and poverty. The school is relieved of responsibility for everything except success.

Much of the research proceeds as though it were outside any political framework. The responsibility of dominant governing groups for schools and school performance is denied implicitly by a sweeping failure even to consider the possibility. Ignored is the seeming commonplace that public education is part of the structure of government and thus subject to the push and pull of democratic politics as much as are police, fire, and garbage-collection services. Communitywide decisions not to educate minority children effectively are far from unknown in American history. Yet, researchers only rarely seem to grasp this fact and its possible relevance for contemporary schooling. Instead, they posit a benevolence that is all too frequently absent.

The existing research literature is characterized by a profusion of investigatory techniques. Accorded a high status in academic circles is survey research which involves selection of random stratified samples of a national population. Both the wide scope and the representativeness of such studies ensure close attention in the literature. On the other hand, these very features also mean that the survey will tend to slight any effects of individual schools as well as ignore the dynamics underlying the findings as a whole. The findings are always correlations rather than causal relations.

The loftiest status is accorded experimental studies which permit manipulations of some factors while holding others unchanged. There are few such studies concerning the education of minority children. At times, the findings of experimental studies concerning nonminority children are applied without change to minority children. This fairly thoughtless procedure assumes away the operation of racial factors, a heroic assumption.

Case studies are the bread and butter of research in this field. Since investigators usually work singly, in dissertation research especially, a single case is usually appropriate. Research studies of single cases tend to use the apparatus of survey research and experimentation. By the nature of the case, however, the singularity of the experience studied precludes much quantitative generalization. The greatest potential of these studies is exploration of the dynamics of whatever changes are discovered. Prevailing academic evaluation tends to rank such studies rather low since they are criticized for achieving neither wide scope nor experimental status.

Vast quantities of data have been gathered by the use of questionnaires, and the literature reflects this feature. Indeed, many studies are hardly more than this. Responses are arranged and rearranged according to the requirements of statistical procedure. The responses are rarely, if ever, audited for simple truthfulness. Consequently, the factual foundation of many an educational generalization is quite insecure. More recently, some studies have found a wide discrepancy between the two. Yet, numerous analyses have been based on responses alone.

Within the past decade, the literature has come to include increasing numbers of studies labeled "ethnographic." Essentially first-hand detailed observation of a classroom or other schooling experience, such studies have a clear advantage over survey or case studies. Using an anthropological term, however, does not resolve problems of this technique. Researchers cannot study a subculture without explicitly attending to some conceptual assumptions that presumably underlie both the research techniques and the subculture. Data are not "out there," waiting to be observed. Concepts appropriate to the observed reality have to be developed. Without this, the recorded first-hand observations are not much more valuable than bare questionnaire responses.

Any researcher would like it said that her or his study was crucial or a landmark. The chances are, in fact, exceedingly slight. As a result, investigators should be modest about the implications of their specific study. Yet, a great number of case studies are declared by their makers to decide this or that general problem. Sometimes, this misimpression reflects simple lack of knowledge of other case studies that came to opposite conclusions.

In a broad sense, the literature of anything is simply all that has been written on the subject. In a research sense, however, a more selective conception is required. It is, for example, of little value to read countless expressions of the same finding or lack of finding. After a point, we are entitled to stop. Needed are a specification of the central problems of a field, the leading studies of those problems, and a listing of problems yet to be resolved.

In this sense, the education of minority children is not a unified subject with a research literature. It is, instead, a congeries of research findings, few of which have yet been coordinated into a meaningful structure that both records what is known and points in new directions that may prove productive of new knowledge.

Research literature, no matter how elaborate or elegant, must ultimately be assessed for its practical import. In general, many American researchers seem hesitant either to submit their work to such a test or to formulate their project in anticipation of such a test. (In Britain, where applied research in education seems more accepted, such tests are more routine.) Now, when minority students comprise about one out of every four students, and the majority in a number of places, the practical import of research on minority children is of considerable interest. The research literature is weak in this kind of content.

Historical Studies

Still standing at the peak of their genre are Carter G. Woodson's *The Education of the Negro Prior to 1861* (Associated Publishers, 1919), and Horace Mann Bond's *The Education of the Negro in the American Social Order* (Octagon Press, 1966, reprint). Together, these works cover colonial times until 1930 and are indispensable. The works of W.E.B. Du Bois remain vitally important. See especially the new collected edition of the works of W.E.B. Du Bois, edited by Herbert Aptheker and published by Kraus-Thomson in Millwood, New York. Louis R. Harlan's *Separate and Unequal Public School Campaigns and Racism in the Southern Seaboard States, 1901–1915* (University of North Carolina Press, 1958), remains an exemplary study. On higher education it is still helpful to refer to Frank Bowles and Frank A. De Costa, *Between Two Worlds, a Profile of Negro Higher Education* (McGraw-Hill, 1971), and Michael R. Winston, "Through the Back Door: Academic Racism and the Negro Scholar in Historical Perspective" (*Daedalus*, 100 [Summer, 1971]). Meyer Weinberg's *A Chance to Learn: A History of Race and Education in the United States*, is of value (Cambridge University Press, 1977).

First-rate scholarly treatments of more recent vintage are Albert M. Camarillo, *Chicanos in a Changing Society: From Pueblos to American Barrios in Santa Barbara and Southern California, 1848–1930* (Harvard University Press, 1979); Arnoldo De Leon, *The Tejano Community, 1836–1900* (University of New Mexico Press, 1981); Robert J. Rosenbaum, *Mexicano Resistance in the Southwest: "The Sacred Right to Self-Preservation"* (University of Texas Press, 1981); and Douglas E. Foley and others, *From Peones to Politicos: Ethnic Relations in a South Texas Town, 1900 to 1977* (University of Texas Press, 1977).

A recent work, Robert G. Sherer, Jr.'s *Subordination or Liberation: The Development and Conflicting Theories of Black Education in Nineteenth Century Alabama* (University of Alabama Press, 1977), demonstrates the relative lack of influence by Booker T. Washington over Alabama schools operated by black churchmen. An outstanding history of discrimination in northern schools is Charles M. Wollenberg, *All Deliberate Speed: Segregation and Exclusion in California Schools, 1855–1975* (University of California Press, 1977).

A splendid educational history of the *Aspira* court ruling on bilingual education is Asaura Santiago Santiago, *A Community's Struggle for Equal Educational Opportunity: Aspira v. Board of Education* (Educational Testing Service, 1978).

Hispanic and Indian Children

The standard historical analysis of legal segregation of Hispanic children remains that by Jorge C. Rangel and Carlos M. Alcala, "De Jure Segregation of Chicanos in Texas Schools," *Harvard Civil Rights—Civil Liberties Law Review*, 7 (March 1972). Six volumes of the U.S. Commission on Civil Rights' Mexican-American Education Study, published during 1970–1974, still constitute the most comprehensive treatment. Volume 5, *Differences in Teacher Interaction with Mexican-American and Anglo Students*, has been almost totally ignored by educational researchers and journals. The encyclopedic *The Mexican-American People. The Nation's Second Largest Minority,* by Leo Grebler and associates (Free Press, 1970), is helpful for demographic settings, although the data are aging rapidly. Richard J. Margolis's *The Losers. A Report on the Puerto Ricans and the Public Schools* (Aspira, 1968), a report written for Aspira, is about fifteen years old but tragically up to date.

A basic work, even if somewhat idealized, is George A. Pettit, *Primitive Education in North America* (University of California Press, 1946). The only general history of recent Indian education is Margaret Szasz, *Education and the American Indian. The Road to Self Determination, 1928–1973* (University of New Mexico Press, 1974). The political realities of enforcing pro-Indian legislation are nowhere more graphically portrayed than in *An Even Chance*, by the NAACP Legal Defense and Educational Fund with the cooperation of the Harvard Center for Law and Education (NAACP Legal Defense Fund, 1971).

Legal Studies

The unaccountably unpublished study by Butler Jones "Law and Social Change: A Study of the Impact of New Legal Requirements Affecting Equality of Education in the South, 1938–1955," doctoral dissertation, New York University, 1955) remains one of the best studies of the legal culture of school segregation and desegregation. Completed three decades ago, it is still unmatched. The publications of the U.S. Commission on Civil Rights are outstanding. These include reports of investigations, transcripts of public hearings, studies of many topics directly related to schools, and recommendations for legislation. Gary Orfield's *The Reconstruction of Southern Education: The Schools and the 1964 Civil Rights Act* (Wiley, 1969), is a classic study of the politics of civil rights enforcement. The development of de jure and de facto concepts in school segregation law is traced in Meyer Weinberg's *Race and Place: A Legal History of the Neighborhood School,* (U.S. Government Printing Office, 1967). A helpful compilation is Jesse P. Guzman's *Twenty Years of Court Decisions Affecting Higher Education in the South, 1938–1958* (Tuskegee Institute, 1960).

Intellectual Functioning

"On Account He Ain't Had a Normal Home": An Intellectual History of the Concept of "Disadvantagedness" in Education (doctoral dissertation, Northwestern University, University Microfilms Order No. 73-30,573), by Dallas P. Dickinson, is

an acerbic analysis of a prevailing myth of American education. Central to the propagation of that myth was James S. Coleman and others' *Equality of Educational Opportunity* (U.S. Government Printing Office, 1966), and two supporting studies: Christopher Jencks and others, *Inequality: A Reassessment of the Effect of Family and Schooling in America* (Basic Books, 1972), and Daniel P. Moynihan and F. Mosteller (eds.), *On Equality of Educational Opportunity*. These latter two works, usually described as restudies of the Coleman study, are in reality extensions of it since they did not ask any radically different questions of the Coleman data and thus, quite expectedly, came to very similar conclusions.

Exceedingly few books have been written in this field. The overwhelming mass of writings are individual articles, each of which tends to specialize in a rather restricted subject matter. Such research is the brick and mortar of larger structures which remain unbuilt.

Learning in the Classroom

The central repository of data and interpretations hostile to the possibility of minority children learning effectively remains Arthur R. Jensen's 1969 article, "How Much Can We Boost I.Q. and Scholastic Achievement?" (*Harvard Educational Review*, 39 [1969]). Empirically based research evidence pointing in an opposite direction can be found in studies by William D. Rohwer and associates ("Learning, Race, and School Success," *Review of Educational Research*, 41 [1971]; and "The Population Differences and Learning Proficiency," *Journal of Educational Psychology*, 62 [1972]). The 1971 study by James W. Guthrie and associates, *Schools and Inequality* (MIT Press, 1971), is still a reliable guide to the issue of school-to-school differences. The 1973 study by the Crain group, *Southern Schools: An Evaluation of the Effects of the Emergency School Assistance Program and of Desegregation* (National Opinion Research Center, October 1973), remains an authoritative source. A newer emphasis was introduced by John U. Ogbu's *The Next Generation. An Ethnography of Education in an Urban Neighborhood* (Academic Press, 1974), which stressed the effect on minority children of socially induced discrimination patterns.

Desegregation and Achievement

Two overviews of the evidence as of the mid 1970s are Nancy St. John, *School Desegregation: Outcomes for Children* (Wiley, 1975), and Meyer Weinberg, *Minority Students: A Research Appraisal* (U.S. Government Printing Office, 1977). A study which is uniformly lauded is Thomas M. Goolsby, Jr. and Robert B. Frary, *Enhancement of Educational Effect through Extensive and Intensive Intervention* (Gulfport, Miss., Municipal Separate School District, July 1969); it deals with Gulfport, Mississippi.

Student and Teacher Interracial Interaction

A pioneer study by Joan H. Criswell, *A Sociometric Study of Race Cleavage in the Classroom* (Archives of Psychology, January 1939), is still worth consulting. The research of Elizabeth G. Cohen into the operations of interracial interaction disability is available in article form: "The Effects of Desegregation on Race Relations," *Law and Contemporary Problems*, 39 (Spring 1975); and "Interracial Interaction Disability, A Problem for Integrated Education," *Urban Education*, 5 (January 1971). Calvin Trillin's report on how white students dealt with the entrance of the first two black students at the University of Georgia can be found in *An Education in Georgia. The Integration of Charlayne Hunter and Hamilton Holmes* (Viking, 1963). Two reports by the Southern Regional Council during 1970–1971 (Robert E. Anderson, Jr., *The South and Her Children: School Desegregation 1970–1971*; and Betsy Fancher, *Voices from the South. Black Students Talk About their Experiences in Desegregated Schools*) recorded the words of many black students or interpreted their experiences in desegregated schools. A study of Goldsboro, North Carolina, by Robert R. Mayer and associates (*The Impact of School Desegregation in a Southern City*, Lexington Books, 1974) is highly regarded by most researchers.

In a generally neglected work, *Black Teachers in Urban Schools. The Case of Washington D.C.* (Praeger, 1973), by Catherine Bodard Silver, the author analyzes the problem of teacher morale in a generally black school system. Ogbu, in *The Next Generation*, mentioned earlier, also touches significantly on the role of teachers. An unheralded, indeed ignored, work that captured the spirit of the '60s better than any other study of urban education is Miriam Wasserman's *The School Trip, NYC, USA* (Outerbridge and Dienstfrey, 1970).

Social Context of Schooling

During the 1960s James S. Coleman and colleagues established an interpretation of schooling and social class which has endured until the present. In *Equality of Educational Opportunity* (U.S. Government Printing Office, 1966), it was contended that schools more or less processed students in accordance with their social class as expressed by family background and social composition of school enrollment. Academic achievement was said to vary with social class and, to a much smaller extent, with race. School-to-school differences in physical resources were said to contribute in a very slight way to achievement differences. All in all, readers gained an impression that existing learning disparities between poor and middle-class students or between blacks and whites were more or less unchangeable features of American schooling. What contribution changes in individual schools or school systems could make was not explored.

No attempt was made to construct studies of the contribution of school or school system changes. As a result, conceptions of schools as inherently incapable of modifying class-originated handicaps upon students thrived. Nor was it long before critics of public schooling argued that little financial support need be given institutions that had putatively such a small educational effect. As indicated in Chapter 13, above, this viewpoint was matched on the left by a contention that the schools intended to perpetuate class differences in school achievement as one means of reproducing the capitalistic system. Thus, the schools were once more viewed as educationally negative. Such a perspective helped deprive public schools, the sole educative mechanism open to most poor and minority children, of defenders when they were most sorely needed.

The research tradition of impotent schools remains dominant today. It is upheld even by its challengers. A recent study by Crain and associates (*Making Desegregation Work: How Schools Create Social Climates*, Ballinger, 1982), which is designed to stress the autonomous role of individual schools in effective secondary education, nevertheless declares that "no amount of improvement in the educational system will create impressive gains in tested achievement in large numbers of students." No evidence is cited other than the existing record of unequal achievement. Instead, an appeal to realism is made. Presumably, this was the original claim found in the Coleman research.

Racism

Judging from the literature of our subject, racism has been an inconsequential factor. Only the rarest study manages to mention it, let alone undertake a systematic analysis of it. This suspension of American reality is not a feature of educational research alone but of American social science and humanities as well.

Desegregation

In 1981, a national research group organized at Vanderbilt University's Institute for Public Policy Studies completed a multiyear study of desegregation in fourteen stably desegregated school districts. The central concern of the study was to discover practical activities that contributed to the relative success of desegregation in each city. Among persons interviewed by senior research personnel in each city were municipal authorities, central school officials, principals and teachers, minority parent leaders, lawyers, newspaper reporters, and others. The project also combed the research literature and classified its findings into a number of subjects significant for educational practice. Thus far, nine mimeographed volumes have appeared. Some, at least, are expected to be printed at a later time. The project, known as the "Assessment of Current Knowledge About the Effectiveness of School Desegregation Strategies," is by far the largest-scale analysis yet of the research literature of desegregation. Gary Orfield's *Must We Bus?* (Brookings Institution, 1978) is the most comprehensive study of the politics of desegregation.

Another important study is *Conditions and Processes of Effective School Desegregation* (Educational Testing Service, July 1976), by Garlie A. Forehand, Marjorie Ragosta, and Donald A. Rock. Several collections of original articles are Derrick Bell (ed.), *Shades of Brown: New Perspectives on School Desegregation* (Teachers College Press, 1980); Adam Yarmolinsky and others (eds.), *Race and Schooling in the City* (Harvard University Press, 1981); and Walter G. Stephan and Joe R. Feagin (eds.), *School Desegregation. Past, Present, and Future* (Plenum Press, 1980). A helpful recent study is Laurence R. Marcus and Benjamin D. Stickney, *Race and Education. The Unending Controversy* (Charles C. Thomas, 1981).

Race and Higher Education

The literature of race in higher education is growing rapidly. Much valuable material can be found in Jeff E. Smith (ed.), *The Impact of Desegregation on Higher Education* (North Carolina Central University, 1981). Scarce statistics for one state are supplied in *A Comparison of the Retention and Completion Rates of Black and White Freshmen Who Enrolled at Virginia's State Supported Institutions of Higher Education in Fall, 1975* (State Council of Higher Education For Virginia, December 1980). Marvin W. Peterson and associates, in *Black Students on White Campuses: The Impacts of Increased Black Enrollments* (Institute for Social Research, University of Michigan, 1978), trace carefully the minimal changes in university curricula and structure occasioned by the advent of black students. Gail E. Thomas has edited a valuable collection of studies and essays, *Black Students in Higher Education; Conditions and Experiences in the 1970s* (Greenwood, 1981). Historical backgrounds can be reviewed in Allen B. Ballard, *The Education of Black Folk: The Afro-American Struggle for Knowledge in White America* (Harper & Row, 1973); and Meyer Weinberg, *A Chance to Learn* (Cambridge University Press, 1977), Chapter 7.

Race and Intelligence

Especially worthwhile treatments of race and intelligence can be found in Kenneth M. Ludmerer, *Genetics and American Society: A Historical Appraisal* (Johns Hopkins University Press, 1972); U.S. Congress, 92nd, 2nd session, Senate, Select Committee on Equal Educational Opportunity, *Environment, Intelligence, and Scholastic Achievement* (U.S. Government Printing Office, 1972); T. Dobzhansky, *Genetic Diversity and Human Equality* (Basic Books, 1973); and Stephen J. Gould, *The Mismeasure of Man* (Norton, 1981).

Intradistrict Inequalities

Studies of intradistrict inequalities are beginning to multiply. See M. Weinberg, "Intradistrict inequalities," *Research Review of Equal Education*, 3 (Winter and Spring, 1979); Patricia C. Sexton, *Education and Income Inequalities in Our Public Schools* (Viking, 1961); W. Norton Grubb and Stephan Michelson, *States and Schools: The Political Economy of Public School Financing* (Lexington Books, 1974); John D. Owen, *School Inequality and the Welfare State* (Johns Hopkins University Press, 1974); and Roger Fox and Bernard Lacour, *The Issue of Resource Equalization: Funding the Education of Economically Disadvantaged Children* (Chicago Urban League, 1977).

Other Sources

Further references to studies on all subjects discussed in this book can be found in the author's *The Education of Poor and Minority Children: A World Bibliography* (Greenwood Press, 1981), two volumes. The cutoff date for inclusion was early 1979. Later citations can be found in the bibliography appearing in each issue of *Integrateducation* magazine since that date.

Two well-indexed guides to educational journals and nonbook materials are produced by the ERIC system. (The acronym stands for Education Resources Information Center.) *The Current Index to Journals in Education* lists abstracts of articles appearing in educational and related journals. For leading journals, all articles are abstracted; for others, selective abstracting is done. *Resources in Education* abstracts material that is neither a journal nor a book. Included, for example, are abstracts of papers read at annual meetings of various learned societies. Many are not otherwise available. Its coverage is quite uneven. Desegregation is poorly covered. Unfortunately, when collective works are abstracted, authors of separate contributions fail to be listed and thus are excluded from any "ERIC search." However, both the *Index* and *Resources* are important sources.

Psychological Abstracts, published by the American Psychological Association, in the last decade or so has begun to list works on racial integration. Many of the entries in the *Current Index to Journals in Education* can also be found in *Psychological Abstracts*. The latter, in fact, is more far-ranging but perhaps only moderately so. Ideally, both guides should be used.

Doctoral dissertations, a principal repository of research on the subject of this book, are listed, with authors, in the monthly *Dissertation Abstracts*. While an abstract is not an acceptable substitute for the entire dissertation, reading it generally gives one an accurate perception of the viewpoint and orientation of the author. (In the present work, only complete dissertations were used.) *Dissertation Abstracts* also lists dissertations from Canada and, curiously, South Africa. A subject index facilitates location of specific works.

What with the growing public importance of research in the areas treated in this book, reference to public documents issued by various governments is increasingly necessary. Unmatched for usefulness is the *Monthly Catalog of United States Government Publications*, which is exhaustively indexed; an annual index is also available. Printed transcripts of congressional hearings as well as studies commissioned by congressional and executive bodies are also indexed in this source.

In a class by itself is the work of the U.S. Commission on Civil Rights. Since 1957 it has published far more on the topics of this book than any other part of the federal government, including the Office (now, Department) of Education, which has always been skittish about racial issues, even during the supposed heyday of the 1960s. The Commission, of course, is not a prime producer of research but many of its informational publications are the only ones on the subject. Also, its printed transcripts of public hearings contain detailed testimony by minority activists, representatives, and practitioners. This kind of documentation is generally absent from social science and educational studies. Best of all, many of the Commission's publications are available at little or no cost to the user.

Indispensable for keeping track of newly published books is the Bowker publication, *The Weekly Record*. It lists "conscientiously" every book published or distributed within the United States, week by week. Over a year, the *Record* is by far the most comprehensive listing available.

Certain types of research tend to filter through the nets set for them. Such, for example, are studies performed by research contract or by research employees of school or university boards. At present, almost the sole listing of these is found in Weinberg, *The Education of Poor and Minority Children*, and in various issues of *Integrateducation*.

Bibliographic guides, however, are not substitutes for reading journals and the actual research works. The latter in particular contain up-to-date lists of references, and usually notation of earlier works by the same author.

Index

About the Author

MEYER WEINBERG has had a distinguished career as an educator, editor, author, and consultant. Currently, he is both a Professor in the School of Education at the University of Massachusetts, Amherst, and Director of its Horace Mann Bond Center for Equal Education. His writings on educational issues include *Race and Place: A Legal History of the Neighborhood School, Desegregation Research: An Appraisal,* and *A Chance to Learn.* His award-winning two-volume bibliography, *The Education of Poor and Minority Children* was published by Greenwood Press in 1981. Weinberg also has held the position of editor at *Integrateducation* for the last twenty years.